Stockholm Arbitration Yearbook 2022

Stockholm Arbitration Yearbook

VOLUME 4

Editors

Axel Calissendorff is a partner in and founder of the law firm Calissendorff Advokatbyrå. Prior to that he was a partner in major Swedish law firms. He was the Solicitor to H.M. the King of Sweden and former President of the Swedish Bar Association. His focus is on Corporate and Public M&A. He often sits as an arbitrator. He has authored numerous articles.

Patrik Schöldström is a Judge of Appeal of the Svea Court of Appeal. He is also an Associate Professor of the Faculty of Law of Stockholm University. He has a doctorate in arbitration law and is a former member of the Swedish Bar. He regularly writes articles and case notes. He has extensive experience as an arbitrator – chairman, sole arbitrator, co-arbitrator and emergency arbitrator – in international and domestic disputes, ad hoc and institutional.

Introduction

The Yearbook is published under the auspices of the Stockholm Centre for Commercial Law, a part of the Stockholm University Faculty of Law. It is designed to meet the information needs of arbitration practitioners and parties from all over the world. The first volume was published in 2019.

Objective

The Yearbook is designed to meet the information needs of arbitration practitioners and parties from all over the world. It provides authoritative articles, some of them with a Swedish angle, that address current matters of global concern in arbitration. Each volume includes one or more chapters accounting for developments in Swedish case law and legislation since the previous volume.

Frequency

The publication is annual.

The titles published in this series are listed at the end of this volume.

Stockholm Arbitration Yearbook 2022

Edited by

Axel Calissendorff
Patrik Schöldström

Assistant Editor

Bruno Gustafsson

Editorial Committee

Christer Danielsson
James Hope
Kristin Campbell-Wilson
Niklas Berntorp

Stockholm Centre for Commercial Law
Faculty of Law

Stockholm
University

Wolters Kluwer

Published by:
Kluwer Law International B.V.
PO Box 316
2400 AH Alphen aan den Rijn
The Netherlands
E-mail: lrs-sales@wolterskluwer.com
Website: www.wolterskluwer.com/en/solutions/kluwerlawinternational

Sold and distributed by:
Wolters Kluwer Legal & Regulatory U.S.
920 Links Avenue
Landisville, PA 17538
United States of America
E-mail: customer.service@wolterskluwer.com

Printed on acid-free paper.

ISBN 978-94-035-1876-3

e-Book: ISBN 978-94-035-1966-1
web-PDF: ISBN 978-94-035-1976-0

Editors

Axel Calissendorff is a Partner and founder of Calissendorff Advokatbyrå, a law firm in Stockholm, Sweden. Prior to that, he was at major law firms, Mannheimer Swartling (1981–2005); (Executive Partner 2003 and 2004) and Roschier (2005–2013); (Senior Partner 2009–2012). He was the Solicitor to H.M., the King of Sweden (2009–2021) and President of the Swedish Bar Association (2001–2004). His focus is on Corporate and M&A. He is a frequently appointed arbitrator. He has authored numerous articles.

Patrik Schöldström is a Judge of Appeal of the Svea Court of Appeal, and an Associate Professor of the Faculty of Law of Stockholm University, Sweden. He has a doctorate in Arbitration Law and is a former member of the Swedish Bar. He regularly writes articles and case notes. He also sits as an arbitrator, and has participated in a number of domestic and international arbitrations (ad hoc and institutional) as chair of arbitral tribunal, sole arbitrator, emergency arbitrator, wing arbitrator, and counsel.

Contributors

Ginta Ahrel, Partner of the Dispute Resolution Group at Westerberg & Partners.

Simon Arvmyren, Partner at Delphi law firm in Stockholm within the field of dispute resolution, acting as counsel and arbitrator within most business sectors. He is a member of the Swedish ICC National Committee and currently serves as a member of the ICC Commission on Arbitration and ADR.

Crina Baltag, Associate Professor (Docent) in International Arbitration at Stockholm University, Sweden, and qualified attorney-at-law, with close to twenty years of practice in various aspects of international dispute resolution, private and public international law. A board member of the SCC Arbitration Institute, Crina has been appointed as sole and co-arbitrator in numerous arbitrations under the rules of the ICC, LCIA, SIAC, FAI, VIAC and CCIR-Romania, and she has acted as an expert in various international commercial and investment arbitrations.

Sara Bengtsson Urwitz is an Associate with Mannheimer Swartling Advokatbyrå's dispute resolution practice. She is specialized in public international law, with experience from, e.g., the department for public international law at the Swedish Ministry for Foreign Affairs and with degrees from Columbia University, New York, and Lund University, Sweden.

Amund Bjøranger Tørum is a Professor and Deputy Head of the Scandinavian Institute for Maritime Law and Independent Arbitrator. His expertise concerns the Law of Obligations, Construction/infrastructure Law, Insurance /Reinsurance Law, Maritime Law, Petroleum/Energy Law and Comparative Law. He is admitted to the Norwegian Supreme Court, Chartered Arbitrator (C. Arb) and Fellow of the Chartered Institute of Arbitrators, Member of the SCC Arbitrators' Council, and Head of Arbitration and Dispute Resolution at the Oslo Centre for Commercial Law. Until being appointed full professor in 2021, he was, for more than a decade, a partner and arbitration specialist at a leading Nordic law firm and Head of the Practice Groups for Dispute Resolution and Arbitration.

Mikal Brøndmo, Partner at Haavind in Norway and specializes in arbitration and litigation. He also acts as an arbitrator in international and domestic arbitrations. In addition, he is a Lecturer in the Faculty of Law at the University of Oslo, Norway.

Andrea Carlevaris, Partner at BonelliErede and an Adjunct Professor of International Law. Between September 2012 and May 2017, he has been the Secretary General of the ICC International Court of Arbitration and the Director of the ICC Dispute Resolution Services. He is currently the President of AIA (the Italian Arbitration Association) and a member of the Board of the Arbitration Institute of the Stockholm Chamber of Commerce. Mr Carlevaris is the author of a monograph on *Conservatory and Provisional Measures in International Arbitration* and of numerous articles on international law, conflict of laws and international arbitration. He regularly contributes to several journals, serving on the Board of Directors of the European International Arbitration Review, Rivista dell'arbitrato, Diritto del commercio internazionale and Giustizia civile.

Christer Danielsson, Independent Arbitrator and former President of the Swedish Bar Association.

Alexander Foerster, Swedish Advokat and German Rechtsanwalt acts now as Independent Arbitrator in Stockholm. Previously, he was a Partner at Mannheimer Swartling Advokatbyrå and had a broad experience in international arbitration and cross-border litigation from more than twenty-five years' of work as counsel and arbitrator. He is a member of the SCC Arbitrators Council and the DIS Council. He also lectures on International Arbitration at the Frankfurt University of Applied Sciences, Germany.

Maria Fogdestam Agius, Partner of the Dispute Resolution Group at Westerberg & Partners.

Chloé Heydarian, French jurist and former Dispute Trainee with Delphi law firm in Stockholm. She has an LLM in International Commercial Arbitration Law from the University of Stockholm, Sweden.

Jennie Hjellström, Associate in Mannheimer Swartling's Dispute Resolution practice group, based in Gothenburg. She has acted as counsel in a variety of commercial litigation and arbitration cases, with a specific focus on investment treaty cases.

Olof Larsberger, Advokat, FCIArb, partner at Kastell Advokatbyrå AB in Stockholm, specializes in public procurement, arbitration and commercial litigation. In the arbitration field, he has many years of experience acting as counsel in domestic and international disputes, both ad hoc and institutional. He also accepts assignments as an arbitrator. In the public procurement field, he has acted as counsel in a large number of judicial review cases, as well as public procurement-related damages claims and contract disputes.

Jan Heiner Nedden, Rechtsanwalt and Managing Partner at HANEFELD, a leading dispute resolution boutique with offices in Hamburg and Paris. He acts as counsel and arbitrator in complex disputes and has, among others, been involved in numerous arbitrations in the Nordic region. Prior to joining HANEFELD, Heiner served as Counsel at the Secretariat of the ICC International Court of Arbitration in Paris.

Tero Poutala, Licensed legal counsel, Finland.

Jakob Ragnwaldh, Partner in Mannheimer Swartling's Dispute Resolution practice group focusing on international arbitration and investor-state disputes, based in Singapore.

Lauri Railas, Attorney-at-Law, Railas Attorneys Ltd, Adjunct Professor (Docent) of Civil Law, University of Helsinki, The Average Adjuster in Finland.

Aron Skogman, Partner in Mannheimer Swartling's Dispute Resolution practice group, based in Malmö. He is specialized in commercial litigation and arbitration, with a particular focus on investment treaty cases.

Johan Tufte-Kristensen, Assistant Attorney at Gorrissen Federspiel's dispute resolution group and external lecturer in private international law at the University of Copenhagen, Denmark, previously working as an Assistant Professor in Private and Procedural Law at the University of Copenhagen and representing Denmark at UNCITRAL's Working Group II.

Christopher Vajda KC, Monckton Chambers, London, Visiting Professor at King's College, London, Professor at the College of Europe, Bruges and Judge at the Court of Justice of the European Union (2012–2020). He specializes in providing expert Opinions and sitting as an arbitrator.

Inga Witte, Rechtsanwältin and Associate at HANEFELD, a leading dispute resolution boutique with offices in Hamburg and Paris. She acts as counsel in a variety of litigation and arbitration cases, as arbitrator and tribunal secretary, and has particular expertise in the renewables sector. Inga previously worked with a leading Swiss law firm in Zurich and clerked with the European Commission and the German Constitutional Court.

Summary of Contents

Table of Contents

Preface

Welcome to the fourth edition of the Stockholm Arbitration Yearbook!

You will find articles on arbitration law in general and Swedish arbitration law in particular. Some contributions are by senior and well-known authors, others by more junior ones.

We are happy to receive – at any time of the year – proposals for future contributions in the form of a short abstract.

Axel Calissendorff
Patrik Schöldström

CHAPTER 1

Swedish Arbitration-Related Case Law 2021–2022

Christer Danielsson

§1.01 INTRODUCTION

This chapter will account for court cases relevant to arbitration law from the Swedish Supreme Court and Swedish appellate courts for the period 1 May 2021–30 April 2022. It does not purport to be exhaustive; the aim is to highlight cases that can be assumed to be of interest to a non-Swedish reader.

§1.02 BACKGROUND

The Swedish Arbitration Act of 1999[1] (the 'Act') applies to all arbitration proceedings seated in Sweden, whether the parties have any connection to Sweden or not.[2] The Act also sets out the requirements for foreign arbitral awards to be recognized and enforced in Sweden.[3]

Sweden has a three-tier court system: district courts, six regional appellate courts and the Supreme Court. However, district courts are only rarely involved in arbitration cases since the appellate courts are *Court of First Instance* for invalidity and set aside cases as well as for enforcement cases.

A Swedish arbitral award can be *declared invalid* if it determines an issue which under Swedish law cannot be decided by arbitrators or if the award, or the manner in

---

1. Lagen (1999:116) om skiljeförfarande, as amended 1 March 2019.
2. The Act, s. 46.
3. The Act, ss 52 et seq.

1

which it came about is clearly incompatible with the basic principles of the Swedish legal system, i.e., *ordre public*.[4]

An arbitral award can be *set aside* (wholly or partially) at the request of a party, *inter alia*, when the arbitrators have exceeded their mandate and when, without fault of the party, an irregularity has occurred in the course of the proceedings which probably influenced the outcome of the case.[5]

An action to invalidate or set aside an arbitration award shall be considered by the Court of Appeal within whose district the arbitral proceedings were seated.[6] The Court of Appeal's permission is required in order to appeal its judgment.[7] Such leave to appeal is denied in the large majority of cases. For the case to be tried by the Supreme Court, leave is also required from that court.[8]

Historically, invalidity and set aside actions have very rarely been successful. A statistical survey for the period 1 January 2004–31 May 2014 shows that seven arbitral awards were set aside pursuant to section 34 of the Act while one award was declared invalid pursuant to section 33 of the Act, equal to 6% of all decided cases.[9]

In the period covered by this chapter, one award was set aside in its entirety and one partially. No award was declared invalid.

§1.03   *REPUBLIC OF POLAND v. PL HOLDINGS S.A.R.L.*

[A]   Introduction

As reported in the 2019, 2020 and 2021 Stockholm Arbitration Yearbook,[10] the Svea Court of Appeal in February 2019 rendered a judgment in a case similar to *Achmea*,[11] the *Republic of Poland v. PL Holdings S.a.r.l.* ('PL Holdings').[12] The Court of Appeal's judgment was appealed to the Supreme Court. The Supreme Court granted leave. On 4 February 2020, the Supreme Court decided to request a preliminary ruling from the Court of Justice of the European Union (CJEU). On 26 October 2021, the Grand Chamber of the CJEU handed down its award.

---

4. The Act, s. 33. In addition, under this provision an award is invalid if it does not fulfil the Act's requirements with regard to written form and signature.
5. The Act, s. 34(1), items 3 and 7. Section 34 provides for five other grounds for setting aside an arbitral award, but the two mentioned are those most frequently invoked in set aside proceedings.
6. The Act, s. 43(1). The large majority of invalidity and set aside proceedings are brought before the Svea Court of Appeal. The reason for this is that most Swedish arbitrations are seated in Stockholm.
7. The Act, s. 43(2), which provides that leave to appeal shall be granted 'where it is of importance, as a matter of precedent, that the appeal be considered by the Supreme Court'.
8. The Act, s. 43(2). Such requirement was introduced in an amendment to the Act which entered into force on 1 March 2019.
9. Översyn av lagen om skiljeförfarande ('Review of the arbitration act'), SOU 2015:37, p. 79.
10. Pages 9 et seq. in the 2019 edition, pp. 2 et seq. in the 2020 edition and pp. 2 et seq. in the 2021 edition.
11. Judgment by the European Court of Justice of 6 March 2018, *Slovak Republic v. Achmea BV*, Case No. C-284/16.
12. Judgment by the Svea Court of Appeal dated 22 February 2019 in Case Nos T-8538-17 and T-12033-7.

[B] Facts

In 1987, Poland, on the one hand, and Luxembourg and Belgium, on the other hand, entered into an investment treaty (the 'Investment Treaty') with a dispute resolution clause (section 9) pursuant to which investors in any of the states being party to the treaty have the right to initiate arbitration proceedings in accordance with three different options, one of which is the Arbitration Rules of the Stockholm Chamber of Commerce (the SCC Rules). Thus, the Investment Treaty is an intra-EU (European Union) Bilateral Investment Treaty, or BIT for short.

PL Holdings, a company registered in Luxembourg, initiated arbitration proceedings against Poland in accordance with the SCC Rules with Stockholm as the seat of arbitration. This was prior to the CJEU's judgment in *Achmea*. PL Holdings submitted that Poland had violated its obligations under the Investment Treaty by expropriating assets of PL Holdings in Poland. PL Holdings claimed damages from Poland.

In June 2017, the arbitral tribunal rendered a partial arbitral award in which it found that Poland had violated its obligations under the Investment Treaty by expropriating PL Holdings' shareholding in a bank and that PL Holdings was entitled to damages. In the final award in September 2017, the arbitral tribunal ordered Poland to pay substantial damages (app. EUR 150 million).

[C] The Judgment by the Court of Appeal

Poland filed actions with the Svea Court of Appeal with regard to both the partial award and the final award. Poland requested that the awards be declared invalid (section 33 of the Act) or be set aside (section 34 of the Act) in light of *Achmea*. With regard to the set aside claim, Poland submitted that the awards should be set aside since they were not based on a valid arbitration agreement.

The Court of Appeal made the following statement with regard to its understanding of *Achmea*:

> The conclusion from the Achmea ruling is therefore that articles 267 and 344 TFEU[13] would not as such preclude Poland and PL Holdings from entering into an arbitration agreement and participating in arbitral proceedings regarding an investment-related dispute. What the TFEU precludes is that Member States conclude agreements with each other meaning that one Member State is obligated to accept subsequent arbitral proceeding with an investor and that the Member States thereby establish a system where they have excluded disputes from the possibility of requesting a preliminary ruling, even though the disputes may involve interpretation and application of EU law. Since the TFEU thus does not preclude arbitration agreements between a Member State and an investor in a particular case, a Member State is, based on party autonomy, free – even though the Member State is not bound by a standing offer as such as that in article 8 of the Achmea case or article 9 in this case – to enter into an arbitration agreement with an investor regarding the same dispute at a later stage, e.g. when the investor has initiated arbitral proceedings. An arbitration agreement and arbitral proceedings

---

13. The Treaty on the Functioning of the European Union (TFEU).

between, on the one hand, an investor from a Member State and, on the other hand, a Member State, is therefore as such not in violation of the TFEU.[14]

The Court of Appeal found that the awards should not be declared invalid pursuant to section 33 of the Act.

With regard to setting aside the awards pursuant to section 34 of the Act, PL Holdings, *inter alia*, argued that Poland was precluded from invoking that the arbitral awards were not covered by a valid arbitration agreement since Poland had participated in the arbitral proceedings without raising this objection. Under the applicable rules for the proceedings, PL Holdings argued that Poland was obligated to raise an objection concerning the alleged invalidity of the arbitration agreement no later than in its statement of defence, which Poland had not done.

The Court of Appeal found that pursuant to the applicable SCC Rules, the objection should have been made no later than in the statement of defence. Since it was not made until in the statement of rejoinder, the court concluded, with reference to section 34(2) of the Act, that Poland must be considered to have waived its right to raise the objection.

[D]   The Supreme Court's Request for Preliminary Ruling

The judgment was appealed to the Supreme Court which, as noted, requested a preliminary ruling from the CJEU. In its decision, the Supreme Court stated the following under the heading 'The need for a preliminary ruling'.[15]

The question is what the implications of the principles elaborated by the CJEU in *Achmea* have for the outcome of the case before the Supreme Court.

It is clear that the provision regarding dispute resolution in the investment agreement of relevance in this case before the Supreme Court is invalid. Thus, a possible conclusion is that the standing offer to initiate arbitration proceedings, which the state can be said to have extended to an investor through the dispute resolution provision, is also invalid, considering that the offer is closely linked to the investment agreement.

In the case before the Supreme Court, it has also been argued that the situation is different in this case since it is the request for arbitration that constitutes an offer. The state would then, as a result of its freely expressed wishes, expressly or tacitly, be able to accept the jurisdiction of the arbitral tribunal, in accordance with the principles explained by the CJEU with regard to commercial arbitration.

The Supreme Court does not consider it to be clear, or clarified, how EU law shall be interpreted with regard to the issues that arise in this case. Therefore, there are reasons for requesting a preliminary ruling from the CJEU in order to avoid the risk of an incorrect interpretation of EU law.

The Supreme Court formulated the question to the CJEU as follows:

---

14. Unofficial translation.
15. Decision by the Supreme Court 21 February 2020 in Case No. 1568-19 (unofficial translation).

Do Articles 267 and 344 TFEU, as interpreted in [the judgment of 6 March 2018, *Achmea* (C-284/16, EU:C:2018:158)], mean that an arbitration agreement is invalid if it has been concluded between a Member State and an investor – where an investment agreement contains an arbitration clause that is invalid as a result of the fact that the contract was concluded between two Member States – by virtue of the fact that the Member State, after arbitration proceedings were commenced by the investor, refrains, by the free will of the State, from raising objections as to jurisdiction?

[E]   Opinion by Advocate General Kokott

On 22 April 2021, Advocate General Kokott issued her opinion.[16] She proposed the following answer to the questions put by the Supreme Court.

Individual arbitration agreements between Member States and investors from other Member States concerning the sovereign application of EU law are compatible with the duty of sincere cooperation under Article 4(3) TFEU and the autonomy of EU law under Articles 267 and 344 TFEU only if courts of the Member States can comprehensively review the arbitration award for its compatibility with EU law, if necessary after requesting a preliminary ruling under Article 267 TFEU. Such arbitration agreements must furthermore be compatible with the principle of equal treatment under Article 20 of the Charter of Fundamental Rights of the European Union.

[F]   Judgment by the CJEU[17]

The CJEU answered the questions put by the Supreme Court as follows:

Articles 267 and 344 TFEU must be interpreted as precluding national legislation which allows a Member State to conclude an ad hoc arbitration agreement with an investor from another Member State that makes it possible to continue arbitration proceedings initiated on the basis of an arbitration clause whose content is identical to that agreement, where that clause is contained in an international agreement concluded between those two Member States and is invalid on the ground that it is contrary to those articles.

Thus, the CJEU firmly shut the door to the reasoning advocated by Poland and accepted by the Svea Court of Appeal.

For further details and an analysis of the CJEU's judgment, reference is made to the articles by Andrea Carlevaris (Chapter [5]) and Christopher Vajda (Chapter [3]) of this yearbook.

Here, only the following shall be added with regard to the temporal effects of the judgment. PL Holdings requested that, were the CJEU to find that Articles 267 and 344 TFEU must be interpreted as precluding an arbitration agreement concluded between a Member State and a private investor from another Member State, it should limit the temporal effects of the judgment that it delivers so that the latter does not affect

---

16. CJEU Case C-109/20.
17. Judgment by the Grand Chamber on 26 October 2021.

arbitration proceedings that have been initiated in good faith on the basis of ad hoc arbitration agreements and concluded before the delivery of that judgment. This request was denied by the CJEU, observing, *inter alia*, the following (paragraphs 65 and 66):

> Indeed, to allow a Member State to replace an arbitration clause, included in an international agreement between Member States, by concluding an ad hoc arbitration agreement in order to make it possible to pursue arbitration proceedings initiated on the basis of that clause, would, as has been held in paragraph 47 above, amount to circumventing that Member State's obligations under the Treaties and, specifically, under Article 4(3) TEU and Articles 267 and 344 TFEU, as interpreted in the judgment of 6 March 2018, *Achmea* (C-284/16, EU:C:2018:158). Thus, a limitation of the temporal effects of the present judgment would, in actual fact, entail limiting the effects of the interpretation of those provisions provided by the Court in the judgment of 6 March 2018, *Achmea* (C-284/16, EU:C:2018:158).

The Supreme Court has not yet rendered its final award.

§1.04   *AO TYUMENNEFTEGAZ v. FIRST NATIONAL PETROLEUM CORPORATION*

In an award rendered on 30 March 2018 (and corrected on 15 April 2018) in an SCC case seated in Stockholm, the arbitral tribunal ordered Russian company AO Tyumenneftegaz (TNG) to pay damages to the amount of USD 70 million to Houston based First National Petroleum Corporation (FNP), together with default interest pursuant to the Swedish Interest Act from 25 December 1998. The dispute concerned a 1992 cooperation agreement between the parties to set up a joint venture to explore an oil field in the Russian Federation.

TNG initiated proceedings before the Svea Court of Appeal, requesting the award to be declared invalid or set aside in its entirety. As a secondary claim, TNG requested that the provision ordering it to pay interest be set aside. The Court of Appeal denied the primary request but set aside the interest part, pursuant to which TNG had been ordered to pay default interest for a twenty-year period.[18] The Court of Appeal found that the interest awarded was in excess of the interest claims forwarded by FNP in the arbitration (based on damages in the amount actually awarded) and that the arbitral tribunal did not have authority to award interest in its absolute discretion. The Court of Appeal did not give TNG permission to appeal the judgment.

§1.05   *TURKISH COMPANIES v. GAZPROM EXPORT LLC*

In the period covered by this chapter, the Svea Court of Appeal handed down judgments in three very similar set aside cases, with different Turkish companies as

---

18. Judgment by the Svea Court of Appeal on 2 June 2021 in Case No. T-7070-18.

claimants and Gazprom export LLC ('Gazprom') as respondent.[19] The underlying disputes concerned Gazprom's claim to have prices under gas delivery contracts adjusted. In all three cases, such adjustments were partially granted by the arbitral tribunals.

A common issue in the set aside cases was whether Gazprom's claim in the arbitration proceedings for changes of the price formula had been an 'all or nothing' claim, and that the tribunals, therefore, had exceeded their mandate when they approved only part of the claim (a removal of a specific rebate). The Court of Appeal found that this was not the case in all three cases. Nor were any other set aside grounds invoked by the Turkish companies successful.

Another common feature is that the Court of Appeal in all three cases (with separate sets of judges) drastically cut the costs claimed by Gazprom for counsel (which were the same in all cases). Gazprom was awarded only between 25% and 40% of costs sought.

In none of the cases did the Court of Appeal give permission to appeal the judgment.

§1.06 NET AT ONCE SWEDEN AB v. TRESVE FIBER IDEELL FÖRENING

In a small domestic case, the Göta Court of Appeal set aside an award rendered by a sole arbitrator on the basis that the claimant in the arbitration proceedings was considered to lack legal capacity (Sw. 'rättskapacitet') and therefore could not be a party to the arbitration agreement on which its claim was based. The Court of Appeal allowed appeal to the Supreme Court. The Supreme Court, in its turn, has granted leave.[20] The Supreme Court has not yet decided the case.

§1.07 ASCOM GROUP S.A. AND OTHERS v. REPUBLIC OF KAZAKHSTAN AND NATIONAL BANK OF KAZAKSTHAN

In a case of importance for determining sovereign immunity, the Swedish Supreme Court has held that a sovereign state was not immune against enforcement of an arbitration award in listed shares since the purpose of holding those assets was not of a sufficiently qualified nature so as to protect the assets from seizure.[21]

For further details and an analysis of the Supreme Court's decision, reference is made to the chapters in this yearbook by Maria Fogdestam Agius and Ginta Ahrel (Chapter [8]), and Alexander Foerster and Sara Bengtsson Urwitz (Chapter [9]).

---

19. Judgment by the Svea Court of Appeal on 8 June 2021 in Case No. T-1806-19 with Akfel Gaz Sanayi Ve Ticaret Anonim Sirketi as claimant; Judgment on 6 October 2021 in Case No. T-1040-19 with Enerco Enerji Sanayi ve Ticaret A.S. as claimant; and Judgment on 1 December 2021 in Case No. T-7865-19 with Kibar Enerji Anonim Sirketi as claimant.
20. Judgment by the Göta Court of Appeal on 2 November 2021 in Case No. T-2236-20.
21. Decision by the Supreme Court on 18 November 2021 in Case No. Ö 3828-20, NJA 2021 p. 850.

§1.08   OTHER

In a case brought already in 2020[22] but not yet decided by the Svea Court of Appeal, a party requested that an arbitration award be set aside, *inter alia,* on the basis that the arbitral tribunal during the pandemic ordered a virtual hearing to be held against the objection of the party. The party took the position that the Act gives parties the right to an in-person physical hearing and that it was denied this right by the decision of the tribunal to proceed virtually. This issue has been the subject of intense discussion within the Swedish arbitration community and the judgment, which can be expected in time for the next edition of the Stockholm Arbitration Yearbook, is much anticipated. The large majority of Swedish arbitration practitioners take the view that a virtual hearing can be organized despite objections by one of the parties, but former Chief Justice of the Supreme Court Stefan Lindskog, who has written the leading commentary to the Act, holds the opposite view.

---

22. Svea Court of Appeal Case No. T-7158-20.

CHAPTER 2

Global Trends in Arbitration 2022: Conference Report

Crina Baltag

The third joint biennial Conference organized by the Stockholm Centre for Commercial Law (SCCL)[1] and Oxford Institute of European and Comparative Law (IECL) took place on 2-3 June 2022 in Stockholm.

This edition of the Conference was set to highlight the latest developments and trends in international commercial arbitration in light of the experiences gained during the pandemic as well as looking at the future of investment treaty arbitration in Europe.

The Conference kicked off with the welcome addresses by André Andersson, Senior Adviser at Mannheimer Swartling and Chair of the SCCL; Ciara Kennefick, Associate Professor of Law at the University of Oxford and Research Fellow at the IECL; and Axel Calissendorff, independent arbitrator, Chair of the Organising Committee, immediate past Head of the Arbitration Research Panel at the SCCL.

§2.01 INVESTMENT TREATY ARBITRATION IN EUROPE: A CHANGING LANDSCAPE

The first session of the Conference began with the keynote addresses of Christopher Vajda, QC, Monckton Chambers, Visiting Professor at King's College, London, and previously United Kingdom (UK) Judge at the Court of Justice of the European Union (CJEU) 2012-2020, and of Robin Oldenstam, Partner at Mannheimer Swartling, Head of the firm's International Arbitration Practice, Swedish member of the International

---

1. In particular, the Research Panel for Arbitration and Other Forms of Dispute Resolution of the SCCL is tasked with bringing together academics, judges and practicing lawyers with a view to promoting research and education in arbitration law, both in Sweden and international legal relationships. The immediate past Head of the Research Panel was Axel Calissendorff; the current Head of the Research Panel is James Hope, Partner, Vinge.

Court of Arbitration of the International Chamber of Commerce (ICC) 2015-2021, Chair of the Arbitration Institute of the Stockholm Chamber of Commerce (SCC). The panel of the first session lined up Veronika Korom, Assistant Professor at Essec Business School, France; Crina Baltag, Associate Professor in International Arbitration, Stockholm University, board member of the Arbitration Institute of the SCC; Paschalis Paschalidis, Counsel at Arendt & Medernach, previously Référendaire at the CJEU, Associate Professor of EU law at the University of Lyon III Jean Moulin; and Lucy Reed, independent arbitrator based in New York and Hong Kong, and was moderated by Axel Calissendorff.

The first session was dedicated to investor-state arbitration, assessing the impact of the development after CJEU's *Achmea* ruling[2] and the subsequent ones upholding *Achmea,* and considering the further impacts these may have in the future. Christopher Vajda provided an overview of the CJEU case law – from *Achmea* to *Komstroy,*[3] and began his keynote by explaining that while Article 3(5) of the Treaty on the European Union (TEU) provides that the European Union (EU) 'shall contribute ... to the strict observance and development of international law', the CJEU has held that this is not an absolute obligation and can be displaced where international law does not respect the basic constitutional charter of the EU, or, as known, the principle of the autonomy of EU law. The judgments in *Achmea* and *Komstroy* have created a tension between EU law and international law. For a future international commitment of the EU, Article 218(11) of the Treaty on the Functioning of the European Union (TFEU) provides a mechanism for avoiding such a tension whereby the CJEU can be asked to rule on an *ex ante* basis whether there is an incompatibility between the proposed international agreement and EU law. Robin Oldenstam's keynote focused on the tension between treaty and commercial arbitration, and, respectively, between public international law and EU law, and whether there is mutual trust at all. Robin Oldenstam highlighted that arbitral tribunals, generally, have not been persuaded to decline jurisdiction based on *Achmea* and have found no incompatibility between bilateral investment treaties (BITs) or the Energy Charter Treaty (ECT) and the TFEU as a matter of treaty interpretation. Undertaking a review of these arbitrations, Robin Oldenstam concluded on the following points: (a) *Achmea* was invoked by the respondent EU Member State in some sixty + intra-EU investment cases; (b) no arbitral tribunal has so far declined jurisdiction; (c) initially, the objection raised by the respondent Member State was dismissed as belated on procedural grounds; (d) also initially dismissed in ECT cases on the basis of *Achmea* not applying to a multilateral investment treaty where the EU itself is a party; (e) some variation in dismissals based on substantive reasoning, but certain common themes have emerged as arbitral tribunals refer to and rely on the reasonings of other arbitral tribunals.

---

2. *Slowakische Republik v. Achmea BV*, CJEU, Judgment of 6 March 2018, https://curia.europa.eu /juris/document/document.jsf;jsessionid = 0C69D499907EEDAC556EA774CB5D8D6E?text = &d ocid = 199968&pageIndex = 0&doclang = EN&mode = lst&dir = &occ = first&part = 1&cid = 213188 (last visited, 21 July 2022).

3. *République de Moldavie v. Komstroy LLC*, CJEU, Judgment of 2 September 2021, https://curia. europa.eu/juris/document/document.jsf?text = &docid = 245528&pageIndex = 0&doclang = EN& mode = lst&dir = &occ = first&part = 1&cid = 213599 (last visited, 21 July 2022).

Veronika Korom began the panel discussion by addressing the future for arbitration investor-state disputes within the EU, looking in particular at four side developments after *Achmea:* (i) the termination of intra-EU BITs, in particular in the light of the Agreement for the termination of BITs between the Member States of the EU entered into force on 29 August 2020; (ii) the set aside proceedings against intra-EU BIT arbitral awards: recently, in *Poland v. Strabag* and *Poland v. Slot*,[4] the Paris Court of Appeal set aside two arbitral awards arising out of intra-EU BITs; (iii) the enforcement of intra-EU BIT arbitral awards, with reports on intra-EU arbitral awards being honoured by respondent EU Member States, as in *Sodexo Pass International SAS v. Hungary*;[5] and (iv) the future of intra-EU investment protection regime, which must include an alternative for the terminated intra-EU BITs, noting that the European Commission has recently launched public consultations on this matter.[6]

Crina Baltag continued the discussion by addressing the future of investment protection and arbitration in the post-Brexit UK, focusing on the relevance of the EU-UK Trade and Cooperation Agreement (TCA), as well as the EU-UK Withdrawal Agreement. Crina Baltag mentioned at the outset that the UK, in the context of CJEU's clear position on intra-EU investment arbitration, may be seen as a preferred jurisdiction for restructuring investments and for transforming intra-EU investments into extra-EU ones. In this context, the post-Brexit relation between UK and the EU is very much relevant. The TCA is a sui generis Free Trade Agreement, which was signed on 24 December 2020, and became applicable, first on a provisional basis, since the end of the transition period on 31 December 2020. The TCA contains limited substantive protections for investors from the EU and the UK and no investor-State dispute-resolution mechanism. Furthermore, the TCA contains no direct reference to the fate of the UK-EU Member States BITs, but it does refer, in its different parts, to bilateral instruments: for example, 'this Agreement and any supplementing agreement apply without prejudice to any earlier bilateral agreement between the United Kingdom … and the Union' etc. Furthermore, the topic must also be approached in the context of the UK not signing the Agreement for the termination of intra-EU BITs, which in October 2020 triggered the infringement proceedings by the European Commission against the UK.[7]

Continuing, Paschalis Paschalidis focused on the impact of the *Komstroy* ruling on the ECT and the international legal order. In doing so, Paschalis Paschalidis

---

4. *Republique de Pologne v. Société STRABAG SE, Société RAIFFEISEN CENTROBANK AG, and Société SYRENA IMMOBILIEN HOLDING AG*, Paris Court of Appeal, Judgment of 19 April 2022; and *Republique de Pologne v. Société CEC PRAHA and Société SLOT GROUP AS C/O M. DAVID JANOSIK*, Paris Court of Appeal, Judgment of 19 April 2022.

5. *Sodexo Pass International SAS v. Hungary*, ICSID Case No. ARB/14/20, Award of 28 January 2019.

6. European Commission, *Cross-border investment within the EU – clarifying and supplementing EU rules*, https://ec.europa.eu/info/law/better-regulation/have-your-say/initiatives/12403-Investment-protection-and-facilitation-framework/public-consultation_en (last visited, 21 July 2022).

7. European Commission, *Intra-EU BITs: Commission calls on THE UNITED KINGDOM to terminate Bilateral Investment Treaties with EU Member States*, https://ec.europa.eu/commission/presscorner/detail/en/inf_20_1687 (last visited, 21 July 2022).

highlighted that the CJEU in *Komstroy* specifically focused on the interpretation of Article 26(2)(c) of the ECT, meaning that the other options for intra-EU disputes, i.e., the courts or administrative tribunals of the Contracting Party party to the dispute, or any previously agreed dispute settlement procedure, would still remain available post-*Komstroy*. Furthermore, the question remains whether the CJEU should interpret treaties as domestic EU acts, at the same time considering EU's obligation to 'strictly observe' international law.

Concluding the first session and the panel discussion, Lucy Reed addressed the views on investment treaty arbitration in Asia and the Americas, in the light of the intra-EU latest developments. Lucy Reed clarified at the outset that while there was considerable focus on the EU and the intra-EU investment disputes, one must be reminded that there is a world beyond Europe. However, as Lucy Reed explained, there is an increasing divergence within each of these regions, as States enter into investment treaties with an increasing variety of dispute resolution procedures and consider reform options. Nowhere is this more evident than in the United Nations Commission on International Trade Law (UNCITRAL) Working Group III (WG III).[8] At the same time, there are some glimmers of convergence between Asia and the Americas. Discussing the convergence, Lucy Reed referred to a statement made by China in WG III, introducing its position on investor-State dispute settlement (ISDS) reform:[9]

> The present investor-State dispute settlement (ISDS) mechanism plays an impor-tant role in protecting the rights and interests of foreign investors and promoting transnational investment. It also helps to build the rule of law into international investment governance and to avoid economic disputes between investors and host countries escalating into political conflicts between nations. Therefore, China believes that the ISDS mechanism is one that is generally worth maintaining.

As such, Lucy Reed explained, certain States in Asia and the Americas defend the ISDS system and do not support the creation of a Multilateral Investment Court, meaning that there may be some points of (semi-)convergence in the future of investment arbitration.

§2.02   ADEQUATE DISPUTE RESOLUTION AND THEIR INTERACTION IN INTERNATIONAL COMMERCIAL DISPUTES

The second session was devoted to 'adequate dispute resolution', which may include expert adjudication, early independent evaluation, and the use of technology in risk analysis. The session was moderated by Geneviève Helleringer, Lecturer in Law at the

---

8. As background, UNCITRAL WG III has identified the following concerns about ISDS: (i) inconsistency in arbitral decisions; (ii) limited mechanisms to ensure the correctness of arbitral decisions; (iii) lack of predictability; (iv) appointment of arbitrators by parties; (v) the impact of party-appointment on the impartiality and independence of arbitrators; (vi) lack of transparency; and (vii) increasing duration and costs of the procedure.
9. Possible reform of ISDS, Submission from the Government of China, 19 July 2019, https://do cuments-dds-ny.un.org/doc/UNDOC/LTD/V19/073/86/pdf/V1907386.pdf?OpenElement (last visited, 21 July 2022).

University of Oxford, Research Fellow of Lady Margaret Hall, Oxford, and Law Professor at Essec Business School, France. Sir Geoffrey Vos, Master of the Rolls for England and Wales, and author of a report for the EU Commission on mediation in Alternative Dispute Resolution (ADR) and in charge of designing the future of justice in the UK, gave the keynote address on the visions for a digital justice reform. Sir Geoffrey Vos emphasized that the reform of justice in the digital era must be a reform of the overall system, rather than focusing only on the judicial decision-making process. In his address, Sir Geoffrey Vos brought up the role online dispute resolution had in the past, as well as the reality of congested dockets of the UK courts, in explaining why the digitalization of justice can offer a speedy and solid solution. The second keynote address was delivered by Catherine Kessedjian, Professor at the University of Paris II (Panthéon-Assas), Deputy Secretary General of the Hague Conference on Private International Law 1996–2000 on the new developments on mediation and settlements. Catherine Kessedjian first asked the question of whether mediation, as a process, is currently in a fashionable period, ending up being used for the wrong reasons. On the same line, various concerns can be raised with respect to the mediator, as a central figure of the mediation process: should the mediator be a generalist or an expert having knowledge of the substance of the dispute? Catherine Kessedjian also highlighted the current push for mediation in the context of the ISDS reform, including training States and mediators for a sensible implementation of this dispute-resolution mechanism for investment disputes.

The panel discussion continued with Christopher Newmark, Partner at Spenser Underhill Newmark, former Chair of ICC Commission on Arbitration and ADR, addressing mediation as a dispute-resolution mechanism for the settlement of international commercial disputes. Christopher Newmark eloquently explained that every dispute has certain moments in which a settlement can be pursued successfully. Identifying the 'settlement curve', Christopher Newmark indicated that to be able to facilitate the settlement agreement by way of mediation, parties – generally including here executives, management, in-house and external counsel – should be able to reach an agreement to mediate the dispute. Few disputes would actually go through the gates of mediation, as metaphorically suggested by Christopher Newmark.

Representing the views of in-house counsel, Jonas Bengtsson, Head of Corporate Affairs at Polarium Energy Solutions, board member of the Arbitration Institute of the SC, continued the panel discussion by looking into various options available to users in commercial disputes. Jonas Bengtsson explained that there are useful dispute-resolution mechanisms, including arbitration, mediation, expert determination, adjudication, early neutral evaluation, and also tailor-made options, such as the SCC Arbitration Institute Express,[10] which allow companies to choose the adequate one for the particular type of dispute and contractual partner. Some users may have a standard approach to disputes, while others would decide on a case-by-case basis.

---

10. 2021 SCC Rules for Express Dispute Assessment – SCC Express, https://sccinstitute.com/media/1800129/scc-rules-for-express-dispute-assessment_20210524.pdf (last visited, 21 July 2022).

The first day of the Conference concluded with a dinner cruise aboard M/S Waxholm III, an opportunity for Róbert Spanó, President of the European Court of Human Rights, to address the audience on *Arbitration and Human Rights – Different Worlds?*. Róbert Spanó's speech emphasized that arbitration and human rights frequently, if not always, interact. In particular, it is undisputed that investors acquire property rights which are recognized and protected as fundamental rights. It is expected that competent bodies may view arbitral awards, too, as acquired property rights and endorse their protection accordingly.[11]

§2.03   THE ORAL HEARING: VISIONS FOR THE FUTURE IN LIGHT OF PANDEMIC EXPERIENCES

The third session featured topical discussions on commercial arbitration, in particular on oral hearings following the pandemic experience, and visions for the future. Moderated by Christer Danielsson, Partner at Danielsson & Nyberg, former president of the Swedish Bar Association, the session began with the keynote addresses by Hilary Heilbron QC, Barrister at Brick Court Chambers, and by Professor Loukas Mistelis, Partner at Clyde & Co, and Clive M Schmitthoff Professor of Transnational Commercial Law and Arbitration. Hilary Heilbron focused on the opportunities for a re-think of arbitral procedure following COVID-19, and highlighted the preparation for the remote hearings, also in light of the digitalization of the dispute resolution process. Hilary Heilbron emphasized the advantages of video meetings and suggested that they should take place more often and be rather used instead of writing emails to discuss various contentious issues regarding the procedure. In his keynote address, Professor Loukas Mistelis addressed the oral hearing post-pandemic and the internal lex arbitri. Professor Loukas Mistelis began by highlighting that any question pertaining to issues of procedure, including virtual hearings, must begin from the applicable lex arbitri. In doing so, Professor Loukas Mistelis explained that the concept of lex arbitri varies from jurisdiction to jurisdiction, with the example of the English courts focusing, in particular, on the relation of arbitration proceedings with the courts that may be deemed to have jurisdiction over the proceedings. However, as essential as this relation with the courts may be, such a view disregards the fact that lex arbitri has two components: the internal lex arbitri, which regulates the arbitration procedure before and within the arbitral tribunal, and the external lex arbitri, which provides the regulatory framework for arbitration proceedings in relation to courts with supervisory role on the arbitration proceedings.

In addressing the oral hearings with the vision on the future, given the lessons learned from COVID-19, the panel discussion lined up Rupert Choat QC, Barrister at Atkin Chambers, giving the international arbitrator's perspective; Kristoffer Löf, Partner and Co-Chair of the Dispute Resolution Group at Mannheimer Swartling, giving

---

11. *See* recently, *BTS Holding, a.s. v. Slovakia*, European Court of Human Rights, Judgment of 30 June 2022.

14

the counsel's perspective; Kristin Campbell-Wilson, Secretary General of the Arbitration Institute of the SCC, on the institutional perspective; and Nicolas Martinez, Stockholm International Hearing Centre, on the 'backstage' of remote arbitration hearings. The panellists were in agreement that virtual hearings were implemented quickly and effectively, with hybrid hearings now benefiting from advanced technology. Furthermore, both counsel and arbitrators have adapted their techniques in advocacy and in the organization of the hearings, respectively. Institutions, equally, have played an essential role in ensuring full digital access to proceedings by providing, as in the case of the SCC with the SCC Platform, access to the file and easy communication with the parties and the arbitral tribunal.

The Conference concluded with lunch and a guided tour of the National Museum of Art in Stockholm. The Organizing Committee, comprised of Axel Calissendorff (chair); André Andersson; Crina Baltag; Christer Danielsson; Geneviève Helleringer; James Hope, Partner and Head of international arbitration at Vinge; Daria Kozlowska Rautiainen, Senior Lecturer at Stockholm University; Anders Reldén, Partner at White & Case, Stockholm; and supported by an administrative assistant, Anna Klasson, would like to express gratitude to all speakers and attendants of the Conference for their valuable contributions.

CHAPTER 3

The Impact of EU Law on Dispute Resolution in International Investment and Trade Agreements

Christopher Vajda KC[*]

§3.01 INTRODUCTION

The resolution of international investment disputes between investors and States through arbitration has been an established feature of public international law (PIL) for many decades. As is well known, Bilateral Investment Treaties (BITs) between States provide, in essence, that investors in one State party are granted certain rights, such as fair and equitable treatment and protection against unlawful expropriation, in the other State party.[1] BITs generally provide a mechanism for investor to state dispute settlement (ISDS) which is by means of an arbitration tribunal. However, this method of dispute resolution has come into conflict with another legal system, namely the European Union (EU) legal system. In this chapter the general relationship between the EU and PIL is analysed first before looking at the case law of the Court of Justice of the European Union (CJEU) on BITs between EU Member States ('intra-EU BITs') and on the Energy Charter Treaty (ECT) and subsequent developments arising from that case law.

§3.02 THE RELATIONSHIP BETWEEN PIL AND EU LAW

PIL lays down a number of rules that apply to Treaties concluded by States and international bodies that are largely now codified in the Vienna Convention on the law

---

[*] All views expressed are in a personal capacity.
1. I refer to BITs but the same is broadly true of Multilateral Investment Treaties like the Energy Charter Treaty (ECT) which entered into force on 1 April 1998.

of treaties (VCLT). Additionally, BITs and multilateral investment Treaties (MITs) contain specific provisions relating to their termination.

[A]   Public International Law

The VCLT places a high value on the binding nature of treaties and their termination in accordance with prescribed procedures. Article 26 provides under the heading '*PACTA SUNT SERVANDA*' that 'Every treaty in force is binding upon the parties to it and must be performed by them in good faith.' The ability of a party to rely on its own internal law to bring an agreement to an end is very limited. Article 27 provides: 'INTERNAL LAW AND OBSERVANCE OF TREATIES A party may not invoke the provisions of its internal law as justification for its failure to perform a treaty. This rule is without prejudice to article 46.' Article 46(1) precludes a State from relying on a violation of its own internal law regarding its competence to conclude treaties to be bound by a Treaty 'unless that violation was manifest and concerned a rule of its internal law of fundamental importance'. A manifest violation is one which 'would be objectively evident to any State conducting itself in the matter in accordance with normal practice and in good faith'.[2] Article 54 permits the termination of a Treaty in conformity with its provisions or by consent of all the parties.[3] Article 65 lays down the procedure to be followed in respect of the invalidity, termination, or suspension of the operation of a Treaty. In the case of a Treaty whose invalidity has been established under the VCLT and is therefore void, Article 69(2) provides what might be termed some form of protection for legitimate expectations: 'If acts have nevertheless been performed in reliance on such a treaty: ...; (b) acts performed in good faith before the invalidity was invoked are not rendered unlawful by reason only of the invalidity of the treaty.'[4] The same rules apply *mutatis mutandis* to multilateral Treaties.[5]

In the case of BITs and MITs, there are specific provisions to protect existing investments made prior to the termination of those agreements. Thus in the case of the ECT Article 47(3) provides that, in the event of a withdrawal by a Contracting Party: 'The provisions of this Treaty shall continue to apply to investments made in the area of a Contracting Party by investors of other Contracting Parties or in the area of other Contracting Parties by investors of that Contracting Party as of the date when that Contracting Party's withdrawal from the Treaty takes effect for a period of 20 years

---

2. Article 46(2).
3. Article 59 also provides for a deemed termination as a result of the conclusion of a later treaty.
4. The principle of good faith also applies to a State prior to the entry into force of a Treaty which it has signed or consented to be bound by, *see* Art. 18 VCLT. In Case T-115/94 *Opel Austria v. Council* EU:T:1997:3 the General Court described 'the principal of good faith ...[as] the corollary in public international law of the principle of protection of legitimate expectations which, according to the case law, forms part of the ... [EU] legal order', para. 93.
5. *See* Arts 41 and 69(4).

from such date.'[6] Likewise, denunciation by a State of the International Convention on the Settlement of Investment Disputes between States and Nationals of Other States (the ICSID Convention) has prospective effect only.[7] Nor can consent to arbitrate between an investor and a State be withdrawn unilaterally.[8]

[B] The EU Treaty Provisions: The Strict Observance of PIL

Article 3(5) of the Treaty on the European Union (TEU) provides that the EU 'shall contribute ... to the strict observance and development of international law, including respect for the principles of the United Nations Charter'. A good illustration of the importance of Article 3(5) TEU arose in *Western Sahara*.[9] The issue in that case was whether the waters adjacent to the Western Sahara fell under the sovereignty or jurisdiction of Morocco and hence within the territorial scope of international fisheries agreements made between the EU and Morocco ('EU-Morocco Agreements').[10] The CJEU rejected the argument that it had no jurisdiction to examine the validity of an international agreement but merely the EU acts approving the conclusion of those agreements. It made three points.[11] First, that such agreements are, from the moment of their entry into force, an integral part of the EU legal order and thus must be compatible with EU law. Second:

> the EU is bound, in accordance with settled case-law, when exercising its powers, to observe international law in its entirety, including not only the rules and principles of general and customary international law, but also the provisions of international conventions that are binding on it (see, to that effect, judgments of 24 November 1992, *Poulsen and Diva Navigation*, C-286/90, EU:C:1992:453, paragraph 9; of 3 September 2008, *Kadi and Al Barakaat International Foundation v Council and Commission*, C-402/05 P and C-415/05 P, EU:C:2008:461, paragraph

---

6. For a similar provision in a BIT, *see* Art. 13(3) of the Netherlands – Slovakia BIT (1991) which provides: 'In respect of investments made before the date of the termination of the present Agreement the foregoing Articles thereof shall continue to be effective for a further period of fifteen years from that date.'
7. *See* Arts 71–72 of the ICSID Convention which provide:
   71. Any Contracting State may denounce this Convention by written notice to the depositary of this Convention. The denunciation shall take effect six months after receipt of such notice.
   72. Notice by Contracting State pursuant to Articles 70 or 71 shall not affect the rights or obligations under this Convention of that State or of any of its constituent subdivisions or agencies or of any national of that State arising out of consent to the jurisdiction of the Centre given by one of them before such notice was received by the depositary.
8. Article 25(1) of the ICSID Convention provides: 'The jurisdiction of the Centre shall extend to any legal dispute arising directly out of an investment, between a Contracting State ... and a national of another Contracting State, which the parties to the dispute consent in writing to submit to the Centre. When the parties have given their consent, no party may withdraw its consent unilaterally.'
9. Case C-266/16 *The Queen, on the application of: Western Sahara Campaign UK v. Commissioners for Her Majesty's Revenue and Customs* EU:C:2018:118.
10. Those agreements were then approved by the EU and then entered into force, *see* para. 14.
11. *See* paras 43–51.

291; and of 21 December 2011, *Air Transport Association of America and Others*, C-366/10, EU:C:2011:864, paragraphs 101 and 123).[12]

Third, the court nevertheless treated the question of the validity of an international agreement concluded by the EU as relating not to that agreement but to the EU act approving the conclusion of that international agreement. Thus, while the CJEU interpreted the EU-Morocco Agreements as a matter of PIL, it confined its response to the question of the validity of the EU's act of ratification.[13]

In the case of international agreements concluded by the EU, Article 216(2) of the Treaty on the Functioning of the European Union (TFEU) provides that such agreements are binding on the EU and its Member States. This reflects the position under PIL as stated in Article 26 VCLT.[14] The effect of Article 216(2) TFEU is that the EU can incur liability at the international level for non-performance of an agreement that it has entered into even if it is in breach of its own internal constitutional rules.[15]

[C]   The EU Law Principle of Autonomy: An Exception to the Strict Observance of PIL

Despite the wording of those TEU and TFEU provisions, the CJEU has held that the EU is not always bound by PIL. Perhaps the most famous example of this approach is *Kadi* where the CJEU held that the importance of fundamental rights in the EU legal order precluded Member States from complying with their own international obligations to impose sanctions on Mr Kadi pursuant to a UN Security Council Resolution. This was because those international obligations did not provide Mr Kadi with his rights of defence, his right to be heard and his right to effective judicial review of such measures, all rights under EU law. The core of the reasoning of the CJEU was as follows:

> In this connection it is to be borne in mind that the Community is based on the rule of law, inasmuch as neither its Member States nor its institutions can avoid review of the conformity of their acts with the basic constitutional charter, the EC Treaty, which established a complete system of legal remedies and procedures designed to enable the Court of Justice to review the legality of acts of the institutions (Case 294/83 *Les Verts* v *Parliament* [1986] ECR 1339, paragraph 23).
>
> It is also to be recalled that *an international agreement cannot affect the allocation of powers fixed by the Treaties or, consequently, the autonomy of the Community legal system*, observance of which is ensured by the Court by virtue of the exclusive jurisdiction conferred on it by Article 220 EC, jurisdiction that the Court has, moreover, already held to form part of the very foundations of the Community (see, to that effect, Opinion 1/91 [1991] ECR I-6079, paragraphs 35 and 71, and Case C-459/03 *Commission* v *Ireland* [2006] ECR I-4635, paragraph 123 and case-law cited).

---

12. Paragraph 47.
13. Paragraph 85.
14. *See* section §3.02[A] above.
15. Case C-327/91 *France v. Commission* EU:C:1994:305 at para. 25. That was a case where France successfully challenged the conclusion of an agreement by the Commission rather than the Council.

In addition, according to settled case-law, fundamental rights form an integral part of the general principles of law whose observance the Court ensures. For that purpose, the Court draws inspiration from the constitutional traditions common to the Member States and from the guidelines supplied by international instruments for the protection of human rights on which the Member States have collaborated or to which they are signatories. In that regard, the ECHR has special significance (see, inter alia, Case C-305/05 *Ordre des barreaux francophones et germanophone and Others* [2007] ECR I-5305, paragraph 29 and case-law cited).

It is also clear from the case-law that respect for human rights is a condition of the lawfulness of Community acts (Opinion 2/94, paragraph 34) and that measures incompatible with respect for human rights are not acceptable in the Community (Case C-112/00 *Schmidberger* [2003] ECR I-5659, paragraph 73 and case-law cited).[16] (emphasis added)

Thus the principle of the autonomy meant that EU law did not need to comply with PIL where PIL did not respect the 'basic constitutional charter' of the EU. The CJEU's reliance on the principle of autonomy in *Kadi* as a reason to depart from PIL did not take away any rights that Mr Kadi had under PIL but rather granted him rights under EU law that did not exist in, or indeed were precluded by, PIL. *Kadi* illustrates that there is tension between the Member States' obligation to comply with PIL and the EU principle of autonomy. Nevertheless, as in *Western Sahara*, the CJEU in *Kadi* made it clear that it was reviewing the EU act implementing the international law measure rather than the international measure itself.[17]

The tension between PIL and the principle of autonomy was explained by Szpunar AG in C-641/18 *Rina*:

it has consistently been held that international conventions which are an integral part of the legal order of the European Union and are binding on the Union have primacy over secondary legislation, which must be interpreted as far as possible in accordance with those conventions. (93) Leaving aside any differences between international conventions and the rules of customary international law, (94) since the latter form part of the legal order of the European Union and are binding upon it, (95) then they must also have primacy over acts of secondary legislation. ...

The co-existence of two obligations, namely that of contributing to the observance of international law and that of ensuring respect for the autonomy of the European Union legal order, can create tensions which the Union must resolve. ...

In that context, in the second place, in order for an obligation imposed by international law, convention or custom to form a part of the legal order of the European Union, that obligation must not call into question the constitutional structure or the values on which the European Union is founded. (98)

Two judgments illustrate that point. ...

The second is the judgment in *Kadi and Al Barakaat International Foundation v Council and Commission*, (100) in which the Court held, in substance, that obligations imposed by an international agreement cannot have the effect of prejudicing the constitutional principle of the European Union that all EU acts must respect fundamental rights.

---

16. EU:C:2008:461 at paras 281–284.
17. Paragraph 286. That is also clear from the *dispositif* in the judgment where the CJEU confines its order to the annulment of the relevant EU Regulation.

Those two apparently contradictory interpretations of the relationship between EU law and international law illustrate the importance of maintaining a balance between safeguarding the European Union's constitutional identity and making sure that EU law does not become hostile to the international community, but is an active part of it. (101).[18]

In summary, the position is that, consistently with Article 3(5) TEU, the EU will comply its obligation to observe PIL but where that obligation calls into question what Szpunar AG called 'the constitutional structure or the values on which the European Union is founded' PIL yields to EU law.

[D]   The Procedure under the TFEU for Eliminating, in the Case of Agreements, any Incompatibility Between PIL and EU Law

It is necessary to look at two provisions of the TFEU: the first relating to agreements with third countries entered into by the Member States prior to their accession to the EU (*ex post* control) and the second relating to proposed agreements to be entered into by the EU (*ex ante* control).

Dealing first with *ex post* control, the first paragraph of Article 351 TFEU provides that 'the rights and obligations arising from agreements concluded before 1st January 1958 or, for acceding States before the date of their accession, between one or more Member States on the one hand, and one or more third countries on the other, shall not be affected by the provisions of the Treaties'. The second paragraph lays down a procedure for eliminating any incompatibility between EU law and the rights and obligations arising from such an agreement. It requires the relevant Member State(s) to 'take all appropriate steps to eliminate the incompatibilities established'. This provision does not, however, apply between the Member States[19] but only between the Member States and third countries. The CJEU has held that such appropriate steps would include denunciation of the agreement in question in a manner that is provided for in the agreement itself.[20] In other words, the obligation in the second paragraph of Article 351, 'to take all appropriate steps to eliminate the incompatibilities' is intended

---

18. EU:C:2020:349 at paragraphs 136–141, footnotes omitted.
19. In a very early case on the standstill provision on custom duties between Member States, the CJEU held that a Member State could not rely, as a defence to the application of the EU Treaty, on what is now Art. 351 TFEU in respect of a multilateral agreement (GATT) to which the Member States were party prior to their accession, *see* Case 10/61 *Commission v. Italy* EU:C:1962:2. 'In matters governed by the EEC Treaty, that Treaty takes precedence over agreements concluded between Member States before its entry into force, including agreements made within the framework of GATT.'
20. Case C-203/03 *Commission v. Austria* EU:C:2005:76 at paras 62–64. Although, in that case, it was found that Austria's obligation under an ILO Convention was incompatible with EU law, Austria had not breached EU law since at the only previous occasion that Austria had the right to denounce that Convention pursuant to the procedure laid down in the Convention was 'when the incompatibility of the prohibition laid down by that convention with [EU Law] had not been sufficiently clearly established for that Member State to be bound to denounce the convention' at para. 62. This suggests a more nuanced approach than in Case 10/61 *Commission v. Italy* where the CJEU considered that a Member State was no longer bound by a multilateral Treaty once the matter was governed by EU law (which was the case in *Commission v. Austria*).

to avoid the abrupt termination of international agreements in breach of the provisions for termination in those very agreements. As the UK Supreme Court observed in *Micula*, Article 351 'is intended to establish, in accordance with principles of international law, that the application of the EU Treaties does not affect the duty of a member state to respect the rights of non-member states under a prior agreement and to perform its obligations thereunder'.[21] This also minimises any damage to legal certainty.

However, in *Kadi*, the CJEU held that the procedure in Article 351 TFEU was inapplicable in a case where a derogation is sought 'from the principles of liberty, democracy and respect for human rights and fundamental freedoms enshrined in Article 6(1) EU as a foundation of the Union'.[22] Thus Article 351 did not 'permit any challenge to principles that form part of the very foundations of the Community legal order, one of which is the protection of fundamental rights, including the review by the Community judicature of the lawfulness of Community measures as regards their consistency with those fundamental rights'.[23] The non-applicability of Article 351 did not adversely affect Mr Kadi as he lost no rights under PIL but rather gained additional rights under EU law, namely the right to rely on fundamental rights, that he did not possess under PIL. Article 351 did not, therefore, stand in the way of the CJEU annulling the EU Regulation implementing the UN Security Council Resolution as being incompatible with fundamental rights.[24] It is not, however, clear whether the procedure in Article 351 is inapplicable solely where a derogation is sought 'from the principles of liberty, democracy and respect for human rights and fundamental freedoms' as the CJEU stated in *Kadi* or any case where PIL yields to the principle of autonomy. When EU law overrides PIL law, it does not necessarily follow there should be no period of adjustment to protect the position of those who have relied on PIL and may be adversely affected by such a determination.

Turning to *ex ante* control, Article 218(11) TFEU provides that a procedure whereby an EU Institution or Member State is entitled to seek an Opinion[25] from the CJEU as to whether an agreement that the EU envisages concluding is compatible with the EU Treaties. Such a procedure is extremely useful as it enables any such potential incompatibility to be the subject of a definitive ruling before the EU concludes an agreement. As the CJEU observed in *Opinion 1/75*:

> It is the purpose of the ... of Article [218(11)] to forestall complications which would result from legal disputes concerning the compatibility with the Treaty of international agreements binding upon the Community. In fact, a possible decision

---

21. *Micula and others v. Romania* [2020] UKSC 5 at para. 97. Thus Art. 351 TFEU reflects what is now Art. 26 of the VCLT as well as Art. 30(4)(b) which provides 'When the parties to the later Treaty do not include all the parties to the earlier one: ... as between a State party to both treaties and a State party to only one of the treaties, the treaty to which both States are parties governs their mutual rights and obligations.'
22. Paragraph 303.
23. Paragraph 304.
24. Although the CJEU permitted the Regulation to be kept in force for a period of not exceeding three months so as enable the Council to rectify the procedural defects and to prevent Mr Kadi seeking to move his assets so as to avoid any new measure.
25. The consequence of an adverse Opinion is that the proposed agreement 'may not enter into force unless it is amended or the Treaties are revised', *see* the last sentence of Art. 218(11).

of the Court to the effect that such an agreement is, either by reason of its content or of the procedure adopted for its conclusion, incompatible with the provisions of the Treaty *could not fail to provoke, not only in a Community context but also in that of international relations, serious difficulties and might give rise to adverse consequences for all interested parties, including third countries.*[26] (emphasis added)

§3.03 THE TREATMENT OF INVESTMENT TREATIES UNDER EU LAW

[A] The Background

It is estimated that the EU Member States are party to around 1,400 BITs with third countries.[27] The importance of BITs is illustrated by the encouragement given by the European Commission in the early 1990s to the conclusion of BITs between, on the one hand, the States of central and eastern Europe, who wished to accede in due course to the EU, and, and on the other hand, existing members of the EU. The aim was to attract investment in those mainly formerly communist countries by investors from the EU. Indeed the wide acceptance of the BIT model was underscored by its replication on a multilateral basis of the ECT. The ECT was signed in 1994 and now includes fifty-three Contracting Parties, including the EU and Euratom.[28] Unlike many BITs, the dispute resolution procedure contained in Article 26 ECT provides an investor with the option of bringing proceedings against a Contracting Party either before a court of the Contracting State or before an arbitration panel. A Tribunal shall decide issues under the ECT in accordance with the ECT and principles of PIL.[29] If a breach is established, damages are awarded to the investor according to the normal principles of PIL.[30]

[B] Intra-EU BITs

In *Achmea*[31] the CJEU had its first opportunity to consider the compatibility with EU law of an arbitral award made under an intra-EU BIT. The BIT had been concluded between the Netherlands and Slovakia in 1991 before Slovakia's accession to the EU in 2004. Since that date, it has become an intra-EU BIT. Pursuant to Article 8 of the BIT, the arbitral tribunal was to resolve the dispute by reference, in particular, to the law in

---

26. [1975] ECR 1355, 1360-1, EU:C:1975:145.
27. *See* https://ec.europa.eu/trade/policy/accessing-markets/dispute-settlement/investment-disputes/ last accessed 3 May 2022.
28. *See* https://energy.ec.europa.eu/topics/international-cooperation/international-organisations-and-initiatives/energy-charter_en/ last accessed 3 May 2022. The EU signed the ECT on 17 December 1994 and it was approved by Decision 98/181, OJ 1998 L69/1. Italy notified its withdrawal from the ECT on 31 December 2014 and by virtue of Art. 47(2) ECT that withdrawal took effect on 1 January 2016.
29. Article 26(6) which provides that: 'A tribunal established pursuant to paragraph 4 shall decide the issues in dispute in accordance with this Treaty and applicable rules and principles of international law.'
30. Article 26(8).
31. Case C-284/16 *Slowakische Republik v. Achmea.* EU:C:2018:158.

force of the Contracting Party concerned, the provisions of the BIT, and the general principles of international law. *Achmea* commenced arbitration proceedings in 2008. The Tribunal, sitting in Germany, rejected Slovakia's objection, based both on the VCLT and EU law, that the Tribunal had no jurisdiction in respect of an intra-EU BIT. By a final award made in December 2012, the Tribunal awarded *Achmea* just over EUR 22 million in damages for breach by Slovakia of the BIT.

Slovakia then sought to set aside the award before the German courts on the basis it was contrary to EU law. On a reference under Article 267 TFEU, the CJEU held that EU law was to be interpreted as 'precluding a provision such as Article 8 of the [BIT] … under which an investor from [An EU Member State] may, in the event of a dispute concerning investments in [another EU Member State], bring proceedings against the latter Member State before an arbitral tribunal whose jurisdiction that Member State has undertaken to accept'.[32]

In brief, its reasoning was that the EU has its own autonomous legal order and that an international agreement could not affect the allocation of powers laid down in the EU Treaties. Article 8 of the BIT enabled the tribunal to interpret and apply EU law. However, the principle of autonomy precluded Member States removing from the jurisdiction of their own courts disputes 'which may concern the application or interpretation of EU law'.[33] Further, to allow the Member States to remove such disputes from the jurisdiction of national courts was contrary to the principle of mutual trust between the Member States.[34]

The CJEU's approach was based on a matter of high constitutional principle. It was not necessary to consider whether the tribunal had actually applied or interpreted EU law. In reaching this conclusion, the CJEU distinguished the position under a BIT both from commercial arbitration[35] where it had previously accepted that an arbitration could apply or interpret EU competition law, albeit subject to a broad public policy review by a national court in an EU Member State and also from an adjudication under an international agreement to which the EU itself is party.[36] The CJEU's reasoning in *Achmea* was based exclusively on EU law. There was no discussion as to whether such

---

32. Paragraph 60.
33. Paragraph 55.
34. Paragraph 58. That is to say that the national courts within the EU should trust each other.
35. §54 citing Case C-126/97 *Eco Swiss* EU:C:1999:269. The distinction drawn with commercial arbitration was that such an arbitration agreement originates from 'the freely expressed wishes of the parties' and not from a State Treaty. This does not extend to agreements to arbitrate under investment Treaties, *see* Case C-109/20 *PL Holdings* EU:C:2021:875 at paras 46–55.
36. §57 'The competence of the EU in the field of international relations and its capacity to conclude international agreements necessarily entail the power to submit to the decisions of a court which is created or designated by such agreements as regards the interpretation and application of their provisions, provided that the autonomy of the EU and its legal order is respected (see, to that effect, Opinion 1/91 (EEA Agreement – I) of 14 December 1991, EU:C:1991:490, paragraphs 40 and 70; Opinion 1/09 (Agreement creating a unified patent litigation system) of 8 March 2011, EU:C:2011:123, paragraphs 74 and 76; and Opinion 2/13 (Accession of the EU to the ECHR) of 18 December 2014, EU:C:2014:2454, paragraphs 182 and 183).'

a result would create any 'tensions'[37] between the EU principle of autonomy and PIL, including the specific provisions in the Netherlands and Slovakia BIT on the termination of the BIT.[38] Unlike in *Kadi*, where the effect of the EU law principle of autonomy was to grant additional rights to an individual which he did not possess in PIL, the application of the principle of autonomy in *Achmea* was to remove, as a matter of EU law, rights that an individual has under PIL, namely to settle disputes with a State through arbitration.[39]

In January 2019, twenty-two EU Member States issued a Declaration on the legal consequences of the judgment of the CJEU in *Achmea* and on investment protection in the EU ('the BIT Declaration').[40] This was followed in May 2020 by an agreement between twenty-three EU Member States for the Termination of Bilateral Investment Treaties Between the Member States of the EU ('the BIT Termination Agreement').[41]

Section 2 of the BIT Termination Agreement provides not only for the termination of intra-EU BITs but also the sunset clauses in such BITs.[42] Section 3 deals with awards and claims made under such BITs. Article 6(1) provides that proceedings in 'Concluded Arbitration Proceedings' shall not be reopened. However, the definition of 'Concluded Arbitration Proceedings' is limited to 'any Arbitration Proceedings which ended with a settlement agreement or with a final award issued prior to 6 March 2018 where: (a) the award was duly executed prior to 6 March 2018, ..., and no challenge, review, set-aside, annulment, enforcement, revision or other similar proceedings in relation to such final award was pending on 6 March 2018 [the date of the judgment in *Achmea*]'.[43] Given the narrow definition of Concluded Arbitration Proceedings, awards made before the entry into force of the BIT Termination Agreement and, indeed, awards made before the *Achmea* judgment are not preserved where there is an outstanding challenge.[44] This is in contrast to the sunset provisions in the BITs where termination of the BIT does not affect the right of an investor who made an investment before the date of termination for a further period of years in the future. Thus if the Netherlands and Slovakia BIT had been terminated according to the terms of the BIT, *Achmea* would not have been deprived of its award.[45] For these reasons, the legality of

---

37. The expression used by Szpunar AG in *Rina*, *see* footnote 18 above. It would seem that the issue of PIL was not raised before the CJEU as neither the Judgment nor the Opinion of the Advocate General touch on it.
38. *See* Art. 13(3) of the Netherlands – Slovakia BIT (1991) at footnote 6 above.
39. This issue has been considered by arbitral Tribunals post *Achmea*, *see* section §3.03[D] below.
40. https://ec.europa.eu/info/sites/default/files/business_economy_euro/banking_and_finance/documents/190117-bilateral-investment-treaties_en.pdf.
41. OJ 2020 L 169/1.
42. *See* Art. 2. A 'Sunset Clause' is defined in Art. 1(7) as 'any provision in a Bilateral Investment Treaty which extends the protection of investments made prior to the date of termination of that Treaty for a further period of time'. Thus, in the case of the Netherlands-Slovakia BIT in issue in *Achmea* the sunset clause is to be found in Art. 13(3), *see* footnote 6 above, which provides a further fifteen years of investment protection post-termination.
43. *See* Art. 1(4).
44. For example, the award in *Achmea*, although made on 7 December 2012, would appear to fall outside the definition of Concluded Arbitration Proceedings since it had not been duly executed before 6 March 2018 and there was a pending challenge at that date.
45. Thus, in the case of the Netherlands-Slovakia BIT it is fifteen years. *See* Art. 13(3) at footnote 6 above.

the BIT Termination Agreement has been questioned.[46] In respect of arbitration proceedings that are not Concluded Arbitration Proceedings,[47] Article 7 imposes a duty on the contracting Member States to inform arbitral tribunals about the legal consequences of *Achmea* and where they are party to judicial proceedings concerning an arbitral award issued on the basis of a BIT to ask the competent national court, including in any third country, as the case may be, to set the arbitral award aside, annul it or to refrain from recognising and enforcing it.[48] There are transitional measures in respect of Pending Arbitration Proceedings which permit the extension of national time limits for a claim to be brought on condition that the claimant renounces all rights under the BIT.[49]

Subsequent to *Achmea* the CJEU was asked in *PL Holdings*,[50] *inter alia*, whether *Achmea* was to be interpreted as depriving investors of an award made prior to the delivery of the *Achmea* judgment where the arbitration proceedings had been initiated in good faith. The CJEU declined to impose any such temporal limitation so as to preserve pre-existing awards.[51] Rather it held that an investor's rights which derive from EU law 'must be protected within the framework of the judicial system of the member states'.[52] There are two problems with this approach. First, the investor's rights under EU law are likely to be different from that under a BIT both in terms of substantive rights and remedies.[53] Put shortly, in terms of substantive rights, the rights under EU law are less than under a BIT.[54] Even if an investor seeks to rely on rights under BIT before a national court, a national court is unlikely to have jurisdiction since

---

46. *See*, for example, Nardell and Rees-Evans, *The Agreement Terminating Intra-EU BITs: Are Its Provisions on 'New' and 'Pending' Arbitration Proceedings Compatible with Investors' Fundamental Rights?* Arbitration International Volume 37, 2021, 37, 197.
47. Defined as 'Pending Arbitration Proceedings' and 'New Arbitration Proceedings' in Arts 1(5) and (6) respectively.
48. The CJEU relied, *inter alia*, on this provision in *PL Holdings* at para. 53 (footnote 35 above) for its conclusion that EU law requires Member States to ask a national court to set aside, annul or refrain from recognising or enforcing an intra-EU arbitral award.
49. *See* Arts 8–10. Pending Arbitration Proceedings are defined in Art. 1(5) as any arbitration proceedings initiated prior to 6 March 2018 and not qualifying as Concluded Arbitration Proceedings. In the case of such proceedings an investor is entitled to have access to 'the judicial remedies under national law' and national time limits can be extended but only on condition that the investor withdraws his arbitration proceedings and 'waives all rights and claims pursuant to the relevant [BIT] or renounces execution of an award already issued, but not yet definitively enforced or executed', *see* Art. 10(1)(a).
50. *See* footnote 35 above.
51. *Ibid.*, at paras 57–67.
52. *Ibid.*, at para. 68.
53. *See*, in this context, Paparinskis, *Substantive Standards of Investment Protection under EU Law and International Investment Law* in *EU Law and International Investment Arbitration*, editors Hélène Ruiz-Fabri and Emmanuel Gaillard (Max Planck Institute Luxembourg for Procedural Law (Juris, 2018)).
54. *See* the Opinion of Wathelet AG in *Achmea* at paras 179–228. Since the delivery of that Opinion the CJEU held in Case C-235/17 *Commission v. Hungary* EU:C:2019:432 that a measure which restricts the free movement of capital can only be justified under EU law if it is compatible with the Charter on Fundamental Rights ('the Charter'). The Hungarian measure in issue in that case was a restriction relating to the right of usufruct over agricultural land which infringed Art. 63 TFEU on the free movement of capital and could not be justified under Art. 17 of the Charter on rights to property.

a BIT generally only gives jurisdiction to an arbitral tribunal.[55] In terms of remedies, the threshold for obtaining an award of damages is significantly higher in EU law than under a BIT.[56] There is also the question of whether a claim under EU law can be brought within national limitation periods.[57] Second, there is no consideration in the judgment of whether such an approach, by depriving an investor of an existing award,[58] is compatible with the sunset provisions in BITs and PIL more generally.

[C]   The Energy Charter Treaty

In *Komstroy*,[59] the CJEU applied the principle of the autonomy of EU Law and mutual trust between the Member States to an MIT, namely the ECT, in the same way as it had done in *Achmea*. The dispute in *Komstroy* was not an intra-EU dispute as in *Achmea* but rather one between a non-EU person and Moldova. The non-EU person had obtained an award from an arbitral tribunal sitting in Paris pursuant to Article 26 ECT on the basis that Moldova had breached the ECT. Moldova then brought a challenge to that award on the basis that the tribunal should have declined jurisdiction as there had not been an 'investment' within the meaning of Article 1(6) of the ECT. The Court of Appeal in Paris then made a reference to this question to the CJEU.

The first issue was whether the CJEU had any jurisdiction to answer this question since the dispute was between non-EU parties in respect of events outside the EU which turned on the interpretation of the ECT, an international agreement. The CJEU held it did have jurisdiction. Its reasoning can be distilled into three steps. *First*, it held that agreements, such as the ECT, which are approved by an EU decision constitute acts of the EU and that provisions of those agreements form an integral part of the EU legal order.[60] *Second*, it was in the interests of the EU that, in the case of a provision of an international agreement that can apply both within and without the scope of EU Law, such a provision 'should be interpreted uniformly, whatever the circumstances in which it is to apply'.[61] This was the case here since the referring court 'could find it necessary, in a case falling directly within the scope of EU law, ..., to rule on the interpretation of those same provisions of the ECT'.[62] *Third*, the parties chose to

---

55. The position is different under the ECT, *see* Art. 26 referred to in section §3.03[A] above.
56. The remedy for breach of a BIT is damages. However, consistently with most European national legal systems, damages are only available in EU law where the breach of EU law is a sufficiently serious breach of a superior rule of law for the protection of individuals, *see* Joined Cases 83/76, 94/76, 4/77, 15/77 and 40/77 *HNL v. Council and Commission* EU:C:1978:113, para. 5. The high hurdle for damages is, however, counterbalanced by the available of remedies such as quashing and annulment which are not available under a BIT.
57. The award in *PL Holdings* would appear, like the award in *Achmea*, to fall within the definition of Pending Arbitration Proceedings and so national time limits could only be extended pursuant to the BIT Termination Agreement if the existing awards are definitively renounced, *see* footnote 49 above.
58. In *PL Holdings* the award was EUR 150 million, *see* para. 17 of the Opinion of Kokott AG.
59. Case C-741/19 *Republic of Moldova v. Komstroy* EU:C:2021:655.
60. Paragraphs 22–27. It added since the entry into force of the TFEU the EU has exclusive competence as regards foreign direct investment and shared competence in indirect investment.
61. Paragraph 29.
62. Paragraph 31.

arbitrate their dispute in Paris which made French law the *lex fori* and French law had to comply with EU law.[63]

Prior to answering the specific question on the definition of an investment under the ECT that was asked by the referring court, the CJEU decided that it was necessary 'to specify which disputes between one Contracting Party and an investor of another Contracting Party concerning an investment made by the latter in the area of the former may be brought before an arbitral tribunal pursuant to Article 26 ECT'.[64] The CJEU had in mind disputes between an EU Member State and an investor from another EU Member State, that is to say, an intra-EU dispute. Those observations were, however, *obiter* as the dispute was between a third country and a non-EU investor.[65]

The CJEU's observations on whether an intra-EU dispute fell within the scope of Article 26 ECT broadly followed its approach in *Achmea*. The steps in the analysis can be summarised as follows. *First*, Article 26(6) ECT requires a tribunal to apply the ECT and since the ECT is an act of EU law, the tribunal would be interpreting and applying EU law.[66]

Second, an arbitral tribunal set up under the ECT is not a court or tribunal for the purposes of Article 267 TFEU and so cannot make a reference to the CJEU and any award is not capable of a full review by a court of a Member State so as to guarantee full compliance with EU law. In this respect, the CJEU maintained the distinction that it had drawn in *Achmea* between commercial arbitration, freely entered into by the parties, and arbitration, deriving from a Treaty whereby the Member States remove disputes from the jurisdiction of their own courts.

Third, it confirmed that the EU's capacity to conclude international agreements necessarily entailed the power to accept the jurisdiction of a court to interpret an international agreement that does not extend 'to permitting, in an international agreement, a provision according to which a dispute between an investor of one Member State and another Member State concerning EU law may be removed from the judicial system of the European Union such that the full effectiveness of that law is not guaranteed'.[67] That would call into question the preservation of autonomy, ensured in particular by the preliminary ruling procedure provided for in Article 267 TFEU.

Fourth and finally, the CJEU considered that the multilateral nature of the ECT did not preclude such a result since Article 26 ECT 'is intended, in reality, to govern bilateral relations between two of the Contracting Parties, in an analogous way to the provision of the BIT at issue in [*Achmea*].[68] The conclusion was that "Article 26(2)I ECT must be interpreted as not being applicable to disputes between a Member State

---

63. Paragraphs 32–38. In so doing the CJEU distinguished earlier case law where it had held that it had no jurisdiction to interpret the EEA Agreement on a reference from a national court.
64. Paragraph 40.
65. The CJEU appears to justify this *obiter* by referring to the submissions of Member States who wished to have an answer to this question, *see* para. 40. As to whether the CJEU was right to proceed in this way, *see Republic of Moldova v. Komstroy LCC*: arbitration under Art. 26 ECT outlawed in intra-EU disputes by obiter dictum, Alan Dashwood E.L.Rev 2022, 47(1), 127.
66. Paragraphs 47–50.
67. Paragraph 62.
68. Paragraph 64.

and an investor of another Member State concerning an investment made by the latter in the first Member State.'"[69] In other words, one could legally disconnect intra-EU disputes from other disputes falling within the scope of the ECT.

I will confine my observations on *Komstroy* to the conclusion that the ECT was part of EU law and that Article 26 ECT was inapplicable to intra-EU disputes.

It is to be recalled that the first step in the reasoning as to why the CJEU had jurisdiction was that the ECT was concluded by the EU and so became part of EU law from the moment that it entered into force. While this conclusion is amply supported by the case law of the CJEU,[70] it does not follow that the ECT is not also part of PIL. Indeed Article 26(6) ECT expressly states that a tribunal is to decide a dispute under the ECT in accordance with the law of the ECT and PIL. The conclusion that the ECT is part of EU law is based solely on the position that it is brought into the EU legal order by signature and ratification of the Member States and the EU. The ECT becomes part of the legal system of all the States that have signed and ratified the ECT. But the ECT still remains an instrument of PIL to be interpreted in the manner set out in Article 26(6) ECT. Thus, in the case of the EU legal order, the ECT has a hybrid character: it is both part of PIL and EU law. But when the CJEU was interpreting Articles of the ECT, it was bound to do so by reference to principles of PIL.[71]

When, however, the CJEU stated that Article 26 ECT is intended, in reality, to govern bilateral relations between two of the Contracting Parties as opposed to being part of a multilateral obligation, in an analogous way to the provision of a BIT, it is not clear whether that conclusion was based on EU law or PIL.

If the CJEU was interpreting that Article as a matter of PIL, then it is striking that there was no analysis of the rules of interpretation under the VCLT, including the *travaux préparatoires* of the ECT.[72] By contrast, when faced with a similar argument as to whether, in the context of an enforcement of an award made under a BIT, the ICSID Convention involved multilateral or simply bilateral obligations between States, the UK Supreme Court in *Micula* analysed the Convention, including the *travaux préparatoires*, before concluding that it contained multilateral obligations.[73] On its face, there is nothing in the ECT that suggests that Article 26 is not to apply to intra-EU disputes. Although the Commission did submit a statement to the ECT Secretariat in respect of Article 26 which is appended to the ECT, there was no suggestion in that statement that Article 26 could not apply to intra-EU disputes.[74] Thus the better view must be that the CJEU in *Komstroy* was not interpreting Article 26 as a matter of PIL but rather as a

---

69. Paragraph 66.
70. *See*, e.g., *Western Sahara* discussed in section §3.02[B] above.
71. This was made clear by AG Szpunar who referred explicitly to the need to interpret those provisions in the light of Art. 31 VCLT, *see* para. 109 of his Opinion.
72. One might add that if the CJEU had intended to rule on this as a matter of PIL, it would have sought submissions from the parties on PIL but there is no indication that this occurred.
73. *See* footnote 21 above at paras 103–108. The Commission has announced that it has brought proceedings against the UK in respect of this judgment but it is unclear if those proceedings extend to the UKSC's interpretation of the ICSID Convention, *see* https://ec.europa.eu/commission/presscorner/detail/en/ip_22_802 (last accessed 3 May 2022).
74. *See* the Statement submitted by the European Communities to the Secretariat of the Energy Charter pursuant to Art. 26(3)(b)(ii) of the ECT:

matter of EU law. This is also consistent with the whole *obiter* passage which refers solely to EU law and indeed what the CJEU subsequently stated in Opinion 1/20.[75] Viewed in this light, what the CJEU appears to have been saying is that EU law precludes Article 26 from being applied to an intra-EU dispute. Expressed in those terms, there is a tension between the interpretation of the ECT, as an instrument of EU law, and as an instrument of PIL. This tension could have been avoided if either the Commission or a Member State had sought an Opinion from the CJEU, via the procedure laid down in Article 218(11) TFEU, as to whether the EU could accede to the ECT in a manner that was compatible with the EU law. If the CJEU had given the answer that it gave in *Komstroy* the EU and the Member States could not have entered into the ECT without resolving the issue as to whether Article 26 ECT could apply to intra-EU disputes and considerable legal uncertainty could have been avoided.

[D]   The Reaction of Tribunals and Courts to the CJEU's *Achmea* Case Law

The approach taken by the CJEU in *Achmea* and *Komstroy* has had a mixed response. Although *Achmea* has been applied by EU national courts as a matter of EU law, it has largely not been followed by Tribunals who have considered that the CJEU's approach omits any consideration of PIL.

Looking first at Tribunals, by way of example, in *Magyar Farming v. Hungary*[76] an ICSID Tribunal rejected Hungary's argument that, in the light of *Achmea*,[77] the Tribunal had no jurisdiction to adjudicate in a dispute between a UK investor and Hungary. It observed:

> The Parties agree that the question whether the EU Treaties override the dispute resolution clause of the BIT must be assessed under international law, and rightly so. Indeed, the BIT's offer to arbitrate is contained in an international treaty, and its validity and interpretation is governed by the VCLT of which Hungary and the

---

'The European Communities, as Contracting Parties to the Energy Charter Treaty, make the following statement concerning their policies, practices and conditions with regard to disputes between an investor and a Contracting Parties and their submission to international arbitration or conciliation:

'The European Communities are a regional economic integration organisation within the meaning of the Energy Charter Treaty. The Communities exercise the competences conferred on them by their Member States through autonomous decision-making and judicial institutions.'

75. Opinion of 16 June 2022 EU:C:2022:485 at para. 47. 'It is clear from the judgment of 2 September 2021, Republic of Moldova (C-741/19, EU:C:2021:655), and in particular from paragraphs 40 to 66 thereof, that compliance with the principle of autonomy of EU law, enshrined in Article 344 TFEU, requires Article 26(2)(c) of the ECT to be interpreted as meaning that it is not applicable to disputes between a Member State and an investor of another Member State concerning an investment made by the latter in the first Member State.'
76. ICSID Case No. ARB/17/27, award of 13 November 2019. *See* to the same effect *Eskosol v. Italy*, ICSID Case No. ARB/15/50, award of 7 May 2019. This was a case on the ECT not a BIT but the Tribunal's analysis of *Achmea* is equally relevant, *see*, in particular, paras 115–119, 152–186.
77. Case C-284/16 *Slowakische Republik v. Achmea.* EU:C:2018:158.

UK are both contracting parties. In addition, this arbitration is conducted under the ICSID Convention and, thus, is not subject to a national legal system.

...

The Tribunal is not convinced that it is bound by the CJEU's decision [in *Achmea*] over the conflict between the BIT and the EU Treaties. Under Article 41 of the ICSID Convention, the UK, Hungary and the other 155 contracting States, including non-EU States, agreed that an arbitral tribunal constituted under the ICSID Convention 'shall be the judge of its own competence', and that:

> Any objection by a party to the dispute that that dispute is not within the jurisdiction of the Centre, or for other reasons is not within the competence of the Tribunal, *shall be considered* by the Tribunal ...

...

In any event, the CJEU's interpretative authority extends to the interpretation and application of the EU Treaties. The CJEU has no such (arguably) exclusive or ultimate mandate in respect of the interpretation of the BIT or the VCLT rules on treaty conflicts. Yet, in order to determine whether Article 8 of the BIT [the relevant dispute resolution provision] is precluded by the EU Treaties, it does not suffice to interpret the EU Treaties. This determination requires the interpretation of both the EU Treaties and the BIT, in order to answer crucial questions such as (i) whether the BIT and the EU Treaties govern the same subject matter as provided in Article 30 of the VCLT and, if so, (ii) whether there is a normative conflict between these treaties as understood under the VCLT.

Not only does the CJEU have no exclusive authority to answer these questions, but it did not even purport to address them in the Achmea Decision. Even a cursory review of that decision reveals that the CJEU did not undertake a conflicts analysis under the VCLT. Thus, even if the Tribunal were willing to pay deference to the CJEU's reasoning, the Achmea Decision would give no guidance on the issues which must be resolved to determine whether the EU Treaties preclude the application of Article 8 of the BIT as a matter of international law.[78]

The Tribunal then held that the BIT Declaration[79] could not validly retroactively invalidate the valid acceptance under the ICSID Convention by Magyar Farms of Hungary's offer to arbitrate.[80] It concluded:

> The Tribunal's finding that the 2019 Declarations were not the proper procedure to terminate or amend the BIT is not based on mere formalism. The BIT is an international treaty that confers rights on private parties. While the Contracting States remain the masters of their treaty, their control is limited by the general principles of legal certainty and *res inter alios acta, aliis nec nocet nec prodest*. This is evident for instance from Article 13(3) of the BIT, which grants a guarantee of stability to investors who have made investments in reliance on the BIT:
>
> > In respect of investment made whilst the Agreement is in force, its provisions shall continue in effect with respect to such investments for a period of twenty years after the date of termination and without prejudice to the application thereafter of the rules of general international law.
>
> This provision shows that, even where the Contracting Parties terminate the treaty on mutual consent, they acknowledge that long-term interests of investors

---

78. Paragraphs 203, 207, 209–210, original emphasis but footnotes omitted.
79. At the time of the award the BIT Termination Agreement had not been signed.
80. Paragraphs 212–221.

who have invested in the host State in reliance on the treaty guarantees must be respected. This is the purpose served by the 20-year sunset provision. If the protection of existing investments outlives an unambiguous termination of the Treaty, then the protection must continue a fortiori in respect of a decision of an adjudicatory body constituted under a different treaty or of declarations that purport to clarify the legal consequences of that decision.[81]

The Tribunals that have considered Article 26 ECT in the light of *Komstroy* have not all reached the same conclusion as the CJEU did in *Komstroy*. Thus, for example, in *Eskosol* an ICSID Tribunal cited the ILC which has stated that the very function of a 'disconnection clause'[82] is that it 'seek[s] to replace a treaty in whole or in part with a different regime that should be [] applicable between certain parties only', with such clause 'agreed to by all the parties of the treaty'.[83]

Subsequently, an ICSID Tribunal in *Infracapital* stated:

> The Tribunal agrees with Claimants that in interpreting Article 26 ECT the CJEU [in *Komstroy*] made no effort to conduct an interpretive exercise under the VCLT – as would be required under public international law – but rather relied on an alleged need to 'preserv[e] the autonomy and [...] the particular nature of EU law' in order to justify its decision. This is clearly inappropriate.

The last premise essentially proposes that there be a separate treatment for intra-EU disputes (i.e., where investors and the host State are part of the EU) and non-intra-EU disputes. This would imply that investors of an EU Member State could not access arbitration against a Member State for claims relating to a breach of the ECT and international law. But such interpretation is not supported by the provisions of the ECT, nor in the objectives of the ECT.

In the Tribunal's view, nothing in the ECT gives an ECT tribunal the authority to disregard or modify the explicit provisions of the ECT and decline jurisdiction on the basis of a Contracting Party's status or its obligations under a different legal order.

As regards disconnection from the provisions relating to arbitration in Article 26(2)(c) of the ECT, this Tribunal found in the Decision that there is no evidence that the EU and the Member States are disconnected from the ECT for the purpose of intra-EU investment arbitrations, and again rejects the claim by Respondent that the EU and its Member States disconnected from Article 26 ECT subsequent to the ratification of the ECT ' as a necessary effect of the ratification of the Lisbon Treaty by the member states'.[84]

---

81. Paragraphs 222–223, original italics but footnotes omitted.
82. That is to say a clause that disconnects intra-EU disputes from Art. 26.
83. Paragraph 91, footnotes omitted.
84. ICSID Case No. ARB/16/18 at paras 111–114 footnotes omitted. *See* to the same effect *Vattenfall v. Germany* ICSID Case No. ARB/12/12 https://www.italaw.com/sites/default/files/case-documents/italaw9916.pdf at paras 169–208 where the Tribunal concludes 'Having carried out an interpretation under Article 31 VCLT of the ordinary meaning to be attributed to Article 26 ECT, in its context, and in the light of the object and purpose of the ECT, the Tribunal finds that a Contracting Party to the ECT in Article 26 ECT includes EU Member States and non-EU Member States without distinction. There is no carve-out from the ECT's dispute settlement provisions concerning their applicability to EU Member States inter se, in particular regarding the

By contrast in *Green Power v. SCE Sola Don Benito*,[85] in an arbitration conducted under rules of the Stockholm Chamber of Commerce where the seat of arbitration was Stockholm the Tribunal concluded, applying *Komstroy*, that it had no jurisdiction to determine an intra-EU dispute under the ECT. The Tribunal considered that previous ICSID cases to the opposite effect were to be distinguished on the basis that they did not take into account the applicable law of the seat, which in this case was Swedish law which included EU law.[86]

What one sees from the above is that there is still uncertainty about the inter-relationship between EU law post *Achmea* and *Komstroy* and PIL. While plainly the CJEU has the ultimate arbiter of EU law, it would be helpful if the CJEU were, in a future case, to address not only issues of EU law but also PIL in the way that it has done in the past in such cases as *Kadi* and *Western Sahara*. While the CJEU is not able to provide a definitive ruling on PIL,[87] consideration by the CJEU of the position under PIL would be helpful as that would open a dialogue between, on the one hand, the CJEU interpreting both EU law and PIL and, on the other hand, Tribunals interpreting PIL and, it is hoped, reduce the scope for conflicting rulings. It may be that the position of the CJEU is that the principle of autonomy trumps any consideration of PIL. If that is the position, it would nonetheless be helpful to explain why such a result can be reconciled with rights investors consider that they have acquired as a matter of PIL.

Turning to the courts of EU Member States, the German Federal Court of Justice (the *Bundesgerichtshof)* applied the judgment of the CJEU in *Achmea* by setting aside the arbitral award in *Achmea*.[88] More recently, the Court of Appeal in Paris has annulled two awards made by arbitral tribunals, also sitting in Paris, under two intra-EU BITs.[89] It did so on the basis that the Tribunal had no jurisdiction pursuant to *Achmea* and *PL Holdings* to determine an arbitration under such BITs. It held that it was unnecessary to consider the position under PIL and the VCLT.

[E]   Extra-EU Treaties

In contrast to the absence of the request for an Opinion prior to the EU acceding to the ECT, an Opinion was sought on the compatibility with EU law of the ISDS mechanism in the Comprehensive Economic and Trade Agreement between EU and Canada (CETA).[90] The ISDS mechanism in the CETA has its origins in the ISDS provisions found in BITs and the ECT but differs in a number of important respects. It has

---

opportunity for an EU Investor to pursue arbitration against an EU Member State. Indeed, the terms of Article 26 ECT give not the slightest hint that any such exclusion is possible.' at para. 207.
85. Arbitration Institute of the Stockholm Chamber of Commerce, SCC Arbitration V (2016/135) of 16 June 2022.
86. Paras. 413–478.
87. *See* Case C-66/18 *Commission v. Hungary* EU:C:2020:792.
88. Decision of 31 October 2018, Case I ZB 2/15.
89. *Poland v. Strabag and others*, Judgment of 19 April 2022 48/2022 and *Poland v. CEC Praha*, Judgment of 19 April 2022 49/2022.
90. *Opinion 1/17* EU:C:2019:341.

renounced ad hoc arbitration in favour of a permanent Tribunal and an Appellate Tribunal to adjudicate on disputes between investors and the parties to the CETA. In the words of Point 6(f) of the Joint Interpretative Instrument, the 'CETA moves decisively away from the traditional approach of investment dispute resolution and establishes independent, impartial and permanent investment Tribunals, inspired by the principles of public judicial systems'. The Tribunals are to apply the Agreement in accordance with the VCLT and other rules and principles of PIL.[91] They have, however, no jurisdiction to determine the legality of a measure alleged to constitute a breach of the CETA, under the domestic law of a Party but are confined to considering the domestic law of a Party as a matter of fact.[92] They have the jurisdiction to award compensatory damages for breach of a provision in the CETA.[93]

The CJEU held that the adjudication of disputes in the CETA by the CETA Tribunals was, in principle, compatible with EU Law as it was inherent in the ability of the EU to enter international agreements that it would also accept the jurisdiction of an international tribunal set up under that agreement. It distinguished *Achmea* on two grounds. First, the CETA Tribunals do not have jurisdiction to interpret EU law.[94] While they might have to consider EU law, they can only do so as a matter of fact which 'cannot be classified as equivalent to an interpretation, by the CETA Tribunal, of that domestic law'. Second, the CETA Tribunals were not an intra-EU arrangement between the Member States but one between the EU and a third country. By contrast, the tribunal in *Achmea* was set up under an agreement between the Member States and did not involve third States.[95] However, the CJEU's approval of the ISDS mechanism in the CETA was not unconditional. It laid down two main conditions.

First, although the establishment of the CETA Tribunals was not precluded by the principle of autonomy, that principle did preclude such Tribunals from 'call[ing] into question the level of protection of a public interest that led to the introduction of such restrictions by the Union with respect to all operators who invest in the commercial or industrial sector at issue of the internal market'.[96] The reason for this was the remedy of damages for a breach of the CETA would lead the EU to amend or withdraw legislation because of a different evaluation of the level of protection made by a body outside the EU judicial system. This is what has been called 'the chilling effect'.[97] The question of whether the level of protection is unlawful is in effect reserved for the

---

91. Article 8.31.1.
92. Article 8.31.2.
93. Article 8.39.1(a), 3 and 4. The CJEU contrasted the remedy of damages with the remedies available under the World Trade Organization, *see* para. 146.
94. Paragraphs 126 and 130-135. As the CJEU acknowledged, the CETA is part of EU law whose interpretation the CETA Tribunals are entrusted with. However the CETA, like the ECT, is a hybrid of both PIL and EU law as explained in section §3.03[C] above. It is to be interpreted according to its own provisions and PIL and not in accordance with EU law.
95. Paragraphs 127-129. The CJEU added that the principle of mutual trust obliges Member States to consider that all other Member States comply with EU law, including the right to an effective remedy but that this principle does not apply between the EU and third States.
96. Paragraph 148.
97. The CJEU was responding to the argument by Belgium and other Member States that the CETA Tribunals should not be able to undermine the policy choices made by domestic legislators through the chilling effect of damages awards.

courts within the EU.[98] The CJEU then analysed the relevant provisions of the CETA and found that the jurisdiction of the CETA Tribunals did not permit them to review the level of protection but was 'concentrated on, inter alia, situations where there is abusive treatment, manifest arbitrariness and targeted discrimination ...'.[99] The CJEU, therefore, used the principle of autonomy to impose a *limit* on the scope of the substantive review of EU legislation by an outside Tribunal pursuant to an international agreement. This is different from the scope of the principle of autonomy in *Achmea* and previous cases which *precluded* an outside Tribunal from having *any* jurisdiction to engage in any review at all. As has been observed, 'it appears to elevate ... EU measures that may have been adopted via EU secondary legislation to the rank of a constituent element of the 'autonomy of the EU legal order'.[100]

The practical effect of this is that an investor will have to overcome a high hurdle to show a breach of the CETA and obtain damages. In this respect, the hurdle under the CETA is now closer to that under EU law. To obtain damages under EU Law requires one to establish that the breach of EU law is a sufficiently serious breach of a superior rule of law, that is to say, that there has been a manifest and grave disregard by a public body of the limits on its discretion.[101]

The second main condition laid down by the CJEU was that the ISDS provisions in the CETA had to comply with Article 47 of the Charter of Fundamental Rights ('the Charter') which provides for access to an 'independent and impartial tribunal'.[102] As mentioned above, while the CETA ISDS mechanisms had their origins in ISDS mechanisms found in BITs and ECTs, there were a number of innovations which were crucial in the CJEU finding that the ISDS mechanisms complied with Article 47. In essence, the ISDS mechanism in CETA is hybrid in nature, combining characteristics based on traditional arbitration mechanisms as well as those of permanent judicial bodies. It provides for the establishment of a permanent tribunal of fifteen Members and that a division of three Members will '[hear] the case on a rotation basis, ensuring that the composition of the divisions is random and unpredictable'.[103] The CJEU held that the requirements of independence and impartiality 'require rules, particularly as regards the composition of the body and the appointment, length of service and grounds for abstention, rejection and dismissal of its members, in order to dispel any reasonable doubt in the minds of individuals as to the imperviousness of that body to external factors and its neutrality with respect to the interests before it'.[104] The CJEU

---

98. Paragraphs 149–151.
99. Paragraphs 152–160. The quoted passage comes from para. 159.
100. *See* Boelaert in Opinion 1/17 of the Court of Justice on the legality, under EU law, of the investor to state dispute settlement mechanism included in the CETA agreement. A case of legal pragmatism or the dawn of a new era? in Biondi and Sangiuolo eds, *The EU and the Rule of Law in International Economic Relations, an Agenda for an Enhanced Dialogue*, Edward Elgar 2021 p. 37 at p. 61.
101. *See* footnote 56 above.
102. Since CETA would be an agreement to which the EU would bind itself, it was subject to the Charter. It did not matter that the Charter does not apply to the third country with whom the EU had concluded the agreement, *see* paras 190–191.
103. Article 8.27.7.
104. §204.

imposed a high standard since the case law on which the CJEU relied was its case law on the requirement of independence of a court or tribunal of a Member State for the purposes of Article 267 TFEU. The tribunals set up under the CETA met this standard. Article 47 of the Charter applies to agreements, such as CETA, concluded or to be concluded after the entry into force of the Charter[105] but it has also been held to apply to measures that predate it.[106] Thus, in principle, it applies also to dispute resolution bodies in pre-existing agreements to which the EU is a party.

It remains to be seen how the EU will seek to ensure this standard is met in international agreements to which it is party which provides for a dispute resolution mechanism.[107]

§3.04   CONCLUSIONS

The EU principle of autonomy is a constitutional principle of the highest importance in the EU legal order. It needs, however, to be applied in a manner that does least damage to obligations undertaken by the Member States and the EU to comply with PIL. If the Member States had decided to terminate all their intra-EU BITs by means of agreements that were prospective in nature and respected sunset clauses in those BITs this would have been uncontroversial as a matter of PIL. However, the retrospective application of the principle of autonomy in *Achmea,* as then applied by the BIT Termination Agreement, has created, to use the expression of Szpunar AG in *Rina,*[108] 'tensions [between EU law and PIL] which the Union must resolve' as illustrated by a number of arbitral rulings post *Achmea,* which have not been willing to follow the *Achmea* approach as a matter of PIL. Such tensions are particularly unfortunate where the effect of EU law is to deprive investors of awards made under PIL for reasons unconnected to the merits.[109] It is, therefore, to be hoped that the CJEU will use a future occasion to resolve these tensions between EU law and PIL or explain more fully why the principle of autonomy trumps any consideration of PIL. In the case of agreements to which the EU itself wishes to adhere, it is important that the procedure under Article 218(11) TFEU is used as it provides a specific mechanism for avoiding any such future tensions. Given the developing nature of the principle of autonomy, the importance of this procedure cannot be overstated. If the CJEU concludes that there is an incompatibility

---

105. The Charter came into force on 1 December 2009 pursuant to Art. 6(1) of the Treaty on European Union.
106. *See,* for example, Case C-362/14, *Schrems v. Data Protection Commissioner,* EU:C:2015:650 at paras 91–98 where the CJEU annulled Commission Decision 2000/520 on data transfers between the EU and the US on the basis, *inter alia,* that it did not comply with the Charter.
107. *See* Vajda, *The Applicability of Article 47 of the Charter of Fundamental Rights to International Agreements to which the Union is a Contracting Party* in *Evolution des rapports entre les orders juridiques de l'Union européénne, international et nationaux, Liber Amicorum Jiří Malenovský,* Bruylant 2020, pp. 551–572.
108. *See* section §3.02[C] above.
109. There is no suggestion in any of these cases that the Tribunal has misapplied substantive provisions of PIL or indeed has misinterpreted of misapplied any substantive provision of EU law, other than the principle of autonomy which is a principle relating to jurisdiction that does not go to the merits of a dispute.

between an intended agreement and EU law, everyone knows what the legal position is. In the absence of an Opinion under Article 218(11) TFEU, one might ask whether any subsequent court ruling concluding that such an agreement, or part of it, is incompatible with EU law should not be prospective in nature or at least not re-open past transactions entered into in good faith under the agreement. What one can say is that if an Opinion had been sought in respect of the ECT, as it was in the case of the CETA, a great deal of legal uncertainty could have been avoided.

CHAPTER 4

The Exception in Theory, a Unicorn in Practice? Revisiting Security for Costs from a Practitioner's Perspective

Jan Heiner Nedden & Inga Witte

§4.01 ARBITRAL TRIBUNALS HAVE THE POWER: NOW WHAT?

In international arbitration, security for costs (*cautio iudicatum sovlvi*) has long played a fairly limited role. With third-party funding gaining traction in recent years, the international arbitration community has revisited the instrument. Both in theory and in practice, however, these discussions focused primarily on the implications of the non-applicant being funded by a third party. We take this development as a reason to revisit security for costs more generally.

What can be regarded as settled nowadays is that arbitral tribunals *have* the power to order security for costs. Some national arbitration laws[1] or institutional rules[2] explicitly vest the arbitral tribunal with this power. Absent such a provision (or an express agreement between the Parties), the power to order security for costs stems from the arbitral tribunal's broad powers under the applicable national arbitration

---

1. In particular s. 38(3) of the English Arbitration Act; s. 56(1)(a) of the Hong Kong Arbitration Ordinance; s. 12(1)(a) of the Singapore International Arbitration Act. Note that the provision was introduced to the English Arbitration Act in reaction to the famous *Ken-Ren* case.
2. *See* Art. 25.2 of the 2020 LCIA Rules, Art. 24 of the 2018 HKIAC Rules, Rule 27(j) of the 2016 SIAC Rules, Art. 38 of the 2017 SCC Rules, Art. 33(6) of the 2021 VIAC Rules; further Rule 53 of the 2022 ICSID Rules (entry into force on 1 July 2022).

laws[3] and/or the applicable institutional rules[4] to issue provisional and conservatory measures.[5]

What is a lot less clear still is under which circumstances arbitral tribunals should *exercise* that power and grant a security for costs application. International arbitration knows no uniform and universally accepted standard, save for a few recurring factors to consider and a general understanding that ordering security for costs must remain the exception. This leaves practitioners faced with a security for costs application with considerable uncertainty about just how rare of an exception security for costs should be, and especially how to approach such an application in practice.

Naturally, this chapter cannot overcome these difficulties as such, and practitioners will always need to carefully consider the rules applicable to their particular case. This chapter is, however, intended to provide practical guidance by outlining typical considerations and practical pitfalls. It is also a call for more procedural robustness on the part of arbitral tribunals. The observation from our practice, including within arbitral institutions, and reported cases is that arbitral practice has essentially turned a security for costs order into a unicorn. We argue that this result goes beyond the limits prescribed by legitimate policy concerns over its misuse, and that it should be addressed by arbitral tribunals fully embracing a careful and nuanced balancing of interests exercise. Security for costs should remain the exception, but not a unicorn.

Against the backdrop of the parties' competing interests at stake (section §4.02), we analyse the requirements for granting a security for costs application. In particular, we examine the various factors that may be considered in the balancing of interests exercise (section §4.03). Where an arbitral tribunal is satisfied that these requirements for granting an application are met, it needs to be mindful of several further practical modalities and implications (section §4.04). We conclude with a succinct summary and a brief outlook (section §4.05).

§4.02   BACKGROUND: THE PARTIES' COMPETING INTERESTS AT STAKE

Before delving into a more detailed analysis of the various factors that may play a role, we find it useful to outline the parties' competing interests at stake. These form the fundamental backdrop for the overarching balancing of interests exercise and mandate that security for costs remain the exception and not become the rule.

The applicant's legitimate interest is to safeguard the reimbursement of its costs. The claimant has a choice whether, having assessed the strengths and weaknesses of its case and other risk factors (including the other party's financial situation), it wishes to pursue a claim in the first place. The respondent has no comparable choice. It should

---

3. For instance, *see* Art. 183(1) of the Swiss PILA, s. 1041 of the German CCP and Arts 1468, 1506(3) of the French CCP.
4. In particular Art. 28(1) of the 2021 ICC Rules and J. Fry/S. Greenberg/F. Mazza, *The Secretariat's Guide to ICC Arbitration* (2012) para. 3-1036. Further Art. 25 of the 2018 DIS Rules, Art. 29 of the 2021 Swiss Rules, Art. 36 of the 2021 DIA Rules, Art. 38 of the 2020 FAI Rules.
5. Some also refer to the arbitral tribunal's general procedural powers.

not be faced with the unfair choice to either not properly defend itself in the arbitration and risk an adverse award or to defend itself in the arbitration with the knowledge that it will incur considerable costs which it will likely be unable to recover from the other side.[6]

The other party's legitimate interest is to have unhindered access to arbitral justice. A security for costs order bears the risk of stifling genuine claims and effectively depriving the other party of its right to proper legal protection.[7]

Of course, this effect can be desirable from the applicant's point of view and can motivate the applicant to misuse a security for costs application as a tool to delay or even put an end to the proceedings. The purpose of a security for costs order is certainly not to encourage such guerrilla tactics, but to re-establish a level playing field between the parties where appropriate.[8] The means to decide whether the circumstances exceptionally warrant a security for costs order is a careful balancing of interests exercise, taking into account all circumstances of a particular case.[9] The following section analyses the various factors that can play a role in this exercise.

§4.03 REQUISITES FOR ORDERING SECURITY FOR COSTS

Subject to specific provisions in the applicable rules, we suggest that the arbitral tribunal essentially adopt a two-step analysis borrowed from national procedural law that has also proven useful in arbitral practice. In Germany and Switzerland, for instance, courts will consider whether the applicant for interim relief has demonstrated a claim for the injunction (*Verfügungsanspruch*) and a reason for the injunction (*Verfügungsgrund*). The first requirement is usually unproblematic. The applicant must have a potential claim for reimbursement of costs. The real crux comes with the second requirement, at the heart of which lies the balancing of interests exercise. The applicant must establish sufficient grounds to exceptionally grant the security for costs application.

---

6. A. Redfern/S. O'Leary, *Why It Is Time for International Arbitration to Embrace Security for Costs*, 32:3 Arb Int'l (2016) 397, 398; W. Gu, *Security for Costs in International Commercial Arbitration*, 22:3 J Int'l Arb (2005) 167, 168; B. Nalbandian, *Security for Costs*, MPEiPro (April 2020) para. 3. In this regard, N. Rubins, *In God We Trust, All Others Pay Cash: Security for Costs in International Commercial Arbitration*, 11:3 Am Rev Int'l Arb (2000) 307, 361 coined the phrase of preventing an '*arbitral hit and run*'.
7. N. Rubins, *supra* n. 6, at 362; T. Webster/M. Bühler, *Handbook of ICC Arbitration* (4th ed. 2018) at paras 28–50; *see also* Art. 4(2) of the 2016 CIArb Guidelines.
8. P. Karrer/M. Desax, *Security for Costs in International Arbitration. Why, When, and What If …*, *Liber Amicorum Böckstiegel* (2001) 339, 340 para. 7 ('*reestablish the balance*'); W. Gu, *supra* n. 6, at 169 ('*eliminates the unfairness*'); in the context of third-party funding ICC Commission Report, *Decisions on Costs in International Arbitration* (2015) para. 90 ('*put both parties on an equal footing in respect of any recovery of costs*').
9. Cf. The Chartered Institute of Arbitrators, *International Arbitration Guidelines: Applications for Security for Costs* (2016) 4; W. Gu, *supra* n. 6, at 186; N. Rubins, *supra* n. 6, at 313–314; C. Ford, *Kluwer Practical Insights on Security for Costs* (2021) at [III.1.g.]; A. Redfern/S. O'Leary, *supra* n. 6, at 411–412; N. Nalbandian, *supra* n. 6, at para. 4; K. Pörnbacher/S. Thiel, *Kostensicherheit im Schiedsverfahren*, SchiedsVZ (2010) 14, 18; ICCA-QMUL Taskforce, *Report on Third-Party Funding in International Arbitration* (2018) 168.

[A]   Potential Claim for Reimbursement of Costs (*Verfügungsanspruch*)

The applicant must have a potential claim for reimbursement of costs (*fumus boni iuris*). The applicant may be the respondent or, in case of counterclaims, the claimant.

Under the first step (*Verfügungsanspruch*), the arbitral tribunal only needs to be satisfied that the applicant, if successful on the merits, could have a claim for reimbursement of costs. In line with the costs-follow-the-event approach prevailing in international arbitration, this will generally be the case. To the extent a party agreement or the applicable rules foresee that each party shall bear its own costs, or otherwise limit the costs eligible for reimbursement, a security for costs application must already be denied for lacking a claim to be secured.

The same applies where the arbitral tribunal finds that the applicant has failed to demonstrate even a prima facie case on the merits. In these cases, the applicant's claim for reimbursement is so unrealistic that it cannot be considered a potential claim for reimbursement of costs to begin with.[10] Importantly, the arbitral tribunal cannot, as a matter of principle, be required to delve into the merits of the case beyond such a prima facie assessment. A security for costs application is usually filed in the early stages of the proceedings when the arbitral tribunal does not yet have the benefit of a full evidentiary record to properly assess the outcome of the dispute. As a matter of principle, the arbitral tribunal will thus want to refrain from unduly prejudging the merits of the case. However, the opposite scenario, where the arbitral tribunal does find it probable that the applicant may prevail on the merits, can become relevant in the second step of the analysis.

By necessity, the claim for reimbursement of costs is a future and conditional claim. Taking into account the object and purpose of security for costs, a claim of this nature must suffice. To hold otherwise would deprive the instrument of its practical relevance, and be incompatible with the mandate of arbitration to grant the parties effective legal protection.

[B]   Grounds Justifying Security for Costs (*Verfügungsgrund*)

The much more demanding step of the analysis is whether the applicant has established sufficient grounds to exceptionally grant the application. The security for costs order must be necessary to avoid that the applicant suffers irreparable harm.[11] Even when the applicable rules list certain criteria, the arbitral tribunal is left with broad discretion to decide whether (and how) to grant security for costs.[12] Arbitral tribunals

---

10. Note that B. Berger, *Security for Costs: Trends and Developments in Swiss Arbitral Case Law*, 28:1 ASA Bull (2010) 7, 9 considers that the arbitral tribunal does not need to conduct even such a prima facie assessment of the outcome of the dispute in the context of the *Verfügungsanspruch*.
11. A. Redfern/S. O'Leary, *supra* n. 6, at 410; P. Karrer/M. Desax, *supra* n. 8, at 341 paras 9–10; B. Berger, *supra* n. 10, at 10; S. Bachmann, *The Impact of Third-Party Funding on Security for Costs Requests in International Arbitration Proceedings in Switzerland*, 38:4 ASA Bull (2020) 842, 848.
12. Cf. Art. 38(2) of the 2017 SCC Rules and Rule 53 of the 2022 ICSID Rules. Highlighting the arbitral tribunal's broad discretion also N. Rubins, *supra* n. 6, at 368; J. Fry/S. Greenberg/F. Mazza, *supra* n. 4, at paras 3-1037 et seq.

seized with a security for costs application should fully embrace that discretion to carefully assess, based on an overarching balancing of interests exercise, the overall appropriateness of granting such relief based on the circumstances of their particular case.[13]

In the following, we will examine various factors that may play a role in this assessment – many already recurring in arbitral practice and some institutional rules, others with different nuances or neglected to date. Again, our analysis is two-fold: The non-applicant's financial situation must endanger the enforcement of an adverse costs award, and the applicant's interest in obtaining a security for costs must outweigh the other party's interest in unhindered access to arbitral justice.

[1] The Non-Applicant's Financial Situation Endangers the Enforcement of an Adverse Costs Award

The initial focus ties back to the purpose of any security for costs order, that is, to safeguard the applicant's position in relation to a potential costs award in its favour. Accordingly, the arbitral tribunal must first and foremost determine whether there is a serious risk that the non-applicant's financial situation endangers the enforcement of an adverse costs award.

[a] The Non-Applicant's Financial Situation

This question depends on the non-applicant's *ability* to comply with an adverse costs award, including the availability of assets for enforcement, and not its *willingness* to comply with an adverse costs award. The latter may be an additional factor to be taken into account in favour of the applicant, but it does not justify a security for costs order as such because the instrument is not intended to relieve the applicant from having to seek formal enforcement proceedings. For that reason, the location of the non-applicant's assets is usually also irrelevant.[14]

The applicant needs to demonstrate specific indications that the other party has insufficient financial means. This does not necessarily require that the non-applicant be on the verge of insolvency, but it could already be the case where it is an empty shell, or has hardly any attachable assets and low revenues.[15] At the same time, a

---

13. CIArb, *supra* n. 9, at 4; K. Pörnbacher/S. Thiel, *supra* n. 9, at 18; cf. also N. Rubins, *supra* n. 6, at 373–374: poor financial situation as a necessary, but by no means sufficient condition for a security for costs order.
14. Cf. s. 38(3)(a) of the English Arbitration Act, s. 56(2) of the Hong Kong Arbitration Ordinance and s. 12(4)(a) of the Singapore International Arbitration Act prohibiting that the application be granted only on the ground that the other party resides elsewhere.
15. Note that for domestic arbitrations in Switzerland, at least the wording of Art. 379 of the Swiss CCP limits the possibility of security for costs to instances where the claimant appears to be insolvent.

non-applicant in insolvency or under the threat of insolvency does not automatically have insufficient financial means to comply with an adverse costs award.[16]

In multi-party-arbitrations, the arbitral tribunal will need to assess whether the non-applicants are jointly and severally liable for the applicant's potential claim for reimbursement of costs. If this is the case, the arbitral tribunal must look at all of them combined. If this is not the case, the arbitral tribunal must look at each of the non-applicants individually.[17]

[b]   Requirement of a Serious Deterioration?

Yet, the applicant cannot always rely on the other party's insufficient financial situation. Specifically, it would violate the *venire contra factum proprium* principle if the applicant could base its application on risks of which it knew or should have known and which it must thus be deemed to have assumed at the time of contract conclusion.[18] It is against this background that, in the reported cases, the success of a security for costs application often depended on whether or not the arbitral tribunal found a serious deterioration of the other party's financial situation.

We submit that the existence of such a serious deterioration strongly argues in favour of granting the security for costs application, but that it should not be postulated as a general requirement. This criterion cannot be applied schematically. In particular, arbitral tribunals should carefully consider to which extent the applicant can truly be deemed to have assumed certain risks at the time of contract conclusion, especially the type and size of the claim(s) now brought in the arbitration proceedings.

Some argue that the applicant has assumed the risk of not being able to collect on a costs award if it has entered into an agreement with a party that was already insolvent, a mere shell, or only holds assets in a jurisdiction that is not a signatory to the New York Convention or a comparable international treaty. It would have been upon the applicant to protect its interests by obtaining some form of guarantee at that point in time. Accordingly, the applicant can only succeed if it can demonstrate a

---

16. *X Holding in Bankruptcy (Switzerland) v. Y Co Ltd (Yemen)*, Procedural Order No. 4 dated 17 June 2003, 28:1 ASA Bull (2010) 23, 27 at para. 30 [ad hoc, Geneva]: Claimant in bankruptcy, but still holding liquid assets of more than CHF 100 million and even ready to put up a CHF 500,000 bank guarantee if the applicant had agreed to a reciprocal guarantee.

    In this regard, arbitral tribunals will also need to be mindful of special protections under the applicable national insolvency law, whereby the claim for reimbursement of costs incurred in proceedings conducted by the insolvency administrator are obligations of the estate and as such given priority over regular insolvency claims, cf. *ABC AG v. Mr X*, Procedural Order No. 14 dated 27 November 2002, 23:1 ASA Bull (2005) 108, 114 [ZCC, Zurich].

17. P. Karrer/M. Desax, *supra* n. 8, at 349 paras 46–50.

18. Cf. Art. 3(2) of the 2016 CIArb Guidelines (*'accepted business risk'*); further O. Sandrock, *The Cautio Judicatum Solvi in Arbitration Proceedings or the Duty of an Alien Claimant to Provide Security for the Costs of the Defendant*, 14:2 J Int'l Arb (1997) 17, 28. C. Sim, *Eight Key Points from the ICCA-QM Task Force's 2018 Third-Party Funding Report* (Kluwer Arbitration Blog 28 May 2018) http://arbitrationblog.kluwerarbitration.com/2018/05/28/8-key-points-icca-qm-task-forces-2018-third-party-funding-report/ (accessed 20 October 2022) rightly noted that the underlying reasoning of upholding the bargain struck between commercial parties does not translate to the investment context.

serious deterioration in circumstances.[19] In our view, this purported assumption of risk is incorrect in its absoluteness.

We agree that the location of the other party's assets is an example where the arbitral tribunal must require a serious deterioration of circumstances because it is otherwise for the applicant to take proper precautions. A security for costs order may thus be appropriate in response to, for example, an international embargo, exchange control legislation effectively prohibiting the transfer of recovered monies elsewhere, and extreme currency devaluations.[20]

We do not agree that the applicant can sweepingly be said to have accepted the other party's financial position. In principle, it may be the case that the parties accept the respective other party's general risk of insolvency when entering into the contract, and more specifically also the cost risks inherent to the conduct of arbitration proceedings when entering into the arbitration agreement. However, with the arbitration agreement also comes the possibility of a security for costs order. We fail to see why the former should necessarily trump the latter, and why security for costs should hence only be available in case the non-applicant's financial position seriously deteriorated after the conclusion of the arbitration agreement.[21]

Indeed, the specific procedural constellation in the arbitration will oftentimes not be foreseeable for either side, and the applicant may well find itself in a situation it could not reasonably anticipate at the time it entered into the arbitration agreement. Therefore, the arbitral tribunal should not reflexively turn to frequently used authorities that require a serious deterioration of the other party's financial situation. Instead, it should carefully consider to which extent the applicant can really be said to have assumed certain risks. In doing so, the arbitral tribunal should pay heed to the subject and nature of the parties' contractual relationship, in particular their respective obligations under the contract, and consider whether the applicant could reasonably anticipate the type and the size of the claim now brought against it.

If, for instance, the other party was only obliged to render certain services over a limited period of time and the applicant did not have to fear any material prejudice in the event of a defective performance by the other party, then the applicant had little reason to concern itself with the other party's financial situation at the time of contract conclusion. If the applicant declares the agreement terminated with retroactive effect due to an alleged fundamental breach of contract by the other party, and if the other party now claims its (sizeable) fees under the contract, should the applicant be denied the opportunity to obtain security for costs just because the other party's financial situation was poor from the start? We submit: Not *necessarily*.

---

19. P. Karrer/M. Desax, *supra* n. 8, at 346 para. 35; O. Sandrock, *supra* n. 18, at 28; ICCA-QMUL Taskforce, *supra* n. 9, 168; at least '*in principle*' also K. Pörnbacher/S. Thiel, *supra* n. 9, at 18; '*generally*' T. Webster/ M. Bühler, *supra* n. 7, at paras 28–49; '*usually*' N. Nalbandian, *supra* n. 6, at para. 51; considerably more flexible CIArb, *supra* n. 9, at 7 ('*may*').
20. P. Karrer/M. Desax, *supra* n. 8, at 347 paras 39–41; K. Pörnbacher/S. Thiel, *supra* n. 9, at 18.
21. Similarly, A. Redfern/S. O'Leary, *supra* n. 6, at 411 ('*logic is flawed*' and '*no reason to deem that a respondent has consented to pay the costs of defending an unmeritorious claim, without the benefit of security for those costs*').

Another even more acute and illustrative example is the following hypothetical case: With the objective to jointly bid in a tender for a large project, the parties entered into a heads of terms agreement and a letter of intent. If successful in the tender, and only then, the parties intended to form a joint venture for the execution of the project. If unsuccessful in the tender or if one of the parties changed its mind in the preparation of the tender and did not wish to continue with the joint bid, each of the parties could go its separate way. The parties ultimately did not prevail in the tender. The other party, an investment vehicle with very limited assets of its own, accuses the applicant of having breached the terms of the agreements. In the arbitration proceedings, it raises a claim in the millions for loss of profits that it allegedly would have made over many years once the joint venture was established. Should the applicant be denied the opportunity to obtain security for costs just because it entered into a heads of terms agreement and a letter of intent with an investment vehicle? We submit: The arbitral tribunal should take a closer look and duly consider the actual circumstances. Among others, the arbitral tribunal should bear in mind that both agreements – and hence the parties' (financial) exposure to each other – were strictly limited in time and purpose.

[c]   In Particular: Third-Party Funding

In recent years, the implications of third-party funding for a security for costs application have been the subject of debate among scholars and in arbitral practice. The emerging consensus appears to be that the existence of third-party funding as such does not suffice to justify security for costs. Indeed, where the other side is funded by a third party, this may well prompt the applicant to take a closer look and encourage a security for costs application on its part. However, it cannot relieve the applicant from establishing the requisites for granting the application. The mere existence of third-party funding also does not justify a less onerous burden of proof or even a rebuttable presumption for the other party's impecuniosity.[22]

This does not mean that the existence of a third-party funding arrangement would not need to be taken into account at all when assessing the other party's ability to comply with an adverse costs award. In cases where the third-party funder is under an obligation to cover adverse costs and where it is also not entitled to freely terminate the funding agreement and be relieved of its obligations, a financially strong funder actually argues against ordering security for costs. Yet, the opposite constellation does not automatically warrant the opposite conclusion. The reason is that financially stable

---

22. In detail ICCA-QMUL Taskforce, *supra* n. 9, 163–183; further 2017 SIAC Practice Note on External Funding, para. 9; S. Bachmann, *supra* n. 11, at 856–857; W. Kirtly/K. Wietrzykowski, *Should an Arbitral Tribunal Order Security for Costs When an Impecunious Claimant Is Relying upon Third-Party Funding?*, 30:1 J Int'l Arb (2013) 17, 30. With a focus on investment cases also B. Gustafsson, *Article 38 of the SCC Rules: An Analysis of Security for Costs in TPF Arbitration*, 1 Swedish Arb Yb (2019) 137, 143–153. Disagreeing A. Redfern/S. O'Leary, *supra* n. 6, at 412: strong prima facie basis for acceding to an application; more cautious in the latest edition G. Born, *International Commercial Arbitration* (3rd ed. 2021) 2681 compared to G. Born, *International Commercial Arbitration* (2nd ed. 2014) 2496: only *'often'* a strong prima facie case; further T. Webster/M. Bühler, *supra* n. 7, at paras 28–53 (*'likelihood … presumably much higher'*).

parties also increasingly use third-party funding as a means to preserve their liquidity and reduce the risks associated with a litigious enforcement of their claims.[23]

In order to put the applicant in a position to properly assess the implications of the other party being funded, the arbitral tribunal can order the funded party to disclose the relevant terms by producing the pertinent sections of the funding agreement or an affidavit from the funder.[24] If the funded party fails to comply with this order, the arbitral tribunal can make the adverse inference that the involvement of the funder does not argue against the security for costs order. Again: The arbitral tribunal cannot automatically infer that the financial situation of the funded party endangers the enforcement of an adverse costs award.

[2] The Applicant Prevails in the Balancing of Interests Exercise

The applicant's interest in obtaining a security for costs must also outweigh the other party's interest in unhindered access to arbitral justice. The various factors discussed in this section are neither conclusive nor relevant in each and every case.

[a] The Parties' Respective Prospects of Success on the Merits

First, the arbitral tribunal may consider the parties' respective prospects of success on the merits of the case.[25] The lesser the other party's prospects of success on the merits, the more readily the applicant's interest in obtaining security can prevail. Conversely, the greater the uncertainties regarding the outcome on the merits, the more the applicant needs to establish other grounds justifying its application.[26]

Any such assessment would be without prejudice to the arbitral tribunal's final decision, and thus not lead to a prejudgment of the merits in the strict sense of the word because it would be based solely on the submissions and evidence on record at the time, and thus remain of a preliminary and summary nature. Nonetheless, the arbitral tribunal will oftentimes be hesitant to disclose any indication of its position at such an early stage of the proceedings.

However, especially in cases tantamount to frivolous claims and in cases with grossly overvalued claims, arbitral tribunals should demonstrate more procedural robustness and take a hands-on approach that affords the applicant's interests sufficient protection. In egregious cases where the non-applicant's claim would be utterly excessive or outright *abusive or extravagant*', the advance on costs alone may

---

23. *See only* ICCA-QMUL Taskforce, *supra* n. 9, 180 (*'increasingly a tool of choice, not of necessity'*).
24. ICCA-QMUL Taskforce, *supra* n. 9, 181; further ICC Commission Report, *Decisions on Costs in International Arbitration* (2015) para. 89.
25. This criterion is explicitly mentioned in Art. 38(2)(i) of the 2017 SCC Rules. *See also* Art. 2 of the 2016 CIArb Guidelines.
26. K. Pörnbacher/S. Thiel, *supra* n. 9, at 20; similar in approach also CIArb, *supra* n. 9, at 6; N. Rubins, *supra* n. 6, at 369; J. Waincymer, *Procedure and Evidence in International Arbitration* (2012) 649.

sometimes suffice to prevent such claims from being brought into arbitration.[27] At the same time, institutional rules increasingly offer special tools to deal with frivolous claims, in particular allowing for the early dismissal or expeditious determination of such claims.[28] This suggests that, in a significant enough number of cases, the advance on costs alone does not suffice as a safeguard. While such tools, and the relevant provisions and guidelines thereon, have no direct bearing on a security for costs application, we submit that the arbitral tribunal may take guidance from their spirit when assessing a security for costs application. Similarly to the aforementioned tools, the instrument of security for costs can be used to adequately safeguard the applicant's interest, while being less onerous in terms of its legal consequences on the other party than an early dismissal or expeditious determination.[29]

This applies all the more with respect to (likely) grossly overvalued claims. We submit that the arbitral tribunal is well advised to seriously consider a security for costs order where it has strong indications that the amount claimed is far off from any reasonable ballpark figure. Admittedly, the arbitral tribunal will expose itself to a certain extent when relying on such considerations, but sometimes only a courageous choice can ensure an effective and fair process for both parties. As a side effect – not as the objective – such a pragmatic decision at the beginning of the proceedings could also benefit the overall efficiency of the arbitration. It would be a helpful hint for the claimant, who could either pursue the claim as is and reinforce its efforts to properly substantiate the quantum, or adjust the claim as necessary and all involved could conduct the remainder of the proceedings in a manner that is proportionate to the real amount in dispute.

[b]   The Parties' Conduct

Second, the arbitral tribunal can take into account the parties' respective conduct.[30]

Where the arbitral tribunal is prima facie satisfied that the applicant contributed to the other party's poor financial position, the applicant is highly unlikely to succeed with its security for costs application.[31] By contrast, where the applicant has not yet paid its share of the advance on costs, it is in breach of its contractual duties, but the

---

27. Stronger J. Lew/L. Mistelis/S. Kröll, *Comparative International Commercial Arbitration* (2003) 601–602 (*'is considered to be a sufficient safeguard'*).
28. *See*, for example, Art. 22(1) of the 2021 ICC Rules and the Note to Parties and Arbitral Tribunals on the Conduct of the Arbitration under the ICC Rules of Arbitration in force as from 1 January 2021, paras 109–114 (expeditious determination); Art. 39(2)(i) of the 2017 SCC Rules (summary procedure); Art. 22.1(viii) of the 2020 LCIA Rules (early determination); Art. 43.1(a) of the 2018 HKIAC Rules (early determination procedure); Rule 29 of the 2016 SIAC Rules (early dismissal); Rule 41 of the 2022 ICSID Rules.
29. Sceptical in this regard and emphasizing the purpose to redress the risk of non-enforceability K. Pörnbacher/S. Thiel, *supra* n. 9, at 19.
30. This criterion is explicitly mentioned in Rule 53(3)(c) of the 2022 ICSID Rules.
31. CIArb, *supra* n. 9, at 10; C. Ford, *supra* n. 9, at [III.2.b.ii.]; P. Karrer/M. Desax, *supra* n. 8, at 348 para. 44; N. Rubins, *supra* n. 6, at 362; depending on the prima face strength of the parties' respective cases on the merits also T. Webster/M. Bühler, *supra* n. 7, at paras 28–49. From arbitral practice recently *Unionmatex v. Turkmenistan* (ICSID Case No. ARB/18/35), Decision on Security for Costs dated 27 January 2020, paras 77–78 (dissenting opinion).

arbitral tribunal should normally not penalize this breach by simply dismissing the application.[32]

As regards the other party's conduct, the arbitral tribunal should factor in any specific indications that the other party has made '*bad faith manoeuvres*'[33] designed to frustrate the enforcement of an adverse costs award. This includes (i) the assignment of the claims to a special purpose vehicle, which is not necessarily impecunious but has comparatively few assets, (ii) the significant disposal of assets, and (iii) the relocation of its domicile in a jurisdiction substantially complicating the enforcement of the costs award.[34] The closer in time to the commencement of the arbitral proceedings the other party takes these actions, the more reason the arbitral tribunal has to suspect foul play and the more of an explanation the other party will need to provide to rebut this suspicion. Where the arbitral tribunal is satisfied that foul play was involved, it should grant the security for costs application even if it were to consider, based on its preliminary assessment, that the other party and not the applicant will prevail on the merits. In these circumstances, the other party is simply not in need of any protection.[35] In addition, the arbitral tribunal can consider granting the security for costs application where the applicant demonstrates that the other party has a notable history of resisting compliance with costs decisions rendered in other proceedings.[36] All of these examples attest to the non-applicant's unwillingness to comply with an adverse costs award.[37]

[c]   Consequences of Failure to Comply with Security for Costs Order

Third, the arbitral tribunal should be mindful of what consequences the non-applicant's failure to comply with the security for costs order would entail under the applicable rules, and should already factor in the severity of these consequences in the balancing of interests exercise.

Notably, section 41(6) of the English Arbitration Act and section 56(4) of the Hong Kong Arbitration Ordinance allow the arbitral tribunal to make an award *dismissing* the claim if the claimant has failed to comply with the security for costs

---

32. Similar *X Sarl (Lebanon) v. Y AG (Germany)*, ICC Case No. 15218, Procedural Order No. 3 dated 4 July 2008, 28:1 ASA Bull (2010) 37, 44 at para. 31 [Berne]. Disagreeing *Westacre (UK) v. Jugoimport (Yugoslavia)*, ICC Case No. 7047, 13:3 ASA Bull (1995) 301; CIArb, *supra* n. 9, at 11 ('*may*' be considered).
33. B. Berger, *supra* n. 10, at 12; S. Bachmann, *supra* n. 11, at 850.
34. CIArb, *supra* n. 9, at 10; N. Rubins, *supra* n. 6, at 374–375, W. Gu, *supra* n. 6, at 196 with fn. 180; S. Bachmann, *supra* n. 11, at 850; K. Pörnbacher/S. Thiel, *supra* n. 9, at 19–20. From arbitral practice, for example, *X SA (Panama) v. A, B, C and D AS (Czech Republic)*, Procedural Order No. 6 dated 25 July 2003, 28:1 ASA Bull (2010) 28, 34 at para. 21 [CCIA-TI]: assignment.
35. In agreement K. Pörnbacher/S. Thiel, *supra* n. 9, at 20.
36. *See RSM v. Saint Lucia* (ICSID Case No. ARB/12/10), Decision on St. Lucia's Request for Security for Costs dated 13 August 2014, para. 86, where the majority granted the application based cumulatively on Claimant's failure to comply with cost orders and awards in previous treaty and annulment proceedings, its lack of sufficient financial resources and the existence of a third-party funder which might not comply with an adverse costs award.
37. This criterion of unwillingness is explicitly mentioned in Rule 53(3)(b) of the 2022 ICSID Rules.

order without showing sufficient cause.[38] Similarly, Article 24(2) of the 2020 LCIA Rules and Article 38(3) of the 2017 SCC Rules allow the arbitral tribunal to either stay or dismiss the claims. A dismissal of the claims by award has res judicata effect. In our view, such a sweeping consequence has to find a legal basis in the applicable arbitration law and/or the applicable rules.

Where no such legal basis for a dismissal exists, the arbitral tribunal may rely on its either express or inherent procedural power to order the (partial) stay of the proceedings, which may ultimately also be discontinued.[39] Alternatively, some consider that the arbitral tribunal could (partially) dismiss the claims as currently inadmissible or treat the failure to comply with the security for costs order as a fictitious withdrawal of the claims.[40] In both of these cases, the claimant could refile its claims.[41] This consequence can create undue benefits for the claimant, but in our view, these undue benefits cannot overcome the lack of a legal basis for the drastic res judicata effect.[42] In any event, the arbitral tribunal should decide on the consequences of a non-compliance with much care and due regard to the applicable law. In particular, the arbitral tribunal should err on the side of caution and opt for the milder consequence if it is uncertain about the extent of its powers.

How do these consequences tie in with the balancing of interests exercise? Where the arbitral tribunal can and potentially will dismiss the claims with res judicata effect, the harsh consequence for the non-applicant mandates that a security for costs order remains the absolute exception. Where the arbitral tribunal can and potentially will discontinue the proceedings but the non-applicant would at least be able to refile its claims, the arbitral tribunal might be slightly more inclined to grant an application. Conversely, where the arbitral tribunal will stay the proceedings, the non-applicant is less in need of protection and the arbitral tribunal can more readily grant the security for costs application.[43]

---

38. Note that s. 41(5) of the English Arbitration Act interposes a peremptory order and that the dismissal only comes into play once the claimant has failed to comply not only with the first time limit under the security for costs order but also the subsequent time limit under this peremptory order. The Hong Kong Arbitration Act does not require such an interim step.
39. Expressly Art. 34(7) of the 2021 VIAC Rules; Rule 53(6) of the 2022 ICSID Rules. Cf. also S. Bachmann, *supra* n. 11, at 849 (stay or termination); N. Rubins, *supra* n. 6, at 315; C. Ford, *supra* n. 9 at [III.3.] (stay until provision of security); M. O'Reilly, *Order for Security for Costs: From the Arbitrator's Perspective*, 61:4 J Int'l Arb, Med and Disp Man (1995) 247, 250 (stay).
40. In detail from a German perspective K. Pörnbacher/S. Thiel, *supra* n. 9, at 14–16.
41. The follow-up question of what effect this order has on the running of the statutory limitation period will again depend on the applicable law.
42. In favour of a dismissal with prejudice: P. Karrer/M. Desax, *supra* n. 8, at 352 para. 59; W. Gu, *supra* n. 6, at 167,200; probably also N. Nalbandian, *supra* n. 6, at paras 28, 48. Note that in *RSM v. St. Lucia* (ICSID Case No. ARB/12/10), Decision on Annulment dated 29 April 2019, paras 183–201, the annulment committee partially annulled the award, ruling that the arbitral tribunal had manifestly exceeded its powers when sanctioning the non-compliance with its security for costs order not just by suspending and eventually discontinuing the proceedings, but by dismissing the claims with prejudice.
43. Similar K. Pörnbacher/S. Thiel, *supra* n. 9, at 21.

Some authors seem to suggest that where the financial situation of the other party is so poor that it is unable to provide the security for costs, the arbitral tribunal should not grant the application to begin with.[44] The absurd consequence of this position would be that the applicant would be deprived of any possibility to safeguard its interests when it needs such protection the most. This result is hardly tolerable. Accordingly, an inability to pay the security for costs cannot, against the will of the applicant, lead to a sub-exception and the unsecured continuance of the arbitral proceedings, at least not in the setting of commercial arbitrations.[45] In Germany, for example, a party's impecuniosity renders the arbitration agreement inoperable and allows the other party to pursue its claims before the competent state courts;[46] this may then also be the 'way out' in case the other party is unable to comply with the security for costs order.

[d]   Further Weighing of Consequences for Each Side

Finally, the arbitral tribunal should consider and weigh the consequences of its decision more generally, in particular the prejudice each side would suffer depending on whether the application is granted or not.

The greater the applicant is in need of protection, the more it is dependent on the security for costs order being granted. Where the applicant has other means available to ensure enforcement of its potential claim for reimbursement of costs, the arbitral tribunal can be more hesitant to grant the application. Specific examples include

---

44. S. Camilleri, *Between Rags and Riches: Rethinking Security for Costs in International Commercial Arbitration*, 37 Arb Int'l (2021) 851, 852. In the recent *Unionmatex* case (*supra* n. 31), the arbitral tribunal had, by majority decision, first granted a security for costs application in the amount of USD 3 million, only to rescind its order a few months later. The majority stated from the beginning that it would reconsider the order if the investor furnished sufficient evidence that it was financially incapable of posting security. According to reports, the arbitral tribunal later found that it would indeed be commercially impossible for the insolvency administrator to secure a bank guarantee in that amount, or, due to the terms of the funding agreement, even an ATE insurance policy for USD 1.5 million. In circumstances where the actions of the State allegedly caused the company's insolvency to begin with, the arbitral tribunal held that maintaining the security for costs order would amount to a denial of access to justice and rescinded the order (again by majority decision). *See* C. Sandersen, *ICSID Panel Rescinds Security for Costs Order* (12 June 2020) https://globalarbitrationreview.com/icsid-panel-rescinds-security-costs-order (accessed 20 October 2022).
45. Similar CIArb, *supra* n. 9, at 11–12 ('*may not of itself lead to a refusal*'). In investment arbitration cases, deferring the claimant to the competent state court is not foreseen and would run counter to the very idea of adjudicating the dispute with the host state in a fully neutral forum. Essentially depriving the investor of this forum may indeed not be adequate.
46. German Federal Court of Justice, Judgment of 14 September 2000 – III ZR 33/00 – NJW 2000, 3720–3722. Cf. also Art. II(3) of the 1958 New York Convention ('*incapable of being performed*'). Not accepting a party's impecuniosity as grounds for releasing it from the arbitration agreement the English Court of Appeal in *Paczy v. Haendler & Natermann GmbH*, IX Yb Comm Arb (1984) 445, 447. Disagreeing with the German approach also S. Wilske/T. Fox, *New York Convention Commentary* (R. Wolff, 2012) Art. II NYC para. 315. In detail M. Cardoso, *Impecunious Parties in International Commercial Arbitration*, 36:1 Arb Int'l (2020) 123–146.

another claim that the applicant can use for setoff,[47] or other rights the applicant can exercise against the other party's assets to satisfy its potential claim for reimbursement.[48]

Similarly, the arbitral tribunal might also consider the impacts of the proceedings on the applicant's financial situation. Arguably, where the applicant is dragged into proceedings of a magnitude which it could hardly anticipate when entering into the contractual relationship and which will likely have a dire or even crippling impact on its financial situation and could even determine its future operations, it might in very exceptional cases be appropriate to grant an application with the primary objective of facilitating the enforcement of an adverse costs award. However, the arbitral tribunal should not lightly meddle with the enforcement of any decision it may render because its mandate to render an enforceable award does *not* extend to interfering with the actual enforcement of its decision. Accordingly, the arbitral tribunal should only grant the application where the overall balancing of interests exercise so warrants. In the context of this overall assessment, the impacts of the proceedings on the applicant's financial situation may exceptionally also be a relevant factor.[49]

In addition, the arbitral tribunal should consider the subject of the dispute before it. It is likely inappropriate to grant the application where the applicant is really the claimant because of the nature of the claim, or where the applicant has raised a counterclaim which it intends to pursue and which essentially involves the same facts and issues as the other party's claim.[50]

Conversely, the arbitral tribunal should also take into account the extent and severity of the consequences a security for costs order will inflict on the non-applicant. A disproportionate prejudice will unduly curtail the non-applicant's access to arbitral justice. In this regard, the duration of the proceedings may play a role. A security for costs order will be less onerous in expedited proceedings than in an arbitration expected to last for several years. Moreover, the arbitral tribunal can, at least to a certain extent, alleviate the burden on the non-applicant by exploring different forms of security with the parties and leaving the choice between various options to the non-applicant. While payment to an escrow account may be particularly burdensome to cash-flow-sensitive parties, others may find it less troublesome than obtaining a bank guarantee or the like in a jurisdiction far away from its place of business.[51] Finally, the amount of security and its due date also contribute to the level of stress a security for costs order will put on the non-applicant.[52]

---

47. The claim to be used for setoff does not necessarily have to be due already, and be undisputed or legally binding. However, the arbitral tribunal should take into account the nature of the claim when determining the practical viability of a setoff as a means of protection.
48. C. Ford, *supra* n. 9, at [III.1.g.].
49. More generous S. Camilleri, *supra* n. 44, at 860–861.
50. CIArb, *supra* n. 9, at 5; C. Ford, *supra* n. 9, at [III.2.b.ii.]; *Parties not Indicated*, Procedural Order No. 4 dated April 2009, 28:1 ASA Bull (2010) 59, 70 at paras 169–172 [ICC, Geneva].
51. On possible forms of security and other modalities *see* below section §4.04[A].
52. K. Pörnbacher/S. Thiel, *supra* n. 9, at 21 highlighting the possibility to order security for costs in stages.

§4.04 GRANTING THE APPLICATION: FURTHER PRACTICAL CONSIDERATIONS

Where an arbitral tribunal is satisfied that the requirements for granting an application are met, it needs to be mindful of several further practical modalities and implications.

[A] Practical Modalities of a Security for Costs Order

As regards the further practical modalities of a security for costs order, the arbitral tribunal enjoys a broad discretion allowing it to account for the particularities of any given case.[53]

For one, the arbitral tribunal needs to decide on the proper form of its decision. Subject to specific provisions in the applicable institutional rules, arbitral tribunals can typically decide on a security for costs application in the form of a reasoned order.[54] Accordingly, the security for costs order will not have any final effect, and can easily be modified in the further course of the proceedings if so required. It is also not subject to an institutional scrutiny mechanism as foreseen, for instance, under the ICC Rules for draft awards.

The arbitral tribunal further needs to decide on the permissible form(s) of the security. The most common forms are payment to an escrow account administered by the arbitral institution, an irrevocable on-demand bank guarantee or a standby letter of credit.[55] Usually, the party ordered to provide the security may choose – within the limits set out by the security for costs order, which in turn should consider reasonable requests from the applicant[56] – the form of security because it is in the best position to assess which form of security has the least impact on its business dealings. The applicant, in turn, will generally not have any legitimate interest in one form of security being chosen over the other. Where payment to an escrow account is one of the options, the order should include a time limit by which the non-applicant shall indicate its choice for this form of security so that the administering body can set up the escrow account in time (e.g., one week before the time limit for providing the security as such). Especially in case of a bank guarantee, the arbitral tribunal should also be mindful that it might be very difficult for the non-applicant to obtain a bank guarantee with unlimited duration. Accordingly, it should allow for bank guarantees being provided

---

53. See only CIArb, supra n. 9, at 13–14.
54. For Switzerland explicitly B. Berger, supra n. 10, at 10.
55. However, arbitral tribunals should be open to exploring other forms of security in order to minimize the burden on the party ordered to provide security for costs. Where applicable, counsel for the non-applicant should clearly outline potential alternatives when commenting on the security for costs application. Cf. CIArb, supra n. 9, at 14 also mentioning parent company guarantee, bond, liens on property, insurance coverage, or assignment of a financial instrument; ICCA-QMUL Taskforce, supra n. 9, at 182–183 mentioning a club letter of guarantee or an insurer's bond.
56. For example, the arbitral tribunal should specify in case of a bank guarantee which types of banks (place of business, international ratings, etc.) are acceptable.

on an extend-or-pay basis.[57] Finally, the arbitral tribunal will need to consider whether to explicitly foresee a cross-indemnity and demand a security also from the applicant for this purpose.[58]

With respect to the amount of the security, the arbitral tribunal needs to anticipate the quantum of its costs decision, and estimate the costs of arbitration for which the applicant will be able to claim reimbursement if it prevails on the merits. In this context, the arbitral tribunal will also need to factor in considerations of procedural equality. If, for example, the other party engages specialized counsel in several jurisdictions, it may well be appropriate for the applicant to take a similar approach so as to be on equal footing. In any event, the applicant is well advised to assist the arbitral tribunal in its assessment by properly substantiating its quantification of the amount sought (indication of approximate costs for the upcoming procedural steps, and for the legal costs potentially also the expected number of hours and the hourly rate).[59] The arbitral tribunal can opt to order security for costs in stages and increase the amount of security as the proceedings evolve.[60] When doing so, however, the arbitral tribunal should strive to ensure that, from the start, the party ordered to provide security for costs has a fair picture of the total amount of security it will likely be asked to put up in the course of the proceedings. Security for costs is normally ordered for costs incurred going forward.[61] Nonetheless, the arbitral tribunal can consider extending the security to exceptionally also encompass costs incurred prior to its security for costs order.

In cases where the applicant has – again, in breach of its obligations – declined to pay its share of the advance on costs until it is afforded security for its costs, the other party could be requested to substitute this share for the proceedings to continue.[62] Depending on the procedural calendar, the arbitral tribunal may wish to move the proceedings forward straight away, and to account for this possibility by allowing the non-applicant to reduce the amount of security if and to the extent it pays the applicant's share of the advance on costs.

[B]   Further Implications of a Security for Costs Order for the Proceedings

Turning from the practical modalities of the security for costs order as such to its implications for the arbitral proceedings more generally, three considerations are worth highlighting:

---

57. In further detail with drafting proposal P. Karrer/M. Desax, *supra* n. 8, at 350–351 paras 55–56.
58. *See* Art. 25.2 of the 2020 LCIA Rules.
59. C. Ford, *supra* n. 9, at [III.1.d.]. In particular, it may be helpful for the applicant to disclose the legal costs it incurred up to the date of the application as a benchmark.
60. Cf. CIArb, *supra* n. 9, at 15; J. Waincymer, *supra* n. 26, at 652.
61. ICC Bulletin (Special Supplement), *Procedural Decisions in ICC Arbitration: Security for Costs* (2014) 7; T. Webster/M. Bühler, *supra* n. 7, at paras 28–51; C. Ford, *supra* n. 9, at [III.1.].
62. *See*, for example, Art. 37(5) of the 2021 ICC Rules.

(1) A security for costs application is likely made early on and ideally still prior to the first case management conference, allowing the arbitral tribunal to take the application into account when determining the procedural timetable. The arbitral tribunal should foresee reasonably short time limits for any comments on the application, and should strive to render a swift decision. This applies all the more in case of expedited proceedings.

(2) The arbitral tribunal may, prior to rendering the decision on the security for costs application as such, be asked to require further information from the non-applicant based on its broad procedural powers to establish the facts of the case. In principle, it is upon the applicant alone to substantiate its application and furnish sufficient proof for its allegations. However, the arbitral tribunal may in certain circumstances find that the non-applicant bears a secondary burden of proof in relation to information solely within its possession. Specifically, the arbitral tribunal may find a need to order the non-applicant to provide information (including supporting documentation) on its financial situation where such information is neither public nor otherwise available to the applicant, and where the applicant has established, on a prima facie basis, that the non-applicant lacks sufficient financial means. If the non-applicant should fail to provide such information, the arbitral tribunal could make an adverse inference in favour of the applicant's interest to obtain a security for costs.

(3) The arbitral tribunal has to tie up any loose ends in relation to the security for costs order when rendering its final award. This includes a decision on the allocation of the parties' legal costs incurred in connection with the security for costs application (unless already done in the order as such). It may also include a decision to release the security to the successful party or to both parties in specific proportions, as the case may be. The decision to release the security will normally not need to be reflected in the operative section and may not even need to be included in the award at all. In our experience, however, it can be useful to include instructions in the body of the award.[63]

---

63. *See also* CIArb, *supra* n. 9, at 16. Where the security was paid to an escrow account administered by the ICC, for example, these instructions (including a time limit for the applicant to request that the security be paid out to its account, failing which the security can be repaid to the other party) allow the Secretariat to proceed accordingly and to close the account without undue delay, cf. Note to Parties and Arbitral Tribunals on the Conduct of the Arbitration under the ICC Rules of Arbitration in force as from 1 January 2021, para. 252. Where the security was provided in the form of a bank guarantee, the terms of the bank guarantee will likely foresee that the applicant needs to present the final award and a written confirmation that the other party has not paid the awarded costs.
   B. Berger, *supra* n. 10, at 13 with reference to *X SARL (Lebanon) v. Y AG (Germany)*, Final Award of 20 April 2009, 28:1 ASA Bull (2010) 46, 47 at (4.) [ICC, Berne] suggests that in order to exclude any risk of the unsuccessful non-applicant having to pay the same amount twice, the arbitral tribunal should order that the security be set off against the applicant's cost claim. Whether the arbitral tribunal can order such a setoff on its own motion will depend on the

In cases where the applicant is (partially) unsuccessful, the arbitral tribunal may additionally be required, if so requested, to decide on the costs the non-applicant incurred for providing the security. Subject to the applicable rules, these costs should be considered as reasonable other costs incurred for the arbitration proceedings.[64]

§4.05   WHERE TO? MAKE IT THE EXCEPTION, NOT A UNICORN

Where does that leave us? The instrument of security for costs is rightly conceptualized as the exception. It is a deviation from the principle that each party bears its own costs until the arbitral tribunal renders its costs decision. As such, it should only be granted where special circumstances leave the applicant in particular need of protection and justify burdening the other party with a security for costs order. It goes without saying that the instrument should not be misused for tactical manoeuvres, and that arbitral tribunals should be vigilant in this regard. After all, the integrity of the proceedings is of paramount importance. However, we question whether arbitral practice has not shown too much reluctance in the past and effectively turned the exception into a unicorn.

An arbitral tribunal faced with a security for costs application should not content itself with falling back on the mantra of security for costs being an exception that is to be used '*rarely and restrictively*'.[65] Instead, arbitral tribunals are encouraged to take a closer and indeed a wider look at such applications, and to show procedural robustness where appropriate in the circumstances. Taking a normative approach to carefully assess the circumstances of its particular case and to balance the parties' competing interests allows the arbitral tribunal to determine whether it is exceptionally appropriate to order security for costs. In this regard, the various but non-conclusive factors discussed in this contribution may warrant consideration – in one direction or the other. As arbitral practice evolves, future security for costs applications and decisions

---

applicable law. Alternatively, the arbitral tribunal could order the applicant to release the security concurrently against the other party's payment of the costs award. In our view, however, the arbitral tribunal should generally be hesitant to include such orders on its own motion because it could end up unduly complicating matters. Double recovery is a commonplace risk, and the other party will likely have sufficient other means available under national procedural law to defend itself against such attempts.

64. By contrast, to the extent that the non-applicant wishes to claim other losses it suffered as a consequence of providing the security, it would need to resort to a claim for damages. Arbitral tribunals should allow the non-applicant to introduce such a claim within a reasonable time period after the provision of the security as a subsidiary request for relief, upon which the arbitral tribunal is only requested to decide in the event that the applicant is (partially) unsuccessful on the merits and in the proportion that the security is thus released to the non-applicant.

65. ICC Bulletin (Special Supplement), *Procedural Decisions in ICC Arbitration: Security for Costs* (2014) 7.

will ideally be approached with a broader view and appreciation instead of the often too narrow Maslow's hammer approach of the past.[66]

---

66. Addressing the phenomenon of Maslow's hammer in the context of international arbitration generally, Ms. Claudia Salomon (President of the ICC Court of International Arbitration) in her recent keynote speech *Maslow's Hammer: An Over-Reliance on Familiar* Tools, available at https://iccwbo.org/content/uploads/sites/3/2022/03/tel-aviv-arbitration-week-keynote-claud ia-salomon-140322-1.pdf (accessed 20 October 2022). Ms. Salomon called upon arbitration practitioners to remain open to thinking about how to improve, to explore new ideas and tools, and find new answers instead of falling back on the 'we've always done it this way' bias.

CHAPTER 5

The CJEU's Case Law on Intra-EU Investment Arbitration and the Importance of the Place of Arbitration

Andrea Carlevaris

§5.01 *ACHMEA* AND ITS IMMEDIATE CONSEQUENCES

The landmark ruling of the Court of Justice of the European Union (CJEU) in *Slovak Republic v. Achmea*[1] has been at the core of the debate on the relationships between European Union (EU) law and investor-State arbitration for almost five years.[2] The ruling was followed by several other decisions of the CJEU—examined in the following paragraphs—which confirmed its content and expanded its scope.

Departing from Advocate General Wathelet's Opinion,[3] the March 6, 2018 judgment held that the investor-State dispute settlement provision contained in Article 8 of the Bilateral Investment Treaty (BIT) between the Netherlands and the Slovak Republic is incompatible with fundamental principles of EU law, such as those

---

1. Case No. C-284/16, *Slovak Republic v. Achmea BV*, March 6, 2018.
2. Ex multis, *see* E. Gaillard, *L'Affaire Achmea ou les conflits de logiques* (CJEU 6 mars 2018 aff. C-284/16), 3 Revue critique de droit international privé 616 (2018); B. Hess, *The Fate of Investment Dispute Resolution after the Achmea Decision of the European Court of Justice*, 3 Max Planck Institute Luxembourg for Procedural Law Working Paper Series 2018; J.R. Basedow, *The Achmea Judgment and the Applicability of the Energy Charter Treaty in Intra-EU Investment Arbitration*, 23 Journal of International Economic Law 271 (2020); E. Sipiorski, *Conflicting Conceptions of Constitutionalism: Investment Protection from the European Union and International Perspectives*, 66 Netherlands International Law Review 219 (2019); R.F. Bodenheimer, *K.H. Eller, Unionszentrismus und ISDS*, Recht des Internationalen Wirtschaft 786 (2018); A. Briguglio, *Achmea and the Day after Achmea*, 3 Rivista dell'arbitrato 504 (2018); A. Carlevaris, A. Ciampi, *Beyond Achmea: Implications for EU Member States, Arbitrators, National Courts and European Investors*, 4 Rivista dell'arbitrato 661 (2020).
3. Opinion of AG Wathelet in Case C-284/16, *Slovak Republic v. Achmea BV*, 19.9.2017, ECLI: EU:C:2017:699.

enshrined in Articles 267 and 344 of the Treaty on the Functioning of the European Union (TFEU). Article 267 TFEU empowers—or, in the case of last instance courts, requires—the courts of EU Member States to refer matters pertaining to the interpretation of the EU Treaties or to the validity and interpretation of acts of the EU institutions to the CJEU for a preliminary ruling. Article 344 TFEU prevents Member States from submitting disputes concerning the interpretation or application of the EU Treaties to any other settlement method.

The CJEU took the view that the dispute settlement provision contained in the Netherlands-Slovakia BIT is incompatible with the above-mentioned provisions insofar as an arbitral tribunal established under the BIT may have to apply and interpret EU law but does not qualify as a "court or tribunal of a Member State" in the meaning of Article 267 TFEU, and thus cannot request a preliminary ruling from the CJEU. As a result, intra-EU investment arbitration does not guarantee the uniform application and interpretation of EU law, which the CJEU regards as a fundamental principle of EU law.

The ruling had several immediate consequences, including the following.

Shortly after the CJEU delivered its judgment, the Commission's views on its effects were summarized in the Communication "Protection of intra-EU investment" of July 19, 2018.

On October 31, 2018, the German Federal Supreme Court implemented the judgment and annulled the arbitral award in *Achmea v. Slovak Republic* on the ground of invalidity of the arbitration agreement.[4]

In three declarations published on January 15 and 16, 2019 ("January 2019 Declarations"), the EU Member States declared their intention to terminate intra-EU BITs, draw the attention of arbitral tribunals in ongoing intra-EU arbitral proceedings initiated by "their" investors to the consequences of *Achmea* and pursue annulment or non-enforcement of existing intra-EU arbitral awards. While twenty-two Member States, including the United Kingdom (UK), assumed these obligations also with regard to intra-EU arbitral proceedings on the basis of the multilateral Energy Charter Treaty (ECT), others issued separate declarations stating that they did not wish to anticipate the CJEU's assessment in this respect. The Declaration of January 15, 2019, signed by twenty-two Member States, recognizes that the *Achmea* judgment has legal consequences in intra-EU arbitral proceedings brought not only under BITs but also under the ECT.[5] Finland, Luxembourg, Malta, Slovenia, Sweden and Hungary disagreed as regards the ECT.[6]

---

4. BGH, October 31, 2018—I ZB 2/15, paras. 25–28. On January 24, 2019, the same *Bundesgerichtshof* rejected *Achmea's* complaint and confirmed its previous ruling.
5. *Declaration of the Representatives of the Governments of the Member States, of 15 January 2019, on the Legal Consequences of the Judgment of the Court of Justice in* Achmea *and on Investment Protection in the European Union,* available at https://ec.europa.eu/info/sites/info/files/business_economy_euro/banking_and_finance/documents/190117-bilateral-investment-treaties_en.pdf and https://bit.ly/2QXx36m.
6. *Declaration of the Representatives of the Governments of the Member States, of 16 January on the Enforcement of the Judgment of the Court of Justice in* Achmea *and on Investment Protection in the European Union,* available at https://www.regeringen.se/48ee19/contentassets/d759689c0c804a9ea7af6b2de7320128/achmea-declaration.pdf and https://bit.ly/2Xi4C7H, and *Declaration of the Government of Hungary, of 16 January 2019, on the Legal Consequences of the Judgment of the*

After *Achmea*, numerous arbitral awards based on intra-EU BITs and the ECT were rendered, both by the International Centre for the Settlement of Investment Disputes (ICSID) and non-ICSID arbitral tribunals. Several of these awards have been challenged before ICSID ad hoc committees and national courts. Some decisions, almost systematically rejecting jurisdictional objections based on *Achmea*, have already been rendered in these proceedings.

On May 5, 2020, twenty-three (of the by then twenty-seven) EU Member States signed an international agreement for the termination of intra-EU BITs ("Termination Agreement"),[7] which entered into force on August 29, 2020. It provides for the termination of 123 intra-EU BITs, and, "[f]or greater certainty," it also terminates the sunset clauses contained in those BITs as well as in recently terminated BITs,[8] all of which "shall not produce legal effects" (Articles 2.2 and 3). The Contracting Parties explicitly confirm that arbitration clauses in intra-EU BITs are contrary to EU law and thus inapplicable as of the date on which the last of the parties to the relevant intra-EU BIT became a Member State of the EU (Article 4).

Further to the conclusion of the Termination Agreement, not all of the intra-EU BITs have been terminated and the ratification process is underway. Even if it entered into force with respect to all signatory States, the Termination Agreement would significantly reduce intra-EU investment arbitrations, but not completely eliminate them. Austria, Finland, Ireland, Sweden and the UK have not (yet) signed the Termination Agreement.

§5.02 *KOMSTROY* AND INVESTOR-STATE ARBITRATION UNDER THE ECT

On September 2, 2021, the CJEU issued its ruling in *Republic of Moldova v. Komstroy*[9] concluding that, as a matter of EU law, Article 26 of the ECT is not applicable to intra-EU disputes. The CJEU's Decision largely follows the reasoning in *Achmea*.

In October 2019, the Paris Court of Appeal made a request to the CJEU for a preliminary ruling addressing three questions pertaining to set-aside proceedings

---

Court of Justice in Achmea *and on Investment Protection in the European Union*, available https://ec.europa.eu/info/sites/default/files/business_economy_euro/banking_and_finance/1 90116-bilateral-investment-treaties-hungary_en.pdf. The two January 16, 2019 Declarations note that "the *Achmea* judgment is silent on the question of the investor-state arbitration clause in the ECT … it would be inappropriate, in the absence of a specific judgment in this matter, to express views as regards the compatibility with Union law of the intra-EU application of the Energy Charter Treaty."

7. *Agreement for the Termination of Bilateral Investment Treaties between the Member States of the European Union*, SN/4656/2019/INIT, OJ L 169, May 29, 2020, 1–41, available at https://eur-lex .europa.eu/legal-content/EN/TXT/?uri = CELEX%3A22020A0529%2801%29.
8. Attached to the Termination Agreement is a forty-six-page double annex: Annex A lists the 123 intra-EU BITs in force at the time of the conclusion of the Agreement; Annex B lists the BITs that have already been terminated and with respect to which a sunset clause may be in force.
9. Case C-741/19, *Republic of Moldova v. Komstroy, a company the successor in law to the company Energoalians*, 2.9.2021, ECLI:EU:C:2021:655.

brought by Moldova in respect of an award rendered in a Paris-seated arbitration under the UNCITRAL Rules against it for certain breaches of obligations under the ECT.[10]

Only one of the three questions referred to by the Paris Court of Appeal ultimately was addressed by the CJEU, i.e., whether the definition of "investment" in Article 1(6) of the ECT requires any economic contribution on the part of the investor in the host State. The ruling found, in essence, that an economic contribution was required. However, the CJEU also set out its views on whether Article 26 of the ECT is compatible with EU law insofar as it provides for arbitration between EU-based investors and EU Member States. This question was not referred to by the Paris Court of Appeal, nor was it directly relevant to the questions before the CJEU, which concerned investments in a non-EU Member State. This separate question had, however, been raised by the Commission, together with certain EU Member States acting as interveners in the CJEU proceedings.

The ruling indicates that intra-EU arbitration under the ECT is incompatible with EU law.[11]

First, following its reasoning in *Achmea*, the CJEU explained that in order to preserve the autonomy of EU law, as well as its effectiveness, national courts of EU Member States may make a preliminary reference to the CJEU pursuant to Article 267 of the TFEU. This referral procedure was described as the "keystone" of the EU judicial system with the "objective of securing the uniform interpretation of EU law, thereby ensuring its consistency, its full effect and its autonomy."

Second, the CJEU reasoned that because the EU is a Contracting Party to the ECT, the ECT itself is an "act of EU law." As such, an ECT tribunal would necessarily be required to interpret, and even apply, EU law when deciding a dispute under Article 26. This reasoning seems inconsistent with the Opinion No. 1/17, in which the CJEU accepted that tribunals acting under the EU-Canada Comprehensive Economic and Trade Agreement (CETA)—though standing outside the judicial system of the EU—could nonetheless interpret and apply the CETA itself without running afoul of EU law.[12] In *Komstroy*, the CJEU does not explain how CETA, to which the EU is also a party and should likewise be considered an "act of EU law," is compatible with EU law, but the ECT is not.

Third, having found that an ECT tribunal would need to apply EU law because the ECT is an "act of EU law," the CJEU then ascertained whether an ECT tribunal is situated within the judicial system of the EU such that a preliminary reference could be made to the CJEU to ensure the effectiveness of EU law. The CJEU held that, in "precisely the same way" as in *Achmea*, ECT tribunals are outside the EU legal system,

---

10. Request for a preliminary ruling from the *Cour d'appel de Paris*, Case C-741/19, *Republic of Moldova v. Komstroy, a company the successor in law to the company Energoalians*, October 8, 2019.

11. *See* J. Odermatt, *Is EU Law International? Case C-741/19 Republic of Moldova v. Komstroy LLC and the Autonomy of the EU Legal Order*, available at https://www.europeanpapers.eu/en/system/files/pdf_version/EP_EF_2021_I_025_Jed_Odermatt_00522.pdf; J. Tropper, *From Achmea to Komstroy: The CJEU Strikes Back Against Investment Arbitration under the Energy Charter Treaty*, Völkerrechtsblog, September 22, 2021.

12. Opinion No. 1/17 of the Full Court (*CETA*), April 20, 2019, ECLI:EU:C:2019:341.

thus preventing effective control over the correct and consistent interpretation and application of EU law. The CJEU found that the judicial review that arises in the context of EU-seated investor-State arbitration is limited, since the referring court can only perform a review insofar as its domestic law permits. Hence, according to the CJEU, the full effectiveness of EU law cannot be guaranteed.

Finally, just like *Achmea*, the decision distinguishes investor-State arbitration from commercial arbitration, insofar as commercial arbitration "originate[s] in the freely expressed wishes of the parties concerned," whereas investor-State arbitration is not based on the parties' freely expressed wishes. This conclusion seems incorrect from a legal point of view. First, investor-State arbitration does not find its direct and only source in the bilateral or multilateral investment treaties, which are just vehicles of the host State's consent to arbitrate disputes with investors. Consent is perfected only upon the investor's acceptance of the State's offer. Second, States, as parties to disputes, freely consent to refer disputes with investors to arbitration by entering into the relevant investment treaty. Therefore, given that commercial arbitration tribunals routinely interpret and apply EU law, the CJEU's approach would logically lead to the conclusion that any commercial arbitration involving the application of EU law may be incompatible with the EU legal system.

Komstroy had no direct impact on the EU's and its Members' status as Contracting Parties to the ECT. The ECT remains in force between all Contracting Parties, including all EU Member States and the EU. A modification of the ECT to remove its application between the EU Member States would require the consent not just of the EU and its Member States, but of all the Contracting Parties to the ECT.

As described in greater detail below, to date, all ECT tribunals that have considered jurisdictional objections based on the intra-EU nature of the dispute have, with only one exception, rejected the suggestion that the ECT does not apply on an intra-EU basis. The CJEU did not provide any analysis under the Vienna Convention on the Law of Treaties (VCLT) on the interpretation of the ECT. Nor did the CJEU address the substantial body of case law under the ECT on the interpretation of Article 26 of the ECT, the vast majority of which reached the opposite conclusion.

§5.03 *PL HOLDINGS* AND THE PROHIBITION OF INTRA-EU AD HOC ARBITRATION AGREEMENTS

In yet another anti-intra-EU investment arbitration ruling, on October 26, 2021, in *Republic of Poland v. PL Holdings S.à.r.l,*[13] the CJEU ruled that EU Member States are precluded from entering into ad hoc arbitration agreements with EU-based investors replicating the content of an arbitration agreement in a BIT between the EU Member States.[14]

---

13. Case No. C-109/20, *Republic of Poland v. PL Holdings S.à.r.l.,* October 26, 2021, ECLI: EU:C:2021:875.
14. *See* D. Zasheva, G. Lentner, *ECJ in PL Holdings: Ad Hoc Arbitration Agreement Between EU Investor and Member State Not Compatible with EU Law* (November 8, 2021) https://

PL Holdings brought arbitration proceedings against Poland under the BIT between the Belgium-Luxembourg Economic Union (BLEU) and Poland after a Polish regulator ordered the compulsory sale of its interests in a Polish bank. The seat of the arbitration was Stockholm, and the case was administered by the Arbitration Institute of the Stockholm Chamber of Commerce (SCC). In a 2017 award, the tribunal concluded that Poland had expropriated PL Holdings' investment and awarded damages.

In September 2017, Poland brought set-aside proceedings before the Swedish courts, arguing that, based on *Achmea* the arbitration clause in the Poland-BLEU BIT was incompatible with EU law. The setting aside proceedings before the Svea Court of Appeal led to a surprising outcome.[15] The Swedish Court came to the same conclusion as the German Supreme Court in *Achmea* with respect to the invalidity of the State's offer to arbitrate. However, the same Court found that, by participating in the arbitration without raising a timely objection to jurisdiction based on an alleged violation of EU law, the respondent State and the investor had concluded a tacit arbitration agreement. In the Court's view, Poland tacitly accepted PL Holding's offer to arbitrate by failing to raise an objection based on *Achmea* at the proper stage of the proceedings. This resulted in an ad hoc arbitration agreement between Poland and PL Holdings governed by Swedish law, i.e., the law of the seat.[16] The arbitration agreement was said to be derived from the parties' common intention to resolve the dispute in the same manner as a commercial arbitration agreement. In this respect, the Svea Court relied on the questionable distinction made by the CJEU in *Achmea* and *Komstroy* between commercial arbitration and treaty arbitration, i.e., that, unlike investor-State arbitration, commercial arbitration originates in the "freely expressed wishes of the parties."

Given that Poland had objected that the arbitration agreement violated EU law during the arbitration proceedings, even if not at the outset, and that the CJEU has on other occasions required Member States' courts to annul awards for breach of mandatory EU law regardless of an objection being raised during the course of the arbitration,[17] the Svea Court's approach is questionable and may be regarded as an extreme attempt at preserving the validity of an intra-EU award despite *Achmea*. In any event, its conclusion would not be applicable to the vast majority of intra-EU arbitrations that led to an award after *Achmea*, in which the relevant objection was timely and effectively raised.

---

europeanlawblog.eu/2021/11/08/ecj-in-pl-holdings-ad-hoc-arbitration-agreement-between-eu-investor-and-member-state-not-compatible-with-eu-law.

15. *See* Svea Court of Appeal, *PL Holdings v. Poland*, Case Nos. T-8538-17 and T-12033-17; for an unofficial English translation, *see* https://www.italaw.com/sites/default/files/case-documents/italaw10447.pdf.

16. Poland had initially objected to the jurisdiction of the arbitral tribunal, but on different grounds. It objected that its offer of arbitration violated EU law only at a later stage of the proceedings.

17. *See* Case C-168/05, *Elisa Maria Mostaza Claro v. Centro Móvil Milenium SL*, October 26, 2006, ECLI:EU:C:2006:675; G. Bermann, *Navigating EU Law and the Law of International Arbitration*, 28 Arbitration International 415 (2012).

As a result of Poland's appeal, the Swedish Supreme Court referred to the CJEU the question whether Articles 267 and 344 of the TFEU as interpreted in *Achmea* mean that an intra-EU arbitration agreement is invalid even if a Member State refrains from raising jurisdictional objections after arbitration proceedings are commenced by the investor.

The CJEU held that: "[a]ny attempt by a Member State to remedy the invalidity of an arbitration clause by means of a contract with an investor from another Member State would run counter to the first Member State's obligation to challenge the validity of the arbitration clause."[18] In those circumstances, the CJEU held that a national court is required to uphold an application seeking to set aside an arbitration award made on the basis of an arbitration agreement infringing Articles 267 and 344 TFEU and the principles of mutual trust, sincere cooperation and autonomy of EU law.

Following in the footsteps of *Achmea* and *Komstroy*, the CJEU underscored that an agreement to remove from the jurisdiction of their own courts' disputes which may concern the application or interpretation of EU law may prevent those disputes from being resolved in a manner that guarantees the full effectiveness of EU law. In the CJEU's view, any ad hoc arbitration agreement containing the same terms as the investment treaty would have the same effect. The CJEU observed that the legal approach envisaged by the Svea Court in PL Holdings could potentially be adopted in a multitude of disputes concerning the application and interpretation of EU law, "thus allowing the autonomy of that law to be undermined repeatedly."[19]

The CJEU also relied on the Termination Agreement. It found that, based on the principles of the primacy of EU law and sincere cooperation, not only may EU Member States not undertake to remove disputes from the EU judicial system but also, in a situation like the one in PL Holdings, they are required to challenge the validity of the arbitration clause or the ad hoc arbitration agreement before the competent arbitration body or court. In the CJEU's view, this is further confirmed by Article 7(b) of the Termination Agreement, which provides that Contracting Parties involved in an intra-EU arbitration "shall ask the competent national court, including in any third country, as the case may be, to set the arbitral award aside, annul it or to refrain from recognising and enforcing it."[20]

§5.04 *MICULA* AND THE INTERTEMPORAL DIMENSION OF THE PROHIBITION OF INTRA-EU TREATY ARBITRATION

The CJEU's most recent broadside at intra-EU treaty arbitration is a January 25, 2022, ruling by which the CJEU overturned a decision by the EU's General Court in the fifteen-year-long Micula "saga."[21]

---

18. Case C-109/20, *Republic of Poland v. PL Holdings S.à.r.l.*, October 26, 2021, ECLI-:EU:C:2021:875, at para. 54.
19. *Ibid.*, at para. 49.
20. *Ibid.*, at para. 53.
21. Case C-638/19 P, *Viorel Micula and others v. Romania*, January 25, 2022, ECLI:EU:C:2022:50.

The ICSID arbitration proceedings commenced in 2005, prior to Romania's accession to the EU. The investors argued—and the ICSID tribunal agreed—that Romania had impaired their investments by repealing certain economic incentives with a view to eliminating measures that could constitute State aid shortly before its accession to the EU. In 2013, the tribunal ordered Romania to pay EUR 178 million in compensation, which the State partially paid. In 2015, however, the Commission ruled that such payment constituted unlawful State aid, precluding Romania from making further payments and requiring recovery of amounts already paid.

In June 2019 (after *Achmea*), the General Court quashed the Commission's ruling on the basis that all events relating to the incentive took place before Romania's accession to the EU in 2007, and the right to receive compensation recognized by the ICSID award arose at the time Romania repealed the incentives in 2005.[22] As EU State aid rules were not applicable in Romania prior to accession, the Commission could not exercise powers conferred to it under those rules. In the General Court's view, the fact that payment of the compensation occurred after accession is irrelevant because the payments made in 2014 represent the enforcement of a right which arose in 2005. Therefore, the General Court distinguished *Achmea* and avoided discussing the relationship between EU law and intra-EU investment arbitration: "in the present case, the arbitral tribunal was not bound to apply EU law to events occurring prior to the accession before it, unlike the situation in the case which gave rise to the judgment [in Achmea]."[23]

The Commission and Spain appealed the ruling before the CJEU, claiming that the award breached the EU principle of mutual trust and autonomy of EU law as interpreted in *Achmea*. In parallel, following the General Court's decision, the claimants in the ICSID arbitration sought to enforce the award, including before the courts of England and Wales.

In July 2021, Advocate General Szpunar opined that the *Achmea* dictum could not be applied to arbitration proceedings initiated pursuant to the Sweden-Romania BIT concluded before Romania's accession to the EU or pending at the time of accession.[24] However, the Advocate General held that the alleged State aid should be deemed granted at a time when Romania was required to pay that compensation based on the arbitral award. As the time of payment post-dated Romania's accession, EU law was applicable to that measure and the Commission was competent to make the ruling it did.

The case then reached the CJEU, which took a partially different view. As far as the time at which the alleged State aid should be deemed granted, the Court agreed with Advocate General Szpunar and held that EU State aid rules were applicable to the compensation paid by Romania. Contrary to the General Court's decision, in the CJEU's view, the applicability of EU State aid rules is triggered by the payment of an

---

22. Cases T-624/15, T-694/15 and T-704/15, *Viorel Micula and others v. European Commission*, General Court (Second Chamber), June 18, 2019, ECLI:EU:T:2019:423.
23. *Ibid.*, at para. 87.
24. Opinion of AG Szpunar in Case C-638/19 P, *European Commission v. Viorel Micula and others*, July 1, 2021, ECLI:EU:C:2021:529.

arbitral award even though all the State measures that the ICSID award compensated the investor for were taken before Romania's accession to the EU. Therefore, the CJEU upheld the competence of the Commission.

In light of its finding on the previous point, the CJEU found it unnecessary to rule on the relevance of *Achmea*. However, it stated that the General Court had erred in considering *Achmea* irrelevant. Since the compensation sought by the investors did not relate exclusively to the damage allegedly suffered before Romania's accession in 2007, but rather it extended until 2009, the arbitral proceedings could not be considered as completely confined to the pre-accession period. As such, the system of judicial remedies provided by EU law replaced arbitration upon the State's accession to the EU: "the consent [to arbitration] given to that effect by Romania, from that time onwards, lacked any force."[25]

As a result of the CJEU's ruling, the case will now be remanded to the General Court which will determine whether the Commission was right to consider that the compensation granted by the ICSID award constituted unlawful State aid and the relevance of *Achmea*.

§5.05 INTRA-EU ARBITRATION BEFORE ARBITRAL TRIBUNALS

The relationship between intra-EU investment arbitration and EU law was extremely controversial even before *Achmea*.[26] Prior to the March 6, 2018 ruling, tribunals consistently rejected objections based on the alleged incompatibility of intra-EU treaty arbitration (based on Article 26 ECT or the applicable BIT) with EU law, holding that there was "no legal rule or principle of EU law that would prevent [them] from exercising [their] functions."[27]

Unsurprisingly, the publication of the CJEU's rulings in *Achmea*, followed by those in *Komstroy*, *PL Holding* and *Micula* (jointly, "CJEU's rulings"), prompted the EU Member States to raise objections to the jurisdiction of arbitral tribunals in arbitrations which either were pending at the time the judgment was rendered or were introduced

---

25. Case C-638/19 P, *Viorel Micula and others v. Romania*, January 25, 2022, ECLI:EU:C:2022:50, at para. 145.
26. *See* J. Kokott, C. Sobotta, *Investment Arbitration and EU Law*, 18 Cambridge Yearbook of European Legal Studies 3 (2016); C. Titi, *International Investment Law and the European Union: Towards a New Generation of International Investment Agreements*, 26 European Journal of International Law 639 (2015); A. Dimopoulos, *The Validity and Applicability of International Investment Agreements Between EU Member States under EU and International Law*, 48 Common Market Law Review 63 (2011).
27. *Electrabel S.A. v. Republic of Hungary*, ICSID Case No. ARB/07/19, Award, November 25, 2015; *see also RREF Infrastructure (G.P.) Limited and RREF PanEuropean Infrastructure Two Lux S.a.r.l. v. Kingdom of Spain*, ICSID Case No. ARB/13/30, Decision on Jurisdiction, June 6, 2016; *Novoenergia II—Energy & Environment (SCA), SICAR v. Kingdom of Spain*, SCC No. 2015/063, Final Award, February 15, 2018; *Jan Oostergetel and Theodora Laurentius v. Slovak Republic*, UNCITRAL, Decision on Jurisdiction, April 30, 2010; *Charanne B.V. & Construction Investments S.a.r.l. v. Kingdom of Spain*, SCC No. 2012/062, Award, January 21, 2016; *Eiser Infrastructure Ltd. and Energia Solar Luxembourg S.à.r.l. v. Kingdom of Spain*, ICSID Case No. ARB/13/36; *Blusun S.A., Jean-Pierre Lecorcier and Michael Stein v. Italian Republic*, ICSID Case No. ARB/14/3, Award, December 27, 2016.

thereafter. So far, these objections have almost invariably been rejected.[28] It is worth noting that the Termination Agreement was not applicable to any of the decisions known to date, which either were rendered before its entry into force or involved States between which the Termination Agreement is not (yet) in force. Also, with a few recent exceptions, the States' objections and the available arbitral decisions to date refer to *Achmea*, not to *Komstroy*, *PL Holdings* or *Micula*. However, the latter decisions are likely having, *mutatis mutandis*, an impact on tribunals' jurisdiction similar to *Achmea*.

Without purporting to be exhaustive, the main arguments recurrently raised by investors and rejected by arbitral tribunals are examined below. The only award sustaining an objection based on the CJEU's rulings, the Award in *Green Power Partners v. Spain*,[29] and the other dissenting voices among arbitrators known to date are examined thereafter.

---

28. *See Spółdzielnia Pracy Muszynianka v. Slovak Republic*, PCA Case No. 2017-08, Award on Liability and Quantum, October 7, 2020; *Raiffeisen Bank International AG and Raiffeisenbank Austria d.d. v. Republic of Croatia*, ICSID Case No. ARB/17/34, Decision on the Respondent's Jurisdictional Objections, September 30, 2020 (with dissenting view of Arbitrator Lazar Tomov); *Addiko Bank AG and Addiko Bank d.d. v. Republic of Croatia*, ICSID Case No. ARB/17/37, Decision on Croatia's Jurisdictional Objection Related to the Alleged Incompatibility of the BIT with the EU *Acquis*, June 12, 2020; *A.M.F. Aircraftleasing Meier & Fischer GmbH & Co. KG v. Czech Republic*, PCA Case No. 2017-15, Final Award, May 11, 2020; *GPF GP S.à.r.l v. Republic of Poland*, SCC Case No. V(2014/168), Final Award, April 29, 2020; *The PV Investors v. The Kingdom of Spain*, PCA Case No. 2012-14, Final Award, February 28, 2020; *Sunreserve Luxco Holdings S.à.r.l., Sunreserve Luxco Holdings II S.à.r.l., Sunreserve Luxco Holdings III S.à.r.l. v. The Italian Republic*, SCC V(2016/32), Final Award, March 25, 2020; *Strabag SE, Raiffeisen Centrobank AG and Syrena Immobilien Holding AG v. Republic of Poland*, ICSID Case No. ADHOC/15/1, Partial Award on Jurisdiction, March 4, 2020; *Theodoros Adamakopoulos and others v. Republic of Cyprus*, ICSID Case No. ARB/15/49, Decision on Jurisdiction, February 7, 2020, (with Statement of Dissent of Professor Marcelo Kohen), February 3, 2020; *Magyar Farming Company Ltd., Kintyre Kft, and Inícia Zrt v. Hungary*, ICSID Case No. ARB/17/27, Award, November 13, 2019; *RWE Innogy GmbH and RWE Innogy Aersa S.A.U.*, ICSID Case No. ARB/14/34, Decision on Jurisdiction, Liability and Certain Issues of Quantum, December 30, 2019; *United Utilities (Tallinn) B.V. and Aktsiaselts Tallinna Vesi v. Republic of Estonia*, ICSID Case No. ARB/14/24, Award, June 21, 2019; *UP (formerly Le Chèque Déjeuner) and C.D Holding Internationale v. Hungary*, ICSID Case No. ARB/13/35, Award, October 9, 2018; *Marfin Investment Group v. The Republic of Cyprus*, ICSID Case No. ARB/13/27, Award, July 26, 2018; *Sodexo Pass International SAS v. Hungary*, ICSID Case No. ARB/14/20, Award, January 28, 2019; *Eskosol S.p.A. in liquidazione v. Italian Republic*, ICSID Case No. ARB/15/50, Decision on Italy's Request for Immediate Termination and Italy's Jurisdictional Objection Based on Inapplicability of the Energy Charter Treaty to Intra-EU Disputes, May 7, 2019; *STEAG GmbH v. Kingdom of Spain*, ICSID Case No. ARB/15/4, Decision on Jurisdiction, Liability and Direction on the Quantification of Damages, October 8, 2020; *Watkins Holding S.à.r.l. and Others v. Kingdom of Spain*, ICSID Case No. ARB/15/44, Award, January 21, 2020; *ESPF Beteiligungs GmbH, ESPF Nr. 2 Austria Beteiligungs GmbH, and Infraclass Energie 5 GmbH & Co KG*, ICSID Case No. ARB/16/5, Award, September 14, 2020; *Hydro Energy 1 S.à r.l. and Hydroxana Sweden AB v. Kingdom of Spain*, ICSID Case No. ARB/15/42, Decision on Jurisdiction, Liability and Directions on Quantum, March 9, 2020; *Vattenfall AB, Vattenfall GmbH, Vattenfall Europe Nuclear Energy GmbH, Kernkraftwerk Krümmel Gmbh & Co. oHG, Kernkraftwerk Brunsbüttel GmbH & Co. oHG v. Federal Republic of Germany*, ICSID Case No. ARB/12/12, Decision on the *Achmea* Issue, August 31, 2018.

29. *Green Power Partners K/S and SCE Solar Don Benito APS v. Kingdom of Spain*, SCC Case 2016/135, Award, June 16, 2022.

[A]   Scope and Binding Nature

A first approach taken by arbitral tribunals relies on the non-binding nature of the CJEU's rulings for an adjudicative body which does not belong to the EU legal order, such as an arbitral tribunal whose authority is based on an international treaty.

As a ruling rendered by the institution of a regional organization, *Achmea* is not binding on tribunals constituted under international treaties, such as the ICSID Convention, multilateral investment treaties, such as the ECT, and BITs, which are not part of the EU legal order.[30]

Albeit relevant to establish the status of EU law with respect to the Member States' obligations, the CJEU's rulings cannot be considered dispositive of the jurisdiction of tribunals established outside the EU legal order.[31] As a variant of this approach, tribunals held that EU law, including the TFEU and its interpretation by the CJEU in the CJEU's rulings, is not part of the law applicable to the jurisdiction of an arbitral tribunal, which is based only on the ICSID Convention (where applicable) and other international law instruments for the promotion and protection of foreign investments.[32]

[B]   Intertemporal Application

A second line of reasoning pertains to the applicability of *Achmea ratione temporis*. The relevant arguments are also applicable to the decisions that followed it.

Tribunals held that, regardless of its *ex nunc* or *ex tunc* effect and of it being regarded as merely interpretative of pre-existing EU law or innovative, *Achmea* cannot retroactively invalidate the consent to arbitration effectively expressed before the ruling was rendered.[33] To corroborate this conclusion, tribunals relied on the principle that, under investment law principles, once given consent cannot be withdrawn unilaterally.[34]

---

30. *A.M.F. v. Czech Republic, supra* n. 28, paras. 376–378; *Magyar Farming v. Hungary, supra* n. 28, para. 209; *United Utilities v. Estonia, supra* n. 28, paras. 532–540; *UP v. Hungary, supra* n. 28, para. 253; *Sodexo v. Hungary, supra* n. 28, para. 185; *Eskosol v. Italy, supra* n. 28, paras. 178–186.
31. *Adamakopoulos v. Cyprus, supra* n. 28, paras. 156–162.
32. *Strabag v. Poland, supra* n. 28, paras. 8.112–8.118, holding that, under French law, the jurisdiction of an arbitral tribunal is subject only to international public order, of which EU law is not part; *Vattenfall v. Germany, supra* n. 28, paras. 113–121.
33. *See Raiffeisen v. Croatia, supra* n. 28, para. 227: "The Tribunal readily accepts that a CJEU interpretation of the EU Treaties forms part of the acquis once formally rendered, but that interpretation—even assuming that it has the *ex tunc* effect under EU law that Croatia ascribes to the Achmea Judgment—cannot be in force before it is rendered and comes into existence. An interpretation by the CJEU cannot be in force with binding effect on unknowing parties. Neither states nor investors can fairly be expected to guess what definitive interpretations of EU law may come from the CJEU in the future"; *UP v. Hungary, supra* n. 28, paras. 258, 264; *Eskosol v. Italy, supra* n. 28, paras. 199–206.
34. *Marfin v. Cyprus, supra* n. 28, para. 593.

In a similar vein, tribunals also rejected the argument that, before *Achmea*, EU Member States could possibly anticipate that concluding a BIT which provides for investor-State arbitration was incompatible with EU law, or with the EU "*acquis.*"[35] This was particularly the case after Advocate General Wathelet's opinion, which reflected a state of the EU *acquis* opposite to the CJEU's eventual finding.[36]

[C]   Applicable Law

Given the central role played by applicable law in *Achmea*, several tribunals excluded from the scope of the ruling, and therefore from its invalidating effects, cases in which EU law is applicable neither as such nor as part of the domestic law of the host State, and may at best be relevant as a mere fact.[37] This is typically the case of arbitrations based on BITs that refer to their own provisions and to "international law" as applicable law or of BITs that contain no express choice-of-law clause, and are thus equally governed by international law.[38]

Tribunals also held that, even assuming they would have to apply EU law as part of the law of the (EU Member) host State, they would not be interpreting and applying EU law as such, but rather domestic law, even if founded on EU law.[39]

[D]   The Vienna Convention on the Law of Treaties

Almost all tribunals which heard jurisdictional objections based on *Achmea* so far examined arguments based on the VCLT, particularly Articles 30(3), 59(1), 46 and 31(3).

Article 30(3) VCLT, in case of successive treaties among the same States "relating to the same subject-matter," makes the earlier treaty applicable only to the extent its provisions are not incompatible with those of the later one. Arguments based on this provision were consistently rejected by tribunals, which found that, in the relations between the EU treaties and bilateral or multilateral investment instruments, neither the "same subject-matter" nor the "incompatibility" requirements are met.[40] Notably, both the "same subject-matter" and the "incompatibility" arguments were rejected on

---

35. *Raiffeisen v. Croatia, supra* n. 28, paras. 238–239; *Addiko v. Croatia, supra* n. 28, paras. 270–273.
36. *Raiffeisen v. Croatia, supra* n. 28, para. 243; *Addiko v. Croatia, supra* n. 28, paras. 274–276.
37. *A.M.F v. Czech Republic, supra* n. 28, paras. 368–375, especially 368: "Nothing in the Achmea judgment suggests that EU Member States were prohibited to offer arbitration under intra-EU BITs not governed even in part by EU law, but only by express treaty provisions and by general principles of international law. The CJEU did not consider that EU law could form part of either of these sources."
38. *Addiko v. Croatia, supra* n. 28, paras. 267, 269; *Sodexo v. Hungary, supra* n. 28, paras. 181–184, 188; *Eskosol v. Italy, supra* n. 28, paras. 172–177.
39. *Adamakopoulos v. Cyprus, supra* n. 28, para. 185.
40. *Addiko v. Croatia, supra* n. 28, para. 293; *GPF v. Poland, supra* n. 28, paras. 363–381; *Magyar Farming v. Hungary, supra* n. 28, paras. 228–248; *Marfin v. Cyprus, supra* n. 28, paras. 588–591.

the grounds that, unlike BITs, the TFEU governs neither the resolution of disputes[41] nor cross-border investments.[42]

Likewise, tribunals invariably held that the conditions for the application of Article 59(1) VCLT,[43] which, for a treaty to be terminated, in addition to the "same subject-matter" and incompatibility, requires that the intention of the State parties to the later treaty that the later treaty override the earlier one be established, were not satisfied.[44] Moreover, termination under Article 59 VCLT is not automatic as this provision refers to a specific procedure described in the same VCLT, which none of the EU Member State parties to the investment instruments in question ever activated.[45]

Some tribunals noted that the scope of the notion of incompatibility under Article 59(1) VCLT (*"so far incompatible ... that the two treaties are not capable of being applied at the same time"*) is narrower than under Article 30(3), which merely refers to the two treaties being compatible.[46] Regardless of the scope of the notion, incompatibility does not result from the fact that intra-EU BITs allegedly discriminate between EU nationals per se. If EU law recognizes a more favorable treatment, all EU investors may invoke it. If, however, an intra-EU BIT gives more rights to certain EU investors, it would be for nationals of those other countries to claim for equal rights. In any event, this circumstance does not per se make EU law and intra-EU BITs incompatible under either provision of the VCLT.[47]

Respondent States also relied on Article 46 VCLT, which prevents a State from invoking a violation of its domestic law to invalidate its consent to be bound by a treaty unless such violation is "manifest" and concerns a rule of domestic law "of fundamental importance." To reject this objection, tribunals relied on the uncertainty as to the

---

41. *GPF v. Poland, supra* n. 28, para. 370; *Strabag v. Poland, supra* n. 28, paras. 8.129–8.139; *Adamakopoulos v. Cyprus, supra* n. 28, paras. 168, 170: "BITs deal with investment and dispute settlement. The EU Treaties also deal with investment and dispute settlement. Thus, at a certain, general, level the treaties deal with the same subject matter. But at a more specific level they deal with different subject matters ... Applying this test, the Tribunal has difficulty in seeing the BITs and the EU Treaties as being of the same subject-matter. The existence of a procedure allowing the nationals of one state to bring a claim against another state under a BIT does not prevent the EU Treaties from operating. The fact that both have provisions relating to obligations on states in respect of foreign investors does not mean that the functioning of one prevents the functioning of the other. They can both operate side by side." Both decisions relied on the International Law Commission's Report on Fragmentation of International Law, which provides that the "same subject matter" precondition requires the two treaties at issue to be "institutionally linked" or "part of the same regime."
42. *Magyar Farming v. Hungary, supra* n. 28, para. 234; *United Utilities v. Estonia, supra* n. 28, para. 543; *Adamakopoulos v. Cyprus, supra* n. 28, para. 171.
43. Article 59(1) VCLT: "A treaty shall be considered as terminated if all the parties to it conclude a later treaty relating to the same subject-matter and (a) it appears from the later treaty or is otherwise established that the parties intended that the matter should be governed by that treaty; or (b) the provisions of the later treaty are so far incompatible with those of the earlier one that the two treaties are not capable of being applied at the same time."
44. *Addiko v. Croatia, supra* n. 28, paras. 295–296; *Adamakopoulos v. Cyprus, supra* n. 28, para. 178.
45. *United Utilities v. Estonia, supra* n. 28, para. 551; *Marfin v. Cyprus, supra* n. 28, para. 594; *Eskosol v. Italy, supra* n. 28, paras. 194–198.
46. *United Utilities v. Estonia, supra* n. 28, paras. 549–550.
47. *Ibid.*, para. 553.

compatibility of dispute resolution clauses contained in intra-EU BITs with EU law at least until *Achmea*. Even if established, the violation would have been far from "manifest" and such to affect a rule of internal law "of fundamental importance."[48]

Finally, another provision of the VCLT potentially relevant to the interpretation of the investment instrument on which a tribunal's jurisdiction is based is Article 31(3)(c), which provides that "any relevant rule of international law applicable in the relations between the parties" shall be taken into account in interpreting a treaty. Respondent States have argued that this provision requires that the relevant instruments (BIT or ECT) be interpreted in light of the EU treaties, which constitute precisely "rule[s] of international law applicable in the relations between the parties." While recognizing that EU law, particularly the TFEU, is part of international law and is therefore potentially relevant to treaty interpretation under Article 31(3)(c) VCLT, tribunals held that this provision has a limited scope. It does not permit to substitute EU law, as interpreted by the CJEU, to the treaty to be interpreted, but merely constitutes a subsidiary rule of interpretation, subject to the general rule that treaties are to be interpreted "in good faith in accordance with the ordinary meaning to be given to the terms in their context and in the light of its object and purpose" (Article 31(1) VCLT).[49]

[E]   The January 2019 Declarations and the Termination Agreement

A fifth series of arguments examined and rejected were those based on the January 2019 Declarations and/or the Termination Agreement. As mentioned above, the Termination Agreement was per se not applicable to any of the cases.

Tribunals were unable to draw from these instruments any conclusion as to the validity of intra-EU BITs' dispute resolution clauses, either because the Member States in question were not signatories of either instrument or because neither instrument was considered part of the EU *acquis*.[50] Moreover, the January 2019 Declarations were not regarded as a "subsequent agreement between the parties regarding the interpretation of a treaty" in the meaning of Article 31(3)(a) VCLT.[51]

---

48. *Raiffeisen v. Croatia, supra* n. 28, paras. 245–248; *Addiko v. Croatia, supra* n. 28, paras. 277–278; *A.M.F. v. Czech Republic, supra* n. 28, paras. 381–385; *Eskosol v. Italy, supra* n. 28, paras. 190–193.

49. *Vattenfall v. Germany, supra* n. 28, paras. 151–155; *Sunreserve v. Italy, supra* n. 28, paras. 386–394.

50. *Raiffeisen v. Croatia, supra* n. 28, paras. 249–254; *Addiko v. Croatia, supra* n. 28, paras. 281–290; *Magyar Farming v. Hungary, supra* n. 28, paras. 212–224; *Eskosol v. Italy, supra* n. 28, paras. 207–227.

51. *GPF v. Poland, supra* n. 28, paras. 350–353, arguing that the January 2019 Declarations: (a) do not constitute an understanding on the interpretation of the TFEU reached during the negotiations of the TFEU; (b) reveal no concern as to the compatibility between the BIT and the TFEU; (c) record the signatory States' intention to make best efforts to terminate intra-EU BITs and do not purport to have themselves the effect of terminating such BITs; *Strabag v. Poland, supra* n. 28, paras. 8.124–8.128, arguing that Art. 31(3)(a) VCLT does not trump other methods of treaty interpretation, including the ordinary meaning to be ascribed to its terms; *Adamakopoulos v. Cyprus, supra* n. 28, para. 179; *Magyar Farming v. Hungary, supra* n. 28, paras. 215, 224; *Sunreserve v. Italy, supra* n. 28, para. 435.

[F] Distinguishing *Achmea*: ICSID and ECT

Finally, several ICSID tribunals and tribunals constituted under the ECT avoided taking a position on one or more of the above-mentioned issues in general terms and instead rejected the objection by distinguishing *Achmea* from ICSID cases and cases based on the ECT.

In ICSID cases, tribunals dismissed objections based on *Achmea* on the grounds that: (a) unlike the *Achmea v. Slovakia* proceedings, ICSID arbitrations are not seated in any specific jurisdiction and are instead governed exclusively by the international regime of the ICSID Convention; (b) given the autonomous nature of the ICSID arbitration system, ICSID awards are not reviewed by State courts at the stage of annulment or enforcement; and (c) it was precisely in the context of the review process, which is excluded in ICSID arbitrations, that the German Supreme Court examined the award in *Achmea* and requested the CJEU's preliminary ruling.

As for cases based on Article 26 ECT, tribunals observed that *Achmea* did not address the status of intra-EU arbitration thereunder and the compatibility of EU law with the ECT, which contains an investor-State dispute settlement clause different from the one under scrutiny in *Achmea*.[52] Tribunals also observed that although, unlike BITs, the ECT is a "mixed agreement" to which, not only the Member States but also the EU itself is a party, this does not prevent investors from invoking Article 26 ECT in intra-EU disputes.[53] Article 26 ECT contains no exclusion, "carve-out" or "disconnection clause," which would make the offer of arbitration contained in this provision inapplicable in the relationships between the EU Member States.[54] Further to the CJEU's ruling in *Komstroy*, which extended the *Achmea* reasoning to ECT cases, tribunals' reasoning in these cases cannot be considered dispositive of the CJEU's concerns.

[G] An (Isolated?) Exception and Other Dissenting Voices

As stated above, no arbitral tribunal has so far upheld an objection based on *Achmea*, with one notable exception. In June 16, 2022 Award in *Green Power Partners v. Spain*, the tribunal upheld an objection based on the CJEU's rulings in an SCC arbitration based on the ECT.

The tribunal emphasized the importance of going beyond the mere juxtaposition of EU law and public international law and the determination of which legal system should prevail, favoring instead "the combined operation of certain specific norm,

---

52. *UP v. Hungary*, *supra* n. 28, paras. 253–258; *Sodexo v. Hungary*, *supra* n. 28, paras. 186–187, 189; *Vattenfall v. Germany*, *supra* n. 28, paras. 162, 213; *Sunreserve v. Italy*, *supra* n. 28, paras. 427–432.
53. For the observation that "even though the EU itself is a Contracting Party of the ECT, this does not eliminate the EU member States' individual standing as respondents under the ECT," *Novoenergia II v. Spain*, *supra* n. 27, para. 453.
54. *Sunreserve v. Italy*, *supra* n. 28, paras. 448–458; *Vattenfall v. Germany*, *supra* n. 28, paras. 169–206; *Hydro Energy 1 v. Spain*, *supra* n. 28, para. 502.

whether from international or domestic law."[55] After ascertaining that Article 26 ECT, interpreted "in accordance with [its] ordinary meaning" (Article 31(1) VCLT), may be applicable to disputes between Danish investors and Spain, the tribunal examined Article 26 ECT in the "context" of provisions it considered relevant, as also required by Article 31(1). In this respect the tribunal considered relevant: (i) other provisions contained in the ECT (Articles 1(3), 1(10), 25), which refer to the notion of "Regional Economic Integration Organizations" (REIO) and recognize that membership of a REIO may be subject to special requirements and the relationships between members of the ECT which are also members of a REIO may be different from relationships between other members of the ECT;[56] (ii) instruments "made by one or more of the parties in connection with the conclusion of the treaty and accepted by the other parties as an instrument related to the treaty" (Article 31(2)(b) VCLT), such as "Declaration 5" included in the Final Act of the ECT Conference in relation to Article 25 ECT, the "Statement submitted by the European Communities to the Secretariat of the Energy Charter pursuant to Article 25(3)(b)(ii) of the Energy Charter Treaty," which, in the tribunal's analysis, supports the conclusion that EU Members intended to withhold consent to intra-EU investment arbitration;[57] (iii) "(a) any subsequent agreement between the parties regarding the interpretation of the treaty or the application of its provisions; (b) any subsequent practice in the application of the treaty which establishes the agreement of the parties regarding its interpretation" (Article 31(3)(a) and (b) VCLT), such as the January 2019 Declarations, which, even if they cannot be regarded as "subsequent agreements" or "subsequent practices" in the meaning of Article 31(3)(a) and (b) VCLT, nonetheless constitute authentic interpretation of EU Members' "authentic interpretation" of the operation of the investor-State dispute settlement provisions of Article 26 ECT under both the same ECT and EU law.[58]

One can predict a similar fate for any objection based on *Komstroy*, *PL Holdings* or *Micula*. The only dissenting positions known are those of Mr. Lazar Tomov in *Raiffeisenbank v. Croatia* and Prof Marcelo Kohen in *Adamakopoulos v. Cyprus*.

Mr. Tomov's dissent is reflected in a succinct statement contained in the award.[59] He argued that, by entering into the BIT, the contracting States agreed that, insofar as the BIT is incompatible with the EU *acquis* in force at any given time, they are not bound by it. Mr. Tomov interpreted the notion of "EU *acquis*" broadly, as "shorthand for the EU legal system as a whole." He argued that incompatibility is to be determined also by reference to the CJEU's authoritative interpretation of EU law, including with respect to its scope *ratione temporis*. Furthermore, dispute resolution clauses in intra-EU BITs must have been reasonably understood by contracting States as incompatible with Articles 267 and 344 TFEU because, based on previous decisions of the CJEU, this conclusion was "predictable and likely."

---

55. *Green Power Partners v. Spain*, *supra* n. 29, para. 333.
56. *Ibid.*, paras. 350–355.
57. *Ibid.*, *supra* n. 29, paras. 359–363.
58. *Ibid.*, *supra* n. 29, paras. 364–387.
59. *Raiffeisenbank v. Croatia*, *supra* n. 28, paras. 255–258.

Conversely, Prof Kohen's dissent resulted in a substantial and articulated statement.[60] While accepting that *Achmea* is not directly binding on an arbitral tribunal constituted under a different BIT, Prof Kohen emphasized that the ruling is an "authoritative interpretation of EU Treaties and of their impact on other rules of international law." He also accepted that accession of the respondent State to the EU did not result in automatic termination of the relevant BIT concluded prior to it under Article 59 VCLT, as, at the time of the tribunal's award, termination negotiations were still pending.

The core of Prof Kohen's reasoning is that Article 30 VCLT, read in light of Article 351 TFEU, leads to the conclusion that the TFEU is indeed a treaty on the "same subject-matter" and the BIT and is incompatible with it. The dissent put particular emphasis on Article 351(3) TFEU,[61] which, in Prof Kohen's reading, reveals the nature of EU law, including the equality of advantages enjoyed by investors of all Member States and the role of the CJEU in interpreting EU law, "as a whole" that must be respected in the mutual relationships between EU Members.

As for the "same subject-matter" requirement under Article 30 VCLT, contrary to all tribunals that have examined objections based on the CJEU's rulings so far, and also to many others before *Achmea*,[62] the dissenting opinion finds that both the TFEU and the BIT deal with the substantive treatment of foreign (EU) investors and the settlement of disputes, even if their respective regimes differ. Hence, both treaties deal with the "same subject-matter."

According to Prof Kohen, even the second requirement under Article 30(1), i.e., incompatibility, is satisfied because intra-EU investment arbitration: (a) undermines the role of the CJEU as the sole and authentic interpreter of EU law; and (b) discriminates between EU investors who can benefit from arbitration and those who cannot, contrary to Article 18 TFEU.

A further point of dissent with numerous prior rulings lies in the role of the January 2019 Declarations, which Prof Kohen regarded as the "authentic interpretation" by EU Member States of "their own Treaties" and their relationships with the BIT. As such, regardless of their constituting an agreement amending prior treaties, the January 2019 Declarations should be "taken into account" in interpreting the BIT under Article 31(3) VCLT.

---

60. *Adamakopoulos v. Cyprus*, ICSID Case No. ARB/15/49, Statement of Dissent of Prof. Marcelo G. Kohen, February 3, 2020.
61. *See* Art. 351(1) TFEU: "the advantages accorded under the Treaties by each Member State form an integral part of the establishment of the Union and are thereby inseparably linked with the creation of common institutions, the conferring of powers upon them and the granting of the same advantages by all the other Member States."
62. *See European American Investment Bank AG v. Slovak Republic*, PCA Case No. 2010-17, Award on Jurisdiction, October 22, 2012, paras. 168–169, 178, 184; *Eastern Sugar B.V. v. Czech Republic*, SCC No. 088/2004, Partial Award, March 27, 2007, paras. 164–165; *Oostergetel v. Slovak Republic*, paras. 74–79.

§5.06   ANNULMENT AND ENFORCEMENT

Unsurprisingly, numerous arbitral awards, issued both before and after *Achmea*, have been challenged before ICSID ad hoc committees or, for cases not governed by the ICSID Convention, State courts.[63] Also unsurprisingly, investors are trying to enforce awards before the courts of the respondent States and elsewhere.

Although States chose a variety of procedural tools to challenge awards, including requests for annulment under Article 52 ICSID Convention or domestic law rules, revision under Article 51 ICSID Convention[64] and rectification under Article 49(2) ICSID Convention,[65] the following sections will examine the prospects of these challenges from the point of view of the most typical forms of award review, i.e., requests for annulment and enforcement.

For the purpose of this analysis, arbitration proceedings and awards governed by the ICSID Convention should be distinguished from non-ICSID proceedings and awards.

The analysis is carried out without considering the impact of the Termination Agreement, which has already been examined above and, albeit not applicable to any of the awards rendered so far, may become relevant to future awards.

[A]   Awards Governed by the ICSID Convention

The arbitration system governed by the ICSID Convention is virtually autonomous from the legal order of its contracting States. Requests for annulment of ICSID awards are brought before other arbitral bodies (ad hoc committees), against whose decisions no recourse is available.[66] While the ICSID Convention dispenses prevailing parties with the need to obtain the *exequatur* of awards, enforcement is governed by the law of the State in whose territory it is sought.[67]

For the purpose of assessing the fate of intra-EU awards after the CJEU's rulings, annulment and enforcement should be distinguished.

---

63. Under the ICSID Convention and Arbitration Rules, only "awards" can be subject to annulment proceedings (Art. 52 ICSID Convention). Decisions dismissing objections to the jurisdiction of arbitral tribunals can be challenged only with the award on the merits.
64. *See Republic of Hungary v. Dan Cake (Portugal) S.A.*, ICSID Case No. ARB/12/9, Decision on Applicant's Request for the Continued Stay of Enforcement of the Award, December 25, 2018.
65. *See*, e.g., *Masdar Solar & Wind Cooperatief U.A. v. Kingdom of Spain*, ICSID Case No. ARB/14/1, Decisions on the Respondent's Request for a Supplementary Decision, November 29, 2018.
66. *See* Art. 52 ICSID Convention.
67. *See* Art. 54(3) ICSID Convention: "Execution of the award shall be governed by the laws concerning the execution of judgments in force in the State in whose territory such execution is sought." *See also* Art. 55: "Nothing in Art. 54 shall be construed as derogating from the law in force in any Contracting State relating to immunity of that State or of any foreign State from execution."

[1] Annulment

Several ICSID ad hoc committees have already rejected challenges brought against awards on the basis of an EU law objection.[68] The analysis and conclusions may obviously differ depending on the factual and legal context of individual cases.

Except for *Micula*, all the CJEU's rulings originated from arbitration proceedings that were not subject to the ICSID Convention.[69] As for all cases not governed by the ICSID Convention, the arbitral award was therefore subject to (limited) judicial review under domestic law at annulment stage, with the possibility for the competent Member State's court to request a preliminary ruling from the CJEU pursuant to Article 267 TFEU.

Since this possibility does not even exist under the ICSID Convention, the *Achmea*, *Komstroy* and *PL Holdings* reasoning may be considered *a fortiori* relevant to ICSID cases. Given the self-contained nature of the ICSID arbitration system, the CJEU's intervention to ensure the correct application and interpretation of EU law, which constitutes the main rationale of the CJEU's rulings, is completely excluded because ICSID awards are not even subject to limited judicial review at annulment or enforcement stage. The CJEU's concerns about the alleged threat to the effectiveness and consistent interpretation of EU law would therefore be even more applicable to ICSID arbitrations. Therefore, it is not surprising that the CJEU eventually extended its reasoning to ICSID cases in *Micula*.

However, all arbitral decisions known to date refrained from engaging in a discussion of the merits of the ruling and instead concluded either for its inapplicability or irrelevance.

[2] Enforcement

Pursuant to Article 54(1) ICSID Convention, an ICSID arbitral award is not subject to judicial review by State courts and is enforceable within the territory of all Member States of the Convention "as if it were a final judgment of a court in that State."[70] Pursuant to Article 53(1) ICSID Convention, Convention awards are not subject to "any other remedy except those provided for in this Convention."

---

68. *Dan Cake v. Hungary*, ICSID Case No. ARB/12/9, Decision on Annulment, July 16, 2021 (unpublished; *see* https://globalarbitrationreview.com/achmea/hungary-fails-upend-another-intra-eu-bit-award); *Sodexo Pass International SAS v. Hungary*, ICSID Case No. ARB/14/20, Decision on Annulment, May 7, 2021 (unpublished; *see* https://globalarbitrationreview.com/intra-eu-award-against-hungary-upheld); *Edendred S.A. v. Hungary*, ICSID Case No. ARB/13/21, Decision on Annulment, March 9, 2020 (unpublished); *UP and C.D Holding Internationale (formerly Le Cheque Dejeuner) v. Hungary*, ICSID Case No. ARB/13/35, Decision on Annulment, August 11, 2021 (unpublished).
69. *Achmea v. Slovak Republic* was governed by the UNCITRAL Rules and seated in Germany *Komstroy v. Moldova* was also an UNCITRAL case seated in Paris, and *PL Holdings v. Poland* was an SCC case with Stockholm as place of arbitration.
70. Article 54(1) ICSID Convention: "Each Contracting State shall recognize an award rendered pursuant to this Convention as binding and enforce the pecuniary obligations imposed by that award within its territories as if it were a final judgment of a court in that State."

Several ICSID tribunals considered their own duty to render an enforceable award and the likely difficulties of enforcement in light of *Achmea*. However, they did not consider these difficulties sufficient to uphold objections to their jurisdiction, *inter alia*, because they found that: (a) enforcement is separate from, and does not impinge on, jurisdiction;[71] (b) difficulty of enforcement does not amount to total "unenforceability";[72] (c) enforcement and jurisdiction are governed by different rules: enforcement is governed by the law of the jurisdiction where it is sought, whereas jurisdiction depends on the ICSID Convention and the relevant investment treaty;[73] (d) whether acts of enforcement may constitute breaches of EU law, as argued by certain Member States, is outside the scope of a jurisdictional decision;[74] and (e) enforcement is not limited to the courts of the host State or of EU Member States, as the prevailing party may seek to enforce the award in the territory of a third State, where enforcement may be possible or easier.[75]

The prospects of enforcement of an ICSID award after the CJEU's rulings may depend on whether enforcement proceedings are brought within or outside the EU.

As a matter of general international law, and regardless of the CJEU's position, the enforcement regime of the ICSID Convention is also applicable to intra-EU investment treaty arbitrations in the relationships between EU Member States.

However, the hierarchy of norms within the EU legal order is nevertheless likely to hinder the enforcement of intra-EU investment arbitration awards by EU courts under Article 54 ICSID Convention. Since primary EU law prevails, not only over national law but also over other international treaties,[76] an EU Member State's court may refuse to apply Article 54 ICSID Convention.[77] Moreover, at the enforcement stage, EU courts may refer the matter to the CJEU for a preliminary ruling. In this case, after *Achmea*, *Komstroy*, *PL Holdings* and *Micula*, the CJEU's finding would be predictable.

This conclusion seems corroborated by a number of court decisions rendered in *Micula* even before the January 22, 2022 ruling, in which the claimants tried to enforce the ICSID award against the State within and outside the EU. Notwithstanding Article 54 ICSID Convention, the competent EU courts stayed in enforcement proceedings in

---

71. *United Utilities v. Estonia, supra* n. 28, para. 541; *Vattenfall v. Germany, supra* n. 28, para. 230.
72. *Eskosol v. Italy, supra* n. 28, para. 233.
73. *Marfin v. Cyprus, supra* n. 28, para. 596; *Eskosol v. Italy, supra* n. 28, para. 234; *RWE Innogy v. Spain, supra* n. 28, para. 374: "the Tribunal is naturally concerned that its award should be capable of enforcement, and notes the statement in the Declaration of 15 January 2019 … However, the issue of recognition and enforcement are ultimately a matter for the courts of concerned ICSID Contracting States in accordance with Art. 54 of the ICSID Convention, and the Tribunal cannot determine its jurisdiction by reference to how differing Contracting States may understand and apply their obligations under Article 54."
74. *Vattenfall v. Germany, supra* n. 28, para. 231.
75. *Adamakopoulos v. Cyprus, supra* n. 28, para. 181.
76. *See*, among others, CJEU Case 235-87, *Matteucci v. Communauté française de Belgium*, September 27, 1988, ECLI:EU:C:1988:460; Case C-3/91, *Exportur v. LOR*, November 10, 1992, ECLI:EU:C:1992:420.
77. P. Goldsmith, B. Yin, *Intra-EU BITs: Competence and Consequences*, in N. Kaplan, M. Moser (eds.), *Jurisdiction, Admissibility and Choice of Law in International Arbitration: Liber Amicorum Michael Pryles*, 2018, 241: "it would be necessary to consider separately the position of EU Member States and non-EU Member States."

view of a potential conflict with EU State aid rules.[78] As a result, there seems to be no prospect of enforcing an ICSID award based on an intra-EU investment treaty within the EU.

The prospects of enforcement of an award outside the EU are quite different. Enforcement of arbitral awards in jurisdictions other than the respondent State may prove problematic due to the absence of assets not covered by State immunity. Moreover, courts outside the EU may still consider the incompatibility of the award with EU law under the doctrine of comity. This may particularly be the case after the January 2019 Declarations, whereby "member States will request the courts, *including in any third country*, which are to decide in proceedings relating to an intra-EU investment arbitration award, to set these awards aside or not to enforce them due to a lack of valid consent."[79] Also, following the January 2022 CJEU's ruling in *Micula*, and subject to the upcoming decision the General Court will render in such case, the Commission may require the Member State to recover amounts paid which it concludes constitute incompatible State aid or are otherwise contrary to EU law, as interpreted by the CJEU. In this respect, it is noteworthy that the Commission recently announced its investigation into the arbitral award rendered in *Infrastructure Services v. Spain* in July 2021, which it considers, on a preliminary view, constitutes State aid.[80]

However, courts outside the EU are bound by neither EU law nor CJEU's rulings. It is unlikely that the above-mentioned considerations will take precedence over ICSID Member States' obligation under Article 54(1) ICSID Convention. Therefore, intra-EU treaty awards governed by the ICSID Convention will most likely remain enforceable outside the EU.

[B] Awards Not Governed by the ICSID Convention

Awards not governed by the ICSID Convention, but rather by the UNCITRAL, SCC, ICSID Additional Facility or other arbitration rules, are subject to the *lex arbitri* of the place or arbitration and to the jurisdiction of the relevant courts at the annulment stage.[81] Their enforcement is governed by the 1958 New York Convention on the

---

78. *See* Judgment of the English Court of Appeal, July 27, 2018; Judgment of the Brussels Court of Appeal, March 12, 2019.
79. *See Eskosol v. Italy, supra* n. 28, para. 232: "non-EU courts may face certain pressure not to enforce an intra-EU investment arbitration award, based on the undertaking by Italy and others in the January 2019 Declaration … Alternatively, if a non-EU court proceeds to enforce an award against Italy, the Commission eventually could deem any amounts collected to be unlawful State aid, and require Italy to seek recovery from Eskosol in an equivalent amount." J. Scheu, P. Nikolov, *The Setting Aside and Enforcement of Intra-EU Investment Arbitration Awards after Achmea*, 36 Arbitration International 253, 271 (2020).
80. *See Infrastructure Services Luxembourg S.à.r.l. and Energia Termosolar B.V. (formerly Antin Infrastructure Services Luxembourg S.à.r.l. and Antin Energia Termosolar B.V.) v. Kingdom of Spain*, ICSID Case No. ARB/13/31. *See* European Commission Press Release, *State aid: Commission opens in-depth investigation into arbitration award in favour of Antin to be paid by Spain*, available at https://ec.europa.eu/commission/presscorner/detail/en/IP_21_3783.
81. K. Bondar, *Annulment of ICSID and Non-ICSID Investment Awards: Differences in the Extent of Review*, 32 Journal of International Arbitration 621 (2015).

Recognition and Enforcement of Foreign Arbitral Awards (NYC) and domestic law. Annulment and enforcement require separate analyses.

[1]   Annulment

The grounds based on which an award not governed by the ICSID Convention can be set aside differ from jurisdiction to jurisdiction. However, there is substantial convergence across different jurisdictions.

The grounds for setting aside relevant objections based on the CJEU's rulings are those reflected in Article 34(2)(a)(i), 34(2)(b)(i) and 34(2)(b)(ii) of the UNCITRAL Model Law or analogous provisions of domestic law, i.e., that the arbitration agreement is "not valid under the law to which parties have subjected it, or, failing any indication thereon, under the law of th[e] State [where annulment is sought]," "the subject-matter of the dispute is not capable of settlement by arbitration" under the law of the jurisdiction where annulment is sought or "the award is in conflict with the public policy" of such jurisdiction.[82]

If the arbitration is seated within the EU, the court seized for the annulment of the award will base its decision on EU law as part of its own domestic law, which is relevant to all three above-mentioned grounds. In light of Achmea, Komstroy, PL Holdings and Micula, all three grounds are likely to provide sufficient basis for annulment.

The invalidity of the arbitration agreement is a consequence of the invalidity of the EU Member State's offer of arbitration contained in the applicable treaty. Pursuant to the most common choice-of-law approach, also reflected in Article 34(2)(a)(i) of the Model Law, in the absence of an agreement of the parties, the arbitration agreement is governed by the law of the place of arbitration.[83] Therefore, having been found incompatible with EU law by the CJEU, the arbitration agreement on which an intra-EU investment award is based is likely to be considered invalid under the law of the Member State in which the arbitration is seated. Even adopting an alternative approach, which subjects the arbitration agreement to the law applicable to the substance

---

82. As of December 2020, legislation based on the Model Law has been adopted in 84 countries and 117 different jurisdictions: see https://uncitral.un.org/en/texts/arbitration/modellaw/commercial_arbitration/status. Even non-Model Law jurisdictions tend to provide for grounds for annulling arbitral awards identical or similar to those of the Model Law.
83. G.B. Born, International Commercial Arbitration, Alphen aan den Rijn, 2014, 514. For a Dutch ruling, see Arrondissementsrechtbank of Rotterdam, September 28, 1995, in Yearbook Commercial Arbitration, 1997, 762; H. Grigera-Naón, Choice-of-Law Problems in International Commercial Arbitration, 289 Récueil des Cours 71 (2001); in England, for the view that the presumption that an express choice-of-law provision contained in a contract extends to the arbitration agreement can be rebutted whenever other elements point to the existence of a closer connection with another jurisdiction, as is the case when there is an express choice of the place of arbitration, see Sulamérica Cia Nacional de Seguros SA v. Enesa Engenharia SA (2012) EWCA Civ 638; in Singapore, FirstLink Investments Corp Ltd v. GT Payment Pte Ltd (2014) SGHCR, 12: "the arbitral seat is the juridical centre of gravity which gives life and effect to an arbitration agreement."

of the dispute,[84] the outcome would likely be the same. Depending on the applicable treaty, such law would be the law of the host State and/or international law. Given the above-mentioned principle which, within the EU, gives priority to EU law over domestic law and other international treaties, an EU Member State's court will most likely abide by the CJEU's findings and declare the consent to arbitration invalid. The same conclusion as to the invalidity of the arbitration agreement is likely to be reached also on the basis of yet a different approach, such as the one elaborated by the French case law, according to which an international arbitration agreement is governed by a substantive rule which preserves its validity unless the agreement is contrary to the public policy of the jurisdiction where annulment is sought.[85] For the reasons stated below, even an EU Member State's court following this approach is likely to find that intra-EU investment arbitration agreements are contrary to public policy and thus invalid.

The German *Bundesgerichtshof* in *Achmea* was directly bound by the CJEU's ruling. Regardless of the binding nature of the judgment, however, it is unsurprising that the Federal Supreme Court set aside the arbitral award pursuant to section 1059(2)(1) of the German Code of Civil Procedure, which sanctions precisely the invalidity of the arbitration agreement, on the ground that Slovakia's offer to arbitrate was not validly made. As stated above, in *PL Holdings*, the Svea Court of Appeal came to the same conclusion as the German Supreme Court in *Achmea* with respect to the invalidity of the State's offer to arbitrate, even if it refused to set aside the award based on its finding that the respondent State and the investor had concluded a tacit arbitration agreement.

Alternatively, or cumulatively, the "incompatibility" of intra-EU arbitration with EU law may be framed in terms of arbitrability. From this perspective, disputes arising from the alleged breach of EU Member States' obligations under BITs or the ECT may be regarded as "not capable of settlement by arbitration."[86] The language of the CJEU's

---

84. For recent English case law holding that, in the absence of a specific choice-of-law agreement, the arbitration agreement is governed by the same law which governs the contract in which it is contained pursuant to the parties' agreement, *see Kabab-Ji SAL (Lebanon) v. Kout Food Group (Kuwait)* [2020] EWCA Civ. 6 (January 20, 2020); in the same case, the Paris Court of Appeal took a different view and relied on French law as the law of the arbitration agreement: Paris Court of Appeal, June 23, 2020, *Kout Food Group v. Kabab-ji SAL*; *Enka Insaat Ve Sanayi AS v. OOO Insurance Company Chubb* [2020] UKSC 38; in the U.S., *see Motorola Credit Corp. and Nokia Corp. v. Uzan et al.*, 388 F.3d (2d Cir. 2004).

85. R. Nazzini, *The Law Applicable to the Arbitration Agreement: Towards Transnational Principles*, 65 International and Comparative Law Quarterly 681 (2016); French Court of Cassation, December 20, 1993, *Municipalité de Khoms El Mergeb v. Dalico Contractors*, *Revue de l'arbitrage*, 1994, 116; "according to a substantive rule of international arbitration law, the arbitration agreement is legally independent of the main contract in which it is included or which refers to it, and its existence and effectiveness are to be assessed, subject to the mandatory rules of French law and international public policy, on the basis of the parties' common intention, without it being necessary to make reference to a national law"; *see also* French Court of Cassation of March 20, 2004, *Unikod v. Ourakali*, Revue de l'arbitrage, 2005, 961.

86. An arbitrability objection was raised by Poland in the setting aside proceedings before the Svea Court in *PL Holdings v. Poland*. The Swedish Court rejected the objection holding that the substantive issues in dispute in the arbitration, i.e., whether Poland had breached the BIT and was liable to the investor and, if so, for what amount, are per se capable of settlement by

rulings is compatible with this approach because it purports to sanction only the investor-State dispute settlement provision of the relevant BIT, not also the BITs' substantive obligations. The breach of the BITs' substantive standards of treatment may be considered enforceable in other *fora* that guarantee the consistent interpretation and application of EU law through the CJEU's role in the context of preliminary rulings under Article 267 TFEU.

Finally, an intra-EU investor-State award not governed by the ICSID Convention is likely to be set aside on the ground of a breach of the Member State's public policy. Applying the standard set by the CJEU in *Eco Swiss*, which held that a norm of EU law "which is essential for the accomplishment of the tasks entrusted to the Community and, in particular, for the functioning of the internal market" must be considered as forming part of the public policy of Member States for the purpose of the annulment and enforcement of arbitral awards,[87] one easily reaches the conclusion that the *vulnus* identified in the *Achmea* ruling does indeed constitute a breach of public policy. Since *Achmea*, the CJEU made clear that it considers intra-EU treaty-based arbitration to be in violation of some of the most fundamental principles of EU law, such as the autonomy of EU law from national and international law, the EU's constitutional structure and the principle of mutual trust and sincere cooperation between the Member States, potentially affecting "the fundamental freedoms, including freedom of establishment and free movement of capitals."[88]

Given Member States' obligation to interpret the concept of public policy in light of EU law and the CJEU's position in this respect, it is difficult to escape the conclusion that giving effect to an intra-EU investor-State award constitutes a breach of EU Members' public policy and is likely to lead to the annulment of the award.[89]

Conversely, considering that all three above-mentioned potential grounds for annulment depend on the impact of the CJEU's rulings on the domestic law of EU Member States, unlike EU courts, courts outside the EU, based on their domestic law, will likely reject requests for setting aside of awards.

[2]   Enforcement

To the extent the debtor has assets in several jurisdictions, the creditor may consider enforcing an award both within and outside the EU. Although the CJEU's rulings have a significant impact in both cases, the prospects of enforcement may differ greatly

---

arbitration. However, the Svea Court failed to address the arbitrability of the claims in light of the specific context, which might have led to the conclusion that EU law, as part of Member States' law, precludes the arbitrability of intra-EU claims based on investment treaties.

87. Case C-126/97, *Eco Swiss China Time v. Benetton International NV*, June 1, 1999, ECLI: EU:C:1999:269, para. 38.
88. *Slovak Republic v. Achmea BV*, *supra* n. 1, paras. 32, 33, 34, 42.
89. The Svea Court's ruling in *PL Holdings* reached a different conclusion. Distinguishing *Eco Swiss* and *Mostaza Claro*, the court held that the notion of public policy refers to the "substantive contents" of the award, and not to the arbitration agreement. This reasoning does not seem convincing. The notion of public policy is generally interpreted as covering both substantive and jurisdictional norms considered contrary to fundamental principles of a given (in this case, EU) legal system.

depending on the place of enforcement. As discussed below, also the place of arbitration may be relevant in this respect.

If enforcement is sought within the EU, courts are likely to deny enforcement on grounds similar to those already examined with respect to annulment, which are also reflected in the NYC, i.e., the invalidity of the arbitration agreement (Article V(1)(a) NYC), lack of arbitrability (Article V(2)(a)) and violation of the public policy of the jurisdiction where enforcement is sought (Article V(2)(b)).

Article V(1)(a) NYC allows the competent court to refuse enforcement where the arbitration agreement is not valid "under the law to which the parties have subjected it or, failing any indication thereon, under the law of the country where the award was made." If the place of arbitration is within the EU, since EU law is part of the law of EU Member States, unless the parties agreed that the arbitration agreement be governed by the law of a non-EU Member State,[90] the award is likely to be denied enforcement on the ground that the arbitration agreement is invalid under the *lex arbitri*. Conversely, if the arbitration is seated outside the EU, Article V(1)(a) NYC is unlikely to constitute a valid basis for refusing enforcement as the applicable *lex arbitri* will not recognize the invalidity of the arbitration agreement.

Article V(2)(a) NYC provides that enforcement may be denied if "the subject-matter of the difference is not capable of settlement by arbitration under the law of th[e] country [where enforcement is sought]." If enforcement is sought within the EU, as stated above with respect to annulment, the subject matter of the dispute may indeed be considered non-arbitrable and enforcement may be denied on this basis.[91] The situation is different if enforcement is sought outside the EU as the CJEU's rulings would not be binding on the enforcement court and may not render a dispute brought under an investment treaty inarbitrable.

As far as public policy is concerned (Article V(2)(b) NYC), as discussed above with reference to setting aside, the threshold relevant for the purpose of a violation of EU's and Member States' public policy seems clearly met from the CJEU's perspective, as the CJEU stated that intra-EU investment arbitration is incompatible with the most fundamental principles of EU law and with the very institutional architecture of the EU. A violation of the public policy would result, not from the award itself,[92] but rather from its effects on the legal order of the place of enforcement. However, in *Achmea, Komstroy, PL Holdings* and *Micula*, the CJEU left no room for doubt that it regards the mere risk for the consistent application and interpretation of EU law which results from intra-EU investment arbitration as contrary to the most fundamental principles of the

---

90. Following the recent case law referred to above, there seems to be growing awareness among users of the potential consequences of the law applicable to the arbitration agreement and growing recourse to choice-of-law agreements. However, such agreements remain relatively rare. Moreover, an agreement subjecting the arbitration agreement to a law which preserves its validity despite its invalidity under the law otherwise applicable may circumvent mandatory rules of law and, as such, be deemed ineffective.

91. *Contra*, in the sense that "the scope of the *Achmea* judgment is limited to the ISDS clause," J. Scheu, P. Nikolov, *supra* n. 74, 270.

92. *See* D. Otto, O. Elwan, *Article V(2)*, in H. Kronke et al. (eds.), *Recognition and Enforcement of Foreign Arbitral Awards: A Global Commentary on the New York Convention*, 2010, 365–366.

EU legal order. Therefore, the enforcement of any intra-EU award, regardless of whether and how it applied EU law, would conflict with Members States' public policy. Conversely, if enforcement is sought outside the EU, there seems to be no reason to consider it in violation of the public policy of the place of enforcement, which would not be affected by the CJEU's rulings.

If the place of arbitration was in the EU, the potential annulment at the place of arbitration may constitute a ground for refusing enforcement also under Article V(1)(e) NYC.[93] Under this provision, annulment at the place of arbitration would significantly reduce enforceability outside the EU, but not necessarily exclude it altogether, given the well-known case law in certain jurisdictions which permits enforcement of awards annulled at the place of the arbitration.[94]

§5.07   CONCLUSION

The recent case law of the CJEU makes the enforcement of intra-EU investor-State arbitration awards much more problematic, but not impossible.

Awards rendered in proceedings governed by the ICSID Convention remain protected from annulment by the completely autonomous regime created by the Convention. Conversely, their enforcement will be virtually excluded within the EU, but *Achmea* and the rulings that followed its principle and expanded its scope are unlikely to get in the way of enforcement outside the EU.

As for non-ICSID cases, the relevance of the CJEU's case law and the fate of awards will largely depend on the place of the arbitration. All grounds potentially relevant to the setting aside of awards are likely to provide sufficient basis for the annulment of awards rendered in EU-based arbitrations, but not in proceedings seated outside the EU. Likewise, enforcement of intra-EU treaty awards not governed by the ICSID Convention is virtually precluded within the EU, whereas it seems possible outside the EU if the place of the arbitration is also outside the EU, as this would result in neutralizing, not only the grounds for refusing enforcement under Article V(2)(a) (arbitrability) and V(2)(b) (public policy) NYC but also those under Article V(1)(a) (invalidity of the arbitration agreement) and V(1)(e) (annulment at the place of arbitration) NYC.[95]

---

93. In *Novoenergia II v. Spain, supra* n. 27, the US District Court for the District of Columbia decided to stay enforcement proceedings in the US pending the setting aside proceedings against the award in Sweden. *See Novoenergia II—Energy & Environment (SCA) v. Kingdom of Spain*, US District Court for the District of Columbia, Civil Action No. 18-cv-01148 (TSC).
94. *See* G. Born, *supra* n. 78, 3621 et seq.
95. S. Lemaire, *Chronique de la jurisprudence arbitrale en droit des investissements*, Revue de *l'arbitrage*, 2018, 435. For the position in awards rendered within the EU, *see Strabag v. Poland, supra* n. 28, para. 8-142 (award rendered in France): "the Tribunal is not able to predict the future validity or enforceability of its award before French courts or other enforcing courts"; *Sunreserve v. Italy, supra* n. 28, para. 371 (award rendered in Sweden): "the Tribunal does not foresee any hindrances to the validity or enforceability of its Award before Swedish courts. In any event, at this stage, is not in a place to predict the future validity or enforceability of its Award before Swedish courts or other enforcing courts." For the position of an award rendered outside the EU (Switzerland) *see A.M.F. v. Czech Republic, supra* n. 28, paras. 393–395: "It is true

In the absence of a choice of seat in the relevant investment treaty and of an agreement of the parties in this respect, the arbitral tribunal's or administering institution's decision on the place of arbitration may thus have far-reaching consequences on the validity and enforceability of awards. Traditionally arbitration-friendly EU jurisdictions may not be the safest seats for intra-EU treaty arbitrations, whereas extra-EU jurisdictions, now including the UK, may prove more reliable. Institutions and tribunals would be well advised to consider these aspects when fixing the place of arbitration.

---

that there exist a limited number of scenarios, under which the enforcement of the Arbitral Tribunal's award might be challenging [sic] or create further disputes. However, this does not make the award unenforceable. A truly unenforceable award can only exist if it is rendered in violation of Article 190 of the PILA governing the setting aside of awards rendered by arbitral tribunals seated in Switzerland. The PILA provides for no other remedy against such awards. The only two grounds under which the award rendered by the present Arbitral Tribunal could be set aside are (i) where it would have wrongly accepted jurisdiction or (ii) its award would be incompatible with public policy due to its decision that the Achmea judgment does not preclude Article 10 of the Germany-Czech Republic BIT. The Arbitral Tribunal considers that its decision is well-founded and not contrary to Swiss international public policy."

CHAPTER 6

Post M&A Disputes: Recent Nordic Case Law, Especially Regarding Loss Calculation

Mikal Brøndmo

§6.01 INTRODUCTION

Arbitration is the main dispute resolution method used in Sale and Purchase Agreements (SPAs) between a buyer and seller concerning company shares or the asset itself. In recent years, especially in Denmark and Norway, several arbitral awards rendered have great importance outside the awards commented on.

Post mergers and acquisitions (M&A) disputes can typically be divided into two main categories. The first category, earn-out disputes, concerns the seller's entitlement to additional compensation in the future depending on the target company achieving certain results and will not be dealt with here.[1] The article will instead focus on the second category, damage claims in case of breach of warranties.

Loss calculation in awards occasionally seems to be handled less thoroughly than other parts of the case. Tribunals typically focus most of their attention on the liability question, at least on the basis of a review of awards and their reasoning.[2] As post M&A disputes are mainly handled by arbitration, there is a shortage of publicly available case law, at least in Nordic countries, including case law regarding the way in which loss calculation after the breach of warranties in SPAs is carried out.

This chapter presents three post M&A awards, focussing on the issue of loss calculation. The tribunals' thorough and solid analyses in these cases, especially regarding loss calculation, should be of interest to a wider audience. Several of these awards also focus quite intensively on the calculation aspects.

---

1. *See,* for example: Niels Schiersing, *Earn-Out Disputes* (Ex Tuto 2020).
2. This observation is also supported by the 2015 PwC report *International Arbitration damages research,* although the report mainly covers investor-state disputes under the ICSID rules.

The aim of the chapter is to show how loss calculation has been carried out for post M&A disputes in recent Nordic case law. The fact that the awards are not public is reflected in the way in which they are presented here, although quotes from the awards are included wherever possible – without disclosing the parties involved – in order to make it easier for readers to assess the tribunals' reasoning. However, they are quoted to different extents, partly because of the above and partly because different reasoning styles are used: some go into more detail than others; some make more general remarks, and others mainly provide more case-specific comments.

The article begins with a short overview of the basic principles in Nordic countries as compared with English law, with the goal of drawing together different readers' legal backgrounds. While tribunals are guided by these general principles, damages must be determined on the basis of the facts in each individual case.

The three awards are presented in sections §6.03, §6.04 and §6.05. While several commentators have viewed them as clarifying how loss calculation in post M&A disputes should be undertaken, space constraints make it impossible to include my own position here.

§6.02   BASIC PRINCIPLES FOR THE CALCULATION OF DAMAGES IN CONTRACTS

[A]   Introduction

The basic principle for calculating damages in contracts is that the damages for breach of contract by one party must consist of a sum equal to the loss suffered by the other party as a consequence of the breach. This principle of full compensation applies not only in Nordic countries but also in English law[3] and more internationally, as illustrated by Article 74 of the CISG[4] and UNIDROIT Principles Article 7.4.2.[5]

[B]   Positive Interest/Expectation Interest

When damages are claimed as the contract was not fulfilled as agreed, this is often referred to in Nordic countries as claiming the positive interest of the contract.[6] Positive interest means that the sufferer must be left in the same financial position as he would have been if the contract had been fulfilled properly, and the damages are, therefore,

---

3. Kåre Lilleholt, *Kontraktsrett og obligasjonsrett* (Cappelen Damm Akademisk 2017) pp. 349–351 with further references, and for English law: *Robinson v. Harman* (1848) 1 Ex 850.
4. The United Nations Convention on Contracts for the International Sale of Goods, Vienna 1980. For the sake of order, pursuant to Art. 2 (d), CISG does not apply to sales of stocks and shares.
5. UNIDROIT (formally the International Institute for the Unification of Private Law) Principles of International Commercial Contracts 2016.
6. Norway: Lilleholt, *supra* n. 3, Sweden: Jan Ramberg & Christina Ramberg, *Allmän avtalsrätt*, 11th edition (Norstedts juridik 2019) pp. 261 and 267–268, and Denmark: Torsten Iversen, *Obligationsret 2. del på grundlag af Bernhard Gomards obligationsret*, 5th edition (Jurist- og økonomforbundets forlag 2019) p. 225.

a performance substitute. In English law, this is covered by *'expectation interest'*, which focuses on the fundamental reasoning.[7]

In Nordic countries, positive interest is normally used as the opposite of negative interest, whereby the claimant is left in a position as though the contract had never been entered into; *'reliance interest'* in English law.[8] In the three awards discussed, the claimants were seeking positive interest.

[C] The Differential Principle

In German law, what is known as 'differential principle' (*Differenzhypothese*) is often used to explain the content of the principle of full compensation.[9] The differential principle is normally defined as the difference between the actual and the hypothetical situation, and the difference constitutes the loss. The principle is based on the roman law of *id quod interest* and is often referred to in Nordic countries, although there has been some debate about it in recent years.[10]

The differential principle has been criticised for being too abstract and for complicating issues. It is said to be too abstract as the principle is modified by various rules that apply differently for various heads of damages, and by that complicating issues when trying to compile these into a general principle. However, this does not prevent the differential principle from serving as a starting point and for examining the loss calculation that has been carried out.[11]

Under certain circumstances, the loss to be calculated does not typically consist of several types of losses (heads of damages). This could apply in post M&A disputes where the loss claimed could be the difference between the value that was agreed and the value that would have been agreed if the contract breaches had been known about prior to entering into the contract.

That said, it may still be useful to bear in mind the criticisms of the differential principle, especially the observation that it involves a significant risk of prejudicing the solution to several problems. These may be generic problems such as compensation *lucre cum damno* and concurring causes or more specific issues such as a claim for compensation for parts of period costs.[12]

---

7. Guenter Heinz Treitel, *Remedies for Breach of Contract: A Comparative Account* (Oxford University Press 1988) p. 82, Hugh G. Beale ed., *Chitty on Contracts Volume I General Principles,* 34th edition (Sweet & Maxwell 2021) pp. 2080–2081.
8. Iversen, *supra* n. 6, pp. 307–309 and Jack Beatson, Andrew Burrows & John Cartwrigh, *Anson's Law of Contract,* 31st edition (Oxford University Press 2020) pp. 540–541.
9. Schlechtriem & Schwenzer, edited by Ingeborg Schwenzer, *Commentary on the UN Convention on the International Sale of Goods (CISG),* 4th edition (Oxford University Press 2016) p. 1059.
10. Viggo Hagstrøm, *Obligasjonsrett* (Universitetsforlaget 2021) 3rd edition by Herman Bruserud, Ivar Alvik, Harald Irgens-Jensen og Inger Berg Ørstavik pp. 564–565 and Torsten Iversen, *Erstatningsberegning i kontraktsforhold* (Thomson Reuters 2000) pp. 113 et seq.
11. Hagstrøm, *supra* n. 10, p. 564, Johnny Herre, *Ersättningar i köprätten: särskilt om skadeståndsberåkning* (Nordstedts Juridik 1996) pp. 315–317 and Iversen, *supra* n. 10, p. 115–121.
12. Iversen, *supra* n. 10, p. 120.

[D]   Concrete Assessment

The principle of full compensation guides tribunals in the same way as positive interest (expectation interest) and the differential principle can do. However, none of these clarifies how damages should be calculated, and the differential principle could be viewed as the name of the result rather than a detailed guide as to how to actually calculate the loss.

In addition to these general guidelines, the type of contract in question is often guiding when damages are calculated. Where cases regarding damages for breach of warranty in an SPA are concerned there seem to be several similarities in the approaches taken by courts and tribunals in Nordic countries and under English law.[13]

Three awards presented below illustrate how this could be done in post M&A disputes; in practice, the loss has to be determined in every single case on the basis of the facts presented.

As the assessment of the evidence is often decisive for the final calculation of the buyer's claim for damages,[14] it is useful to run through the rules for the burden of proof and the standard of proof before looking at the three awards.

[E]   The Burden of Proof and the Standard of Proof

In Nordic countries, the burden of proof lies in general with the party making the claim or assertion for both breach of contract and the loss claimed, as it does in English law.[15] However, if the burden of proof requirements are met for breach of contract, causation and loss as such, Nordic case law contains examples of cases in which the compensation was set at the court's discretion.[16]

The general principles of evidence are similar in Swedish, Danish, Norwegian and English law at the outset, although several differences emerge when the more specific rules are examined. There is, however, one main difference that could be relevant: under Norwegian and English law, the standard of proof is the balance of probabilities.[17] This is different under Swedish and Danish law.

In Swedish law, the standard of proof is 'styrkt', which is more than the balance of probabilities, and in principle, this also applies to claims for damages. The Swedish Supreme Court has confirmed that 'styrkt' means a higher standard than the balance of

---

13. Margrethe Buskerud Christoffersen, *Kjøp og salg av virksomhet: risiko og ansvar for mangler* (Gyldendal akademisk 2008), Part 5 with further references and Harvey McGregor, edited by James Edelman, *McGregor on Damages*, 21st edition (Sweet & Maxwell 2021) pp. 960–961, and *Chitty on Contracts, supra* n. 7, p. 2197.
14. Iversen, *supra* n. 10, p. 166 and Christoffersen, *supra* n. 13, p. 584.
15. Bernhard Gomard & Michael Kistrup, *Civilprocessen*, 8th edition (Karnov Group 2020) p. 564, Per Olof Ekelöf, Henrik Edelstam & Lars Heuman, *Rättegång. Fjärde häftet*, 7th edition (Nordstedts Juridik 2009) pp. 94–95, Jens Edvin A. Skoghøy, *Tvisteløsning*, 3rd edition (Universitetsforlaget 2017) p. 911, Sidney L. Phipson & Hodge M. Malek ed., *Phipson on Evidence*, 20th edition (Sweet & Maxwell 2021) para. 6-06, p. 171.
16. Iversen, *supra* n. 6, p. 270 with further references.
17. English: *Miller v. Minister of Pensions* [1947] 2 All ER 372, 373–374. Norwegian: HR-2019-1225-A [73].

probabilities, but has not ruled exactly how much higher, while Swedish legal scholars state that 'styrkt' is more than likely and the balance of probabilities, but less than evidently and beyond a reasonable doubt.[18]

In Danish law, there is no general standard of proof, and it may vary not only depending on the rule applied but also for different assertions of facts under the same rule. In spite of the fact that the standard of proof can vary, it is seldom solely the balance of probabilities and is thus often greater than this.[19]

The fact that the threshold for the standard of proof in Swedish and Danish law is higher may make it more difficult for claimants to prove claims for damages for breach of contract from the outset under Swedish and Danish law than under Norwegian and English law.

§6.03 THE FSN AWARD

[A] Introduction

In June 2020, an arbitral tribunal seated in Copenhagen rendered an award in a post M&A dispute under the rules and administration of the Danish Institute of Arbitration. The SPA was governed by Danish law and the tribunal consisted of Torstein Iversen, Mads Bryde Andersen and Torben Melchior, all from Denmark.

The case concerned a buyer's claim against the seller for losses caused by alleged breaches of the seller's warranties resulting from the seller's fraud and wilful misconduct in connection with the buyer's acquisition of the entire share capital of a holding company and its subsidiaries ('the target company').

The buyer was awarded damages for the loss as the tribunal found that there had been wilful misconduct by the seller. The loss consisted of the difference between the market value (price paid) without the warranty breaches and what the market value (price) would have been if the warranty breaches had been known prior to the SPA. As it is public knowledge that the successful buyer was FSN Capital, the case was later referred to as the FSN Award, and this term will be used here as well.

[B] The Seller Was Found Liable

Pursuant to the SPA, the seller's responsibility for warranty breaches was covered by warranty and indemnity insurance, so the buyer could only claim directly against the seller in cases of fraud or wilful misconduct.

Before deciding on whether there had been any warranty breaches, the tribunal had to decide who was covered by the exception in the SPA for seller fraud or wilful misconduct. As the seller was a holding company, information was given by other individuals on the seller's behalf, in particular, the target company's top management. The tribunal interpreted the SPA in such a way that wilful misconduct or fraud on the

---

18. NJA 2013 p. 524 [21] and *Rättegång, supra* n. 15, p. 85.
19. Gomard & Kistrup, *supra* n. 15, p. 560.

part of the target company's top management concerning the information provided by the seller could be considered to be provided either by the seller or on the seller's behalf, and was thus attributable to the seller in both instances.

The tribunal next decided whether there had been any warranty breaches and, if so, whether they involved fraud or wilful misconduct. It concluded in the buyer's favour in both matters. The tribunal found that the financial information provided to the buyer on the seller's behalf had been systematically manipulated through fictitious write-ups and cut-off misstatements,[20] all carried out with the intention that the buyer should not discover the underlying facts.

In addition to the question of loss due to breach of warranty, the tribunal had to decide whether the seller should pay the purchase price adjustment amount to the buyer in accordance with an independent accountant's final decision. Although this second main issue will not be discussed further here, its relation to the loss calculation due to breach of warranty will be commented on.

[C]   Causation

The tribunal found that the buyer would not have acquired the target company if it had known about the misstatements due to wilful misconduct, and therefore found that the wilful misconduct as such was the root cause of the buyer's loss. Causation was therefore proven.

Furthermore, the tribunal stated:

> The Tribunal does not agree with the Seller that the Buyer has 'to prove a causal link between each alleged warranty breach and the amount claimed'. It suffices if the Buyer proves a causal link between the Warranty breaches in toto and Buyer's decision to acquire the Group, which resulted in a loss because the Buyer bought at a price exceeding the value.
>
> A different result would be conceivable only if the warranty breaches found to constitute wilful misconduct on the part of the Seller were held to have played a minor or immaterial role for Buyer's decision to enter into the SPA compared to other warranty breaches. This is not the case, and generally speaking, this case does not give rise to other problems of causation than those mentioned above. As a starting point, the Warranty breaches invoked by the Buyer must be seen in their totality in relation to causation.[21]

[D]   The Valuation Methods Applied by the Buyer for Its Bid

[1]   Introduction

The tribunal found that the buyer had based its bid for the target company on a market value assessment using several valuation methods. The key methods used were

---

20. Cut-off misstatements could be explained to be misleading information given in relation to the end of relevant accounting periods.
21. Paragraphs 1286–1287, p. 402.

Discounted Cash Flow (DCF) and leveraged buyout (LBO) (long and short exit horizons), whereas the multiples analysis and liquidation value were used as sense-checks and inputs to DCF and LBO. As these methods are relevant not only for this case but also for the two others and for cases of this kind in general, what follows is a brief introduction to the buyer's methods.

[2]   *Discounted Cash Flow*

The DCF method can be explained as a valuation method that is used to estimate an investment's value based on its expected future cash flows. The DCF approach uses estimates of future financial performance in order to estimate free cash flows for future years. In other words, a DCF analysis attempts to calculate the value of an investment today on the basis of projections as to how much money it will generate in the future.[22]

[3]   *Leveraged Buyout*

A LBO may be used if the acquisition of a company is financed by substantial amounts of debt – hence the term 'leveraged'. The cash flow generated by the company acquired is used to finance the acquisition, interest and principal on outstanding debt. An LBO analysis may be used to obtain an LBO market value for a company by analysing the alternative sources of funds in terms of their contribution to the net internal rate of return. This analysis is carried out by the financial buyer to project the enterprise value[23] of a company.[24]

[4]   *Multiple*

The multiple approach is a valuation method in which key figures from the target company's accounts are multiplied using a multiple that is normally based on comparable companies or similar companies within the same industry. To be more specific: to calculate a company's value, a multiple is used on the cash flow, balance sheet or result that reflects the industry's required rate of return, typically based on publicly listed companies' multiples or multiples that could be obtained from transactions.[25]

---

22. For a more thorough presentation of DCF; *see* Olle Flygt, *Värderingstvister: något om vad som kan göras för att domstolars och skiljenämnders avgöranden ska bli så högkvalitativa som möjligt. Del 1*, Juridisk Tidskrift No. 3 of 2020/2021 pp. 590 ff (pp. 602–607).
23. The enterprise value is in short the total value of the company including equity and liabilities.
24. Victoria Ivashina, Alexey Tuzikov & Abhijit Tagade, *Valuation Techniques in Private Equity: LBO Model* (Harvard Business School Background Note 218-106, June 2018).
25. Christoffersen, *supra* n. 13, p. 70. *See also* section §6.04[D][7] below.

[5]   *Liquidation*

Liquidation valuation is an asset-based method that calculates the amount that the business would receive by selling the assets on the open market. The liquidation value is the net value of a company's assets if the assets are sold or the company goes out of business. The liquidation value is notably different from the book value, as assets with no book value may still have a liquidation value.

[E]   Loss Calculation

[1]   *Introduction*

As mentioned above, the buyer had based its bid for the target company on a market value assessment using several valuation methods. To find the enterprise value, these methods were used together via triangulation, i.e., by taking different valuation methods into account and collating the results in order to achieve a more solid basis for the value. The original enterprise value based on the information that the buyer originally possessed was named the *as warranted* situation.

After the warranty breaches were discovered, a similar market value analysis was carried out using several valuation methods, taking into consideration the new information about the actual situation, which was named *as is*.

The claim for damages was calculated on the basis of the difference between the company value *as warranted* and *as is*. The latter was based on an *ex ante* assessment, i.e., the date of the breach, using forecasts, as opposed to taking into consideration later developments in an *ex post* assessment. For the *ex ante* assessment of the *as is* valuation, a key question was what the situation would have been if the *as is* had been known when the bid was made and the price agreed on.[26]

To carry out the *as is* valuation, the target company management revised its estimates of anticipated future performance, termed the revised case, which reflected the management's best estimate of the forecasts it would have made at the time of the acquisition had all the issues identified since the acquisition been known then. On the basis of the revised case, an expert carried out an *as is* market value assessment by using similar valuation methods to those used by the buyer prior to entering into the SPA.

The tribunal stated that the loss claimed by the buyer was essentially the difference between the enterprise value as it was and as it ought to have been had there been no wilful warranty breaches:

---

26. As this article is included in the Stockholm Arbitration Yearbook it is useful to mention that the *ex ante* and *ex post* reasoning in economic topics was introduced by the Swedish economist Gunnar Myrdal in *Monetary Equilibrium* (William Hodge & Company Ltd. 1939).

Thus, the value difference is the difference between the Enterprise Value agreed upon at the time of the SPA and paid by the Buyer, and the actual value at the same time, calculated on the basis of reasonably correct information.[27]

The seller does not seem to have disputed the valuation methods applied by the buyer as such. That such an assessment of this difference should be the basis for calculating the compensation appears to have been taken as a matter of course.

[2] The *as Warranted* Valuation

The tribunal found that the enterprise value agreed on reflected the target company's market value had there been no warranty breaches, and emphasised three factors: first, this was the value agreed on between two independent parties with opposing interests; second, the sales process was organised as an auction process with the aim of obtaining the best possible bid from a buyer, and third, there was another buyer in the running almost to the end of the process.

According to the tribunal, this implied that all the known risks should have been factored into the enterprise value, including known unknowns such as uncertainties of results and projections, but not unknown unknowns such as the risk of falling victim to wilful misconduct.

[3] The *As Is* Valuation

For the *as is* valuation, the tribunal stressed that the position in which buyer found itself involved in a situation very different from its acquisition case and referred to it as a turnaround case in which the target company was loss-making. Furthermore, the tribunal stated that the buyer's only option was to replace the company's top management, causing additional disruption.

The tribunal found no grounds for dismissing the revised case prepared by the target company's new management as a basis for the comparison between *as warranted* and *as is*. They also saw no reason for setting aside the explanations given for the revised case, and commented that the seller's objections to the revised case were of a general nature and contained no specific relevant criticism.

Moreover, the tribunal found that the buyer had presented extensive evidence that had been prepared by an expert in support of its proposition that the real enterprise value *as is* of the target company should be calculated on the basis of the revised case. Prior to the acquisition, the buyer had prepared a detailed business case to project the target company's expected performance in future years under the buyers' expected ownership period, including key financial statement items such as revenue, costs, capital expenditures, net working capital etc. Following the acquisition, the buyer made a revised business case in which the expected performance in future years, including key financial statement items such as revenue, costs, capital expenditures,

---

27. Paragraph 1247 on p. 394.

net working capital etc. were adjusted for the information discovered by the buyer subsequent to the closing ('the revised case').

In the tribunal's opinion, the severe setbacks regarding revenue and EBITDA[28] significantly reduced the enterprise value. In addition, the tribunal found that the seller's objections were mostly of a general nature and had not convinced the tribunal that the loss was overstated. Accordingly, the award did not focus on the later developments of the target company's when calculating the loss.

[4]   The Asserted Overlap with the Purchase Price Adjustment

The seller had asserted that the above-mentioned purchase price adjustment decision made by the independent accountant overlapped with the buyer's claim for damages. To deal with this issue, the tribunal referred to the report and to testimony from the buyer's expert. The expert submitted that when calculating the market valuation, using mainly the DCF model and the LBO model, which are both forward-looking, he had relied on the target company's future expected cash flows and had calculated the target company's enterprise value as the present value of these future cash flows. According to the expert, the revised case represented these future estimated cash flows. However, the purchase price adjustment in accordance with the Purchase Price Calculation (PPC) neither measures the target's market value nor relies on future expected cash flows. The PPC is a pure accounting-based calculation of the seller's equity value given several items on an agreed closing balance sheet per an agreed balance sheet date, and is, therefore, a result of past financial performance. The tribunal thus found that there was no overlap between the buyer's claim no. 1 (damages for loss incurred by warranty breaches) and claim no. 2 (calculation of the final purchase price).

[5]   Should the Amount Paid for W&I Insurance Be Deducted?

On the basis of the above considerations, the tribunal concluded that the buyer had documented a total loss of EUR 103,700,000 as claimed. The buyer had received EUR 50 million from the warranty & indemnity (W&I) insurer as part of a settlement.

W&I insurance has become a familiar feature of M&A transactions in recent years. Although it is usually taken out by the buyer, it is frequently proposed by the seller, who often wants a clean exit, including removing/reducing the need to hold part of the purchase price in escrow, or for the seller to retain large amounts of cash to cover post-closing liability.

The parties in the FSN case disagreed over the consequences of the insurer's payment for the buyer's damages claim against the seller. The buyer submitted that neither the SPA nor the W&I insurance policy limited the seller's liability in the event of fraud or wilful misconduct. The seller submitted that the SPA rules stated that any amount paid out by the W&I insurer must be subtracted when calculating the loss as the buyer cannot claim compensation for the same loss twice, and that these SPA

---

28. Earnings Before Interest, Taxes, Depreciation and Amortization.

provisions were no limitation on liability that was not applicable in cases of fraud/wilful misconduct.

The tribunal agreed with the seller that the SPA provisions were not limitations on the seller's liability for loss. Hence, pursuant to the SPA, the amount of insurance paid to the buyer should be deducted when calculating the loss. As a consequence, the EUR 50 million paid by the W&I insurer reduced the loss that the buyer could claim from the seller to EUR 53,700,000.

[6] Calculation of Interest

The tribunal found that the buyer also was entitled to a statutory interest in accordance with Danish law. It could be mentioned that the seller had not objected to the buyer's interest claims as such.

§6.04 THE OCC AWARD

[A] Introduction

In April 2021, an arbitral tribunal seated in Oslo rendered an award in a post M&A dispute under the rules and administration of the Oslo Chamber of Commerce (OCC). The SPA was governed by Norwegian law. The tribunal consisted of Torben Melchior (Denmark), Axel Calissendorff (Sweden) and Tore Schei (Norway), with Schei as chair. Like many such hearings during COVID-19, the main hearing in February 2021 was held virtually.

The case concerned a claim under W&I insurance for warranty breaches. An investment company had acquired all shares in the target company through a firm which was established for the purpose of acquiring and owning the shares. The buyer entered into an SPA with the sellers of the target company and signed a W&I insurance policy as part of the transaction. Pursuant to the SPA, the claims had to be submitted against the underlying insurers, as only claims due to fraud or wilful misconduct on the seller's part could allow claims against the seller. That was not the case here, and the underlying insurers were thus the respondents in the case.

The buyer was awarded damages for its loss with an amount equal to the limitation of liability in the W&I insurance of NOK 250 million,[29] less payments already made by the respondents. The tribunal's approach to calculating loss in this case is of wider interest. In addition to their legal analyses, the tribunal also referred to other interesting sources for what is a set market approach in determining losses of the type which applies in this case. The tribunal found reason to rely on a DCF approach, and this analysis was held against market-based multiples on acquisitions of other companies when determining the loss to the buyer.

---

29. Equal to approximately EUR 26 million as per 24 March 2022.

The award was rendered in Norwegian, so all the quotes are from an unofficial translation of the award. The original statements have been included in the footnotes for Nordic readers.

[B]   The Respondents Were Found Liable

The SPA included warranties for the correctness of the target company's audited accounts for 2016 and the unaudited accounts for Q1 in 2017. During the arbitration, the respondents acknowledged a warranty breach for the 2016 accounts, while still disputing the other alleged warranty breach. The tribunal found both warranties had been breached.

Furthermore, it was not disputed that losses caused by the warranty breach were covered by the W&I insurance and so the dispute mainly concerned the scope of the loss suffered by the claimant, for which the respondents were liable under the insurance agreement.

[C]   Causation

The tribunal found the causal requirement to be fulfilled. The warranty breaches were the direct reason why the bid was submitted and the agreement was entered into with no knowledge of the accounting errors that constituted the warranty breaches. According to the tribunal, there could be no doubt that the loss could be traced back to the fact that a higher bid was submitted than there was a basis for was foreseeable or adequate. The tribunal found that this is exactly what happens when a company is sold with a warranty stating that it is in better financial condition than it actually is.

[D]   Loss Calculation

[1]   *The Parties' Main Arguments*

The parties agreed that the buyer was entitled to compensation for the positive contractual interest, and that the buyer should be in the same financial situation as it would have been if the terms of the warranty had been fulfilled. However, the parties disagreed on what this actually meant in practice.

The parties agreed that the target company's market value matched the purchase price. The dispute concerned the reduction in value in the *as is* state, and whether the loss should be calculated on the basis of a difference between *as warranted* and *as is* for the target company as a whole.

The buyer argued that the loss should be calculated on the basis of the difference between the target company's *as warranted* and *as is* value. The buyer submitted that three silver bullet points were central to this calculation. First, a reasonable buyer will take an *ex ante* perspective, i.e., assess the values on the basis of information provided at the time of purchase and do the calculations on the basis of recognised methods for valuing companies in connection with acquisitions. Second, a reasonable buyer will assess the effect of financial errors affected by the warranties on the company as a whole. Third, the starting point for assessing the company *as is* must be the valuation method that the buyer actually used as a basis for the purchase.

The respondents submitted that the principle of positive contractual interest did not provide any guidance on a specific valuation method. The respondents submitted that the buyer's valuation method as the starting point, as asserted by the buyer, had no legal or factual basis as the buyer had mentioned several valuation methods in correspondence to the seller prior to concluding the SPA. The analyses and assessments in the recommendation to the investment committee were also based on various methods. Moreover, the respondents submitted that the lack of EBITDA and revenue should be assessed (and dealt with) in isolation, and that the target company as a whole should not be considered. The respondents also maintained that there was no causation between the warranty breaches concerning accounts and revenue from future customers, and submitted that much of the buyer's claim was the future loss that was not covered by the warranty breaches.

[2] The Tribunal's General Introductory Remarks

After confirming that the SPA did not stipulate a particular loss calculation method, the tribunal stated: 'However, this does not mean that, inter alia, the nature of the purchase and the breach cannot indicate that a correct calculation presupposes a specific method.'[30]

As regards the SPA's regulation that compensation was the sole remedy, the tribunal stated:

> It follows from Clause 10.1 d that compensation is the sole remedy that can be claimed. This also means that price reductions cannot be claimed. However, as the Tribunal will return to, compensation and price reductions may in some situations lie fairly close to each other and almost coincide both in justification and scope. This is not in itself sufficient to exclude such a compensation calculation on the basis of Clause 10.1d. The key is that the loss must be attributable to the breach of the warranties in Clauses 8.5 and 8.6, which triggers the claim for compensation – i.e. that there is causation – and also that the condition of foreseeability/adequacy is fulfilled.[31]

The tribunal emphasised that the buyer should be placed in the same financial position as it would have been in without the breach of warranty, stating:

---

30. Page 31, original on p. 33: '*Men det er ikke ensbetydende med at ikke blant annet karakteren av kjøpet og misligholdet kan tilsi at en korrekt beregning forutsetter en bestemt metode.*'
31. Page 32, original on p. 33: '*Det følger av 10.1 d at erstatning er den eneste misligholdsvirkningen som kan gjøres gjeldende. Det vil også si at prisavslag ikke kan kreves. Men som retten kommer tilbake til, vil erstatning og prisavslag i noen situasjoner kunne ligge helt opp til hverandre og nærmest falle sammen både i begrunnelse og i omfang. Det er i seg selv ikke nok til ut fra 10.1 d å utelukke en slik erstatningsberegning. Det sentrale er at tapet må kunne føres tilbake til bruddet på garantiene i 8.5 og 8.6 som utløser kravet på erstatning – altså at det er årsakssammenheng – og også at vilkåret om påregnelighet/adekvans er oppfylt.*'

The breach of warranty has led to the Buyer not having the opportunity to calculate and offer a price that reflected the real state of the company. This has obviously led to the Buyer having paid a higher price than it would have been willing to if it had received the correct information. This higher price is the positive contractual interest in this case.[32]

The tribunal stressed that the higher price caused by the breach of the warranties was precisely what was central in the case: the difference between the value of the company *as warranted* and *as is*. According to the tribunal, this was the difference between what was actually offered and agreed in the SPA and what would have been offered with knowledge of the warranty breaches. The tribunal then stated:

> It goes without saying that the first value ('as warranted') must be an ex ante assessment. And this is not disputed. It is agreed that the 'as warranted' value is what was paid, MNOK [amount]. But it is equally clear that also 'as is' must be an ex ante assessment. The question is: What would the Buyer have paid for the company if the incorrect elements in the accounts that constituted the breaches of the warranty had been clarified before the conclusion of the agreement. It is precisely what the Buyer would have done at this point that should be considered. What would the buyer have done then if he had had this information then? Subsequent information about other matters is not suited to shed light on this.[33]

After referring to legal theory and some case law, including the FSN case, the tribunal stated: '*A loss calculation based on the difference* ex ante *between the value of the Company "as warranted" and "as is" has, as the Tribunal has explained, clear support in the background rules of law.*'[34]

The tribunal also remarked:

> Although it cannot be considered a 'source of law', it is also important that the perception among leading academic economists highlights calculating the differ-ence between the value of the company 'as warranted' and 'as is' as the correct method for calculating the loss. The assessment must be made ex ante, and the company values must be determined on the basis of accepted ways of determining the value – first and foremost DCF calculation held against the use of market-based multiples. The Tribunal refers here to the explanation – in writing and at the main hearing – from Professor [name].[35]

---

32. Page 33, original on p. 34: '*Garantibruddet har ført til at Kjøper ikke fikk anledning til å til å beregne og tilby en pris som reflekterte den reelle tilstanden til selskapet. Dette har åpenbart ført til at Kjøper har betalt en høyere pris enn kjøper ved riktig informasjon ville vært villig til. Denne høyere prisen er den positive kontraktsinteressen i denne saken.*'
33. Page 33, original on p. 34: '*Det sier seg selv at det første må være en ex ante vurdering. Det er heller ikke omstridt. Det er enighet om at as warranted-verdien er det som ble betalt, MNOK [beløp]. Men det er like klart at også "as is" må være en ex ante vurdering. Spørsmålet er: Hva ville Kjøper betalt for selskapet dersom de uriktige elementene i regnskapet som utgjorde garantibrud-dene, var blitt klarlagt før avtaleinngåelsen. Det er nettopp hva Kjøper ville gjort på dette tidspunktet som skal vurderes. Hva ville kjøper gjort den gang om han da hadde hatt denne informasjonen? Etterfølgende informasjon om andre forhold er ikke egnet til å kaste lys over det.*'
34. Page 37, original on p. 38: '*En tapsberegning ut fra differansen ex ante mellom verdien av Selskapet "as warranted" og "as is" har, som retten har redegjort for, klar støtte i bakgrunnsretten.*'
35. Page 36, original on p. 36: '*Selv om det ikke kan betraktes som en "rettskilde", har det også betydning at oppfatningen blant ledende akademiske økonomer fremhever en differanse mellom*

[3]   The *as Warranted* Valuation

The parties agreed that the target company's market value matched the purchase price. Among other observations, the tribunal stated the following regarding the valuation of the target company:

> The buyer based the bid of MNOK [amount] on a DCF analysis compared to market-based multiples taken from other known acquisitions. The Arbitral Tribunal takes as a starting point that this is a standard way of valuing companies. The Tribunal refers in this regard to the statement from the expert witness [name] and also to the witness statements of the representatives of [Parent].[36]

[4]   The *As Is* Valuation

With regard to the disputed *as is* valuation, the tribunal stated, *inter alia*, the following:

> As pointed out, we know what kind of methods the calculated offer and purchase price were based on. It is then, as the Tribunal has also pointed out, a natural starting point to use similar methods as a basis for calculating the value of [Target] 'as is'. We have no basis for assuming that the approach would have been different. Such a valuation 'as is' also has clear support in theory and practice.[37]

Moreover, the tribunal underlined:

> It is not a subjective test that shall be performed in determining the difference between 'as warranted' and 'as is'. It must be considered how an ordinary reasonable buyer would act. This is not a big point in this case. [Parent] based its bid on a general and professional procedure for company acquisitions, and must be presumed to have acted reasonably and rationally in a determination 'as is'.[38]

The respondents had argued that the negotiations and the situation up to the conclusion of the SPA indicated that it was not tenable to carry out the loss calculation

---

verdien av selskapet "as warranted" og "as is" som den korrekte metoden for tapsberegningen. Vurderingen må skje ex ante, og selskapsverdiene må fastlegges ut fra aksepterte måter å fastsette verdien på – først og fremst DCF- beregning holdt opp mot anvendelse av markedsbaserte multipler. Retten viser her til forklaringen – skriftlig og under hovedforhandlingen – fra professor [navn].'

36. Page 33, original on p. 34: *'Kjøper baserte sitt bud på NOK [beløp] på en DCF-analyse holdt opp mot markedsbaserte multipler hentet ut fra andre kjente oppkjøp. Voldgiftsretten legger til grunn at dette er en standard måte å verdsette selskaper på. Retten viser på dette punkt til forklaringen fra ekspertvitnet professor [name] og også til vitneforklaringene fra representantene for [mor].'*

37. Page 36, original on p. 37: *'Som påpekt vet vi hva slags metoder kjøper beregnet tilbuds- og kjøpsprisen med grunnlag i. Det er da, som retten også har vært inne på, et naturlig utgangspunkt å legge tilsvarende metoder til grunn ved beregningen av verdien av [target] "as is". Vi har ikke grunnlag for å anta at tilnærmingen ville vært annerledes. En slik verdsettelse "as is" har også klar støtte i teori og praksis.'*

38. Page 33, original on p. 34: *'Det er ikke en subjektiv test som skal foretas ved differansefastleggelsen mellom "as warranted" og "as is". Det må ses hen til hvordan en alminnelig fornuftig kjøper ville handlet. Noe stort poeng i denne saken er ikke dette. [Mor] baserte sitt bud på en alminnelig og profesjonell fremgangsmåte ved selskapsoppkjøp, og må forutsettes å ville ha opptrådt fornuftig og rasjonelt ved en fastsettelse "as is".'*

on the basis of the difference between *as warranted* and *as is*. However, the tribunal stated:

> The Arbitral Tribunal cannot see that these objections from [Insurer] are tenable. A loss calculation based on the difference ex ante between the value of the Company 'as warranted' and 'as is' has, as the Tribunal has explained, clear support in the background rules of law. The fact that the parties have not agreed that the valuation shall take place in this way, or that it has not been pointed out during the negotiations between them, is not an argument against the background rules of law being applied on this point. The significance of the background rules of law is precisely that it is applied where the parties have not expressly or as a background assumption resolved the issue.[39]

As regards the respondents' arguments concerning future profit loss, the tribunal stated:

> As the Arbitral Tribunal will describe when addressing the specific loss calculation, the 'as is' value will be determined by discounting future revenue streams. [Insurer] has claimed that this would be in conflict with Clause X.XX of the SPA regarding 'No other Warranties'. This position is not tenable. The fact that budgets, estimates, prospectuses, etc. cannot be regarded as warrantied, does not mean that one must disregard future assessments that appear to be probable based on moderate and reasonable and sensible considerations.
>
> The fact that there is discounting – a calculation of the present value of future revenue streams – is also not, as [Insurer] has claimed, the same as claiming compensation for future lost profits. This is well illustrated when looking at the 'as warranted' value and how it was determined. There, calculations were made of future revenue streams. The present value of these were, through discounting, used to find the value of [Target] when the purchase was to be completed. It is exactly the same procedure that is followed in determining the 'as is' value. One seeks to calculate the value that [Target] would have had with information about the errors in the warranted accounts. As with the determination of the 'as warranted' value, overall cash flows are estimated, based on the other conditions at the time the contract is entered into. Through discounting, the value of [Target] 'as is' is then determined at the time of entering into the SPA.[40]

---

39. Page 37, original on p. 38: '*Voldgiftsretten kan ikke se at disse innvendingene fra [forsikrer] er holdbare. En tapsberegning ut fra differansen ex ante mellom verdien av Selskapet "as warranted" og "as is" har, som retten har redegjort for, klar støtte i bakgrunnsretten. At partene ikke har avtalt at verdsettelsen skal skje på denne måten, eller at det ikke har vært trukket frem under forhandlingene mellom dem, er ikke noe argument mot at bakgrunnsretten på dette punkt kommer til anvendelse. Bakgrunnsrettens betydning er nettopp at den får anvendelse der partene ikke uttrykkelig eller forutsetningsvis har løst spørsmålet.*'

40. Page 36, original on p. 37: '*Som voldgiftsretten kommer til ved den konkrete tapsberegningen, vil "as is"-verdien fastlegges ved diskontering av fremtidige inntektsstrømmer. [Forsikrer] har hevdet at dette vil være i strid med SPA X.XX om "No other Warranties". Det er ikke holdbart. At ikke budsjetter, estimater, prospekter etc. kan ses på som garantier, kan ikke være ensbetydende med at man må se bort fra fremtidsvurderinger som fremstår som sannsynlige ut fra nøkterne og rimelig og fornuftige betraktninger.*
    At det skjer en diskontering – en beregning av nåtidsverdien av fremtidige inntektsstrømmer – er heller ikke, som [forsikrer] har hevdet, det samme som at man krever erstatning for fremtidstap. Det illustreres godt når man ser på "as warranted"-verdien og hvordan den ble fastlagt. Der ble det foretatt beregninger over fremtidige inntektsstrømmer. Nåtidsverdien av disse ble, gjennom diskontering, brukt for å finne verdien av [target] da kjøpet skulle gjennomføres. Det

[5] Mitigation in Particular

Another interesting statement from the tribunal concerned the buyer's alleged lack of mitigation:

> [Insurer]'s views that the Buyer has not fulfilled its loss mitigation obligation are, in the Arbitral Tribunal's view, irrelevant to the method of compensation to be used. The loss that the Buyer is entitled to have compensated is the loss the Buyer has suffered by not being able to bid and being able to conclude the contract with knowledge of the deviation from the warranted accounts, held up against what the Buyer actually paid for [Target]. Here, the Buyer has no loss to mitigate by taking measures. Any 'mitigation' will result in the Buyer not completely receiving its positive contractual interest.[41]

[6] The Specific Loss Calculation and Its Test Intensity

As regards the specific loss calculation, the tribunal made some general remarks on its test intensity:

> [Claimant] has emphasised that the Tribunal is composed of legal professionals. This is where the Tribunal's competence lies. The Tribunal is not composed of experts in valuation of companies. The Tribunal of course agrees with this, and notes that the composition of the Arbitral Tribunal is the choice of the parties. This provides some guidelines for the loss assessment. The Tribunal must – without any reservations – test whether the method used in the loss calculation fully complies with the legal framework for the valuation that the Tribunal has described above. Both parties have used financial experts for their assessments and estimates of the loss that they believe there is a basis for compensating. The Tribunal must therefore fully test whether the assessments and estimates are based on the correct legal principles. However, the Tribunal must exercise caution in assessing issues of a factual nature, where it is obviously the experts who have the greatest competence. The parties do not challenge the 'mathematics' of the experts' calculations. But there are, as the Tribunal will return to, assumptions in these calculations that are disputed. The Tribunal cannot refrain from trying such objections, but must exercise caution in the review where specialized financial insight is required.[42]

---

er akkurat den samme fremgangsmåten som følges ved fastleggelsen av "as is"-verdien. Man søker å beregne den verdien [target] ville fått med opplysninger om feilene ved de garanterte regnskapene. Som ved fastleggelsen av "as warranted"-verdien, anslår man, basert på forhold ellers ved kontraktsinngåelsen, fremtidige kontantstrømmer. Gjennom diskontering, bestemmes så verdien av [target] "as is" på tidspunktet for inngåelsen av SPA.'

41. Pages 37–38, original on p. 38: '[Forsikrers] synspunkter om at Kjøper ikke har oppfylt sin tapsbegrensningsplikt – mitigation – er, etter voldgiftsrettens syn, uten relevans for den erstatningsmetoden som skal anvendes. Det tapet som Kjøper har krav på å få erstattet, er det tapet Kjøper har lidt ved ikke å få by og kunne slutte kontrakten med kunnskap om avviket fra de garanterte regnskapene holdt opp mot hva Kjøper faktisk betalte for [target]. Her er det ikke noe tap å begrense ved tiltak fra Kjøpers side. Enhver "begrensning" vil føre til at Kjøper ikke fullt ut får oppfylt sin positive kontraktsinteresse.'

42. Page 38, original on pp. 38–39: '[Kjøper] har fremhevet at retten er sammensatt av jurister. Det er der rettens kompetanse ligger. Retten er ikke sammensatt av eksperter i verdivurdering av

After making this general remark, the tribunal assessed the parties' submissions concerning the specific loss calculation. Although it is not possible to go into the details here, the tribunal found that the respondents' different loss calculations were based on valuing what in the case has been characterised as the gap – what was missing, and then first and foremost in subscriptions, and therefore not the company as a whole. In the tribunal's view, this was contrary to what the correct legal starting point in the valuation should be, as commented above.

However, the tribunal concluded that the buyer's expert's *'analyses and assessments of, inter alia, prospects for growth in revenue, EBITDA and EBITDA margins appear to be professionally well-founded, and they are rooted in the situation at the time of purchase'*.[43]

[7]   Multiple in Particular

Central to the buyer's valuation of the target company before the SPA, the value *as warranted*, was a DCF analysis. In addition, to ensure the quality of the valuation, a further valuation was carried out on the basis of a market-based multiples method. The tribunal described the procedure for a marked-based multiples method in five steps, as follows:

> (1) Find comparable companies, (2) Find economic indicators that are relevant in determining the values of these, (3) For each company find the value of these indicators and the amount the company was sold for, (4) Based on the selling price divided by the relevant indicator, determine typical multiples and (5) Based on the same indicator and the typical multiples make an estimate of the value of the relevant purchase object.[44]

It was not disputed that the buyer's expert analysis related to the loss calculation on the basis of a market-based multiples method had followed the method used by the buyer for its analyses and calculations. The tribunal found that the market-based

---

selskaper. Dette er retten selvfølgelig enig i, og bemerker at sammensetningen av voldgiftsretten er partenes valg. Dette gir noen føringer for tapsvurderingen. Retten må – uten noen reservasjoner- prøve om den metoden som anvendes ved tapsberegningen fullt ut samsvarer med de rettslige rammer for verdivurderingen som retten har beskrevet foran. Begge parter har benyttet økonomiske eksperter for sine vurderinger og anslag over det tapet de mener det er grunnlag for å erstatte. Her må altså prøve fullt ut om vurderingene og anslagene er basert på riktige rettslige prinsipper. Men retten må vise forsiktighet i prøving av temaer av faktisk art, hvor det åpenbart er ekspertene som har den største kompetansen. "Matematikken" i ekspertenes beregninger er ikke angrepet. Men det er, som retten kommer tilbake til, forutsetninger – assumptions – i disse beregningene som er bestridt. Retten kan ikke avstå fra å prøve slike innvendinger, men må vise forsiktighet ved prøvingen der det kreves spesialisert økonomisk innsikt.'

43. Page 43, original on p. 46: 'analyser og vurderinger av blant annet utsikter for vekst i revenue, EBITDA og EBITDA-marginer som faglig godt begrunnet, og de er forankret i forholdene på kjøpstidspunktet.'

44. Page 46, original on p. 48: '(1) Finne sammenlignbare selskaper, (2) Finne økonomiske indikatorer som er relevante ved fastleggelsen av verdiene på disse, (3) For hvert selskap finne verdien på disse indikatorene og den sum selskapet ble solgt for, (4) Basert på salgspris delt på den relevante indikatoren, fastlegge en typisk multippel og (5) Basert på den den samme indikatoren og den typiske multippel foreta et anslag over verdien på det aktuelle kjøpsobjektet.'

multiples method supported the tenability of the DCF method's estimate of NOK 245 million.

[8] Risk Premium in Particular

There was a separate question as to whether there was any basis for a markup on a loss amount from a risk point of view – damages for unknown unknowns – a risk premium.

The buyer argued that in a case like this, someone who buys a company whose revenue and EBITDA are incorrect will not only base their offer on correct figures, but their offer will also take into account the possibility that the company may have other weaknesses besides the fact that the actual figures for revenue and EBITDA are different from those shown in the accounts. The buyer submitted that the risk premium should be calculated by marking up the rate for the cost of capital in the DCF analysis by 2%. This led to an additional claim of MNOK 298 on top of MNOK 245, MNOK 543 in total.

The respondents argued that there was no basis for a risk premium, holding that if there were, this would involve double compensation, while also stressing that any risk premium would be affected by an adequacy limitation. The respondents also held that in any event the claim was significantly exaggerated and could be a question of MNOK 5–10 million at most.

The tribunal made reference to the sources of law invoked by the buyer, including legal theory from Johnny Herre and statements from the buyer's expert, concluding as follows:

> In the Arbitral Tribunal's view, it seems probable that a reasonably rational and reasonable buyer will make a deduction for such a risk. That this will have its cause in the breach of warranty seems clear. It is also difficult to see other than that such a loss is foreseeable/adequate when it is in line with reasonable behaviour from a buyer.[45]

As regards the amount of the risk premium, the tribunal stated:

> The Tribunal has a weak factual basis for assessing the size of such a risk deduction. In this regard, the Tribunal notes that it is precisely the uncertainty at the time of purchase that is to be considered. It is no question of giving an estimate of what it will cost to 'fix' the accounting system so that overstatement is avoided for the future. It would be to draw in ex post knowledge.
> The Tribunal finds that it has not been proven that a risk loss, and thereby a risk addition in the compensation, can amount to MNOK 298 or an amount close to it. On the other hand, an addition, given the company's size and business,

---

45. Page 45, original on p. 48: 'Etter voldgiftsrettens syn fremstår det som sannsynlig at en rimelig rasjonell og fornuftig kjøper vil gjøre et fradrag for en slik risiko. At dette vil ha sin årsak i garantibruddet synes klart. Det er også vanskelig å se annet enn at et slikt tap er påregnelig/adekvat når det er i tråd med fornuftig opptreden fra en kjøper.'

cannot constitute a completely trivial amount. In the absence of further evidence, the Tribunal assumes that the risk amounts to at least MNOK 5.[46]

As observant readers will already have noticed, the total amount of MNOK 250 would accordingly be the same as the total limitation of liability for the insurer according to the W&I insurance agreement.

[9]   Calculation of Interest

It should be noted that the award also includes very thorough handling of the interest part of the claim, which is governed by the Norwegian Insurance Contracts Act, in which the parties disputed several legal and factual issues. This part of the award accounts for twenty-six of the eighty-one pages. Pursuant to the Norwegian Insurance Contract Act, the rate set out in the Norwegian Late Payment Act should apply, which was between 8% and 9.5% in the applicable period. Thus, the amount of interest was in the range of NOK 50 million alone.

§6.05   THE AD HOC AWARD

[A]   Introduction

In spring 2021, an arbitral tribunal seated in Oslo rendered an award in a post M&A dispute in an ad hoc arbitration. The SPA was governed by Norwegian law and the tribunal consisted of Anders Arnkværn (Norway), Stig Even Jakobsen (Norway) and Johnny Herre (Sweden), with Herre as chair.

The case concerned a claim under W&I insurance for warranty breaches. The buyer had entered into the SPA with the seller of the target company and had signed a W&I insurance policy replacing the seller's liability for breaches of its warranties as part of the transaction. Pursuant to the SPA, the claims had to be submitted against the underlying insurance companies, which were thus the respondents in the case.

The tribunal found warranty breaches and the buyer was duly awarded damages for its loss. As in the two above awards, the tribunal's handling of loss calculation, including its general remarks concerning the valuation methods, is of wider interest. In this case, the tribunal found reason to rely on a valuation-based approach when calculating the loss to the buyer.

---

46. Page 45, original on p. 48: '*Retten har et svakt faktisk grunnlag for å vurdere størrelsen av et slikt fradrag for risiko. I denne forbindelse minner retten om at det nettopp er usikkerheten på kjøpstidspunktet som skal vurderes. Det er ikke spørsmål om å gi et anslag over hva det vil koste å "fikse" regnskapssystemet slik at overstatement unngås for fremtiden. Det ville være å trekke inn ex post kunnskap.*

Retten finner det ikke godtgjort at et risk-tap, og derved et risk-tillegg i erstatningen, kan utgjøre MNOK 298 eller et beløp i nærheten av det. På den annen side kan et tillegg, hensett til selskapets størrelse og virksomhet, ikke utgjøre et helt bagatellmessig beløp. I mangel av nærmere holdepunkter legger retten til grunn at risikoen iallfall utgjør MNOK 5.'

[B] The Respondents Were Found Liable

The buyer's claim was based on the target's alleged underreporting of software licenses, where the licence costs had not been paid. The respondents disputed the allegation, relying, *inter alia,* on an audit carried out by the licensor which did not support the buyer's claim. The tribunal found that there had been underreporting on the part of the target in 2015 and that this constituted a breach of several of the warranties provided by the seller and insured by the respondents.

[C] Causation

The tribunal found the causal requirement to be fulfilled as the underreporting was the cause of the buyer's receiving less than the value *as warranted,* without making causation a separate issue.

[D] Loss Calculation

[1] The Tribunal's General Introductory Remarks

The parties mainly agreed that if there had been a breach of warranty, the resulting loss was the delta between the target company's value with and without the breach. However, the parties disagreed on how the delta value should be determined.

The SPA defined loss as any reasonably foreseeable loss, liability, claim, damage, cost, or expense. The tribunal pointed out: '*The meaning of these different terms is not further elaborated on in the agreement and must thus be resolved and established by an interpretation of the SPA as a whole with due regard to Norwegian background law.*'[47] After reviewing the SPA and the insurance policy, the tribunal further stated: '*As the term Loss is not defined in any further detail than described above and there are no other interpretative guidelines in the agreements, the further assessment of losses Claimant may claim compensation for and the calculation of such losses must be determined on the basis of the background law.*'[48]

The tribunal went on to state that the '*starting point in Norwegian law is that an aggrieved party is entitled to damages providing full compensation for any financial harm suffered as a result of the breach of contract',*[49] also asserting:

> The starting point for assessing such compensation is to compare the effects of what has happened with what would have happened if the contract was performed as contracted. It follows from this basic principle that the aggrieved party should not through the compensation be placed in a better position than if the contract had been rightfully performed.[50]

---

47. Paragraph 135 on p. 36.
48. Paragraph 146 on pp. 37–38.
49. Paragraph 152 on p. 39.
50. Paragraph 153 on p. 39.

As regards loss calculation, the tribunal, *inter alia,* made the following general remarks in the introduction:

> 'There are different ways to calculate a loss. These differences are mainly due to differences in the factual situations at hand. In some cases, the aggrieved party may also choose the method. §§ 67–70 of the Norwegian Sale of Goods Act provide some guidance for such calculation according to Norwegian law. However, these provisions do not provide the full picture.'[51]
>
> 'The SPA does not, as stated, provide any clear guidance on what kind of consequences that could constitute a Loss to be compensated under the SPA. The starting point must therefore be that the terms used in the SPA and in the insurance policy correspond to applicable law, i.e., general principles of Norwegian contract law (first and foremost the Norwegian Sale of Goods Act, applicable for all other sales contracts than sales of real estate and consumer sales). It is clear that compensation for the difference in market value is a compensable loss under Norwegian law.
>
> As stated above, Section [x.xx] of the SPA stipulates that compensation for Loss pursuant to Section [x.xx] excludes any other claim for damages and a claim for "reduction of the Purchase Price". This provision could not be interpreted to prevent Claimant from claiming damages calculated on the basis of the market value difference. As stated, these remedies are to be regarded as two distinct remedies with differing purposes. Thus, the exception in Section [x.xx] could not prevent and does not influence the assessment of what Claimant may be entitled to receive. If the insurance policy was intended to exclude such losses pursuant to Norwegian law as well, Respondents should have specified this in the insurance policy.'[52]

[2] *The Choice of Valuation Methods*

The tribunal emphasised that the buyer had '*chosen*' to claim the difference between the target's value *as warranted* (i.e., the value of the target shares without any breaches) and the value *as is* (i.e., as delivered to the buyer).

After underlining the point that the main problem is to assess an asset's value *as is*, i.e., in the non-conforming state, the tribunal made the following general remarks regarding the choice of valuation methods:

> In the marketplace there are certain more or less accepted valuation methods to be used for different kinds of assets. Thus, when the task is to assess the market value of assets in a non-conforming state, certain methods are applied by market participants and also in courts and by arbitral proceedings.
>
> The same is true for the valuation of the asset class shares or companies. However, all these methods are based upon assumptions. They only provide more or less strong indications of the value of the company. Thus, it is generally accepted that no method or combination of methods provide an objective value, i.e. a value that would be accepted by all market participants. Instead, each market participant would value a company in its own way based upon propensity to

---

51. Paragraph 155 on p. 39.
52. Paragraphs 161–162 on pp. 40–41.

accept risk and the expectations regarding the future in such complex matters as price and cost development, micro and macroeconomic development etc.

However, the methods for valuation of a company developed, refined and generally used are the best methods available also for a damages calculation, where the purpose is to establish with reasonable certainty the actual loss caused by one or several breaches of warranty.

In general terms there are, in cases where a breach of warranty has an effect on the income generating capacity, two groups of valuation methods used for the assessment. These are methods based upon an income approach and methods based upon a market approach. The former estimates the value of the company by calculating the present value of anticipated benefits in the future, whereas in the market approach the company as delivered (i.e. with the breaches of warranties) is compared to similar business, business ownership interest and securities sold in the market. The most commonly used income-based method is the discounted cash flow (DCF) method, used by both [expert] and [expert], however, in different ways. Also such methods as the adjusted present value and the capitalized cash flow could be used. Among the market approach methods used, comparisons with publicly traded multiples, transaction multiples and stock prices and implicit trading multiples of such quoted companies could be mentioned.

As no method or approach provides a clear answer, most calculations of the value of a company (the 'EV' or 'enterprise value') are based upon the application of several methods and a final appraisal of a reasonable market value. Such an approach also seems to be in line with recommended generally accepted valuation principles. As this is the basis for valuations in the marketplace forming the basis for real transactions, such an approach should also be accepted and preferred when calculating damages for a warranty breach.[53]

[3]   The *as Warranted* Valuation

With regard to the value had there been no breaches, where the value was not disputed, the tribunal stressed that '*the agreed value is a strong indication of the market value of [target] at the time*'.[54] The tribunal pointed out that the buyer chose to pay the enterprise value in an auction process that involved other prospective buyers. As these competitive auction processes are frequently used by professional company sellers in order to calculate the company's market value, and as the buyers participating in these processes are primarily professional company buyers, this indicated that the market value was the agreed enterprise value. In addition, the tribunal stated:

> Furthermore, the legal position in Norwegian law, as well as in Scandinavian law in general, is that there is a rather strong presumption, both in price reduction calculations and in damages calculations based upon value difference, that the agreed price between the parties equals the market value. Already for these reasons, the Tribunal finds that MNOK [amount] could be used as the basis for a value difference calculation.[55]

---

53. Paragraphs 261–265 on pp. 61–62.
54. Paragraph 266 on p. 62.
55. Paragraph 267 on p. 62.

[4]   The *As Is* Valuation

The tribunal's next task was to assess the target's value at the time of the transaction if the true license costs had been reported or disclosed to the buyer prior to signing the SPA.

The buyer submitted that this value would have been MNOK 170 lower. This amount was reached by using different valuation methods and thus not only the EV/EBIT multiple. One such method was the application of the DCF approach, which in the view of the buyer's expert would have had a negative effect amounting to MNOK 198 on the enterprise value. The buyer's expert had also used the implicit EV multiples of the deal and applied them giving a range of values. As the buyer's expert deemed the degree of uncertainty regarding the business's development after 2017 to be significantly higher than it had been for 2015–2017, the expert relied more on the result of the implicit multiples analysis than on the DCF analysis. Furthermore, the buyer's expert's view was that these implicit multiples were supported by observing the trading and M&A multiples of comparable companies, which is usually termed 'peer group' analysis.

The respondent's expert concluded that the reduction in value associated with the underreporting was between MNOK 16.8 and 17.4, mainly on the basis of a DCF model. The respondents, *inter alia*, argued that the target would have renegotiated each customer contract at the end of a four-year period, and that the target would have been able to pass on all additional future costs with the software licences at that point.

In the tribunal's view, it was clear that the methods used by the buyer's expert were in principle the same methods used in the valuations that formed the basis for the transaction, stating that it *'is also clear that such methods are regularly used and accepted in the marketplace'*.[56] The tribunal also found that: *'there are good arguments in favour of a market value difference of approximately MNOK 170 as claimed if the only factor to be considered is that the COGS [cost of goods sold] would have been almost MNOK 17 higher than the COGS reported in 2015 and everything else in would have remained the same'*.[57] However, the tribunal pointed out that other factors also needed to be taken into account.

First, there were some uncertainties regarding the base case and the de facto underreporting. Second, the analysis assumed that the target would not have been able to pass on any costs to the customers, and this second factor was more thoroughly assessed separately. The third and fourth factors are very general in nature:

> Thirdly, [the buyer's expert]'s implicit assumption in its application of the implicit multiple based upon the deal enterprise value is that all market participants would have made the same assumptions as Claimant and that these assumptions therefore could be applied also if the cost base proved to be higher than assumed in the valuations. The deal enterprise value as agreed is a price to be adjusted for at closing. It is based upon a multitude of valuation methods used and especially on Claimant's risk propensity and assumptions about the future. Even if the Seller

---

56. Paragraph 274 on p. 64.
57. Paragraph 275 on p. 64.

accepted the price offered, it does not follow from this decision that the Seller also accepted all underlying assumptions made by Claimant when Claimant made the decision to accept to pay a price based upon an enterprise value of MNOK [amount]; it was the price that was accepted and not the assumptions and the importance of these for the different calculations. Thus, [the buyer's expert]'s approach in this regard is in some respects a problematic assumption as this would from a legal perspective mean that the Seller actually assumed or accepted these assumptions made by Claimant when accepting a stated enterprise value and the purchase price.

However, it is clear law that the assumptions made by a buyer when accepting to buy something at a certain price are the buyer's risk. Therefore, one has to take into account that a seller would not necessarily have accepted the same assumptions forming the basis for the different valuation methods (e.g. the peer companies to be used for the comparison or the WACC or other factors).

Fourthly, it is not the best approach for a calculation of damages due to a breach of this nature to assume that the costs would have been higher at the beginning of the negotiations – and thus when the transaction was initiated – and that these costs would have been treated in the same way as other costs on an aggregate level even if disclosed just prior to the signing of the SPA.[58]

The tribunal also made the following statement concerning the valuation assessment performed:

It is in this respect of relevance that a breach of warranty would have been avoided if the Seller had disclosed the underreporting to the Buyer prior to signing of the SPA (i.e. not necessarily when the transaction was initiated) and that the decisive question for the claim for damages is how a rational buyer in such a case would have valued [target]. It is fair to assume that a rational buyer would have adopted the valuation methods adopted by as a starting point, but it is also fair to assume that the valuation would have been affected by an assessment as to which extent the additional costs would be considered to be recurring losses or not and to some extent whether the loss could be mitigated without affecting the upside of the business already paid for by the buyer through the valuation of the company.

Thus, the valuation has to be based upon how reasonable market participants would have treated disclosed higher license costs. However, as the calculation should be objective, no assumptions should be made regarding the reasonable reactions of the parties (however, see below). Therefore, it must for example be ignored if the buyer could reasonably be assumed to have treated the surprising information about non-compliance with its most important supplier's license rules as a deal-breaker.[59]

The tribunal made a thorough assessment of whether the target would have been able to pass on the part of the increase in costs to its customers and concluded that only a limited part could have been passed on. This assessment also included other general remarks of interest.

As regards facts about the target's development after the transaction, the tribunal stated:

---

58. Paragraphs 280–282 on pp. 64–65.
59. Paragraphs 284–285 on p. 65.

These statements indicate that neither in 2016 nor later managed to pass on any significant portion of the extra costs incurred as a result of the correction of the underreporting. However, in the view of the Tribunal, this information is of minor importance for the assessment of the compensation. One should not, in principle, consider facts about the development after the transaction as part of the market difference assessment. This assessment should be made based upon the situation at the time of delivery (i.e. closing of the transaction) and the assumed assessment of a rational buyer at this stage. Thus, the actual reporting of [name] licenses in 2016, 2017, 2018, 2019 and 2020 is of minor importance for the calculation as such. The same is true for the results of the efforts made by [target] to pass on costs.

By contrast, evidence from the period when the underreporting was discovered is of importance for how the issue would have been handled by a rational market participant at the time of the contract if the information would have been available. In this regard, the Tribunal notes the following from the correspondence and the investigations made at that time.[60]

The tribunal concluded as follows: '*Considering all relevant circumstances, the Tribunal concludes that the market value difference loss amounts to MNOK 145.*'[61] The buyer was therefore compensated with MNOK 135, from which the agreed MNOK 10 retention had been deducted.

[5]   *Calculation of Interest*

The tribunal found that the buyer was entitled to late payment interest in accordance with the Insurance Contract Act.

In addition, the buyer was awarded loss of use interest (Nw: avsavnsrente) from the closing of the transaction until the date on which late payment interest started to accrue, a fact which may be surprising in some jurisdictions.

The tribunal stressed that in Norwegian law, it is clear that loss of use interest should in principle be treated in the same way other losses to be compensated as damages, reasoning as follows: as the loss is the difference between the value paid for *as warranted* and the value received, this means that the buyer was entitled to compensation for the loss from the time at which the transaction was closed. As no such compensation was paid by either the seller or the respondents at the time, the buyer made a loss in the form of the interest costs suffered. The buyer was awarded an additional amount.

§6.06   CONCLUDING REMARKS

These awards show how tribunals in the Nordic countries have handled loss calculation after finding warranty breaches and give highly useful insight to parties involved in such cases. As mentioned in the introduction, these three recent awards have been viewed by several commentators as clarifying how loss calculation in post M&A disputes should be undertaken.

---

60. Paragraphs 290–291 on pp. 66–67.
61. Paragraph 311 on p. 71.

At the same time, the awards also show that there may be some differences between the approaches taken by the tribunals to some of the issues at hand. One example may be the relevance for loss calculation of circumstances that arise after the transaction. In the OCC Award, the tribunal stated that subsequent information was not suited to shed light on what the buyer would have done if he had had the information prior to the transaction.[62] In the ad hoc Award, the tribunal stated one should not, in principle, consider facts about the development after the transaction as part of the market difference assessment. However, the tribunal continued to state that evidence from the period when the underreporting was discovered is of importance for how the issue would have been handled by a rational market participant at the time of the contract if the information had been available.[63]

Furthermore, there are also issues that only appear to be dealt with in one of the awards and on which the tribunal's reasoning seems less elaborated and provides less clarification than other issues in the award. One such example could be the calculation of the risk premium part in the OCC Award.[64] For the sake of good order, it is important to stress that while the OCC Award was the only one to explicitly deal with a risk premium in the award's reasoning, it cannot be ruled out that a risk premium was included in the loss calculation presented by the experts in the other cases, as this could be part of the experts' view on the weighted average cost of capital (WACC), even though the tribunals did not refer to it.

In an article in 2018, Claes Zettermarck wrote that the multiple question had not been forgotten and that it would turn up again.[65] These awards, and perhaps especially the ad hoc Award, show that the multiple question has indeed turned up again, and the last word on loss calculation in post M&A disputes has not yet been spoken.

---

62. *See* section §6.04[D][2].
63. *See* section §6.05[D][4].
64. *See* section §6.04[D][8].
65. Claes Zettermarck, *Var är multipeln?*, pp. 827–834, in Lars Edlund, eds et al., *Festskrift till Stefan Lindskog* (Jure Förlag AB, 2018).

CHAPTER 7

Investment Protection under the Energy Charter Treaty in the Early Stages of an Underwater Gas Pipeline Project

Jakob Ragnwaldh, Aron Skogman & Jennie Hjellström

§7.01 INTRODUCTION

The Energy Charter Treaty (the ECT) is a multilateral treaty for international long-term cooperation within the energy sector. The treaty was signed in 1994 and entered into force in 1998. Pursuant to the ECT, the Contracting Parties have undertaken to promote and protect investments in the energy sector by investors from other Contracting Parties and to facilitate the transit of energy through their respective 'Areas'.[1] The ECT stands out in comparison to other investment treaties, not only because of its focus on the energy sector but also because of its large number of Contracting Parties. There are currently fifty-three signatories and Contracting Parties to the ECT, including both states and organisations such as the EU and EURATOM.

The laying down of an underwater gas pipeline will generally require significant resources, even at the very early stages of the project. Before the first section of the gas pipeline is placed on the seabed, the investor will often have spent significant funds preparing and obtaining necessary approvals for the project. Early-stage investments may include hiring consultants and contractors to analyse the environmental effects of the project, dealing with permit processes, and preparing, designing and planning for the manufacture, delivery and assembly of the pipeline.

---

1. The definition of 'Area' is discussed below, *see* section §7.02[A].

This chapter will first examine whether the construction of a gas pipeline on the seabed within the continental shelf or in the exclusive economic zone (the EEZ)[2] of a Contracting Party to the ECT constitutes an 'Investment' within the meaning of the ECT.[3] Following this, the chapter will discuss *when* an investor's early measures to prepare for the construction of a pipeline may reach the point where the investor is considered to have made an 'Investment' protected by the ECT.[4] In particular, this chapter aims to discuss whether it is possible to recognise an 'Investment' within the meaning of the ECT before a permit for the construction of a pipeline has been obtained.

The ECT provides no firm obligations on the part of the Contracting Parties with regard to the 'Making of Investments',[5] which is a term used to describe a project that is still in a 'pre-investment phase'.[6] The treaty's provisions concerning the 'Making of Investments' are often described as 'soft-law' obligations, which do not offer effective protection against unfair treatment by the host state. Notably, the drafters of the ECT were explicit that firm obligations relating to the 'Making of Investments' would be subject to a separate treaty.[7] However, no such treaty has ever been concluded.

In the absence of any firm obligation of the Contracting Parties to provide protection at the pre-investment phase, the question of *when* an early-stage project has progressed to the point where it may be recognised as an 'Investment' (at least in some part) may be of great significance to an investor embarking on an underwater pipeline project. For example, access to remedies under the ECT may be of considerable value for investors facing obstacles in the permit process with authorities in one of the states where the pipeline is to be laid down. Once the project, at least in part, *does* qualify as an 'Investment' within the meaning of the ECT, the investor is protected by the ECT's protection standards, such as the guarantee of fair and equitable treatment and the protection against unreasonable or discriminatory measures impairing the investment. At that stage, the investor will also gain access to the treaty's dispute resolution mechanisms, including the right to bring a claim before an international arbitral tribunal against the host state. Thus, the question of whether the project qualifies in some part as an 'Investment' under the ECT may have important implications for an investor subjected to unfair, unreasonable or discriminatory treatment in the process of obtaining a permit for its pipeline project.

---

2. Pipelines intended to be laid down on the seabed of the coastal states' internal waters and territorial sea are excluded from the scope of this article.
3. *See* section §7.02 below.
4. *See* section §7.03 below.
5. *See* e.g., Arts 1(8) and 10(1) ECT and C. Baltag, *The Energy Charter Treaty: The Notion of Investor*, Wolters Kluwer, 2012, pp. 206f.
6. *See* further Art. 1(8) ECT, where 'Making of Investments' is defined as 'establishing new Investments, acquiring all or part of existing Investments or moving into different fields of Investment activity'.
7. Article 10(4) ECT.

§7.02 IS THE PIPELINE PROJECT PER SE CAPABLE OF BEING RECOGNISED AS AN 'INVESTMENT' PROTECTED BY THE ECT?

One of the key elements of the ECT is its provisions on the protection of foreign investments in the energy sector. These provisions set forth a number of protection standards, including the aforementioned guarantee of fair and equitable treatment and protection against unreasonable and discriminatory measures.

If the host state acts in violation of one or several of the protection standards, the affected investor may claim compensation and initiate legal proceedings pursuant to the investor-state dispute mechanisms set forth in Article 26 ECT. Under this provision, the investor may choose either to bring a claim before the national courts of the host state of the 'Investment' or to initiate international arbitration proceedings.

To benefit from the ECT's provisions on investment protection and access the mechanisms of dispute resolution, the investor must pass the test of having made an 'Investment' in the 'Area' of the host state. The definition of an 'Investment' in Article 1(6) ECT is broad and includes virtually 'every kind of asset' that is 'owned or controlled [...] directly or indirectly' by an investor, provided that the investment is 'associated with an Economic Activity in the Energy Sector'.

In the following subsections §7.02[A]–§7.02[B], it will be examined whether the laying down of an underwater gas pipeline on the seabed located within the continental shelf/EEZ of an ECT Member State is capable per se of fulfilling these criteria.

[A] Does a Gas Pipeline Located on the Continental Shelf/EEZ of an ECT Member State Satisfy the 'Area' Requirement in the ECT?[8]

The first question that must be addressed is whether a gas pipeline located on the continental shelf/EEZ of an ECT Member State is capable of satisfying the 'Area' requirement set out in Article 1(10) ECT, which reads:

> [W]ith respect to a state that is a Contracting Party: (a) the territory under its sovereignty, it being understood that territory includes land, internal waters and the territorial sea; and (b) subject to and in accordance with the international law of the sea: the sea, sea-bed and its subsoil with regard to which that Contracting Party exercises rights and jurisdiction.

The question of whether the part of the seabed located within a coastal state's continental shelf/EEZ falls within Article 1(10)(b) ECT is thus dependent on whether the host state exercises 'rights and jurisdiction' with regard to such areas pursuant to the international law of the sea.

---

8. Although the 'Area' requirement is not expressly included in the 'Investment' definition (other than with respect to 'investments or classes of investments designated by a Contracting Party *in its Area* as "Charter efficiency projects" and so notified to the Secretariat') an investment must have been made in the 'Area' of a Contracting Party to the ECT in order for the protections standards to apply and the mechanisms of dispute resolution to be available, cf. Arts 10 and 26 ECT.

Articles 56(1) and 77(1) of the United Nations Convention on the Law of the Sea (UNCLOS) provide as follows:

Article 56(1):

In the exclusive economic zone, the coastal State has:

(a) sovereign rights for the purpose of exploring and exploiting, conserving and managing the natural resources, whether living or non-living, of the waters superjacent to the seabed and of the seabed and its subsoil, and with regard to other activities for the economic exploitation and exploration of the zone, such as the production of energy from the water, currents and winds.[9]

Article 77(1):

The coastal State exercises over the continental shelf sovereign rights for the purpose of exploring it and exploiting its natural resources.[10]

In view of the wording of Article 1(10) ECT and Articles 56(1) and 77(1) UNCLOS, it would seem beyond doubt that the ECT's definition of 'Area' includes the seabed within the continental shelf as well as the EEZ of a Contracting Party to the ECT. The drafting history of the ECT, particularly the discussion that took place following Norway's objection to the use of the term 'Area', further supports this conclusion. Although the discussion concerned the use of the term in the context of Article 7(10) ECT (regarding the Transit of Energy Materials and Products), Norway's suggestion was to use the word 'territory' instead of 'area' in order to limit the territorial scope of Article 7(10) to land territory, internal waters and territorial sea, and thus to exclude the continental shelf and EEZ from the scope of the provision.[11] Norway's proposal was not accepted, and the discussion supports the notion that the drafters' intention was for the term 'Area' to cover the continental shelf and EEZ of a Contracting Party.[12]

---

9. The EEZ is defined in Art. 55 UNCLOS: 'The exclusive economic zone is an area beyond and adjacent to the territorial sea, subject to the specific legal regime established in this Part, under which the rights and jurisdiction of the coastal State and the rights and freedoms of other States are governed by the relevant provisions of this Convention.' It is worth noting that, pursuant to Art. 77(3) UNCLOS, the EEZ must be claimed by states, in contrast to the continental shelf which exists *ipso facto*, *see* K. Hobér, *The Energy Charter Treaty: A Commentary*, Oxford University Press, 2020, p. 138.
10. The continental shelf is defined in Art. 76(1) UNCLOS: 'The continental shelf of a coastal State comprises the seabed and subsoil of the submarine areas that extend beyond its territorial sea throughout the natural prolongation of its land territory to the outer edge of the continental margin, or to a distance of 200 nautical miles from the baselines from which the breadth of the territorial sea is measured where the outer edge of the continental margin does not extend up to that distance.' The criteria by which a coastal state is allowed to establish the outer limits of its continental shelf are set out in the remainder of Art. 76.
11. *See* the Energy Charter Treaty's Secretariat's 'CCDEC201607 – Adoption of the Commentary to the Rules Concerning the Conduct of Conciliation of Transit Disputes', dated 20 June 2016, at para. 22. *See* further, e.g., V. Pogoretskyy, *Freedom of Transit and Access to Gas Pipeline Networks under WTO Law*, Cambridge University Press, 2017, p. 266.
12. *See* further e.g., K. Hobér, *supra* n. 9, at p. 139.

[B] Is the Requirement of an 'Economic Activity in the Energy Sector' Satisfied?

The next question to address in order to establish whether the construction of a gas pipeline on the continental shelf/EEZ of an ECT Member State qualifies as a protected 'Investment' under the ECT, is whether such a project is 'associated with an Economic Activity in the Energy Sector', as required by Article 1(6) ECT.

A definition of 'Economic Activity in the Energy Sector' is provided in Article 1(5) ECT:

> 'Economic Activity in the Energy Sector' means an economic activity concerning the exploration, extraction, refining production, storage, *land transport, transmission,* distribution, trade, marketing, or sale *of Energy Materials and Products except those included in Annex NI,* or concerning the distribution of heat to multiple premises. (Emphasis added.)

'Petroleum gases and other gaseous hydrocarbons' are expressly covered by the definition of 'Energy Materials and Products'.[13] Moreover, a gas pipeline can be said to 'transmit' gas. Intuitively, therefore, one would expect an underwater gas pipeline project to qualify as an 'Economic Activity in the Energy Sector' under the ECT.

Notably, however, Understanding No. 2[14] with respect to Article 1(5) ECT casts doubt on this conclusion. The Understanding includes a list of activities which, although stated to be no more than 'illustrative' of what constitutes an 'Economic Activity in the Energy Sector', could be interpreted as excluding the transmission of gas through an underwater pipeline from the scope of Article 1(5) ECT.

Understanding No. 2 includes the following example of an 'Economic Activity in the Energy Sector':

> (iii) *land transportation,* distribution, storage and supply of Energy Materials and Products, *e.g., by way of transmission* and distribution grids and *pipelines* or dedicated rail lines, *and construction of facilities for such,* including the *laying of* oil, *gas,* and coal-slurry *pipelines;* (Emphasis added.)

The wording of Understanding No. 2 could potentially be construed as indicating that 'transmission' through a gas pipeline should be considered merely as a form of 'transport' ('land transportation [...] e.g. *by way of* transmission') and, thus, that 'transmission' (of gas) must occur on *land* ('*land* transportation [...]') in order to qualify as an 'Economic Activity in the Energy Sector'. Such an interpretation would, in turn, mean that the transmission of gas by means of an *underwater* pipeline (as well as the 'construction of facilities for such')[15] would not be recognised as an 'Economic Activity in the Energy Sector'. Neither Article 1(5) nor the Understanding, provides a clear answer as to whether the ECT drafters intended to exclude gas transmission

---

13. *See* ECT Annex EM I.
14. As expressed by one commentator, the so-called Understandings issued with regard to some of the ECT provisions 'are helpful in that they provide guidance for the interpretation of various Treaty provisions', *see* K. Hobér, *supra* n. 9, at p. 5.
15. This is another illustrative example provided in the Understanding.

through underwater gas pipelines (and hence, the construction of such pipelines) from the purview of Article 1(5) ECT.

To determine whether gas transmission through underwater gas pipelines constitutes an 'Economic Activity in the Energy Sector', guidance should be sought in the Vienna Convention on the Law of Treaties (the VCLT). Pursuant to Article 31 VCLT, a treaty shall be interpreted in good faith in accordance with the ordinary meaning to be given to the terms of the treaty in their context and in the light of its object and purpose. Instruments accepted by the parties to the treaty (such as the aforementioned Understanding) may also be taken into consideration.[16] According to Article 32 VCLT, the preparatory work of the treaty (such as drafts of the treaty and records of the treaty negotiations) and the circumstances of its conclusion may be taken into account either to confirm the meaning established by applying the principles of Article 31 or to avoid arriving at a meaning that would be ambiguous or obscure, or would lead to a manifestly absurd or unreasonable interpretation. As expressed by one commentator, an interpretation based on the wording and context of a treaty must ultimately be 'submitted to the test of reasonableness'.[17]

Having regard to the above principles of treaty interpretation, the following observations can be made:

(i) Although the Understanding on Article 1(5) ECT may indicate that 'transmission' could be regarded as a subcategory of 'transportation', the wording of Article 1(5) in itself does not clearly indicate that 'transmission' (as opposed to 'transport') must take place *on land* in order to be covered.

(ii) It is the authors' understanding that 'transmission', rather than 'transport' or 'transportation', is the phrase more commonly used in the industry to describe the flow of gas through a gas pipeline.

(iii) The fact that 'land transport' in Article 1(5) ECT is followed not only by the word 'transmission' but also by 'trade, marketing, or sale' indicates that the word 'land' should be read together with 'transport' only, and not with the subsequent words in the provision, such as 'transmission'. An interpretation to the contrary would indicate, for example, that 'marketing' is covered only to the extent that it could be categorised as 'land marketing', which would arguably be an unreasonable and absurd interpretation within the meaning of Article 32 VCLT.

(iv) The drafting history of the ECT indicates that the reason for adding the word 'land'[18] to the definition of 'Economic Activity in the Energy Sector' in Article 1(5) ECT was to exclude 'maritime transportation' rather than to exclude underwater gas pipelines as a transmission (or 'transport') method.[19]

---

16. *See* K. Hobér, *supra* n. 9, at pp. 31f.
17. *See* the commentary to Art. 31 VCLT in O. Dörr & K. Schmalenbach (eds), *Vienna Convention on the Law of Treaties: A Commentary*, 2nd ed., Springer, 2018, at pp. 579–588.
18. '*[L]and* transport, transmission, distribution [...]'.
19. The insertion of 'land' to the definition of 'Economic Activity in the Energy Sector' was addressed by the ECT drafters in the context of discussing whether 'air transport' should be

(v) The conclusion in (iv) above seems to be consistent with the fact that Article 1(5) refers to both 'transport' and 'transmission', which would arguably not have been necessary if the drafters had regarded 'transmission' as merely a form of 'transport'.

To conclude, in the authors' view, a reasonable, good faith interpretation in accordance with Articles 31–32 VCLT is that the transmission of gas through an underwater gas pipeline constitutes an 'Economic Activity in the Energy Sector' within the meaning of Article 1(5) ECT.

Accordingly, the construction of an underwater gas pipeline on the seabed within the continental shelf or EEZ of an ECT Member State is indeed capable per se of qualifying as an 'Investment' pursuant to Article 1(6) ECT.

§7.03 CAN THE PIPELINE PROJECT BE A PROTECTED 'INVESTMENT' BEFORE A PERMIT HAS BEEN OBTAINED?

[A] Are Early Steps in Advance of a Permit Application Capable of Being Recognised as 'Investment[s]' under the ECT?

Article 1(6) ECT provides, in part, the following definition of an 'Investment':

'Investment' means every kind of asset, owned or controlled directly or indirectly by an Investor and includes:

(a) tangible and intangible, and movable and immovable, property, and any property rights such as leases, mortgages, liens, and pledges;
(b) a company or business enterprise, or shares, stock, or other forms of equity participation in a company or business enterprise, and bonds and other debt of a company or business enterprise;
(c) claims to money and claims to performance pursuant to contract having an economic value and associated with an Investment;
        [...]
(f) any right conferred by law or contract or by virtue of any licences and permits granted pursuant to law to undertake any Economic Activity in the Energy Sector.
        [...]

'Investment' refers to any investment associated with an Economic Activity in the Energy Sector [...]

As mentioned in the introduction to this article, the ECT makes an important distinction between 'Investment[s]' and the 'Making of Investments'. The latter is defined in Article 1(8) ECT as 'establishing new Investments, acquiring all or part of existing Investments or moving into different fields of Investment activity'.

---

covered, which suggests that the term 'transport' was understood by the drafters to refer to transport of goods by trucks, airplanes or ships rather than a broader term that would comprise all types of 'transmission', such as that of gas through a gas pipeline, see 'CONF 98, Draft ECT – Chairman's Compromise Text' dated 22 April 1994, p. 4. See also K. Hobér, supra n. 9, at p. 65.

The definition of the 'Making of Investments' in Article 1(8) ECT suggests that the ECT drafters intended that at least some concrete steps would need to be taken by the potential investor before an 'Investment' is considered to have been made. However, the 'Investment' definition in Article 1(6) ECT is extremely broad, which suggests that the threshold for having made an 'Investment' is relatively low. As noted by one commentator:

> [I]n practice the process of distinguishing the two notions [i.e., the post- and pre-investment phases] is facilitated by the broad definition of 'Investment' in Article 1(6). If something does not qualify as an Investment, it falls into the pre-investment category. As a consequence, *the pre-investment measures covered by the ECT are rather limited.*[20] (Emphasis added.)

Notably, there are no publicly available cases in which an ECT tribunal has determined whether a project would fall within the category of 'Making of Investments' pursuant to Article 1(8) ECT.[21] However, there are a number of awards rendered under investment protection treaties where arbitral tribunals were faced with the more general question of whether an 'Investment' had been made or if additional steps were required in order for a protected 'Investment' to come into existence. Those awards suggest that it is not imperative that the most important step of an investment project has been taken (such as entering into an essential agreement or the granting of a permit) in order for an investor to be deemed to have made an 'Investment'.[22] In the view of the authors, there is no basis in the language of the ECT to impose such a requirement. Rather, the notion that early measures and steps in preparation for the construction of a pipeline could suffice to establish an 'Investment' finds support in the broad 'Investment' definition in Article 1(6) ECT, as well as in the above-mentioned Understanding No. 2 with respect to 1(5) ECT. The following observations can be made in this regard.

First, in addition to providing that 'every kind of asset' is capable of being recognised as an 'Investment' (including, e.g., 'claims to money and claims to performance pursuant to contract having an economic value and associated with an Investment'), Article 1(6) ECT states that '"Investment" refers to any investment *associated with* an Economic Activity in the Energy Sector [...].'[23] It could be argued already on this basis that measures such as entering into contracts concerning, e.g., research on the environmental effects of a pipeline project, as well as early design-related issues, are 'Investment[s]', as they are 'associated with' an Economic Activity in the Energy Sector, namely the construction of a pipeline.

Second, as for the aforementioned Understanding No. 2 on the meaning of 'Economic Activity in the Energy Sector', the list of 'illustrative' examples provides that

---

20. K. Hobér, *supra* n. 9, at p. 132.
21. *Ibid.*, at p. 135.
22. *See*, e.g., *Chevron Corporation (U.S.A.) and Texaco Petroleum Corporation (U.S.A.) v. Republic of Ecuador II*, PCA Case No. 2009-23, Third Interim Award on Jurisdiction and Admissibility, 27 February 2012, at para. 4.13, and *Plama Consortium Ltd v. Republic of Bulgaria*, ICSID Case No. ARB/3/24, Decision on Jurisdiction, 8 February 2005, at para. 128.
23. Emphasis added.

the 'construction of facilities' for the transmission of gas through a pipeline, as well as measures such as 'research, consulting, planning, management and design activities *related to the activities mentioned above*'[24] (i.e., *inter alia*, the construction of a pipeline) in and of themselves qualify as 'Economic Activity in the Energy Sector'. Hence, such activities would not only be '*associated* with an Economic Activity in the Energy Sector'[25] but would be a direct investment into such an activity, providing further support to the proposition that such measures are capable of being recognised as 'Investment[s]'.

Thus, considering that measures such as 'research, consulting, planning, management and design activities' will generally have been taken before a permit application is filed, 'Investment[s]' in an underwater pipeline project capable of protection under the ECT may have been made already before a permit is obtained.

In turn, this would mean that there could be a basis for the investor to launch a claim against an ECT Contracting Party, in whose 'Area' the pipeline is to be placed, in cases where the investor has been subjected to unfair treatment in connection with the application process.

Notably, however, it has been suggested that 'studies, visits, the opening up of development offices or negotiations' carried out before the investor has obtained a 'right conferred by law or contract or by virtue of any licenses and permits granted pursuant to law to undertake any Economic Activity in the Energy Sector'[26] are 'business development risk, which falls under the pre-investment regime'.[27] As noted by the same author, however:

> Given the very expansive concept of investment [...] and the typically long lead-time from first contact to start-up of a commercial operation, with the many steps in between, it will be quite difficult to distinguish clearly the two phases and their legal treatment. A restrictive approach would use the establishment of a productive operation as the threshold, where pre-investment business development, undertaken at the risk of the investor, converts into a completed investment falling under the Treaty's protection. *This view, however, does not do justice to the long sequence of increasingly capital-intensive activities by which an investment incrementally matures*; companies, for example in energy exploration and development, will carry out desk studies, in situ investigations, preliminary drilling, intensive drilling, appraisal and, finally, move to feasibility studies and erection of plant, testing and producing from it. *Each stage involves an investment, i.e. a risky, long-term oriented commitment of money which is done, as the investment increases, with increasing need of confidence in the legal stability of the operation.* This modern notion of investment is reflected in Article 1(6) [...].[28]

Considering the wording of Article 1(6) (in particular the part clarifying that ''Investment' refers to any investment associated with an Economic Activity in the

---

24. Emphasis added.
25. Emphasis added.
26. Article 1(6)(f) ECT.
27. *See* T.W. Wälde; 'Chapter 13. International Investment under the 1994 Energy Charter Treaty', in T.W. Wälde (ed.), *The Energy Charter Treaty: An East-West Gateway for Investment and Trade*, Kluwer International, 1996, pp. 251–320, at p. 280.
28. *Ibid.*, at pp. 279f.

Energy Sector'), together with the fact that 'research, consulting, planning, manage-ment and design activities [...]' can themselves qualify as 'Economic Activity in the Energy Sector',[29] there is arguably no basis for concluding categorically that 'studies, visits, the opening up of development offices or negotiations' carried out in the early stages of a project would fall under the pre-investment regime. Rather, each measure taken during the initial phase of a project must be individually analysed to determine whether the requirements of an 'Investment' are met in the circumstances. In the authors' view, measures relating to early-stage research and design of the pipeline, which may be necessary, *inter alia*, for the purpose of applying for a permit, may indeed qualify as 'Investment[s]' under the ECT.

In order for an investor to establish that a protected 'Investment' has come into existence before a permit is obtained, it may be worth considering also other support-ing circumstances. This may include arguments based on Article 1(6)(f) ECT, which stipulates that '*any right conferred by law or contract* or by virtue of any licences and permits granted pursuant to law *to undertake any Economic Activity in the Energy Sector*'[30] is to be considered an 'asset' capable of being recognised as an 'Investment'.

Certain rights relating to the laying down of pipelines on the seabed within the continental shelf/EEZ of coastal states are provided for in UNCLOS. Below, we will discuss whether such rights, depending on the circumstances, may suffice to establish the existence of an 'Investment' pursuant to Article 1(6)(f) ECT.

[B]   May 'Rights' under UNCLOS Constitute an 'Investment' under the ECT?[31]

Article 79(1) UNCLOS stipulates that '[a]ll States are *entitled* to lay submarine cables and pipelines on the continental shelf, in accordance with the provisions of [Article 79]'. The provision establishes a right for all UNCLOS states to lay submarine pipelines (and cables) on the continental shelf of other states, which is conditioned only by (i) the coastal state's right to take reasonable measures for the exploration of the continental shelf, the exploitation of its natural resources and the prevention and the reduction and control of pollution from pipelines pursuant to Article 79(2) and (ii) the requirement of the coastal state's consent to the delineation of the course for the pipeline pursuant to Article 79(3).[32] UNCLOS thus provides for a 'right' under public

---

29. *See* the above-mentioned Understanding No. 2 with respect to Art. 1(5) ECT.
30. Emphasis added.
31. Where the investor is a state-owned entity, it may also be considered whether 'rights' relevant to the existence of an 'Investment' could be derived from the ECT transit provisions (Art. 7 ECT). It appears unlikely, however, that an ECT tribunal would find that the ECT transit provisions provide obligations and rights relating to the laying down of submarine pipelines derogating from those set forth in UNCLOS.
32. *See* D. Langlet, 'Nord Stream, the Environment and the Law: Disentangling a Multijurisdictional Energy Project', *Scandinavian Studies in Law*, 59, 2014, pp. 79–108, at pp. 86f. Although the *delineation* of the course for the pipeline is indeed subject to the coastal state's consent, it should be emphasised that pursuant to Art. 300 UNCLOS, the coastal state has to exercise that right in good faith and in a manner which would not constitute an abuse of rights.

international law to lay down pipelines on the continental shelf of other UNCLOS states.[33]

On the face of it, the rights under UNCLOS appear to be granted only to the state parties to the convention. However, the term 'States' is to be given a broad meaning, encompassing not only the states themselves but also their nationals.[34] Thus, although an 'Investor' under the ECT cannot be a state party to UNCLOS,[35] an investor may rely on the rights conferred by UNCLOS to lay down pipelines on the continental shelf/EEZ of a state party to UNCLOS.

The issue to be considered is whether this 'right' may constitute an 'Investment' within the meaning of Article 1(6) ECT. More specifically, the relevant question is whether a right under UNCLOS to lay down pipelines on the continental shelf/EEZ may constitute a 'right' under Article 1(6)(f) ECT, i.e., a 'right conferred by law or contract [...] to undertake any Economic Activity in the Energy Sector'.[36] For reasons already addressed above, the latter part of the requirement – that the right must relate to an 'Economic Activity in the Energy Sector' – should reasonably be met.

It, therefore, remains to determine whether the right under UNCLOS to lay down pipelines on the continental shelf/EEZ is 'conferred by law or contract' within the meaning of Article 1(6)(f) ECT.

Although UNCLOS is an international 'convention', a convention is indeed a 'contract' between states. Applying the principles of treaty interpretation described above, including the starting point of focusing on the 'ordinary meaning' of the text of the treaty, it could thus be argued that rights under UNCLOS are indeed 'right[s] conferred by [...] contract'.[37] A potential objection against such an argument could be that a 'right *conferred* by contract',[38] at least when read in conjunction with the first sentence of Article 1(6) ECT ('... every kind of asset, *owned or controlled* directly or indirectly *by an Investor* ...'),[39] suggests that the contract at issue must have been

---

33. With respect to the EEZ, Art. 58(1) UNCLOS stipulates that 'all States' enjoy the 'freedoms [...] of laying down submarine cables and pipelines'. However, the freedoms in Art. 58(1) are 'subject to relevant provisions of this Convention', which for the laying of pipelines are the provisions of Art. 79. Thus, Art. 79 UNCLOS will apply regardless of the distinction between the continental shelf and the EEZ. See A. Proelss, 'Article 58: Rights and Duties of Other States in the Exclusive Economic Zone', in A. Proelss (ed.), *United Nations Convention on the Law of the Sea: A Commentary*, Hart Publishing, C.H. Beck Verlag, Nomos Verlagsgeschellschaft, 2017, pp. 449f.

34. *See* D.R. Burnett, R.C. Beckman & T.M. Davenport, *Submarine Cables: The Handbook of Law and Policy*, Martinus Nijhoff Publishers, 2014, pp. 79f.; and D.J. Englender, 'Article 79: Submarine Cables and Pipelines on the Continental Shelf', in A. Proelss (ed.), *supra* n. 33, at p. 623.

35. Cf. Art. 1(7) ECT.

36. It must be recalled, however, that the assets listed in Art. 1(6) ECT are mere examples of assets qualifying as 'Investment[s]' under the ECT. Accordingly, whether the right under UNCLOS to lay down pipelines on the continental shelf/EEZ may constitute an Investment under the ECT does not necessarily hinge on the list of examples set out in Art. 1(6)(f).

37. *See* e.g., Cambridge Dictionary, in which a 'contract' is defined as 'a legal document that states and explains a formal agreement between two different people or groups, or the agreement itself' and a 'convention' as 'a formal agreement between country leaders, politicians, and states on a matter that involves them all'.

38. Emphasis added.

39. Emphasis added.

entered into by the investor itself (which is obviously not the case with UNCLOS). However, such an argument would be difficult to reconcile with the fact that rights 'conferred by law' are also covered by Article 1(6)(f) ECT. On balance, therefore, a right conferred under an international convention such as UNCLOS should reasonably be considered as a 'right conferred by [...] contract' within the meaning of Article 1(6)(f) ECT.

One commentator has noted that the question of whether a right pursuant to Article 1(6)(f) ECT has come into existence depends on the legal status of that right. The commentator furthermore appears to suggest that there is a distinction to be made between, on the one hand, the situation where an investor has signed a document containing a legally binding right to undertake an Economic Activity in the Energy Sector (a 'contract'), and, on the other hand, the situation where the right is conferred merely 'by law'. In the first situation, the contract itself may represent an independent value for the investor capable of qualifying as an 'Investment', and even pre-contractual rights may constitute 'Investments' if such rights are 'created effectively under the law [...] and [...] [have] some financial value ("asset")' for the foreign investor. As for 'right[s] conferred by law', the commentator adds that such a right may also qualify as an 'Investment', but only provided that 'the investor has acted and committed resources' in reliance of such right.[40] Since it is difficult to say that a right conferred by law has a financial value to an individual or entity unless the individual or entity has, at least in some manner, 'acted and committed resources' relating to such right, there seems to be merit to this proposition.

With respect to the rights conferred by UNCLOS, they are indeed of a character unlikely to represent 'independent' financial value to an investor, in the same manner, that a contract signed by the investor may represent. Therefore, it is not unlikely that an ECT tribunal would require the potential investor to have, at least to *some* extent, 'acted and committed resources' in reliance of the UNCLOS rights, in order to characterise such UNCLOS rights as 'rights' under Article 1(6)(f) ECT. Notably, however, 'acts and committing of resources' would not necessarily have to include entering into contracts with third parties. Rather, resources committed internally to prepare for the permit application, or work on the design of the contemplated pipeline, would arguably also suffice.

In summary, rights under UNCLOS have the potential to qualify as 'rights conferred by law or contract' under Article 1(6)(f) ECT. It is likely, however, that an arbitral tribunal would require some concrete steps to have been taken by the investor in reliance of such rights and in pursuing a project. Since such steps will normally have been taken once a permit application is submitted, an investor in a project concerning the laying down of an underwater gas pipeline on the continental shelf/EEZ of a state party to the ECT will generally be fairly well-positioned to argue that an 'Investment' has already been made before a permit has been granted.

---

40. *See* T.W. Wälde, *supra* n. 27, at p. 272.

§7.04 CONCLUSION

It would seem beyond doubt that an underwater gas pipeline laid down on the continental shelf or EEZ of an ECT Member State is located within the 'Area' of the state, as required in order for an 'Investment' to be protected under the ECT. It would seem equally clear that the transmission of gas by means of an underwater pipeline, as well as the construction of the pipeline, constitute an 'Economic Activity in the Energy Sector' pursuant to Article 1(5) ECT. It follows that investments associated with such activities are capable of being recognised as 'Investment[s]' pursuant to Article 1(6) ECT.

Depending on the preparatory measures and steps taken by the Investor in advance of its permit application, there are compelling reasons in favour of the position that a pipeline project is, as a matter of principle, capable of reaching the point where an 'Investment' has already been made before a permit is obtained. For example, the Understanding with respect to Article 1(5) ECT clarifies that 'research, consulting, planning, management and design activities' related to, *inter alia*, the construction of an underwater gas pipeline constitutes 'Economic Activity in the Energy Sector'. Thus, an investment in such an activity, such as entering into contracts concerning 're-search', 'consulting' or 'design' in preparation for a permit application, would arguably qualify as an 'Investment' in accordance with the ordinary meaning of those terms.

It appears, however, more uncertain whether the right to lay down underwater pipelines on the continental shelf/EEZ pursuant to UNCLOS, when considered in isolation, constitutes a 'right conferred by law or contract' within the meaning of Article 1(6)(f) ECT. However, considering the preparatory steps and measures that investors will generally have taken before submitting a permit application, investors will often be in a fairly good position to argue that an 'Investment' has been established on the basis of Article 1(6)(f) – even in cases where contracts with third parties, enabling the investor to establish an investment under Article 1(6)(c), may not yet have been signed.

If the investor succeeds in establishing that an 'Investment' protected by the ECT has come into existence before a permit is obtained, this may have important implications in instances where the investor is subjected to unfair, unreasonable or discriminatory treatment in connection with the permit application process. Instead of having to resort to possible remedies under domestic law before the courts of the host state, the investor would be protected under the ECT and may submit its claim(s) arising out of such treatment to international arbitration.

Thus, and in conclusion, an investor preparing to embark on a project involving the laying down of an underwater gas pipeline on the continental shelf/EEZ passing through one or several ECT Member States is wise to carefully document any and all steps involving committing resources, entering into contracts and spending time (even internal time) on researching, planning and designing the pipeline to demonstrate that the project should enjoy the 'Investment' protection status of the treaty.

CHAPTER 8

Execution of Arbitral Awards Against Sovereign Wealth Fund Assets: Enforcement Against States and the Supreme Court's Decision in *Ascom*

*Maria Fogdestam Agius & Ginta Ahrel**

§8.01   INTRODUCTION

A party alighting victorious from arbitration realises soon enough that if payment is not forthcoming, the award will only be as effective as its opportunities for being enforced. If the award is against a sovereign State – as it commonly will be in investment treaty arbitration – this complicates things. Enforcing in the respondent State's jurisdiction may present difficulties. However, the competence of foreign courts and authorities to enforce the award is subject to the respondent's sovereign immunity. An award creditor seeking to enforce its claim against a sovereign State must, therefore, not only ensure the recognition of its title to execution in a jurisdiction that is the location of suitable assets but must also ensure that these assets are not protected by State immunity.

In November 2021, the Swedish Supreme Court (the 'Swedish Supreme Court' or 'Court') issued an important clarification of the law on sovereign immunity from execution in *Ascom and Others v. Republic of Kazakhstan and National Bank of*

* The authors' law firm is representing Ascom and others in the Swedish enforcement proceedings discussed in this article. The views expressed herein are those of the authors only and do not necessarily correspond to the views of any of their affiliations, the firm of Westerberg & Partners or any of its clients.

Kazakhstan (the '*Ascom*' case).[1] Adhering to the restrictive theory of sovereign immunity in respect of enforcement measures, the Court acknowledged the legitimate interest of an award debtor to have the award satisfied and denied immunity from execution of assets held for purposes of general State saving and investment. The decision confirms that Sweden is a favourable jurisdiction for the enforcement of arbitral awards against States.

The Court's decision arose in an enforcement action in Sweden, brought by Moldovan investors seeking payment under an arbitral award against the Republic of Kazakhstan. The award was given in 2013, in an arbitration under the Energy Charter Treaty (ECT).[2] A Stockholm-seated tribunal operating under the rules of the Arbitration Institute of the Stockholm Chamber of Commerce (SCC) found Kazakhstan liable for breaches of the fair and equitable treatment standard under the ECT and awarded damages of close to USD 500 million plus interest for Kazakhstan's seizure in 2010 of the investors' petroleum and gas operations in Kazakhstan. Enforcement action ensued in numerous jurisdictions, including Belgium, the Netherlands and Sweden.

In 2018, at the investors' request, the Swedish Enforcement Agency seized assets in the form of shares in listed Swedish corporations valued at approximately USD 90 million. These assets formed part of a savings portfolio[3] of the National Fund of Kazakhstan (NFK), a sovereign wealth fund (SWF) owned by the Kazakh Finance Ministry but placed under management by the National Bank of Kazakhstan (NBK). Kazakhstan and NBK challenged the seizure, arguing, *inter alia*, that the funds belonged to the NBK – its central bank – and therefore enjoyed immunity.

The District Court upheld the Enforcement Agency's decision to seize the assets to satisfy the award. Upon appeal, the Svea Court of Appeal found that the assets were indeed protected by sovereign immunity based on its finding that the assets were the property of a central bank and consequently could not be seized.[4] The Swedish Supreme Court granted leave to appeal in respect of the issue of whether sovereign immunity barred execution against the seized assets and found, overruling the Court of Appeal on this issue, that this was not the case. Accordingly, the Court concluded that

---

1. *Ascom Group S.A. and Others v. Republic of Kazakhstan and National Bank of Kazakhstan,* Sweden, Supreme Court, Case No. Ö 3828-20, Decision, 18 November 2021.
2. *Anatolie Stati, Gabriel Stati, Ascom Group S.A. and Terra Raf Trans Traiding Ltd. v. Republic of Kazakhstan,* SCC Case No. V 116/2010, Award, 19 December 2013.
3. A Decree of the President of the Republic of Kazakhstan No. 385 on the Concept for Creating and Using Funds of the Republic of Kazakhstan's National Fund, 8 December 2016 ('Decree No. 385'), establishes that the NFK shall have two portfolios: a stabilisation portfolio capped at USD 10 billion, with the aim of maintaining an adequate level of liquidity for the fund, and a savings portfolio, with the aim of accumulating and preserving funds generated through the sale of non-renewable energy for future generations to ensure long-term returns with an appropriate level of risk. Excess funds of the stabilisation portfolio are transferred to the savings portfolio and funds of the savings portfolio can be transferred to the stabilisation portfolio. Only funds from the stabilisation portfolio may be withdrawn to boost the government budget and meet public expenses.
4. The ownership of the shares remains contentious. At the time of writing, this issue is still being examined by the Svea Court of Appeal, to which the case was remanded following the Swedish Supreme Court's decision.

execution could take place on the condition that certain criteria under Swedish execution law were met.[5]

This article analyses the Swedish Supreme Court's decision in the *Ascom* case in light of public international law and the comparative jurisprudence of national courts from other jurisdictions.

The precedent set by the Court in the *Ascom* case provides useful guidance to any party seeking to enforce an arbitral award against a sovereign entity through execution in Sweden. The decision is, however, also of wider interest, being one of the first in international jurisprudence that explicitly addresses SWF assets under central bank management. SWFs are ambiguous investment vehicles with both public and private characteristics. As a result, they are poorly understood in the context of sovereign immunity. SWFs and their property have been considered to exist in an 'international law black hole'.[6] The article will therefore focus particularly on the immunity of SWFs and the effect of management arrangements involving central banks.

The extent to which States recognise enhanced immunity to central bank property differs considerably.[7] In particular, the legal effect of various arrangements to place SWF assets under central bank management has so far been uncertain.[8] By weighing in on this issue, the Court has arguably contributed significantly to the development of the law in this field.

§8.02 SWFS UNDER INTERNATIONAL LAW

Over the past few decades, States have increasingly used SWFs as vehicles to manage their excess funds. As a result, SWFs are now major participants in the global financial markets.[9]

However, this is not without its problems. SWFs are sparsely regulated. Although they are subject to a certain degree of self-regulation through the so-called Santiago

---

5. The case was remanded to the Svea Court of Appeal to address these criteria, discussed in the footnote immediately above. As a result of the finding of sovereign immunity, the Court of Appeal for reasons of judicial economy did not consider these criteria.
6. *See* Shu Shang & Wei Shen, *When the State Sovereign Immunity Rule Meets Sovereign Wealth Funds in the Post Financial Crisis Era: Is There Still a Black Hole in International Law* (2018) 31 Leiden Journal of International Law 915 ('Shang and Shen, *When the State Sovereign Immunity Rule Meets Sovereign Wealth Funds*').
7. *See*, generally, Ingrid Wuerth, *Immunity from Execution of Central Bank Assets*, in: The Cambridge Handbook of Immunities and International Law, ed. Ruys, Angelet and Ferro (Cambridge University Press, 2019) 266 ('Wuerth, *Immunity from Execution of Central Bank Assets*').
8. *See* Wuerth, *Immunity from Execution of Central Bank Assets*, n. 103 ('The extent to which a state can protect the assets of sovereign wealth funds by administering them through their central bank is unclear. The purposes and functions of the sovereign wealth funds differ somewhat from those of central banks.').
9. *See* Victorino J. Tejera, *The U.S. Law Regime of Sovereign Immunity and the Sovereign Wealth Funds* (2016) 25 University of Miami Business Law Review 1 ('Tejera, *The U.S. Law Regime of Sovereign Immunity and the Sovereign Wealth Funds*'), p. 7.

Principles,[10] there is no general regulation of SWFs under international law. Moreover, their treatment in national and international jurisprudence varies to a large degree.

Arguably, this is (at least in part) a result of the fact that there is no common design for SWFs. Historically, SWFs were set up to: (i) manage surplus revenue from, for example, the extraction of natural resources such as oil and gas; (ii) diversify the economy of States overly dependent on singular commodities; and (iii) ensure inter-generational equality in the benefits to the population from natural resources (i.e., that current generations do not deplete such assets without ensuring that also future generations benefit from the gains therefrom).[11] The first SWF was established by Kuwait already in 1953.[12] In the decades that followed, a limited number of other resource-rich countries followed suit and pursued ways to invest excess revenue and foreign exchange reserves.[13] Over time, countries with large foreign exchange reserves began using SWFs to hedge currency risk as well as generate equity returns as opposed to fixed income returns.[14] Since 2000, the use of SWFs has spread considerably.

SWFs may generally be understood as special purpose investment funds or arrangements owned by the government.[15] SWFs hold, manage, and/or administer assets to achieve financial objectives, and employ a set of investment strategies to do so, including investing in foreign financial assets.[16] However, SWFs may be set up in quite diverse ways. While it is common to speak of SWFs as 'investment vehicles'[17] which may be set up as entities endowed with separate legal personality, either in incorporated form or functioning as an instrumentality of the State, SWFs may also be virtually formless and consist merely of a pool of assets owned or managed directly or indirectly by governments, government agencies or central banks.[18]

SWFs are publicly funded and therefore composed of wealth raised through sovereign activities. Such activities may include the accumulation of foreign exchange reserves or balance of payments surpluses, privatisations of public entities, collection

---

10. International Working Group of Sovereign Wealth Funds, *Generally Accepted Principles and Practices* ('Santiago Principles'), October 2008. *See* further Régis Bismuth, *The 'Santiago Principles' for Sovereign Wealth Funds: The Shortcomings and the Futility of Self-Regulation* (2017) EUROPEAN BUSINESS LAW REVIEW 69.
11. *See* Hussein Haeri, Yarik Kryvoi, Camilla Gambarini and Robert Kovacs, *Sovereign Wealth Funds: Transnational Regulation and Dispute Resolution*, WITHERS LLP/BRITISH INSTITUTE OF INTERNATIONAL AND COMPARATIVE LAW, September 2021 ('Haeri et al., *Sovereign Wealth Funds: Transnational Regulation and Dispute Resolution*'), pp. 10–11.
12. *See* website of the Kuwait Investment Authority, available at: http://www.kia.gov.kw.
13. *See* EU Commission, *A Common European Approach to Sovereign Wealth Funds*, Communication from the Commission to the European Parliament, the Council, the European Economic and Social Committee and the Committee of the Regions, 27 February 2008, COM(2008) 115 ('*Common European Approach to Sovereign Wealth Funds*'), p. 2.
14. Tejera, *The U.S. Law Regime of Sovereign Immunity and the Sovereign Wealth Funds*, p. 10.
15. *See Santiago Principles*, p. 27 (Appendix I. Defining Sovereign Wealth Funds).
16. *See Santiago Principles*, p. 27 (Appendix I. Defining Sovereign Wealth Funds).
17. *See*, e.g., *Common European Approach to Sovereign Wealth Funds*, p. 2.
18. *See*, e.g., Adrian Blundell-Wignall, Yu-Wei Hu and Juan Yermo, *Sovereign Wealth and Pension Fund Issues*, OECD WORKING PAPERS ON INSURANCE AND PRIVATE PENSIONS No. 14, January 2008. In 2008, approximately half of SWFs were established as pools of assets whereas the other half were set up as entities endowed with separate legal personality. *See* Cornelia Hammer, Peter Kunzel and Iva Petrova, *Sovereign Wealth Funds: Current Institutional and Operational Practices*, IMF WORKING PAPER No. WP/08/254, November 2008, p. 4.

of tax, granting of concessions and earnings from commodity exports and natural resource exploitation.[19] Although SWFs regularly are kept under State ownership and control,[20] they are usually managed separately from the official reserves of the State[21] as well as from the official reserves of central banks or monetary authorities.[22] The funds are invested domestically or internationally, with a long-term investment outlook and with the chief objective of generating returns.[23]

SWFs clearly engage in commercial activities by investing directly or indirectly in a wide range of asset classes, such as shares and securities, fixed income, structured products, private equity, real estate, hedge funds and derivatives for the purpose of optimising their portfolios and hedging unwanted risks. Through SWFs, States have thus come to engage in transactions in international financial markets very different from commercial operations of the kind that States have traditionally engaged in.[24]

The dual status of SWFs as commercial investors in financial markets and State-controlled entities has led to some uncertainty as to whether SWFs are protected by sovereign immunity from execution.[25] It has often been assumed that SWFs should enjoy immunity from execution.[26] However, the limited jurisprudence that exists on this issue is diverse and there are known examples where execution has been ordered against SWFs.[27] For example, in 2019, the Paris Court of Appeal denied immunity to two Libyan SWFs on the basis that the assets were not used or intended to be used for governmental non-commercial purposes.[28] Moreover, in certain jurisdictions, the

---

19. See *Santiago Principles*, p. 27 (Appendix I. Defining Sovereign Wealth Funds). *See also* Locknie Hsu, *Sovereign Wealth Funds: Investors in Search of an Identity in the Twenty-First Century* (2015) INTERNATIONAL REVIEW OF LAW 1 ('Hsu, *Sovereign Wealth Funds: Investors in Search of an Identity*'), p. 5.
20. See Haeri et al., *Sovereign Wealth Funds: Transnational Regulation and Dispute Resolution*, p. 11.
21. See *Common European Approach to Sovereign Wealth Funds*, p. 3.
22. See Tejera, *The U.S. Law Regime of Sovereign Immunity and the Sovereign Wealth Funds*, p. 10.
23. See Haeri et al., *Sovereign Wealth Funds: Transnational Regulation and Dispute Resolution*, p. 11.
24. See Tejera, *The U.S. Law Regime of Sovereign Immunity and the Sovereign Wealth Funds*, p. 7; *see also* Joel Slawotsky, *Sovereign Wealth Funds and Jurisdiction under the FSIA* (2009) 11 UNIVERSITY OF PENNSYLVANIA JOURNAL OF BUSINESS LAW 967 ('Slawotsky, *Sovereign Wealth Funds and Jurisdiction under the FSIA*'), pp. 976–977 (noting that whereas SWFs traditionally invested their assets in conservative investments, SWFs today have come to develop a greater appetite for risk, shifting, e.g., towards investments in flagship international corporations and stakes in global businesses in a variety of sectors).
25. See Tejera, *The U.S. Law Regime of Sovereign Immunity and the Sovereign Wealth Funds*, pp. 16–17; Slawotsky, *Sovereign Wealth Funds and Jurisdiction under the FSIA*, p. 996.
26. See, e.g., Claire Milhench, *Kazakhstan's frozen billions sound alarm for sovereign funds*, REUTERS, 20 February 2018; Abdullah Al-Hassan et al., *Sovereign Wealth Funds: Aspects of Governance Structures and Investment Management*, IMF WORKING PAPER No. WP/13/231, November 2013, p. 9.
27. See Haeri et al., *Sovereign Wealth Funds: Transnational Regulation and Dispute Resolution*, p. 34.
28. See *Société Mohamed Abdel Moshen Al-Kharafi et Fils v. Société Libyan Investment Authority and Société Libyan Arab Foreign Investment Company*, Paris Court of Appeal, Case No. 18/17592, 5 September 2019. The French enforcement action arises out of a substantial award rendered against Libya, awarding USD 935 million plus interest in damages, *see Mohamed Abdulmohsen Al-Kharafi & Sons Co. v. the State of Libya and Others*, Award, 22 March 2013.

extent of SWF immunity may vary depending on its structure, as funds organised in different ways may be treated differently under domestic law.[29]

The immunity of States and State entities is generally determined based on the nature of the conduct in which the State has engaged. A key distinction in this respect is that between *acta jure imperii* (acts that only a sovereign entity is capable of undertaking) and *acta jure gestionis* (acts that any private party could equally undertake). By contrast, State immunity from execution is governed primarily by for what purpose the property against which execution is sought is used or intended to be used.[30] In the context of SWFs, this has led to considerable uncertainty, as SWF assets are used or intended for different purposes. Some may be created to achieve certain national objectives while others may buy, hold and sell securities and assets on behalf of their citizenry but ultimately in the pursuit of generating profit (with little or no direct connection with sovereign purposes).

SWFs themselves may have contributed to this uncertainty. SWFs are often prone to underline their commercial (rather than sovereign) nature to avoid burdensome investment screenings motivated by suspicions about foreign State interference.[31] A guiding objective of the Santiago Principles is that SWF investments should be made solely on the basis of economic and financial considerations and not further political objectives. The Santiago Principles further provide that SWFs must have a sound governance structure, which ensures that the fund is operationally independent and that investment decisions and operations are free of political influence.[32] At the same time, SWFs or their owner States have sometimes asserted immunity in enforcement actions on the basis that the purpose and activity of SWFs are inextricably linked to the fulfilment of public functions and core economic sovereign responsibilities.[33]

Some SWFs have very clearly defined goals and manage assets that are earmarked for special expenditures. This may include macroeconomic stabilisation schemes, programmes to guarantee the State's future wealth and offset the effects of dwindling natural resources, pension schemes, plans for regional development or

---

29. *See*, generally, e.g., Tejera, *The U.S. Law Regime of Sovereign Immunity and the Sovereign Wealth Funds*.

30. *See* August Reinisch, *European Court Practice Concerning State Immunity from Enforcement Measures* (2006) 17 EUROPEAN JOURNAL OF INTERNATIONAL LAW 803 ('Reinisch, *European Court Practice Concerning State Immunity from Enforcement Measures*'), p. 807.

31. *See further* Shang and Shen, *When the State Sovereign Immunity Rule Meets Sovereign Wealth Funds*, p. 932 (describing ways in which SWFs may pursue political rather than economic goals in host States). *See also* Slawotsky, *Sovereign Wealth Funds and Jurisdiction under the FSIA*, pp. 967, 980 and 986.

32. *See* Tejera, *The U.S. Law Regime of Sovereign Immunity and the Sovereign Wealth Funds*, p. 11; *Santiago Principles*, p. 27 (Appendix I. Defining Sovereign Wealth Funds).

33. *See* Slawotsky, *Sovereign Wealth Funds and Jurisdiction under the FSIA*, p. 1000 ('SWFs will likely argue that the SWFs' activity is inextricably linked with basic essential public functions, and therefore, the nature of their activity is the same as the purpose – a sovereign governmental function.'); *but cf.* Tejera, *The U.S. Law Regime of Sovereign Immunity and the Sovereign Wealth Funds*, pp. 22–24. *See* moreover Wuerth, *Immunity from Execution of Central Bank Assets*, n. 103 (observing, with reference to *AIG v. Kazakhstan*, discussed below, that where courts emphasise the overall purpose of SWF funds, there is a better chance at such funds enjoying immunity from execution).

industrialisation, and similar strategic and political objectives.[34] Others, however, are intended to manage funds for uses not yet defined and have no particular assigned purpose beyond generating returns and diversifying assets. SWFs may serve a number of these potential objectives at the same time, and it is not always easy to attribute a particular objective to a particular fund.[35] Because the objectives, structures and management models are so diverse, one must evaluate, in each individual case, 'whether the nature of the SWF's conduct really reflects a basic governmental duty to its citizens'.[36]

The matter is not only of academic interest. In the context of enforcement, award creditors with claims against States have begun to view SWFs with increasing attention due to their wealth, accessibility and ambiguous nature.[37] At the same time, for the past twenty years, there has been a notable surge in the establishment of SWFs. The number of SWFs has increased from around 20 worldwide in the year 2000 to more than 140 as of today.[38] The assets currently under management by SWFs are estimated to be around USD 10 trillion.[39] SWF assets increased by over 200% between 2008 and 2021, according to a report published in 2021.[40] When compared with reports from the late 2010s, it is suggested that assets held by SWFs have increased sharply even in the last few years.[41] With SWFs accounting for about one-tenth of the world's total assets

---

34. *See* Tejera, *The U.S. Law Regime of Sovereign Immunity and the Sovereign Wealth Funds*, p. 11; Haeri et al., *Sovereign Wealth Funds: Transnational Regulation and Dispute Resolution*, pp. 10–11.
35. *See* Slawotsky, *Sovereign Wealth Funds and Jurisdiction under the FSIA*, p. 981 (accounting for five types of SWFs identified by the International Monetary Fund: stabilisation funds, savings funds, reserve investment corporations, development funds and contingent pension reserve funds) and 999 ('SWFs may have more than one purpose: These objectives may be multiple, overlapping, or changing over time.').
36. Slawotsky, *Sovereign Wealth Funds and Jurisdiction under the FSIA*, p. 1000, *see also* at p. 981 ('Courts will need to examine the purpose of the SWF to determine whether a claim of sovereign ownership is colorable or merely a label invoked to avoid liability.').
37. *See* Tejera, *The U.S. Law Regime of Sovereign Immunity and the Sovereign Wealth Funds*, p. 16; Anne-Catherine Hahn, *State Immunity and Veil Piercing in the Age of Sovereign Wealth Funds* (2012) 2 Swiss Review of Business and Financial Market Law 103 ('Hahn, *State Immunity and Veil Piercing in the Age of Sovereign Wealth Funds*'), p. 105.
38. Haeri et al., *Sovereign Wealth Funds: Transnational Regulation and Dispute Resolution*, pp. 11–12. The Sovereign Wealth Fund Institute reports 143 SWFs, *see* at: https://www.swfinstitute.org/.
39. Shang and Shen, *When the State Sovereign Immunity Rule Meets Sovereign Wealth Funds*, p. 917, report that SWFs in the early 2000s managed approximately USD 0.5 billion, whereas in 2018, the assets under management were approximately USD 7 trillion. In December 2020, a practice note published for Herbert Smith Freehills by Andrew Cannon and Hanna Ambrose, *Dealing with Sovereign Wealth Funds: Immunity Concerns and Practical Steps to Mitigate Them*, estimated assets under management in SWFs across the world at USD 15 trillion. Haeri et al., *Sovereign Wealth Funds: Transnational Regulation and Dispute Resolution*, reported in September 2021, with reference to Global SWF listings, just over USD 10 trillion in assets under SWF management. A lack of transparency may contribute to the somewhat disparate reporting, but the trend towards considerable growth in managed assets is clear.
40. *See* Haeri et al., *Sovereign Wealth Funds: Transnational Regulation and Dispute Resolution*, p. 12.
41. *See* Tejera, *The U.S. Law Regime of Sovereign Immunity and the Sovereign Wealth Funds*, p. 7; Shang and Shen, *When the State Sovereign Immunity Rule Meets Sovereign Wealth Funds*, p. 917.

under management,[42] this category of State property is no doubt of increasing importance for the enforcement of investment awards.

A coinciding trend is that certain States have assigned the management of their SWFs to their monetary authorities.[43] The motivations for doing so are not clear, but it cannot be excluded that, at least in some instances, the objective is to shield these funds from enforcement on the basis of sovereign immunity. Whether or not merely assigning the management to, for example, a central bank is enough to confer immunity on SWF assets has long been unclear.[44] The Swedish Supreme Court's decision in *Ascom* has now offered a helpful clarification. Following a brief summary of the Court's findings in section §8.03, we highlight in section §8.04 the major points of precedent.

§8.03   THE *ASCOM* DECISION

In the *Ascom* case, the Swedish Supreme Court declared that enforcement may take place against SWF assets designed for the general management of State wealth.

When assessing whether the purpose of the State's possession of the property was of a qualified character – i.e., used for sovereign activities or similar acts of an official nature[45] – the Court held that 'long-term state saving for future needs – not yet defined – in itself cannot be regarded a sovereign activity'.[46] While accepting that SWF assets sometimes may relate to macroeconomic or monetary policy goals, the Court required a showing of a 'concrete and clear connection to a qualified purpose of sovereign character' to justify immunity.[47]

In this case, Kazakhstan and NBK had offered only 'very general' information about any future State purposes of the assets and the regulation of the NFK was not sufficiently concrete as to what those purposes might be. Furthermore, the seized assets – i.e., the listed shares – were not immediately available for unequivocally sovereign activities. They could only be allocated to finance sovereign activity following liquidation and transfers in multiple steps appropriating them to the State budget. In the Court's assessment, '[t]his connection cannot be regarded as sufficiently concrete to justify assets of this kind being covered by immunity'.[48]

Both sources, published in 2018, reported a total of USD 7 trillion in SWF assets. The estimates reported in 2021 suggest an increase of about 50% or more just in the last few years.

42. *See* Tejera, *The U.S. Law Regime of Sovereign Immunity and the Sovereign Wealth Funds*, p. 6.

43. *See Santiago Principles*, at pp. 11 and 15 (noting that certain SWFs are set up as pools of assets held by the central bank, naming, e.g., Chile, Norway, Timor-Leste and Trinidad and Tobago).

44. *See* Wuerth, *Immunity from Execution of Central Bank Assets*, n. 103, quoted above in fn 8. Cf. Tejera, *The U.S. Law Regime of Sovereign Immunity and the Sovereign Wealth Funds*, pp. 60–62.

45. This is what is required under the test devised by the Swedish Supreme Court in *Sedelmayer v. Russian Federation*, NJA 2011 p. 475 ('*Lidingöhuset*' or '*Sedelmayer*'), para. 14. For a discussion of the *Sedelmayer* case, *see* Pål Wrange's Case Note in (2012) 106 AMERICAN JOURNAL OF INTERNATIONAL LAW, pp. 347–353.

46. *Ascom*, paras 44–45 (unofficial translation from Swedish).

47. *Ascom*, paras 45–46.

48. *Ascom*, para. 46.

The Court accepted that the NBK functioned as the Kazakh central bank but found the scope of immunity for central bank property under customary international law to be unclear. The Court further stated that immunity from enforcement is not necessarily limited to property which the central bank legally owns or holds in its own name, but that immunity also should not extend to all assets that a central bank controls regardless of their use. Special protection for central banks is motivated by their monetary policy activities and, therefore, protection should be afforded only to funds that serve this purpose.[49] The Court found 'no clear support in customary international law' for any wider immunity for funds controlled by central banks and also found such wide immunity unjustified.[50] The seized property did not have the requisite connection to monetary policy, since the funds were used exclusively for wealth management on commercial terms. In the Court's view, their management did not constitute 'an instrument for the exercise of the National Bank's monetary policy functions' and 'could equally have been entrusted to a State entity without such a function'.[51]

§8.04   IMPLICATIONS OF THE *ASCOM* DECISION

[A]   Confirming the Restrictive Theory of Immunity from Execution

First, the *Ascom* decision confirms that the restrictive theory of immunity from execution applies in Sweden, in keeping with the attitude held today by most Western States.[52]

Under international law, State immunity from execution is distinct from immunity from jurisdiction. Even where a foreign court finds itself competent to adjudicate a claim against a sovereign, it is not necessarily competent to execute the same against the property of that State. Sovereign immunity from execution must be determined separately[53] and it remains the case that, generally, 'the immunity from enforcement enjoyed by States in regard to their property situated on foreign territory goes further than the jurisdictional immunity enjoyed by those same States before foreign courts'.[54]

The precise scope of immunity from execution afforded by States, however, varies considerably. As noted by the Spanish Constitutional Court in 1992: 'the degree

---

49. *See Ascom*, para. 23.
50. *Ascom*, para. 24.
51. *Ascom*, para. 41.
52. Cf. *Ascom*, paras 13 and 18.
53. *See Ascom*, para. 12. Cf. *Jurisdictional Immunities of the State (Germany v. Italy: Greece intervening)*, Judgment, I.C.J. Reports 2012, p. 99 (*'Jurisdictional Immunities'*), para. 113. *See also* Chester Brown & Roger O'Keefe, *Article 19*, in: The United Nations Convention on Jurisdictional Immunities of States and Their Property, ed. O'Keefe et al. (Oxford University Press, 2013) 308 (*'Brown and O'Keefe, Article 19'*), at p. 315 (referencing the legislation of several States).
54. *Jurisdictional Immunities*, para. 113; *see also Ascom*, at para. 12. *See further* Hazel Fox, QC and Philippa Webb, *The Law of State Immunity* (Revised and Updated 3rd ed., Oxford University Press, 2015) (*'Fox and Webb, The Law of State Immunity'*), pp. 484 et seq.; *see also* Reinisch, *European Court Practice Concerning State Immunity from Enforcement Measures*.

to which property held by a foreign State in the State of the forum [is considered immune from execution] varies from refusal to recognize even the slightest exception to immunity, on the one hand, to notably advanced positions which require that such property be unequivocally allocated to activities *jure imperii*, on the other'.[55]

The major jurisdictions have now embraced the so-called restrictive doctrine on State immunity in respect of both jurisdiction and enforcement,[56] and few States today recognise absolute immunity of foreign States from execution measures within their territory.[57] This is also the principle informing the 2004 United Nations Convention on Jurisdictional Immunities of States and Their Property (UNCSI or the 'Convention').[58]

As noted above, the restrictive doctrine distinguishes between acts performed in the exercise of sovereign authority, which are immune, and acts of a private or commercial nature, in respect of which the State may be subjected to the jurisdiction of national courts in foreign States. The distinction derives from an understanding that when a State enters the marketplace and acts commercially, it does not enjoy sovereign immunity in respect of those acts. Equally, when its property is used for commercial purposes, that property is not protected from execution measures through decisions by foreign courts.

As for measures of post-judgment constraint, such as attachment, arrest or execution, the UNCSI prescribes that States in connection with a proceeding before a court of another State may be subjected to such measures by the forum State's authorities in the circumstances described in Article 19 of the Convention.[59] Article 19(c) exempts from immunity property which the State uses for commercial purposes.[60]

The UNCSI is often used as a starting point for judicial analysis by domestic as well as international courts.[61] However, this instrument is not yet legally binding. In the 18 years since it was adopted, the Convention has attracted only 22 of the requisite 30 ratifications in order to be effective under its own terms and so has not entered into force. Sweden ratified the UNCSI in 2009 and has passed legislation which, once it

---

55. *Abbott v. Republic of South Africa*, Spain, Constitutional Court (Second Chamber), 1 July 1992, 113 INTERNATIONAL LAW REPORTS 411 ('*Abbott v. South Africa*'), p. 420.
56. *See* Fox and Webb, *The Law of State Immunity*, p. 487.
57. *See* Reinisch, *European Court Practice Concerning State Immunity from Enforcement Measures*, p. 804.
58. The UNCSI was adopted by the General Assembly of the United Nations on 2 December 2004. *See* United Nations General Assembly resolution 59/38.
59. Article 19 of the UNCSI allows for execution of a judgment or award against State property when the State has given its consent, when the State has earmarked property for the satisfaction of the claim, or when the property is used for commercial purposes.
60. Article 19(c) of the UNCSI allows for post-judgment measures of enforcement such as seizure and execution against State property specifically in use or intended for use by the State for other than government non-commercial purposes, if such property is located in the territory of the forum State and has a connection with the entity against which the proceeding was directed.
61. *See*, e.g., *Sedelmayer*, paras 12–14 (noting that the UNCSI is not in force, and not in all aspects a codification of customary international law, but nevertheless expresses certain commonly recognised principles). *See also Republic of Kazakhstan and the National Fund of Kazakhstan v. Ascom et al*, Svea Court of Appeal, ÖÄ 7709-19, Decision, 17 June 2020, p. 10.

enters into force, will incorporate the Convention into Swedish law.[62] Since the Swedish law on State immunity will not enter into force until the UNCSI does, sovereign immunity in Sweden is, at present, only regulated through customary international law.[63]

It is widely considered that the UNCSI only partially reflects customary international law.[64] Specifically, as to the status of Article 19(c), this provision gave rise to long and difficult discussions during the drafting process. State practice on immunity from execution remains diverse and the scope of the customary international law obligation to refrain from execution measures against States is not well-defined. In the 2012 *Jurisdictional Immunities* case, the International Court of Justice declined to decide 'whether all aspects of Article 19 reflect current customary international law'.[65] However, it confirmed that measures of constraint may be taken against property belonging to a foreign State, but only if the property is 'in use for an activity not pursuing government non-commercial purposes' (or the State has consented to execution or allocated property for satisfying the claim).[66] This statement preserves immunity for property used for sovereign activities and confirms the customary international law status of the rule that commercial State property may be subject to enforcement measures by other States.

The Swedish Supreme Court came to the same conclusion the year before, in the 2011 *Sedelmayer* case, where it applied 'the principle now recognised by many States that enforcement can take place at least in certain State-owned property, namely in property used for other than governmental non-commercial purposes'.[67] The Court declared that 'immunity from enforcement measures may be invoked at least in respect of property used for the official functions of a State'.[68] It was, however, quick to add that the rule 'should not be regarded as conferring immunity from measures of constraint already on the basis that the property in question is owned by a State and used by it for a non-commercial purpose'.[69] The Court instead set the bar higher, requiring that the property was in use or intended for use in connection with sovereign activity (i.e., *acta jure imperii*).

In *Ascom*, the Court referenced and elaborated on its stance in the *Sedelmayer* case,[70] confirming that Swedish courts apply a relatively high threshold for State

---

62. Sweden signed the Convention on 14 September 2005 and ratified it on 23 December 2009. On 10 December 2009, Sweden passed act (2009:1514) on the immunity of States and their property, incorporating the Convention into domestic law. The law will enter into force upon executive decision.
63. *See Ascom*, para. 16.
64. *See Sedelmayer*, para. 12.
65. *Jurisdictional Immunities*, para. 117.
66. *Jurisdictional Immunities*, para. 118.
67. *Sedelmayer*, para. 14. *See further* UNCSI, Art. 19(c).
68. *Sedelmayer*, para. 14.
69. *Sedelmayer*, para. 14.
70. *See Ascom*, para. 19.

immunity from execution and providing further guidance on what constitutes sovereign activity or 'official functions of a State'.[71]

[B]   Denying Immunity *Ipso Facto* for SWFs

Second, the Court declared that the fact that the seized assets formed part of a SWF did not, as such, affect whether they were immune from enforcement, thereby denying any categorical immunity to this class of State assets.[72] In other words, the very fact that the funds belong to the State or have been accumulated through sovereign activities does not confer immunity.

In confirming that State saving for future needs in itself is not a sovereign activity,[73] the Court overturned the decision of the Court of Appeal, which held that the management of State finances through a SWF should be regarded as *acta jure imperii* and that already on this ground should SWF property be immune.[74]

The Court also departed from similar views adopted by courts in the United Kingdom and the Netherlands. The Dutch Supreme Court held in a decision in late 2020 (pertaining to a related enforcement action but concerning a different Kazakh SWF, Samruk) that increasing the national prosperity of the State constitutes a sovereign purpose in itself.[75] Importantly, the Dutch court held that whether or not the funds were intended for public use had to be ascertained by assessing the fund as a whole and not the specific holding that was subject to seizure.[76] An earlier, much-commented, decision rendered by the English High Court in 2005, *AIG v. Kazakhstan*, took the same view of State saving.[77] This decision also related to the NFK and its arrangement within the NBK but was taken in the context of enforcing an award rendered under the Arbitration Rules of the International Centre for Settlement of Investment Disputes. In its decision, the English court held that the aim 'to enhance the National Fund' was 'part of the overall exercise of sovereign authority'.[78]

Neither the Dutch nor the English decision was referenced in the Swedish Supreme Court's decision, but both cases were pleaded by the parties and submitted as

---

71. *See* below in section §8.04[C].
72. *See Ascom*, paras 30–33.
73. *Ascom*, para. 45.
74. *Republic of Kazakhstan and the National Fund of Kazakhstan v. Ascom and Others*, Svea Court of Appeal, ÖÄ 7709-19, Decision, 17 June 2020, p. 24.
75. *Republic of Kazakhstan v. Ascom and Others*, Netherlands, Supreme Court, Judgment, 18 December 2020, ECLI:NL:HR:2020:2103, paras 3.2.2–3.2.5.
76. *See Republic of Kazakhstan v. Ascom and Others*, Netherlands, Supreme Court, Judgment, 18 December 2020, ECLI:NL:HR:2020:2103, para. 3.2.4 (rejecting the Dutch Court of Appeal's approach to consider the immediate purpose of the seized assets). *See* further below in section §8.04[C].
77. *See AIG Capital Partners, Inc. and Another v. Republic of Kazakhstan*, England, High Court of Justice, 20 October 2005 [2005] EWHC 2239 (Comm) ('*AIG v. Kazakhstan*'), para. 92 ('Management of a State's economy and revenue must constitute a sovereign activity.'). For discussion of this case, *see*, e.g., David Gaukrodger, *Foreign State Immunity and Foreign Government Controlled Investors*, OECD Working Papers on International Investment No. 2010/02, 2010, pp. 21–23.
78. *AIG v. Kazakhstan*, para. 92.

part of the record. The fact that the Swedish Supreme Court came to a diametrically different conclusion must therefore be viewed as a conscious departure from the position taken by these other courts on this point.[79]

[C]   Determining the Purpose for Which Assets Are Used

Third, the Court elaborated on relevant factors for determining the purpose of invested financial assets.

Applying the test devised in *Sedelmayer* to the SWF funds at issue,[80] the court observed that the use for which financial assets are intended may not be immediately apparent.[81] In its analysis of the purpose, the Court considered four related elements: (1) the risk assumed by the State in making the investment; (2) the objective sought with the holding of the specific assets; (3) the expressed objective of the portfolio of which the assets formed part; and (4) the ease with which funds could be withdrawn from the fund to be assigned for clearly sovereign activities.

As to the risk assumed by the State when investing the SWF assets in question, the Court observed that when a State invests in listed shares and similar securities (as was the case with the property in *Ascom*), it becomes 'exposed to the same commercial risks as the undertakings in which the investments are made'.[82] According to the Court, the State's 'primary motivation for exposing itself to such risks can typically be assumed to be the same as those of other equity investors', namely return on investment. This, the Court held, could not be seen as 'an outflow of the State's sovereign activity'.[83]

The Court's position finds support in findings of Belgian courts in related proceedings. In 2018, a court in Brussels denied immunity to the NFK savings portfolio, noting that the 'attached securities and cash must be considered to be long term investment objects' and that the 'increase of the profitability of the assets in the long term is a commercial activity'.[84] In June 2021, a Belgian Court of Appeal concurred that '[p]ure investments do not fall under the protection of state immunity'.[85]

The Swedish Supreme Court was, however, more pronounced in considering how the nature of the property, the inherent risk profile and the kind of transactions the property was involved in could reveal the purpose for which it was intended.

---

79. Cf. *Republic of Kazakhstan and National Bank of Kazakhstan v. Stati et al*, Belgium, Brussels Court of Appeal (Seventeenth Division), Cases Nos 2018/AR/1209 and 2018/AR/1214, Judgment, 29 June 2021, p. 39 (arriving at a similar conclusion to the Swedish Supreme Court and insisting that it was not bound by the December 2020 decision of the Dutch Supreme Court and did not find references to this case law helpful).
80. See *Ascom*, para. 19; cf. *Sedelmayer*, para. 14.
81. See *Ascom*, para. 25.
82. *Ascom*, para. 28.
83. *Ascom*, para. 28.
84. *Republic of Kazakhstan v. Stati et al*, Belgium, Brussels Court of First Instance, Case No. 2017/4282/A, Decision, 25 May 2018, p. 15 (unofficial translation from Flemish).
85. *Republic of Kazakhstan and National Bank of Kazakhstan v. Stati et al*, Belgium, Brussels Court of Appeal (Seventeenth Chamber), Cases Nos 2018/AR/1209 and 2018/AR1214, Judgment, 29 June 2021, p. 40 (unofficial translation from Flemish).

These considerations may be viewed as controversial, walking a fine line between the activity-based test commonly used for the commerciality exception in respect of immunity from jurisdiction and the purpose-based test used for the commerciality exception in respect of immunity from enforcement. Holding stakes in listed companies or other placements on international financial markets is of course an activity that a private individual could equally undertake. However, under Article 19(c) of the UNCSI (and, arguably, customary international law), it is the purpose of the use for which property is intended that is determinative.[86] Indeed, sovereign States may undertake acts that could be undertaken by a private party but with a different, public or sovereign, objective in mind. Interestingly, the Court in *Ascom* expressly drew on the purpose for which a private party would normally hold the same type of assets.[87] Notably, Kazakhstan had not proffered any information about the specific intended purpose of the seized shares.

The basic point of the Court's reasoning is, however, that saving, investment and wealth management per se are not intrinsically sovereign purposes. In line with German jurisprudence, the Court reasoned that the purpose of the property could be determined with reference to the kind of activity in which the property was used.[88] Funds managed through inherently commercial activities can only enjoy immunity if 'qualified purposes of a sovereign nature ... come to concrete and clear expression in the State's regulation of how the property is to be used'.[89] In other words, where indications based on risk appetite and investment horizon suggest a purely commercial purpose, the State will need to produce some evidence that the funds are indeed connected to its sovereign activities.[90]

In this case, Kazakhstan did not produce an official statement as to the sovereign purpose of the assets.[91] The question is, however, whether the Court would have been amenable to rely blindly on the State's own (possibly self-serving) *ex post facto* statement as to the intended use. Notably, in Sweden, there is not, as in, for example, the United Kingdom, legislation and case law providing that a statement by the competent authorities that certain property is intended for public use constitutes authoritative proof of the property's purpose.[92] Such legislation considerably raises the

---

86. *See* Brown and O'Keefe, *Article 19*, p. 323.
87. *See Ascom*, para. 28.
88. Cf. *Central Bank of Mongolia*, Germany, Federal Court of Justice, Decision, 4 July 2013, VII ZB 63/12 ('*Central Bank of Mongolia*'), para. 12 (finding an asset to be in use for sovereign purposes if it is in use for a sovereign activity).
89. *Ascom*, para. 28.
90. Cf. Slawotsky, *Sovereign Wealth Funds and Jurisdiction under the FSIA*, p. 981 ('A record of investments would serve to corroborate whether a stated intended purpose is true. [...] If the SWF's investment record established a pattern of investing in highly speculative derivate transactions betting on continuous increases in that nation's export, that would serve to undermine the stated goal.')
91. Cf. *AIG v. Kazakhstan*, para. 25 (where the Ambassador of Kazakhstan to the United Kingdom had produced a certificate under section 13(5) of the State Immunity Act 1978 to the effect that the assets against which enforcement was sought 'have never been used for commercial purposes [and] are not intended to be used for such purposes').
92. *See* s. 13(5) of the State Immunity Act of 1978. Cf. *Alcom Ltd v. Republic of Colombia and Others*, England, House of Lords, [1984] AC 580, at p. 604.

burden of proof incumbent on the party seeking enforcement against that property to show that the funds in question are earmarked, specifically and exclusively, for commercial transactions.[93]

Instead, the Court examined the arrangements within the NFK and in particular the distinction between its two portfolios and their stated objectives.[94] As discussed above, SWFs sometimes have loftier overarching objectives, but in the Court's view, the regulations of the NFK did not identify concrete sovereign purposes;[95] nor was there any decision issued before the seizure of assets specifying Kazakhstan's intention to use the seized assets for any particular sovereign activity.

The Court's approach would seem to allow States to preserve the immunity of SWFs by setting up such funds to serve more tangibly sovereign objectives and by being more precise about the purposes of such funds. However, to merely manage State wealth to ensure the prosperity and future needs of a country's population is too vague and remote a purpose to justify immunity in accordance with Article 19 of the UNCSI. The Court expressly held that 'the mere fact that the State in the future will have the opportunity to use the value of the property for government activities or that the value of the property shall benefit future generations cannot be considered sufficient'.[96] All funds of a State may in theory be reassigned for sovereign purposes and are in some sense ultimately for the benefit of its people. Immunity for State-controlled assets regardless of whether or not they have been assigned or appropriated for any particular sovereign activity would in essence amount to absolute immunity, negating the restrictive doctrine.

In the final step, the court considered the procedure through which the State could withdraw money from the fund for reallocation, such as, e.g., reinforcing the State budget and financing State actions or public services, and whether this connection was 'sufficiently concrete' to justify immunity.[97] This investigation into the nexus between the seized assets and activities that could be regarded as *acta jure imperii* reflects a sophisticated approach offering reasonable flexibility for the courts to appraise the circumstances that may warrant immunity of State assets in other cases in the future. In *Ascom*, it also allowed the Court to consider not only the purpose of the seized local assets (arguably entirely commercial) or only the objective of the SWF as a whole (which may be more public in nature), but both, and the connection between

---

93. Cf. the similar situation in the Netherlands, *see* Pieter H.F. Bekker and Jacques F. de Heer, *Enforcement of Arbitral Awards Against Sovereigns: The Netherlands*, in: Enforcement of Arbitral Awards Against Sovereigns, ed. Bishop (JurisNet, 2009) 381, at p. 412.
94. *See Ascom*, para. 32.
95. Pursuant to Decree of the President of the Republic of Kazakhstan No. 402 on the National Fund of the Republic of Kazakhstan, 23 August 2000, the NFK was established 'to ensure a stable social and economic development of the country, accumulation of financial resources for future generations [and] reduce the dependence of the economy on the impact of unfavorable external factors'. Decree No. 385 describes the goal of the NFK as being 'to preserve financial resources by accumulating savings for future generations and reducing the national budget's dependence on global commodity markets'.
96. *Ascom*, para. 28.
97. *See Ascom*, para. 46.

the two. This seems preferable to the approach adopted, for example, by the Dutch Supreme Court in 2020, focusing entirely on the overarching goal of the SWF.[98]

A national court considering immunity will normally do so as part of its investigation into its jurisdiction to issue a certain judgment or order. Under international law, States are permitted to act within their jurisdiction unless they are legally obligated to refrain from doing so.[99] The obligation to recognise the immunity of other States and their property is one such restriction on the competence of States to act within their territory.[100] Since immunity applies in relation to a particular forum State, where immunity is invoked as a jurisdictional defence, it makes sense to focus on the immunity of the property located within that jurisdiction, and thus the ascertainable purpose of the same.[101]

The Court's focus on the immediate purpose of the funds (as opposed to the future use the State may make of the value of the same) echoes the views of courts in other jurisdictions. For example, a German district court concluded already in 1975 in a case concerning enforcement against the respondent State's cash and securities accounts that the assets were not 'in the public service' of the State and held that 'a possible use of these assets in the future to finance state business cannot serve to establish their present immunity'.[102] Similarly, the Swiss Federal Tribunal concluded in 2000, in a case concerning enforcement against a bank account of Kazakhstan, that: 'the aim pursued by the State cannot be decisive, since this aim always aims, in the final analysis, at a State interest. The first thing to be examined is the intrinsic nature of the operation set up by the State: it is a question of determining whether the act is a matter of public authority or whether it is a legal relationship which could, in an identical or similar form, be entered into by two private individuals'.[103] The same point was confirmed by a Belgian court in proceedings relating to *Ascom*, referenced above, noting that 'in the long term, a State will always aim for sovereign goals of public interest' and that consequently the 'starting point for the assessment [of immunity of State funds] is the specific, actual, current use of the funds', with appropriate weight

---

98. *See* above in section §8.04[B].

99. *See* Robert Jennings and Arthur Watts, *Oppenheim's International Law* (9th ed. Oxford University Press, 1992), pp. 456 et seq.

100. *See Jurisdictional Immunities*, para. 56.

101. Cf., e.g., *Certain Iranian Assets (Islamic Republic of Iran v. United States of America)*, Preliminary Objections, Judgment, 13 February 2019, I.C.J. Reports 2019, p. 7 ('*Certain Iranian Assets*'), paras 93–97 (where the International Court of Justice held that in order to examine the status of the Iranian central bank as acting in a sovereign or commercial capacity, it needed to consider the bank's activities within the territory of the United States); *see further* on this case below in section §8.04[E]. Whether or not seized assets in *Ascom* are located in the Swedish jurisdiction remains contentious and will be subject to further proceedings before the Svea Court of Appeal.

102. *Non-resident Petitioner v. Central Bank of Nigeria*, Germany, Frankfurt Provincial Court, 1 December 1975, 65 INTERNATIONAL LAW REPORTS 131 ('*Central Bank of Nigeria*'), p. 135.

103. *Republic of Kazakhstan and Another*, Switzerland, Federal Tribunal, Judgment No. 1P.581/2000, 8 December 2000, s. 2(c) (unofficial translation from French).

given to the context.[104] What appears in these jurisdictions is a nuanced, functional approach, similar to that adopted by the Swedish Supreme Court.

[D] Reigning in Central Bank Immunity

Fourth, the decision in *Ascom* clarified that SWF assets cannot enjoy immunity simply because the fund and its assets are held, controlled or managed by a central bank.

It has long been unclear to which extent States can protect their SWF assets by administering them through their central banks.[105]

As State practice has endorsed the restrictive theory on immunity from execution, certain States have carved out exceptions in domestic regulation for certain types of property viewed as by default intended for sovereign use. This practice is reflected in Article 21 of the UNCSI, which preserves immunity for property used for diplomatic missions or military performance, central bank property, cultural heritage or archival property and exhibit objects of scientific, cultural or historical interest. Specifically, Article 21(1)(c) of the UNCSI provides that the property of the central bank or other monetary authority of the State should not be considered as property specifically in use or intended for use by the State other than government non-commercial purposes under Article 19.

However, as set out above, Article 21 is not yet binding; nor is the rule widely regarded as reflecting custom.[106] There is no consistent State practice on central bank immunity from enforcement measures.[107] Certain States treat central bank property as any other property.[108] Others recognise an enhanced or automatic immunity for central banks, albeit in some cases on the condition either that the funds are held by the central bank on its own account or that it is used by the central bank for sovereign purposes or both.[109] Some States grant near-absolute immunity from enforcement against all State property, including central bank property.[110] Consequently, the parties in *Ascom* presented the Court with considerable investigations into State practice and *opinio juris* to establish the customary international law on central bank immunity. The Court, however, concluded that the extent and scope of immunity for central bank property under customary international law is simply unclear, noting in particular the different

---

104. *Republic of Kazakhstan and National Bank of Kazakhstan v. Stati et al*, Belgium, Brussels Court of Appeal (Seventeenth Chamber), Cases Nos 2018/AR/1209 and 2018/AR1214, Judgment, 29 June 2021, pp. 38–39.
105. *See* Wuerth, *Immunity from Execution of Central Bank Assets*, n. 103.
106. *See* Chester Brown & Roger O'Keefe, *Article 21*, in: The United Nations Convention on Jurisdictional Immunities of States and Their Property, ed. O'Keefe et al. (Oxford University Press, 2013) 334, at p. 347.
107. Wuerth, *Immunity from Execution of Central Bank Assets*, pp. 269–278.
108. For example, Australia, Canada and Israel. *See* Wuerth, *Immunity from Execution of Central Bank Assets*, pp. 276–277.
109. For example, US, Germany, Switzerland, France and Belgium. *See* Wuerth, *Immunity from Execution of Central Bank Assets*, pp. 269–271.
110. For example, Argentina, China and Japan. *See* Wuerth, *Immunity from Execution of Central Bank Assets*, pp. 271–276.

views expressed during the drafting of the Convention and the lack of consistent State practice on central bank immunity.[111]

To complicate things, State practice in this area, such as domestic legislation on State immunity and court decisions applying the same, may often derive from other considerations than complying with international law. National immunity laws commonly reflect policy choices based on political or practical considerations, e.g., to attract foreign central bank investments to the jurisdiction,[112] avoid litigation that would be considered embarrassing or harmful to inter-State relations,[113] or ensure reciprocal treatment by other States. While some jurisdictions grant extensive immunity to central bank property, this is usually the result of national legislation: were it not for that, central bank property would often be viewed as property held for a commercial purpose and not enjoy immunity.[114] Legislation passed or applied out of 'considerations of convenience or simple political expediency' does not express the sense of legal obligation needed to establish customary international law.[115] As noted by the International Court of Justice (ICJ) in the *Jurisdictional Immunities* case: 'While it may be true that States sometimes decide to accord an immunity more extensive than that required by international law, for present purposes, the point is that the grant of immunity in such a case is not accompanied by the requisite *opinio juris* and therefore sheds no light upon [the scope of immunity recognised under customary international law].'[116]

Trends in domestic regulation towards enhanced central bank immunity are tempered by various conditions introduced by States, such as reciprocity requirements that extend immunity only to the property of central banks of States that would equally

---

111. *See Ascom*, para. 21.
112. *See* Wuerth, *Immunity from Execution of Central Bank Assets*, p. 274 (noting that France in 2015 enacted legislation with the aim of protecting foreign central banks assets and encouraging investment of such assets in France; and equally that Belgium in 2008 enacted legislation designed to make Belgium an attractive place for foreign central banks to deposit their assets). *See also* generally Fox and Webb, *The Law of State Immunity*, p. 486.
113. *See*, e.g., *AIG v. Kazakhstan*, para. 58 ('The assets of a State's central bank (or monetary authority) would be an obvious target for the enforcement process in relation to judgments against the State or its central bank (etc). This might lead to unwelcome and perhaps embarrassing litigation in UK courts. Therefore this possibility was pre-empted by the all-embracing and imperative immunity granted by section 14(4).')
114. *See*, e.g., *AIG v. Kazakhstan*, para. 53 ('if section 14(4) did not exist, then because central banks and other monetary authorities are not excluded from the scope of section 14(1), a central bank (etc) that is a department of the government of a State and is not a "separate entity", (as defined), and its property could be the subject of an enforcement process in respect of a judgment obtained against the relevant State'.). *See also*, as regards US law, Jeremy Ostrander, *The Last Bastion of Sovereign Immunity: A Comparative Look at Immunity from Execution of Judgments* (2004) 22 BERKELEY JOURNAL OF INTERNATIONAL LAW 541, p. 569 (noting that '[w]ithout section 6011 [of the FSIA], a foreign central bank engaged in almost any investment or deposit in the United States would, by the nature of such an activity be acting as a private player rather than as a regulator, and hence, its property would fall within the commercial exception'.).
115. *Colombian-Peruvian asylum*, International Court of Justice, Judgment, 20 November 1950, I.C.J. Reports 1950, p. 266, at pp. 277 and 286.
116. *Jurisdictional Immunities*, para. 55.

recognise immunity of the forum State's central bank assets[117] or requirements that the property in question is used for typical central banking activities and not for other, commercial, purposes.[118]

In the absence of any customary international law to guide its decision on central bank immunity, the Court in *Ascom* examined the interests involved and the justification for enhanced immunity for central bank property. The court opined that in respect of funds controlled by a central bank, immunity from enforcement should not necessarily be limited to property which the central bank legally owns or holds in its own name. However, nor did it accept that immunity should extend to all assets that a central bank controls regardless of their use.[119] SWF assets that have no specific sovereign purpose would not be immune merely because they are managed by a central bank.

With this functional interpretation, the Swedish Supreme Court again departed from the approach of the Svea Court of Appeal, which had taken an explicitly categorical approach. Guided by Article 21(1)(c), the Court of Appeal held that immunity did not depend on the use the central bank made of the assets in question.[120]

The Swedish Supreme Court's finding also departs from the decision of the English High Court in *AIG v. Kazakhstan* regarding the same arrangement involving the NFK and the NBK. The English court, with reference to provisions under the English State Immunity Act of 1978, found that the central bank held a 'kind of "property" interest', conferring immunity on the property 'irrespective of the capacity in which the central bank holds it, or the purpose for which the property is held'.[121] The Court in *Ascom*, however, having no such domestic legislation to relate to, found no basis for immunity of 'property which the bank controls without there being a connection with the bank's mission in terms of monetary policy'.[122]

Central banks are traditionally responsible for setting and executing monetary policy and overseeing the banking system and financial infrastructure. They do so through interventions that require access to reserve capital and commonly manage funds for this purpose. However, it is less common to entrust central banks with more general wealth management tasks.[123] The fund management that central banks undertake for their own capital is usually guided by a relatively low tolerance for risk

---

117. *See* Wuerth, *Immunity from Execution of Central Bank Assets*, pp. 266 and 270–276. Professor Wuerth consequently stated in an expert opinion filed in the *Ascom* case that '[i]n practice, [certain] important countries would not afford categorical protection of central bank assets of countries like the United States, Germany, Switzerland and the many other countries that do not give categorical protections'. *See* Ingrid Wuerth, *Expert Report in the Republic of Kazakhstan and the National Bank of the Republic of Kazakhstan v. Anatolie Stati, et al Before the Supreme Court in Case No. Ö 3828-20*, 10 February 2021 ('Wuerth Expert Report'), Exhibit S-95, p. 4.
118. *See* further below in section §8.04[F].
119. *See Ascom*, para. 23.
120. *Republic of Kazakhstan and the National Fund of Kazakhstan v. Ascom and Others*, Svea Court of Appeal, ÖÄ 7709-19, Decision, 17 June 2020, at p. 26.
121. *AIG v. Kazakhstan*, para. 61.
122. *Ascom*, para. 24.
123. *See* survey by Bank for International Settlements, Central Bank Governance Group, *Issues in the Governance of Central Banks*, May 2009, pp. 28–31.

and loss and is not driven by financial outcomes as such, in contrast with the diversified investment strategy and higher level of risk generally accepted by SWFs.[124] This longer investment horizon for SWFs is possible precisely because such assets are normally not used for currency interventions or other realisations of monetary policy.[125] Where central banks manage funds through more volatile investment, such funds have in fact sometimes been viewed as SWFs rather than central bank funds, precisely because the purposes are assumed to differ from traditional central bank investments.[126] In the same vein, the standard definition of SWFs under the Santiago Principles explicitly excludes 'foreign currency reserve assets held by monetary authorities for the traditional balance of payments or monetary policy purposes'.[127]

Arguably recognising these fundamental differences, the Court in the *Ascom* case acknowledged that the seized assets were used exclusively for wealth management on commercial terms with no functional connection to central bank activities and therefore did not enjoy immunity.[128] This approach indeed seems more in line with the structure of the UNCSI as regards the immunity of assets, the purpose-oriented test for immunity from execution in Article 19(c) and the enhanced immunity provided by Article 21.

Article 21 does add an extra layer of protection for certain classes of property, but arguably based on the function served by such property and the particular role that it serves in certain sovereign activities. The property classes included in Article 21 have in common that they commonly sit in foreign jurisdictions and may include property that could otherwise be regarded as commercial. Diplomatic missions are by their nature located abroad and may make use of property such as buildings, cars and moneys on account. The property of forces stationed abroad under visiting forces agreements or forces engaged in operations on foreign soil are habitually located in other jurisdictions and may include not just typically military assets but also items such as trucks or supplies. Central banks commonly hold foreign currency reserves to facilitate intervention to stabilise currency rates or inflation and often hold considerable foreign assets to be able to act even if their markets experience volatility or severe downturn. The exceptions for cultural heritage property or other exhibition objects would appear to target museum artefacts on loan to foreign institutions and the like.[129] What is common to the listed items is that this property is of a type that could appear in commercial contexts, but it may also, in a more particular context, allow the State to realise its sovereign or foreign policies, protect its relationships with other States,

---

124. *See* Haeri et al., *Sovereign Wealth Funds: Transnational Regulation and Dispute Resolution*, p. 11.
125. *See* Hsu, *Sovereign Wealth Funds: Investors in Search of an Identity*, p. 4; and Tejera, *The U.S. Law Regime of Sovereign Immunity and the Sovereign Wealth Funds*, p. 11 (both emphasising SWFs' risk appetite).
126. *See* Khalid A. Alsweilem et al., *Sovereign Investor Models: Institutions and Policies for Managing Sovereign Wealth*, BELFER CENTER FOR SCIENCE AND INTERNATIONAL AFFAIRS AND CENTER FOR INTERNATIONAL DEVELOPMENT, HARVARD KENNEDY SCHOOL, April 2015, pp. 12 and 91.
127. *Santiago Principles*, p. 27 (Appendix I. Defining Sovereign Wealth Funds).
128. *Ascom*, para. 41.
129. *See Immunitet för utställningsföremål, Betänkande av utredningen om skydd mot processuella åtgärder mot inlånade kulturföremål*, SOU 2021:28, April 2021.

safeguard its ability to deploy its military, preserve its sense of cultural identity, and so on. As highlighted in one of the expert reports presented to the Court: 'the purpose of Article 21(1)(c) is not to provide blanket immunity for categories of property without reference to the nature or use of that property – the purpose of Article 21(1)(c) is instead to make clear that the nature of some property renders it in use for governmental purposes'.[130] Wealth placed in SWFs may certainly be important to States but in much more general ways. In contrast to central bank property, the function of these funds is not to guarantee their country's monetary and financial system.[131] A seizure of such funds would of course affect the State's general resources in a similar way as a voluntary payment under an award, but it would not appear to deprive the State of any immediate means for fulfilling sovereign functions in the same way as a seizure of property listed in Article 21.

[E] Affirming a Nordic Position on Central Bank Immunity

Fifth, in underscoring the connection with the exercise of monetary authority, the Court appears to have embraced the position previously adopted by the Nordic States in the elaboration of the UNCSI.

During the drafting of the Convention, the Nordic countries proposed language to specify that the provision in Article 21(1)(c) was directed only at funds used for monetary purposes. The Nordic countries were concerned that if the property of central banks in the territory of other States was to be unconditionally excluded from execution, this presumed that 'because central banks are instruments of sovereign authority any activity they undertake must be covered by immunity from execution. However, if the foreign property of a central bank is used or intended for use by the State for commercial purposes, it might be logical not to treat it differently from other State property that fulfils this condition'.[132] The Nordic States thus wished to distinguish clearly between *acta jure imperii* and *acta jure gestionis*, underscoring that the doctrine of restrictive immunity was based on the view that 'once a foreign State has entered the market place it should be treated in the same way as others in the market place'.[133]

The proposal was rejected on the view that central banks were regarded as always being 'instruments of sovereign power' which engaged exclusively in sovereign activity, making further clarification superfluous.[134] However, the reason for the rejection of the clarification does not necessarily support a categorical interpretation decoupled from the purpose for which the property is used. It rather conveyed an

---

130. Wuerth Expert Report, p. 4.
131. Hahn, *State Immunity and Veil Piercing in the Age of Sovereign Wealth Funds*, pp. 116–117.
132. International Law Commission, *Jurisdictional immunities for States and their property*, Yearbook of the International Law Commission (1988), Volume II, Part One, UN Doc. A/CN.4/SER.A/Add.1 (Part 1), p. 78.
133. *See Immunitet för stater och deras egendom*, SOU 2008:2, December 2007, p. 107.
134. *See* International Law Commission, *Jurisdictional immunities for States and their property*, Yearbook of the International Law Commission (1990), Volume II, Part Two, UN Doc. A/CN.4/SER.A/1990/Add.1 (Part 2), p. 42.

understanding (prevailing at the time) of what role central banks play in sovereign governance. By contrast, the pervasive use of SWFs and their some-time management by central banks was arguably not foreseen at the time and, as far as known, not discussed during the drafting of the UNCSI.

State practice shows that central banks today can be given tasks that are not necessarily connected with sovereign activities. For example, in the pending case of *Certain Iranian Assets*, the ICJ undertook to examine the activities of the Iranian central bank Bank Markazi within the territory of the United States (US) in order to determine whether the bank constituted a company for the purposes of the US-Iran Treaty of Amity. The relevant criterion was whether the bank engaged in activities of a commercial nature or whether it carried out exclusively sovereign functions on behalf of Iran. While the ICJ has yet to determine definitively the status of Bank Markazi, it found as a matter of principle that a central bank indeed could pursue not only sovereign but also commercial objectives in the territory of other States.[135]

[F]   Aligning with Germany, the US and Switzerland

Sixth, by requiring a connection between the funds under management and traditional central banking functions, the Court aligned Swedish jurisprudence with certain strands of international practice.

Germany and the US are examples of jurisdictions that also, with some nuance, recognise a separate, enhanced immunity for central bank property but require that the central bank holds such funds for 'sovereign purposes' or 'its own account', thereby restricting central bank immunity to funds used for typical or paradigmatic central bank activities and functions. Both US and German case law has distinguished between traditional paradigmatic sovereign tasks of central banks, i.e., where the bank acts as a regulatory authority, as opposed to tasks where the bank does not fulfil a public mission and does not act as an emanation of the State.[136]

Under German law, central bank property is immune from execution only when used or intended for non-commercial purposes.[137] Consequently, central bank assets used entirely for commercial investments are arguably not immune from attachment under German law. The connection with a sovereign purpose is a long-standing requirement in Germany, which, like Sweden, has no domestic law on State immunity but applies customary international law.[138] Already in 1977, the German Federal Constitutional Court restricted immunity from execution to property used for sovereign purposes.[139] Pursuant to a 2013 decision of the German Federal Supreme Court,

---

135. See *Certain Iranian Assets*, paras 87–92.
136. See, e.g., *EM Ltd and NML Capital Ltd v. Banco Central de República de Argentina*, United States, Judgment, 5 July 2011, 652 F.3d 172 (2d Cir 2011) ('*NML Capital v. Banco Central de Argentina*'); *Central Bank of Mongolia*, para. 10 (finding that sovereign assets are immune from execution to the extent they serve sovereign purposes).
137. *Central Bank of Nigeria*, pp. 135–136.
138. See Art. 25 of the German constitution.
139. See the seminal *Philippine Embassy* case, Germany, Federal Constitutional Court, Judgment, 13 December 1977, 65 International Law Reports 146 ('While general rules of international law

currency reserves owned by central banks are considered immune because and to the extent that they serve sovereign purposes and ensure the State's international capacity to act as a public authority.[140] *A contrario*, funds held by a central bank without a connection to such purposes are arguably not immune.

US law similarly requires a connection with central bank activity. However, the criterion is differently formulated. Pursuant to the Foreign Sovereign Immunities Act of 1976, central bank property is immune from execution if the funds are held by the central bank 'for its own account'.[141] In practice, this has been interpreted to mean that the funds are used for traditional and paradigmatic central bank functions, like the accumulation of currency reserves or bank reserves intended to facilitate interventions in currency or financial markets.[142]

In requiring a concrete connection to sovereign purposes, the Swedish Supreme Court also aligned with Swiss courts, which have held central bank assets to be immune only if the measures of execution concern assets allocated for the performance of acts of sovereignty[143] and required that assets are earmarked for concrete public goals in order to qualify for immunity.[144] Swiss courts have maintained that '[i]mmunity can therefore only be claimed by reason of the nature of the assets subjected to the attachment where those assets are allocated in an identifiable manner for the performance of a sovereign function. [...] [A] plea of immunity is inadmissible, in respect of money and securities, unless the documents or specified sums have been designated for the performance of such tasks'.[145]

[G] Recognising the Award Creditor's Legitimate Interests

Seventh, the Court explicitly acknowledged that the award creditor has a legitimate right of enforcement. State immunity imposes a de facto restriction on the availability of execution measures for parties with a claim against a sovereign entity. Execution measures are recognised as an element of the access to court guaranteed under Article

---

thus impose no outright prohibition on execution by the State of the forum against a foreign State, they do impose material limits on execution. There is an established general custom among States, backed by a legal consensus, whereby the State of the forum is prohibited by international law from levying execution, under judicial writs against a foreign State, on property of the foreign State which is situated or present in the State of the forum and is used for sovereign purposes of the foreign State, except with the latter's consent.'). The approach was followed by constitutional courts in, e.g., Spain and Italy. *See Abbott v. South Africa*; *Condor and Filvem v. Minister of Justice*, Italy, Constitutional Court, Case No. 329, Judgment, 15 July 1992, 101 INTERNATIONAL LAW REPORTS 394.

140. *Central Bank of Mongolia*, paras 10–15.
141. 28 U.S. Code § 1611(b)(1).
142. *See NML Capital v. Banco Central de Argentina*, pp. 194–195.
143. *See Banque Bruxelles Lambert (Suisse) SA and Others v. Paraguay*, Switzerland, Federal Supreme Court, 20 August 1998, ATF 124 III 382, p. 389.
144. Sandrine Giroud, *Enforcement Against State Assets and Execution of ICSID Awards in Switzerland: How Swiss Courts Deal with Immunity Defences* (2012) 4 ASA BULLETIN 758, p. 760.
145. *See Libyan Arab Jamahiriya v. Actimon SA*, Switzerland, Federal Tribunal, Judgment, 82 INTERNATIONAL LAW REPORTS 30, 24 April 1985, pp. 35–36; *Banque centrale de la République de Turquie v. Weston Compagnie de Finance et d'Investissement SA*, Switzerland, Federal Tribunal, Judgment, 15 November 1978, 65 INTERNATIONAL LAW REPORTS 417.

6 of the European Convention on Human Rights (ECHR) because without adequate opportunities for execution, a right to judicial determination of one's claim amounts to precious little. Consequently, the European Court of Human Rights (ECtHR) has declared that the right to access to court encompasses a right to enforcement of judicial decisions rendered: 'The right of access to a tribunal would be illusory if a Contracting State's legal system allowed a final, binding judicial decision to remain inoperative to the detriment of one party. Execution of a judgment given by any court must be regarded as an integral part of the "trial" for the purposes of Article 6.'[146]

Admittedly, this right is not absolute but can be legitimately restricted to accommodate the respect for the equality of States, their sovereign functions and activities and to maintain a sense of comity and good relations in the community of nations.[147] Sovereign immunities is an important element to ensure that respect is grounded in the understanding that States have no jurisdiction over other States.[148]

However, pursuant to the case law of the ECtHR, this restriction on the effect of Article 6 is only acceptable as long as the immunity in question is mandated by international law.[149] Since the legitimate purpose that justifies denying access to a court is to ensure compliance with international law, it would follow that anything that goes further in that direction than what international law requires could be regarded as disproportionate. A mere liberty to treat the foreign State as immune could thus not legitimately restrict that access because the denial of access would be a discretionary choice on the part of the forum State.[150] Immunity gratuitously afforded would thus amount to an illegitimate restriction on access to court as guaranteed by the ECHR.[151]

---

146. *Kalogeropoulou v. Greece and Germany*, pp. 7–8. *See also Golder v. United Kingdom*, European Court of Human Rights, Application No. 4451/70, Judgment, 21 February 1975, paras 28–36. *See also*, in proceedings related to *Ascom*, the decision of the Brussels Court of Appeal in *Republic of Kazakhstan and National Bank of Kazakhstan v. Stati and Others*, Cases Nos 2018/AR/1209 and 2018/AR1214, Judgment, 29 June 2021, p. 37 (holding that the principle of immunity must be assessed against the fundamental right provided for in Article 6 ECHR).

147. *See*, e.g., *Fogarty v. United Kingdom*, European Court of Human Rights, Application No. 37112/97, Judgment, 21 November 2001, paras 33–34 ('*Fogarty v. United Kingdom*'); *McElhinney v. Ireland*, European Court of Human Rights, Application No. 31253/96, Judgment, 21 November 2001, paras 34–35; *Al-Adsani v. United Kingdom*, European Court of Human Rights, Application No. 35763/97, Judgment, 21 November 2001, para. 54; *Sabeh El Leil v. France*, European Court of Human Rights, Application No. 34869/05, Judgment, 29 June 2011, paras 51–54; *Cudak v. Lithuania*, European Court of Human Rights (Grand Chamber), Application No. 15869/02, Judgment, 23 March 2010, para. 60; *Jones and Others v. the United Kingdom*, European Court of Human Rights, Applications Nos 34356/06 and 40528/06, Judgment, 14 January 2014 ('*Jones v. United Kingdom*'), para. 188. *See* further Matthias Kloth, *Immunities and the Right of Access to Court under Article 6 of the European Convention on Human Rights* (Brill/Martinus Nijhoff, 2010), p. 15 ('the Court is usually prepared to consider the granting of immunity as legitimate').

148. Cf. the maxim *par in parem non habet imperium*, 'an equal has no authority over an equal'.

149. *See Fogarty v. United Kingdom*, paras 34–35.

150. *See Benkharbouche v. Secretary of State for Foreign and Commonwealth Affairs and Secretary of State for Foreign and Commonwealth Affairs and Libya v. Janah*, United Kingdom, Supreme Court, Judgment, 18 October 2017, [2017] UKSC 62 ('*Benkharbouche*'), para. 34. *See also Jones v. United Kingdom*, paras 189, 196–198 and 201–215.

151. *See Benkharbouche*, para. 34.

For that reason, it is significant that the Court in *Ascom* explicitly rendered its decision with reference to customary international law and with a view to safeguarding the award creditor's rights.[152] Although the court did not refer to the ECHR in its decision, it thus arguably helped clarify the scope of the right to access to enforcement measures under the ECHR by clarifying the scope of immunity legitimately liming that access.

§8.05   CONCLUDING REMARKS

The *Ascom* case is given in the context of several shifts in the way States act in international commerce. First, States are increasingly involved in investments on commercial terms on foreign markets through ambiguous vehicles such as SWFs. Second, in the same way that States' increasing activity in the marketplace justified a more restrictive view of their immunity from the jurisdiction of local courts, States' increasing involvement in arbitral proceedings with private parties seems to demand that the awards resulting from such proceedings can be made effective.

The fact that the Court made its decision on the basis of customary international law makes the *Ascom* judgment all the more interesting. While it is indeed common for domestic courts to consider sovereign immunity objections to the competence of local authorities to order execution against certain assets, domestic courts will often do so with reference to domestic law and practice and may thus base their determination on, for example, foreign policy or reciprocity considerations. This may result in a broader scope of sovereign immunity than what follows from customary international law. In *Ascom*, the Court engaged clearly and exclusively with customary international law for its decision. The decision thereby constitutes an instance of State practice underpinned by an acceptance of that practice as law (*opinio juris*) and helps identify, define and consolidate the international custom on enforcement immunity.[153]

In our view, the *Ascom* decision strikes a sensible balance in its definition of the competing interests involved. By being guided by the immunity which *must* be recognised under international law, as opposed to the immunity that *could* be recognised, the Court navigated well the inherent tension between the respect for sovereign equality and State immunity, on the one hand, and, on the other, the award creditor's legitimate interest in access to enforcement mechanisms allowing it to be paid under the award. An award that cannot be enforced is worth little more than the paper it is written on. By circumscribing the immunity for commercial assets of States,

---

152. *See Ascom*, paras 13–14.
153. Regarding the formation of customary international law, *see* International Law Commission, *Draft conclusions on identification of customary international law*, YEARBOOK OF THE INTERNATIONAL LAW COMMISSION (2018), Volume II, Part Two, UN Doc. A/73/10, Conclusion 2 ('To determine the existence and content of a rule of customary international law, it is necessary to ascertain whether there is a general practice that is accepted as law (*opinio juris*).'); and *North Sea Continental Shelf*, Judgment, I.C.J. Reports 1969, p. 3, para. 77.

the decision represents a levelling of the playing field for enforcement of awards where States have appeared in arbitration, subject only to the restrictions on enforcement jurisdiction imposed by customary international law.[154] This is an important stance in support of the arbitration process.

---

154. *See Ascom*, para. 13.

CHAPTER 9

The Public International Law Significance of the *Ascom* Case

Alexander Foerster & Sara Bengtson Urwitz[*]

---

§9.01   INTRODUCTION

On November 18, 2021, the Swedish Supreme Court delivered its decision in the case of *Ascom*.[1] Originating in an arbitral dispute under the Energy Charter Treaty, the case had become an opportunity for the court to contribute to the clarity of rules of the public international law on state immunity for the property of central banks and sovereign wealth funds.

The dispute was between Kazakhstan and some foreign investors, resulting in an arbitral award in favor of the latter. Following failed attempts by the state to have the award set aside, the investors successfully requested the Swedish Enforcement Authority that the award be enforced. The district court upheld the decision. The Court of Appeal reversed it. Leave to appeal was granted by the Supreme Court, limited to the question of whether state immunity protected the attached property from enforcement.

The property attached by the Enforcement Authority (financial instruments on a securities depository at a bank, receivables linked thereto, and funds on a cash account) was accumulated in and managed by the Kazakhstan central bank—the National Bank of Kazakhstan—as part of a sovereign wealth fund, the National Fund. The immunity protection for property belonging to a state's central bank is considered

---

[*]   The authors have represented the Republic of Kazakhstan in the discussed enforcement proceedings before Swedish courts. The views expressed in this chapter represent the personal analysis by the authors and do not necessarily correspond to the views of Mannheimer Swartling Advokatbyrå or any of its clients. The authors would like to thank Pål Wrange, professor of public international law at Stockholm University, for insightful comments on a draft of this chapter.
1. Supreme Court Case Number Ö 3828-20.

to be especially strong. There are, however, disagreements about the more precise content of this principle.[2] The Supreme Court was thus called upon to determine this.

In the absence of specific Swedish rules on state immunity, the task before the Supreme Court was purely one of public international law. The question it had to solve involved fundamental international law issues of identification, interpretation, and evolvement of customary international law. Yet, the court did not answer it with reference to public international law and the methods it prescribes. This chapter analyzes what the court did instead. It is argued that the court's failure to take public international law seriously diminishes the decision's potential as an *agent of development* of public international law, limiting its function to *evidence* of such law.

In the following section, the international regime of state immunity is presented. The significance of the United Nations Convention on Jurisdictional Immunities of States and Their Property (UN Convention) is explained, followed by a discussion of the implications hereof for national courts determining cases where the international rules of state immunity are at play. More specifically, the question of how national courts are to go about when solving state immunity cases is discussed, as is the question of what the significance is of national courts determining issues of international law. In light of this discussion, the Supreme Court's reasoning in *Ascom* is subsequently analyzed. The analysis is limited to the court's treatment of the precedential question of how the state immunity protection for the property of central banks is to be construed.

§9.02   THE INTERNATIONAL REGIME OF STATE IMMUNITY

[A]   The UN Convention on Jurisdictional Immunities of States and Their Property

State immunity is a rule of customary international law.[3] States enjoy immunity because they are sovereign. They are equally sovereign, which means that they may not exercise jurisdiction over one another (*"in parem non habet imperium,"* "equals have no sovereignty over each other").[4]

With evolvements in the notion of sovereignty, the idea that states at all times enjoy immunity from other states' jurisdiction—*absolute* immunity—has been contested. Developed and developing states have had diverging views. So has West and

---

2. *See*, e.g., Brown, C. & O'Keefe, R., "Part IV: State Immunity from Measures of Constraint in Connection with Proceedings Before a Court" in *The United Nations Convention on Jurisdictional Immunities of States and Their Property: A Commentary* (eds. O'Keefe, R. & Tams, C.), 1 ed., Oxford University Press, 2013, p. 389.
3. The ILC established the rule's "solidly rooted" character early on in its process of developing the *United Nations Convention on Jurisdictional Immunities of States and Their Property*, *see* Yearbook of the ILC 1980, vol. 2, Part II, p. 147, para. 26. The rule's existence was moreover confirmed by the International Court of Justice (ICJ) in judgment dated February 3, 2012 in *Jurisdictional Immunities of the State (Germany v. Italy: Greece intervening)*, para. 56.
4. *See*, e.g., European Court of Human Rights (ECtHR), judgment dated November 21, 2001 in *Al-Adsani v. the United Kingdom* (2002), para. 54.

East, spurred by ideological differences. Increased commercial activities by states have prompted a wish to ameliorate the status of commercial actors vis-à-vis their sovereign counterparts. Many states have thus adopted a *restrictive* approach to immunity, according to which commercial or private law acts performed by states are not protected.[5]

The International Law Commission (ILC) in 1977 recommended to the UN General Assembly that the topic of jurisdictional immunity be considered for codification.[6] Given the diverging views among states, this was a tricky quest. It took the Commission fourteen years to present a draft set of articles.[7] In 2004, after an additional thirteen years, the General Assembly unanimously adopted the UN Convention.[8] That the Convention finally, and after multiple consultation rounds with all Member States, was capable of coming into being was a result of its essential principles by 2004 being "broadly acceptable to States of all persuasions."[9] As shall be discussed (*see* section §9.05), the Swedish Supreme Court in its reasoning in *Ascom* took no note of either the thorough and inclusive drafting procedure or the unanimous support for the final version.

The restrictive doctrine of state immunity permeates the UN Convention. The Convention indeed allows for private actors to proceed against states in foreign courts with proceedings arising out of commercial transactions. These situations are formulated as exceptions to the main rule, enshrined in Article 5 of the Convention, that a state enjoys immunity. Important, however, is the distinction the Convention makes between immunity for the state itself and immunity for its property.[10]

The threshold for allowing an exception to the main rule of state immunity is set higher for measures of constraint against a state's property than for court jurisdiction over the state. Against certain types of state property, measures of constraints are not allowed at all. The distinction is due to the more intrusive nature of measures of constraint. These are considered to constitute a greater infringement of a state's sovereignty than the exercise of court jurisdiction.[11] While the UN Convention signified the breakthrough of the restrictive doctrine, the immunity protection afforded by the Convention is thus sometimes stronger than what the doctrine prescribes.

---

5. *See*, e.g., O'Keefe, R. & Tams, C., "General Introduction" in *The United Nations Convention on Jurisdictional Immunities of States and Their Property: A Commentary* (eds. O'Keefe, R. & Tams, C.), 1 ed., Oxford University Press, 2013, pp. 38–41. *See also* government bill 2008/09:204, pp. 36–37.

6. Yearbook of the ILC, 1977, vol. 2, Part II, p. 130, para. 110.

7. Yearbook of the ILC, 1991, vol. 2, Part II.

8. UN General Assembly resolution 59/38 of December 2, 2004.

9. *See*, e.g., O'Keefe, R. & Tams, C., "General Introduction" in *The United Nations Convention on Jurisdictional Immunities of States and Their Property: A Commentary* (eds. O'Keefe, R. & Tams, C.), 1 ed., Oxford University Press, 2013, p. 39.

10. Cf. O'Keefe, R. & Tams, C., "General Introduction" in *The United Nations Convention on Jurisdictional Immunities of States and Their Property: A Commentary* (eds. O'Keefe, R. & Tams, C.), 1 ed., Oxford University Press, 2013, pp. 40–42.

11. *See*, e.g., the ICJ, judgment dated February 3, 2012 in *Jurisdictional Immunities of the State (Germany v. Italy: Greece intervening)*, para. 113; and Swedish Supreme Court case reported as NJA 2011 p. 475, para. 9.

With twenty-two states currently parties to the UN Convention and thirty required for its entry into force, the Convention has yet to become a source of law. The UN Convention is nevertheless significant, also without having obtained status as a treaty.[12]

[B]   The Significance of the UN Convention

At least certain of the UN Convention's provisions *reflect*—are textual expressions of—customary international law rules on state immunity. The ICJ's decision in *Jurisdictional Immunities of the State,* for example, must be understood as clarifying that the pivotal parts of Article 19 of the Convention mirror customary international law.[13] The ECtHR has also repeatedly found that the Convention, or provisions thereof, reflect such law.[14]

The UN Convention moreover functions as *evidence* of customary international law: its very existence, unanimously adopted, supports the proposition that at least parts of its content reflect what states consider to be the law of state immunity.[15] A rule obtains customary international law status when it is reflected in widespread, consistent, and representative state practice, which is accepted as law *(opinio juris)*.[16] In the comments to its Draft conclusions on the identification of customary international law, the ILC discussed the significance of treaties not having entered into force. The Commission noted that these may "be influential in certain circumstances, particularly

---

12. Cf. e.g., Webb, P., *Introductory Note to the United Nation Convention on Jurisdictional Immunities of States and Their Property*, United Nations' Audiovisual Library of International Law, 2017; O'Keefe, R. & Tams, C., "General Introduction" in *The United Nations Convention on Jurisdictional Immunities of States and Their Property: A Commentary* (eds. O'Keefe, R. & Tams, C.), 1 ed., Oxford University Press, 2013, pp. 41–42.
13. *See* paras. 117–118 in ICJ, judgment dated February 3, 2012 in *Jurisdictional Immunities of the State (Germany v. Italy: Greece intervening)*, where the court held that it "considers that it is unnecessary for purposes of the present case [...] to decide whether all aspects of Article 19 reflect current customary international law. Indeed, it suffices for the Court to find that there is at least one condition that has to be satisfied before any measure of constraint may be taken against property belonging to a foreign State: that the property in question must be in use for an activity not pursuing government non-commercial purposes [...]."
14. *See*, e.g., ECtHR, Grand Chamber, judgment dated March 23, 2010 in *Cudak v. Lithuania*, paras. 66–67; and ECtHR, Fourth Section, judgment dated November 8, 2016 in *Naku v. Lithuania and Sweden*, para. 60. Albeit not the subject of discussion in the present context, it is worthwhile noting the difference in the approach to what constitutes customary international law regarding state immunity issues according to the ICJ, and, respectively, ECtHR. Compare para. 55 in *Jurisdictional Immunities of the State (Germany v. Italy: Greece intervening)*, and paras. 66–67 in *Cudak v. Lithuania*.
15. Cf. e.g., the New Zealand High Court, judgment dated December 21, 2006 in *Fang and Others v. Jiang and Others*, para. 65, where the UN Convention was referred to as a "very recent expression of the consensus of nations on this topic," and England & Wales High Court of Justice, judgment dated October 20, 2005 in *AIG Capital Partners et al. v. Republic of Kazakhstan and the National Bank of Kazakhstan*, para. 80, where it was called a "powerful [...] demonstrat[ion] of international thinking."
16. *See* ICJ, judgment dated February 20, 1969 in *North Sea Continental Shelf cases (Federal Republic of Germany v. Denmark/Federal Republic of Germany v. the Netherlands)*, para. 74; and ILC, *Draft conclusions on identification of customary international law, with commentaries*, 2018.

where they were adopted without opposition or by an overwhelming majority of States."[17]

Also the process leading to the adoption of the UN Convention functions as evidence of what is customary international law. In *Jurisdictional Immunities of the State*, the ICJ held that state practice of particular significance in the determination of the scope and extent of immunity is to be found, e.g., in the statements made by states in the course of the study of the subject by the ILC, as well as in the context of the adoption of the UN Convention.[18]

The UN Convention is thus partly declaratory of the customary international law of state immunity. As evidence of this law, it has routinely been a starting point for courts determining cases on state immunity.[19] It may hence also be "a catalyst for [...] development" of this law.[20] This prompts two questions of interest for the present article.

First, how should a national court, referring to the Convention as a reflection of and evidence of customary international law, proceed when determining cases on state immunity? What, second, is the significance of such referral by national courts? Are national judgments on state immunity directly contributing to the development of this field of international law? Or, are they merely providing evidence of their states' practice and *opinio juris*? These questions will be discussed in the following, as will the significance of *Ascom*.

§9.03 THE METHODOLOGY OF THE APPLICATION OF THE INTERNATIONAL LAW ON STATE IMMUNITY

Pursuant to Article 38(1) of the Statute of the ICJ, customary international law is a source of international law. The provision refers to its two constituent parts as "a general practice accepted as law." The well-established methodology for the determination of the existence and content of a rule of customary international law is to search for evidence of such general practice and its acceptance as law (*opinio juris*). It is thus a process of *identification*; of discerning a rule in practice.

---

17. ILC, *Draft conclusions on identification of customary international law, with commentaries*, 2018, conclusion 11.
18. ICJ, judgment dated February 3, 2012 in *Jurisdictional Immunities of the State (Germany v. Italy: Greece intervening)*, para. 55.
19. *See*, e.g., The New Zealand High Court, judgment dated December 21, 2006 in *Fang and Others v. Jiang and Others*, para. 65; and England & Wales High Court of Justice, judgment dated October 20, 2005 in *AIG Capital Partners et al. v. Republic of Kazakhstan and the National Bank of Kazakhstan*, para. 80. *See also* Webb, P., *Introductory Note to the United Nation Convention on Jurisdictional Immunities of States and Their Property*, United Nations' Audiovisual Library of International Law, 2017, p. 3. *See also* the Svea Court of Appeal's reasoning on this point, in its final judgment dated June 17, 2020 in matter No. ÖÄ 7709-19, p. 10.
20. O'Keefe, R. & Tams, C., "General Introduction" in *The United Nations Convention on Jurisdictional Immunities of States and Their Property: A Commentary* (eds. O'Keefe, R. & Tams, C.), 1 ed., Oxford University Press, 2013, p. 43.

The requirement on a general practice refers primarily to conduct by states,[21] whether exercised by the executive, judicial, or legislative branch.[22] Available practice from a particular state should, however, be consistent. It must therefore be assessed as a whole.[23] To qualify as general, practice must be "both extensive and virtually uniform."[24] There is no absolute standard for either requirement. Practice must, however, be sufficiently widespread, representative, and consistent to fulfill the requirement of generality.[25]

A general practice does not in and by itself constitute a rule of customary international law. It must moreover be exercised out of a sense of legal right or obligation, *opinio juris*. It must thus be established that states have acted in a certain way because they thought themselves legally compelled or entitled to do so by international law.[26]

The ICJ has specified what constitutes relevant practice and *opinio juris* in the context of state immunity. In *Jurisdictional Immunities of the State*, the court explained that relevant practice includes judgments dealing with the question of whether a foreign state is immune, and the claims to immunity advanced by respondent states. Relevant reflections of *opinio juris* include the acknowledgment, by states granting immunity, that international law imposes upon them an obligation to do so, and, conversely, the assertion by respondent states that international law accords them a right to immunity.[27]

The identification of customary international law is to be distinguished from the *interpretation* hereof. Once a customary rule has been identified, it does not have to be identified anew each and every time it is to be applied. Yet, there will be instances when it is not possible to answer whether a particular situation falls within the scope of the rule. In such situation, the rule must be interpreted.[28] How customary rules in general are to be interpreted is a topic of scholarly debate.[29]

However, in a situation like the present, where a treaty functions as evidence of custom, the tools of *treaty interpretation* are available to determine the content of rules

---

21. *See*, e.g., ICJ, judgment dated June 27, 1986 in *Military and Paramilitary Activities in and against Nicaragua*, para. 183.
22. ILC, *Draft conclusions on identification of customary international law, with commentaries*, 2018, conclusions 4 and 5.
23. ILC, *Draft conclusions on identification of customary international law, with commentaries*, 2018, conclusion 7. *See also* ICJ, judgment dated February 3, 2012 in *Jurisdictional Immunities of the State (Germany v. Italy: Greece intervening)*, paras. 76 and 83.
24. ICJ, judgment dated February 20, 1969 in *North Sea Continental Shelf cases (Federal Republic of Germany v. Denmark/Federal Republic of Germany v. the Netherlands)*, para. 74.
25. ILC, *Draft conclusions on identification of customary international law, with commentaries*, 2018, conclusion 8.
26. *See*, e.g., ICJ, judgment dated February 20, 1969 in *North Sea Continental Shelf cases (Federal Republic of Germany v. Denmark/Federal Republic of Germany v. the Netherlands)*, paras. 76–77.
27. ICJ, judgment dated February 3, 2012 in *Jurisdictional Immunities of the State (Germany v. Italy: Greece intervening)*, para. 55.
28. Merkouris, P., "Interpreting the Customary Rules on Interpretation" in *International Community Law Review* (19) 2017, p. 135.
29. It is currently the subject of a research project, where rules on interpretation are induced from the case law of international courts and tribunals. *See* https://trici-law.com/project/.

of customary international law.[30] As put by Judge Sørensen in his dissenting opinion in the *North Sea Continental Shelf cases*: "If [...] the provisions of [a] convention serve as evidence of generally accepted rules of law, it is legitimate, or even necessary, to have recourse to ordinary principles of treaty interpretation[...]."[31] Because the UN Convention is not necessarily fully congruent with custom, the principles of treaty interpretation should, however, be employed with some caution.

The international rules on treaty interpretation are set out in Articles 31–32 of the Vienna Convention on the Law of the Treaties ("Vienna Convention"), which codify customary international law.[32] Pursuant to Article 31.1 of the Vienna Convention, "[a] treaty shall be interpreted in good faith in accordance with the ordinary meaning to be given to the terms of the treaty in their context and in the light of its object and purpose." With this primary rule of interpretation placed at the beginning of Article 31, the Vienna Convention places priority on textual interpretation. The primacy of the text has also repeatedly been stressed by the ICJ.[33] The intention of the parties only occupies a subsidiary space, with Article 31.4 declaring that "a special meaning shall be given to a term if it is established that the parties so intended."[34] Supplementary means of interpretation, including the preparatory work of a treaty, are moreover tools of last resort. Pursuant to Article 32, recourse hereto may only be had to confirm the interpretation according to Article 31, or when the interpretation in accordance therewith "leaves the meaning ambiguous or obscure, or leads to a result which is manifestly absurd or unreasonable."

As will become apparent in the following (*see* section §9.05), the Swedish Supreme Court in *Ascom* referred to neither the methods of identification of customary international law nor those of treaty interpretation. The failure to engage herein is

---

30. For a discussion of the appropriateness of using the international regime of treaty interpretation for interpretation of customary international law in general, *see* Fortuna, M., "Different Strings of the Same Harp: Interpretation of Customary International Rules, Their Identification and Treaty Interpretation" in *The Theory, Practice and Interpretation of Customary International Law* (eds. Merkouris, P., Kammerhofer, J. & Arajärvi, N.), Cambridge University Press, 2022, pp. 393–413..

31. ICJ, judgment dated February 20, 1969 in *North Sea Continental Shelf cases (Federal Republic of Germany v. Denmark/Federal Republic of Germany v. the Netherlands)*, Dissenting Opinion by Judge Sørensen, para. 13. To be noted is also that, in *Ascom*, all legal experts retained by both sides were in agreement of the suitability of treaty interpretation to determine the content of the relevant rules.

32. *See*, e.g., ICJ, judgment dated February 3, 2015 in *Application of the Convention on the Prevention and Punishment of the Crime of Genocide (Croatia v. Serbia)*, para. 138; judgment dated February 3, 1994 in *Territorial Dispute (Libya/Chad)*, para. 41; and judgment dated November 12, 1991 in *Case Concerning the Arbitral Award of 31 July 1989 (Guinea-Bissau v. Senegal)*, para. 48.

33. *See*, e.g., ICJ, judgment dated February 3, 1994 in *Territorial Dispute (Libya/Chad)*, para. 41. *See also* Sorel, J.-M. & Boré Eveno, V., "Observance, Application and Interpretation of Treaties" in *The Vienna Conventions on the Law of Treaties* (eds. Corten, O. & Klein, P.), Oxford Commentaries on International Law, 2011, para. 32.

34. Sorel, J.-M. & Boré Eveno, V., "Observance, Application and Interpretation of Treaties" in *The Vienna Conventions on the Law of Treaties* (eds. Corten, O. & Klein, P.), Oxford Commentaries on International Law, 2011, para. 48.

directly relevant to what we argue is the decision's limited international law significance. Before turning to the decision, we shall first discuss the role national decisions play in international law.

§9.04   THE SIGNIFICANCE OF DOMESTIC COURTS' APPLICATION OF THE INTERNATIONAL LAW ON STATE IMMUNITY

While state immunity is a rule of international law, by its very nature, pleas hereof tend to come before national courts.[35] Immunity cases are thus often such that national courts may make pronouncements on international law. The significance of such pronouncements may be dual.

First, as indicated in the previous section, the practice of national courts faced with the question of whether the assets of a foreign state are immune may count as *evidence* of state practice. Statements on international law may similarly count as evidence of *opinio juris*. Factors such as the court's hierarchical status, and whether its decision aligns with the position of other branches of government, impact the possibility for a court decision to represent evidence in support of a rule of customary international law.[36]

Second, Article 38(1)(d) of the ICJ Statute mentions judicial decisions as subsidiary means for the determination of international law. In ILC's Draft conclusions on the identification of customary international law, it is specified that also decisions of national courts may constitute such subsidiary means.[37]

As subsidiary means of interpretation, judicial decisions are not formal sources of law.[38] In practice, however, judicial decisions may play an important role in formulating international law.[39] The law of state immunity has perhaps been the primary example hereof, with national courts applying the doctrine of restrictive state immunity, paving the way for the UN Convention.[40] In these situations, national courts thus act as *agents of the development* of international law.

According to the ILC, the status of judicial decisions by national courts as subsidiary means of interpretation is, however, not automatic. Conclusion 13(2) of the Draft conclusions states that "[r]egard may be had, as appropriate" to decisions by national courts. Caution is thus required when turning to national judgments for guidance on the existence and content of customary rules. This is, ILC explains,

---

35. Cf., Fox, H. & Webb, P., *The Law of State Immunity*, 3 ed., Oxford University Press, 2015, p. 20.
36. ILC, *Draft conclusions on identification of customary international law, with commentaries*, 2018, conclusion 6 and 7.
37. ILC, *Draft conclusions on identification of customary international law, with commentaries*, 2018, conclusion 13(2).
38. Thirlway, H., *The Sources of International Law*, 2 ed., Oxford University Press, 2019, p. 131.
39. Roberts, A., "Comparative International Law? The Role of National Courts in Creating and Enforcing International Law" *International and Comparative Law Quarterly* (60) January 2011, p. 63.
40. Fox, H. & Webb, P., *The Law of State Immunity*, 3 ed., Oxford University Press, 2015, p. 17, and Roberts, A., "Comparative International Law? The Role of National Courts in Creating and Enforcing International Law" *International and Comparative Law Quarterly* (60) January 2011, p. 70.

because national courts may lack relevant international expertise, and their judgments may represent particular national interests.[41]

The reasons expressed by the ILC for this conditional status are echoed in scholarship. The role of national courts as agents of international law has since long been a subject of scholarly debate. It has been argued that national courts have a better position to enforce international law, and they have thus been called upon to act as guardians of the international legal order, making every effort to interpret international law "as it would be interpreted by an international tribunal."[42] Concerns have also been raised. Benvenisti has written that national courts tend to skew the interpretation of international law in order to protect national interests.[43] Abrahamson Chigara has rather worried about the abilities of national judges when they face the challenge of solving problems beyond their day-to-day practice. To protect the legitimacy and integrity of international law, he has therefore suggested lower national courts appoint expert academicians to illuminate the contested applicable international law.[44]

More prosaically, in their great volume on state immunity, Webb and Fox have pointed out that the "lasting impact" of all national court decisions will be dependent on their imitation or rejection in practice by other states and by the wider international community.[45] Whether a national decision will serve as a subsidiary means of determination may thus hinge less on the quality or international objectivity of the decision. In practice, factors such as from which state a decision emanates seem to carry more weight: Western and non-Western States alike turn primarily to the case law of Western states as a subsidiary source.[46] As will be returned to, also the *Ascom* court may have had an occidental bias.

There are, however, reasons to take seriously the rationale for ILC's hesitance to resort to national judgments in the determination of the existence and content of international law. Former ICJ judge Simma has written that, with the jurisprudence of domestic courts on questions of international law gaining relevance for the development of the law, there also "arises an increasing responsibility on the part of these courts to maintain the law's coherence and integrity."[47] In our view, this includes carefully abiding by the methodologies that international law prescribes, as well as making use of its recognized sources. Hopefully, "the lasting impact" of national judgments will also be dependent hereof. As mentioned, the decision in *Ascom* fails in

---

41. ILC, *Draft conclusions on identification of customary international law, with commentaries*, 2018, conclusion 13, comment 7.
42. *See* Institut de Droit International, *Resolution on The Activities of National Judges and the International Relations of their State*, September 7, 2003, available at https://www.idi-il.org/app/uploads/2017/06/1993_mil_01_en.pdf, accessed March 15, 2022.
43. Benvenisti, E., "Judicial Misgivings Regarding the Application of International Law: An Analysis of the Attitudes of National Courts" *European Journal of International Law* (4) 1993, p. 161.
44. Abrahamson, C.B., "The Administration of International Law in National Courts and the Legitimacy of International Law" *International Criminal Law Review* (17) 2017.
45. Fox, H. & Webb, P., *The Law of State Immunity*, 3 ed., Oxford University Press, 2015, p. 17.
46. Thirlway, H., *The Sources of International Law*, 2 ed., Oxford University Press, 2019, p. 140.
47. Simma, B., "Universality of International Law from the Perspective of a Practitioner" *European Journal of International Law* (20) 2009, p. 290.

this regard. We now turn to this decision. Some words on the Swedish approach to state immunity, as well as the case leading up to *Ascom*, serve as an introduction.

§9.05   THE *ASCOM* CASE

[A]   Introduction

Sweden has no legislation on state immunity. The UN Convention is ratified, and Sweden has chosen to incorporate it by way of the Act on Immunity for States and Their Property (the "State Immunity Act," SFS 2009:1514, Sw. *lagen om immunitet för stater och deras egendom*) in 2009. The Act is to enter into force when the Convention does.[48] According to the *travaux préparatoires*, state immunity issues are thus "primarily" (*"främst"*) determined with reference to customary international law before the entry into force of the State Immunity Act.[49]

The first case on enforcement immunity following the incorporation of the UN Convention came before the Supreme Court in 2011: Supreme Court case reported as NJA 2011 p. 475 (*"Lidingöhuset"*).[50] The question was whether state immunity protected a real property owned by the Russian Federation from execution. Pursuant to Article 19 of the UN Convention, no post-judgment measures of constraint against the property of a state may be taken in connection with a proceeding before a court of another state unless one of the exceptions enumerated in the provision applies. The exception in Article 19(c) provides that measures of constraint may be taken if it has been established that the property is specifically in use or intended for use by the state for other than government non-commercial purposes.

The Supreme Court held that the Convention constitutes a codification of customary international law "in large—but not all—parts" (*"i stora—men inte alla—delar"*).[51] The principle in Article 19(c) was said to be "recognized by many states" (*"erkänd av många stater"*).[52] By and in itself, recognition by many states is not necessarily sufficient to render it custom. Whether it sufficed in this particular case was not explained. Despite thus not having clarified what source of law it was applying, the court nevertheless went on to apply its interpretation of the principle in Article 19(c).[53]

This lack of clarity regarding the source of law is also attached to the court's view on Article 21, on which the court made pronouncements *obiter dicta*. According to the court, immunity for property for other than government non-commercial purposes requires that the property be "used for the official functions of a state" (*"för en stats*

---

48. Government bill 2008/09:204, p. 109.
49. Government bill 2008/09:204, p. 90.
50. In international articles and commentaries, *Lidingöhuset* is often referred to as *"Sedelmayer,"* named after the German businessman who had won the arbitral award against the Russian Federation, which he in *Lidingöhuset* sought enforcement of.
51. *Lidingöhuset*, para. 14.
52. *Lidingöhuset*, para. 14.
53. As pointed out by Wrange, the rule formulated by the Supreme Court in *Lidingöhuset* is not necessarily fully congruent with Art. 19(c). *See* Wrange, P., "Sedelmayer v. Russian Federation" *American Journal of International Law* (106) 2012.

officiella funktioner").[54] The court held that this does not mean that property is immune only by virtue of being owned by a state and used for non-commercial purposes, but state immunity should impede measures of constraint if the purpose of holding the property "is of a qualified kind" (*"är av ett kvalificerat slag"*). According to the court, this includes the kind of property set forth in Article 21 of the UN Convention.[55]

Property of central banks is one of the categories enumerated in Article 21 of the UN Convention. With the leave to appeal in *Ascom*, the Supreme Court thus had an opportunity to clarify the customary status of the principle in Article 21, as well as to elaborate on its content.

[B] The Supreme Court's Reasoning in the *Ascom* Case

In *Ascom*, the question was whether state immunity protected property accumulated in and managed by the National Bank of Kazakhstan against measures of constraint. The main issue was thus what immunity protection to award to the property of central banks.

The Supreme Court commenced its reasoning by explaining the concept of state immunity and the difference between court and enforcement jurisdiction.[56] In this part of the decision, appropriate but selective references to international law sources were made. The court then noted that there is no Swedish immunity legislation and that Swedish courts are "considered to be obliged" (*"domstolar anses [...] vara skyldiga"*) to observe the immunity that follows from customary international law.[57] Just as in *Lidingöhuset*, the court did, however, not outright say that customary international law was the applicable law in the case at hand. Judging by what the court then de facto did, the remaining ambiguity about the source of law applied appears to have served the purpose of giving the court greater leeway to construe the immunity principles as it pleased.

Next, the court held that, insofar as it shed light on the content of customary international law, the UN Convention was relevant.[58] In this context, the court made no mention of the history of the UN Convention nor discussed how it was the result of a long negotiation process in which all states had taken part and what possible implications that could have.

The court then cited Article 19 of the UN Convention. It referred to the *travaux préparatoires* of the 2009 Act, where it had been stated that there is no common state practice regarding restrictions on the principle of immunity from enforcement, but that the countries of the Western world had developed an approach according to which

---

54. *Lidingöhuset*, para. 14.
55. *Lidingöhuset*, para. 14.
56. *Ascom*, paras. 11–13.
57. *Ascom*, para. 14.
58. *Ascom*, para. 16.

enforcement would be permitted in property used or intended to be used for commercial purposes.[59] Since the court, as shall be seen, failed to explain the international law basis for its conclusion, a possible assumption is that this primarily occidental approach to enforcement immunity permeated its standpoint. That would expose the court to criticism. The sovereign interests at stake were not those of two Western countries, both accepting the standard of restrictive enforcement immunity. Rather, the sovereign interests were those of Sweden (the interest of exercising jurisdiction) and Kazakhstan (the interest of immunity). An expectation on the court in this situation is that it applied what it found was the rule of public international law in force.

The court subsequently turned to Article 21 of the Convention, taking up where it had left off in *Lidingöhuset*. The provision enumerates categories of property of a state which are not to be considered as property specifically in use or intended for use by the state for other than government non-commercial purposes under Article 19(c). Property of the central bank or other monetary authority of the state is one of these categories, mentioned in Article 21(1)(c).

According to the court, the scope of the immunity protection in Article 21(1)(c) "appears unclear in customary international law" ("*framstår [...] som oklart i den internationella sedvanerätten*").[60] The conclusion appears to have been reached through a deductive process. The court made a general reference to the negotiations that preceded the UN Convention, stating that this applies "in particular in light of" ("*särskilt mot bakgrund*")[61] that, during these, there were different views on the issue and no clear state practice has subsequently developed.[62] This gives the impression that the attitudes among states during the development of the Convention, as well as subsequent state practice, had been evaluated. But no reference to any source was made.

Faced with the unclear immunity protection for central banks, the court resorted to a teleological interpretation of the more precise scope of this protection, guided by a purpose which itself formulated, with reference to neither the UN Convention nor its rich drafting history. It held that the reason why the property of central banks is entitled to near absolute immunity "must be considered" ("*måste anses vara*") to be that a central bank conducts activities within the area of monetary policy.[63] According to the court, the great importance of monetary policy to a state's central functions justifies this immunity protection in respect of property used within this activity.[64]

The court then again made a statement which gives the impression that it had evaluated state practice and *opinio juris*. It held that there is no unequivocal support for the position that absolute immunity under international customary law applies also in respect of property which a central bank has at its disposal without any connection to

---

59. *Ascom*, para. 18, referring to government bill 2008/09:204, pp. 45 and 56.
60. *Ascom*, para. 21.
61. *Ascom*, para. 21.
62. *Ascom*, para. 21.
63. *Ascom*, para. 23.
64. *Ascom*, para. 23.

the bank's monetary policy tasks. Yet again, with no reference to any public international law source, the court held that "such far-reaching entitlement to immunity does not appear to be justifiable" ("*[e]tt sådant vittgående immunitetsskydd framstår inte [...] som motiverat*").[65] The court hence concluded that immunity protection for the property with no clear connection to the central bank's activities in the area of monetary policy was instead to be determined according to the principle expressed in Article 19(c).[66]

The court thus treated the problem of the unclear immunity protection for the property of central banks as a matter of interpretation. Nevertheless, it did not resort to the established principles of treaty interpretation, even though the UN Convention at the least is evidence for customary law. According to these principles, moreover, the teleological element is of minor importance.[67] A treaty is a compromise between the wills of the state parties, and the intentions behind the final specific provisions may differ among them. The provision in Article 31(1) of the Vienna Convention that a treaty shall be interpreted in the light of its object and purpose thus refers to the object and purpose of the instrument as a whole.[68] A treaty's preamble is generally useful for the determination hereof. A quick glance in the preamble of the UN Convention reveals that it is difficult to find other purpose of the instrument than legal certainty.[69]

It is not obvious that the scope of immunity protection for the property of central banks even is a question of interpretation. It appears that the lack of a consistent practice—in either a restrictive or absolute direction—was determinative for the Supreme Court's conclusion that the scope of immunity protection is unclear.[70] It held that there is no unequivocal support for the position that absolute immunity under international customary law applies in respect of central banks. It did not say that there neither is unequivocal support for the position that absolute immunity does *not* apply to such property. But it did acknowledge that the situation was unclear. What rule should in such a situation be applied?

In the *Asylum Case*, the ICJ did not accept that a customary rule would no longer be in force only because a certain new practice—not meeting the requirements for such practice to have obtained status as custom—was applied by certain states.[71] This means that a customary rule applies until a new one has replaced it. Faced with the unclear scope of immunity protection for the property of central banks, the Supreme

---

65. *Ascom*, para. 24.
66. *Ascom*, para. 24.
67. *Supra* note 34.
68. Gardiner, R., "The General Rule: The Treaty, Its Terms, and their Ordinary Meaning" in *Treaty Interpretation*, 2 ed., Oxford International Law Library, 2015, p. 37.
69. Cf. the preamble of the UN Convention, which, e.g., reads: "Believing that an international convention on the jurisdictional immunities of States and their property would enhance the rule of law and legal certainty, particularly in dealings of States with natural or juridical persons, and would contribute to the codification and development of international law and the harmonization of practice in this area[.]."
70. Cf. *supra* note 61.
71. ICJ, decision dated November 20, 1950 in *Asylum Case (Colombia v. Peru)*, p. 277. *See also* Wolfrum, R., "Sources of International Law" in *Max Planck Encyclopedias of International Law* (eds. Peters, A. & Wolfrum, R.), 2011, para. 30.

Court could thus have searched for the most recent applicable rule and asked whether this rule had been replaced by a new one. Another approach would have been to discuss whether absolute or restrictive immunity was the main rule (and the other consequently an exception).[72] This would have required a serious engagement with international law sources. Instead, the crucial parts of the decision are completely void of such engagement.

§9.06   CONCLUSION

Unfortunately, the scholarly concerns about judges in national courts applying public international law—that they are not sufficiently familiar with the regime and that they are too influenced by national particularities—appear to have been realized in the *Ascom* decision. The Swedish Supreme Court failed to take the regime seriously. This is despite the rich material available on the subject and despite the explicit guidance provided by the ICJ in the *Jurisdictional Immunities* case on how to go about when solving state immunity issues. The court moreover applied the restrictive doctrine also in respect of the property of central banks, which may align with the practice of some Western states but not necessarily with international law. The court's refusal to be clear about whether international law applied suggests that it was aware of the decision's shortcomings in this regard. Potentially, its intention was less to correctly reflect public international law and more to clarify a Swedish—or at least the Supreme Court's—position on the matter.

In any event, the failure by the Supreme Court to "speak and think" international law limits the decision's possibility of acting as an agent of development of this law; of being considered a subsidiary source of international law. Instead, its significance is limited to being a piece of evidence of the Swedish position on state immunity for the property of central banks, albeit an important one. To also be considered relevant Swedish state practice depends on whether the decision is viewed as congruent with the legislator's decision to incorporate the UN Convention, which is not necessarily the case. In contrast to the principle applied in *Ascom*, Article 21(1)(c) of the Convention after all makes no mention of the property of central banks having to have a clear connection with monetary policy to enjoy immunity protection.

---

72. This approach to the issue was also advocated in the expert opinions submitted to the Supreme Court by professors Pål Wrange and Chester Brown, respectively, both retained by the Republic of Kazakhstan, of which the Supreme Court made no mention. Both opinions are publicly available and could be obtained from the Supreme Court.

CHAPTER 10

Paradigm Shift: Reflections on the Interpretation of International Investment Agreements by National and Supranational Courts Post-*Achmea*

Crina Baltag

The Court of Justice of the European Union (CJEU or the Court) in *Republic of Moldova v. Komstroy,* Case C-741/19, was called upon to answer the questions posed by the Paris Cour d'Appel, essentially addressing the interpretation of the notions of 'investment' and 'investor' under Article 1(6) and 1(7) of the Energy Charter Treaty (ECT),[1] even though the underlying case had no immediate qualifications for the jurisdiction of the CJEU. National courts undertake the interpretation of international investment agreements (IIAs) in connection with the set aside or recognition and enforcement of investment arbitration awards. For example, the Paris Cour d'Appel in *Venezuela v. Serafín García Armas and Karina García Gruber* has set aside an investment arbitration award, deciding that the definitions of 'investment' and 'investor' in the Spain-Venezuela Bilateral Investment Treaty (BIT) required that assets were 'invested by investors' of the other contracting State and, hence, that investors must satisfy the nationality requirement when making the investment. In *Clorox Spain S.L. v. Venezuela*, the Swiss Federal Tribunal set aside an investment arbitration award noting that Article 1(2) of the Spain-Venezuela BIT reflects an asset-based definition of the notion of 'investment', and that the relevant BIT does not include a denial of benefits clause, nor additional requirements in establishing the nationality of an investor, which could

---

1. The Energy Charter Treaty was signed on 17 December 1994 and entered into force on 16 April 1998, 34 ILM 373 (1995).

justify the interpretation of the notion of 'investment' in a narrow sense, with emphasis on the wording 'invested by investors'.[2]

The topic of the interpretation of IIAs by national or supranational courts is relevant for several reasons. First, the choice between an arbitration under the Convention for the Settlement of Investment Disputes between States and Nationals of Other States (ICSID Convention)[3] and non-ICSID Convention arbitration has gained new connotations taking into consideration both the nationality of the claimant-investor in the light of the intra-European Union (EU) concerns in a post-*Achmea*[4] world, as well as any consequences on the set aside and recognition and enforcement of arbitral awards. Second, the standard of review of the investment arbitration awards is considerably different between ICSID and non-ICSID awards. Under the ICSID Convention, the grounds upon which an award can be annulled are set forth in Article 52 of the ICSID Convention and are limited in scope, while the annulment proceedings are within the self-contained system of ICSID, before the ICSID annulment committees. Furthermore, under Article 53(1) of the ICSID Convention, an award shall be binding on the parties and shall not be subject to any appeal or to any other remedy except those provided for in the ICSID Convention. On the recognition and enforcement of awards, Article 54(1) of the ICSID Convention provides for the direct recognition of pecuniary arbitral awards, as if they were final judgments of a court in the State of enforcement. On the contrary, non-ICSID investment arbitral awards, either institutional or ad hoc, would be subject to the scrutiny of the courts at the seat of arbitration, and the recognition and enforcement proceedings submitted, most often, under the Convention on the Recognition and Enforcement of Foreign Arbitral Awards, New York, 1958 ('New York Convention'). It is not only that the set aside grounds and the grounds for the refusal of the recognition and enforcement of an award become more 'national' rather than 'a-national' in the context of a non-ICSID arbitration, given the fact that each national court will have to apply its *lex fori*, but also policy concerns can also become relevant, especially in the context of national courts of Member States that are part of regional economic international organizations, such as the EU. As such, the seat of arbitration for non-ICSID investment arbitrations becomes even more important in this context, and it is particularly important how the courts at the seat approach the interpretation of IIAs and whether they are rather flexible in remitting these issues to the supranational court, such as the CJEU. Last but not least, the exposure to the post-award scrutiny by a national and supranational court may be used to invalidate international treaties validly entered into by their contracting States. The latter point is particularly relevant for the current approach taken by the CJEU, commencing with the ECT and continuing with the EU's possible position on the intra-EU application of the ICSID Convention.

---

2. *Clorox Spain S.L. v. Bolivarian Republic of Venezuela*, Decision of the Swiss Federal Tribunal of 25 March 2020, Case No. 4A_306/2019.
3. Convention for the Settlement of Investment Disputes between States and Nationals of Other States, entered into force on 14 October 1966, 1 ICSID Reports 3 (1993). The ICSID Convention established the International Centre for Settlement of Investment Disputes (ICSID).
4. *Slowakische Republik (Slovak Republic) v. Achmea BV*, Judgment of the CJEU of 6 March 2018, in Case C-284/16.

This analysis will focus first on the power of the interpretation of IIAs by national courts and then move to the *Moldova v. Komstroy* CJEU case and analyse the manner in which the court addressed the interpretation of the relevant provisions in the ECT. The paper is concerned with the manner in which national and supranational courts proceed with such interpretation.

§10.01   NATIONAL COURTS AND TREATY INTERPRETATION

As mentioned, it is undisputed that where national courts are competent to set aside or recognize and enforce arbitral awards, they are also competent to interpret the terms of the underlying treaty.[5]

In *Ecuador v. Occidental*, the English High Court[6] and the English Court of Appeal[7] confirmed that the court can proceed with the interpretation of the relevant BIT in the light of the provisions of the Vienna Convention on the Law of Treaties (VCLT). Similarly, the Swedish courts have endorsed their power to interpret the underlying treaty provisions based on the fact that the relevant BIT provides that the place of arbitration would be a New York Convention state.[8]

The standard of review of the national courts is not uniform, but it certainly does not contemplate a review on the merits of the case. However, jurisdictional matters are often brought before the national courts and then the interpretation of the definitions in an IIA by the court becomes central. In the case of jurisdictional issues, courts in leading arbitration jurisdictions, including France, Sweden and England, take the approach that this is a de novo review.[9]

For example, the Swedish Arbitration Act provides for a de novo standard of judicial review in section 2, for the negative jurisdictional decisions, and in section 36, for the positive jurisdictional decisions. The decision of the Swedish Supreme Court of 21 April 2016 in Case No. Ö 1429-15 concludes that '[t]he most obvious interpretation of this provision [i.e. Section 2 of the Swedish Arbitration Act] is that the jurisdictional issues that can be considered by the court are the same as those that can considered by the arbitral tribunal. Thus, the wording of the provision would imply that the scope of

---

5. Broadly on the compliance by States with the investment arbitration awards against them, *see* Emmanuel Gaillard and Ilija Mitrev Penushliski, *State Compliance with Investment Awards*, 35(3) ICSID Review 2020, 540–594.
6. *The Republic of Ecuador v. Occidental Exploration & Production Company* [2006] EWHC 345 (Comm) (2 March 2006).
7. *The Republic of Ecuador v. Occidental Exploration & Production Company* [2007] EWCA Civ 656 (4 July 2007).
8. *The Russian Federation v. Mr. Franz Sedelmayer*, Decision of the Stockholm District Court on the Set Aside Application of 18 December 2002.
9. *See* further, John Christopher Thomas and Harpreet Kaur Dhillon, *The Foundations of Investment Treaty Arbitration: The ICSID Convention, Investment Treaties and the Review of Arbitration Awards*, 32(3) ICSID Review-Foreign Investment Law Journal 2017, 459–502, at pp. 494 et seq. Also on the approach of the Canadian courts, *see* Céline Lévesque, *Correctness' as the Proper Standard of Review Applicable to 'True' Questions of Jurisdiction in the Set-Aside of Treaty-Based Investor-State Awards Get access Arrow*, 5(1) Journal of International Dispute Settlement (2014), 69–103.

the arbitral tribunal's and the court's jurisdictional review is intended to be identical'.[10] In *Ecuador v. Occidental*, the English High Court further elaborated on the applicable standard of review by the court in the context of jurisdictional matters and interpretation of IIAs being one of a re-hearing, meaning whether the arbitral tribunal was 'correct' in its decision, rather than whether the arbitral tribunal was 'entitled' to reach the decision on its jurisdiction:

> It is now well-established that a challenge to the jurisdiction of an arbitration panel under section 67 proceeds by way of a rehearing of the matters before the arbitrators. The test for the court is: was the Tribunal correct in its decision on jurisdiction? The test is not: was the Tribunal entitled to reach the decision that it did.[11]

As to the interpretation of treaties, the English High Court in *GPF GP S.À.R.L. v. Poland*[12] confirmed the approach of the English courts in *Ecuador v. Occidental* that an arbitration agreement in a bilateral or multilateral IIA is governed by international law.[13] The High Court in *GPF GP S.À.R.L. v. Poland* went further and explained that the interpretation of the arbitration agreement and of the jurisdiction of the arbitral tribunal under the applicable IIA will be done in accordance with the principles of interpretation in the VCLT which codify international law.[14] The High Court then proceeded to analyse Articles 31 and 32 of the VCLT. Looking first at Article 31 of the VCLT,[15] the High Court in *GPF GP S.À.R.L. v. Poland* emphasized that this provision 'sets out the essential primary, or fundamental, rule of interpretation',[16] and that this

---

10. Judgment of the Supreme Court of 21 April 2016, Case No. Ö 1429-15, para. 18.
11. *The Republic of Ecuador v. Occidental Exploration & Production Company* [2006] EWHC 345 (Comm) (2 March 2006), para. 7, emphasis in original removed.
12. *GPF GP S.À.R.L. v. The Republic of Poland* [2018] EWHC 409 (Comm) (2 March 2018).
13. *GPF GP S.À.R.L. v. Poland*, para. 46.
14. *GPF GP S.À.R.L. v. Poland*, para. 47.
15. Article 31 of the VCLT: General rule of interpretation:

> 1. A treaty shall be interpreted in good faith in accordance with the ordinary meaning to be given to the terms of the treaty in their context and in the light of its object and purpose.
> 2. The context for the purpose of the interpretation of a treaty shall comprise, in addition to the text, including its preamble and annexes:
>   (a) any agreement relating to the treaty which was made between all the parties in connection with the conclusion of the treaty;
>   (b) any instrument which was made by one or more parties in connection with the conclusion of the treaty and accepted by the other parties as an instrument related to the treaty.
> 2. There shall be taken into account, together with the context:
>   (a) any subsequent agreement between the parties regarding the interpretation of the treaty or the application of its provisions;
>   (b) any subsequent practice in the application of the treaty which establishes the agreement of the parties regarding its interpretation;
>   (c) any relevant rules of international law applicable in the relations between the parties.
> 3. A special meaning shall be given to a term if it is established that the parties so intended.

16. *GPF GP S.À.R.L. v. Poland*, para. 48.

rule of interpretation is 'textual'.[17] As explained by the High Court, this means that 'the text [of the treaty] is to be presumed to be the authentic expression of the intention of the parties (the textual approach to interpretation) and is not to be substituted for or overridden by the presumed intention of the parties (the teleological approach to interpretation)'.[18] Furthermore, as the High Court emphasized, the good faith interpretation principle under Article 31(1) of the VCLT, while it requires that provisions of treaties are to be interpreted so as render them effective rather than ineffective, does not justify going beyond the text of the treaty. The High Court also addressed the reference to the object and purpose of a treaty in Article 31 VCLT, emphasizing that 'any scope for the application of this principle in any event only arises in the event of their being an ambiguity'.[19] As to the relevance and application of Article 32 of the VCLT,[20] the High Court noted that the supplementary means of interpretation 'is applicable *only* to confirm the meaning resulting from the application of Article 31, or to determine the meaning when the interpretation according to Article 31 leaves the meaning ambiguous or obscure or leads to a result which is manifestly absurd or unreasonable'.[21] As such, the High Court concluded, 'if the meaning resulting from the application of Article 31 is clear ... the supplementary means of interpretation in Article 32 *cannot* be used to change or contradict the meaning resulting from the application of Article 31'.[22]

The position on the interpretation of IIAs by the English courts in *GPF GP S.À.R.L. v. Poland* was later confirmed by the English High Court in *PAO Tatneft v. Ukraine*.[23] As the High Court mentioned, 'the principles governing the construction of a treaty such as the BIT, including its arbitration provision, were as set out in the decision of Bryan J in GPF GP v Poland [2018] EWHC 409'.[24] The High Court summarized the reasoning of *GPF GP S.À.R.L. v. Poland* as follows:

> It is for the Court to interpret the BIT in accordance with international law, and the principles of interpretation contained in Articles 31 and 32 of the Vienna Convention on the Law of Treaties (1969) ('the Vienna Convention'), which codifies customary international law ....
>
> ...

---

17. *GPF GP S.À.R.L. v. Poland*, para. 49.
18. *GPF GP S.À.R.L. v. Poland*, para. 49.
19. *GPF GP S.À.R.L. v. Poland*, para. 59.
20. Article 32 Supplementary means of interpretation:

    Recourse may be had to supplementary means of interpretation, including the preparatory work of the treaty and the circumstances of its conclusion, in order to confirm the meaning resulting from the application of article 31, or to determine the meaning when the interpretation according to article 31:

    (a) leaves the meaning ambiguous or obscure; or
    (b) leads to a result which is manifestly absurd or unreasonable.

21. *GPF GP S.À.R.L. v. Poland*, para. 61, emphasis in original.
22. *GPF GP S.À.R.L. v. Poland*, para. 61, emphasis in original.
23. *PAO Tatneft v. Ukraine* [2018] EWHC 1797 (Comm) (13 July 2018).
24. *PAO Tatneft v. Ukraine*, para. 38.

The rule of interpretation is textual, not teleological .... That is, 'interpretation must be based above all upon the text of the treaty' .... Accordingly, the text is presumed to be the authentic expression of the intention of the parties and is not to be substituted for or overridden by the presumed intention of the parties ....[25]

Before the Swedish courts, the interpretation of IIAs was addressed in the *Russian Federation v. GBI 9000 SICAV S.A, Orgor de Valores SICAV S.A, Quasar de Valores SICAV S.A, ALOS 34 SL*.[26] Stockholm District Court noted that it is undisputed that the ECT shall be interpreted in accordance with Articles 31 and 32 of the VCLT, whereas Article 31 provides general rules for interpretation, and Article 32 contains supplementary aids for interpretation.[27] Further, the Stockholm District Court noted, is the fact that all four elements of Article 31, i.e., good faith, ordinary meaning, context, and object and purpose, are of equal importance.[28]

The French Cour de Cassation in *Venezuela v. Garcia Armas*[29] considered the interpretation of the applicable BIT in the context of the jurisdiction of the arbitral tribunal and the dual nationality of investor, where one of the nationalities was of the respondent State. As such, the Cour de Cassation held that the interpretation of treaties is made under the rules of international law and, in particular, under the VCLT.[30] In particular, the Cour de Cassation held, in determining the coverage of dual nationals by the applicable BIT, the relevant treaty provision must be interpreted in the light of Article 31 of the VCLT, which codifies the customary rules on treaty interpretation.[31] Similarly, in *Etat d'Ukraine v. Société Pao Tatneft*, Paris Cour d'Appel held that the interpretation of the terms of the underlying BIT is made in the light of the rules of treaty interpretation of the VCLT.[32]

It is evident that while national courts in non-ICSID set aside or recognition and enforcement proceedings of investment arbitration awards are not shy in proceeding with a de novo review, they are careful in appreciating that the interpretation of the IIAs must always be based on public international law rules. It is noticeable also that great attention is devoted to the VCLT, as codifying the customary international law rules on treaty interpretation.[33]

---

25. *PAO Tatneft v. Ukraine*, para. 38.
26. Judgment of the Stockholm District Court, 11 September 2014, Case No. T 15045-09, *Russian Federation v. GBI 9000 SICAV S.A, Orgor de Valores SICAV S.A, Quasar de Valores SICAV S.A, ALOS 34 SL.*
27. *Russian Federation v. GBI 9000 SICAV S.A, Orgor de Valores SICAV S.A, Quasar de Valores SICAV S.A, ALOS 34 SL*, p. 26.
28. *Russian Federation v. GBI 9000 SICAV S.A, Orgor de Valores SICAV S.A, Quasar de Valores SICAV S.A, ALOS 34 SL*, p. 26.
29. *Venezuela v. Serafin Garcia Armas and Karina Garcia Gruber*, Judgment No. 157 F-D of 13 February 2019.
30. *Venezuela v. Garcia Armas*, p. 13.
31. *Venezuela v. Garcia Armas*, p. 13.
32. *Etat d'Ukraine v. Société Pao Tatneft*, Paris Cour d'Appel, Judgment of 29 November 2016.
33. For further detailed analysis on the approach of national courts to post-award remedies in the context of investment arbitration awards, *see* further Kateryna Bondar, *Annulment of ICSID and Non-ICSID Investment Awards: Differences in the Extent of Review*, 32(6) Journal of International Arbitration 2015, 621–676; Alexander J. Marcopoulos, *Revisiting the Risk of Undesired Appeal in Investment Treaty Arbitration: Is Deference to the Tribunal's Award Still Less Likely in the ICSID Context?*, 37 Arbitration International, 685–706; Gaëtan Verhoosel, *Annulment and Enforcement*

§10.02 *KOMSTROY* AND THE INTERPRETATION OF THE ECT

As we have now seen the approach of national courts to the interpretation of IIAs, let us proceed with the position of the supranational courts and, in particular, with the CJEU reasoning in *Republic of Moldova v. Komstroy*.

On 3 March 2021, the CJEU Advocate General delivered the Opinion in *Republic of Moldova v. Komstroy* (the 'Opinion'), upon the request for a preliminary ruling by the Paris Cour d'Appel.[34] While most of the attention was captured by the application of *Achmea* to the ECT, the Opinion is also very much relevant in the context of the interpretation of treaties by the CJEU, and of the notions of 'investment' under Article 1(6) of the ECT, and 'investor' under Article 1(7) of the ECT.

In brief, on the underlying facts of the case and the subsequent resolution of the dispute,[35] Ukrenergo, a Ukrainian electricity generator, sold electricity to Energoalians, a Ukrainian electricity distributor, which then sold it to Derimen Properties Limited, a company registered in the British Virgin Islands, which in turn sold it to Moldtranselectro, a Moldovan public undertaking. The sale was made under two contracts concluded on 1 and 24 February 1999 and the volumes of electricity to be supplied were determined each month directly between Moldtranselectro and Ukrenergo. The electricity was supplied in 1999 and 2000, under 'DAF Incoterms 1990', to the border between Ukraine and Moldova, on the Ukrainian side. On 30 May 2000, Derimen assigned to Energoalians the claim which it held against Moldtranselectro, which in turn partially settled its debt by assigning several claims which it held to Energoalians. While initially Energoalians attempted to obtain payment of the remainder of its claims before the Moldovan and the Ukrainian courts, it eventually resorted to arbitration against Moldova under Article 26 of the ECT. The ad hoc arbitral tribunal seated in Paris, France, delivered its majority award on 25 October 2013, deciding that it had jurisdiction and, considering that the Republic of Moldova had failed to comply with its undertakings under the ECT, ordered Moldova to pay a certain amount to Energoalians. The dissenting opinion of the presiding arbitrator concerned the jurisdiction of the arbitral tribunal. Subsequently, Moldova brought an action for annulment against the arbitral award, alleging infringement of a public-policy provision related to the jurisdiction of the arbitral tribunal, pursuant to Article 1520 of the French Code of Civil Procedure. By judgment of 12 April 2016, the Paris Cour d'Appel annulled the award on the ground that the arbitral tribunal had wrongly declared itself to have jurisdiction. That Cour d'Appel held that the dispute between Energoalians and Moldova concerned a claim, assigned by Derimen, having as its sole purpose the sale of electricity and that in the absence of any contribution, such a claim could not be regarded as an investment within the meaning of the ECT. In October 2014, Komstroy became the successor in law of Energoalians and appealed the judgment of the Cour d'Appel to the French Cour de

---

Review of Treaty Awards: To ICSID or NOT to ICSID, 23(1) ICSID Review – Foreign Investment Law Journal, Spring 2008, pp. 119–154.

34. *Republic of Moldova v. Komstroy*, Opinion of Advocate General Szpunar of 3 March 2021 in Case C 741/19.
35. *See* paras 10–22 of the Opinion.

Cassation. By judgment of 28 March 2018, the Cour de Cassation set aside the judgment in the first instance and referred the case back to the Cour d'Appel. In the resubmitted case, Moldova argued that the arbitral tribunal should have declined jurisdiction in the absence of an 'investment', within the meaning of the ECT, 'of' an enterprise of a Contracting Party to the ECT, 'in the area of' Moldova. Further, even if that claim could constitute an investment, it was not 'of' an undertaking of a Contracting Party, since Derimen is an undertaking of the British Virgin Islands. Finally, and in any event, that claim relates to a transaction for the sale of electricity which did not take place 'in the area' of Moldova, since the electricity was sold and transmitted only to the border between Ukraine and Moldova, on the Ukrainian side. The Cour d'Appel decided to stay the proceedings and to refer the following questions to the CJEU for a preliminary ruling:

(1) Must (Article 1(6) of the ECT) be interpreted as meaning that a claim which arose from a contract for the sale of electricity and which did not involve any contribution on the part of the investor in the host State can constitute an 'investment' within the meaning of that article?

(2) Must (Article 26(1) of the ECT) be interpreted as meaning that the acquisition, by an investor of a Contracting Party, of a claim established by an economic operator which is not from one of the States that are Parties to that Treaty constitutes an investment?

(3) Must (Article 26(1) of the ECT) be interpreted as meaning that a claim held by an investor, which arose from a contract for the sale of electricity supplied at the border of the host State, can constitute an investment made in the area of another Contracting Party, in the case where the investor does not carry out any economic activity in the territory of that latter Contracting Party?

Before addressing the questions posed by the Cour d'Appel, the Advocate General had to first clarify how the provisions of the ECT are applicable in the EU legal order and why the CJEU has the interest and the powers to proceed with their interpretation. This is an essential matter dealt with by the Opinion, and subsequently by the CJEU, which may trigger important consequences for comparable situations in the future.

In a nutshell, *Komstroy v. Moldova* concerned neither the EU nor the Member States of the EU. Under Article 267 of the Treaty on the Functioning of the European Union (TFEU), the CJEU has jurisdiction to give preliminary rulings concerning the interpretation of acts of the institutions of the EU.[36] The Advocate General highlighted that it is understood that an international agreement concluded by the European Council, in accordance with Articles 217 and 218 TFEU, constitutes such an act, and that, as from its entry into force, the provisions of such an agreement form an integral part of the EU legal system, and thus the CJEU has jurisdiction to give preliminary

---

36. Opinion, para. 28.

rulings concerning the interpretation of such an agreement.[37] Furthermore, in the special case of the ECT, this treaty was signed by and approved on behalf of the EU, and, as such, this agreement must be regarded as an act of the institutions of the EU for the purposes of Article 267 TFEU, with the CJEU having jurisdiction to rule on the provisions of the ECT.[38] However, the Advocate General found that this is not sufficient to establish that the court has jurisdiction, and that it is, therefore, necessary to examine whether the fact that neither the EU nor the Member States of the EU are involved in the case at hand is likely to affect the CJEU's jurisdiction to answer the questions referred for a preliminary ruling.[39]

However, the specific features of the ECT have been held as having relevance for the discussion. First, the Advocate General looked at the fact that the ECT does not establish any court or tribunal responsible for ensuring the uniform interpretation of its provisions, such as the CJEU, and that such interpretation is only made in the course of the settlement of disputes by various arbitral tribunals and therefore cannot avoid divergences in interpretation.[40] Second, although the ECT is a multilateral agreement, it does consist of a set of bilateral obligations between the Contracting Parties, including the EU and the Member States, and, in theory, those obligations could also govern, within the EU itself, relations between the Member States and, consequently, apply within the EU legal order.[41] In concluding on the interest and the powers of the CJEU to interpret the provisions of the ECT, the Advocate General emphasized that the EU's interest in the uniform interpretation of the provisions of the ECT cannot be excluded and that the CJEU should assume jurisdiction to answer the questions referred for a preliminary ruling.[42] Moreover, as explained by the Advocate General, with specific reference to Article 1(6) of the ECT regarding the notion of 'investment', this provision as it determines the material scope of the ECT also has the effect of triggering the application of the substantive protective provisions of the ECT. Hence, the applicability in the EU legal order of that provision depends essentially on whether the substantive rules to which it gives effect are themselves applicable in the EU legal order, so that investors from one Member State can rely on them in proceedings against another Member State before the courts of that State.[43]

Having established that the CJEU is competent to interpret the provisions of the ECT, the Advocate General proceeded with the first question addressed by the Cour d'Appel:

> Must [Article 1(6) of the ECT] be interpreted as meaning that a claim which arose from a contract for the sale of electricity and which did not involve any contribution on the part of the investor in the host State can constitute an 'investment' within the meaning of that article?

---

37. Opinion, para. 28.
38. Opinion, para. 31.
39. Opinion, para. 32.
40. Opinion, para. 41.
41. Opinion, para. 42.
42. Opinion, para. 45.
43. Opinion, paras 92–93.

As explained by the Opinion, Article 1(6) of the ECT defines the concept of 'investment', and it is one of the introductory provisions of the ECT, which are intended more generally to establish the scope and purpose of that treaty and to define the terms used in its provisions.[44] In looking at the definition of the notion of 'investment' under Article 1(6), the Advocate General immediately concludes that this is 'an imprecise definition which seems, at first sight, to be limited only by the purpose of the activity with which that investment is associated'.[45] Furthermore, as explained by the Opinion, the notion of 'investment' within the meaning of the ECT must be associated with an economic activity in the energy sector,[46] and the definition is supplemented by a non-exhaustive list of specific examples of investments.[47] In looking at the facts of the underlying case, the Advocate General centres his analysis on clarifying the circumstances in which 'contractual claims' would constitute an 'investment' under the ECT. In his view, contractual claims are likely to fall under both Article 1(6)(c) and Article 1(6)(f) of the ECT, which refer to 'claims to money ... pursuant to contract having an economic value and associated with an investment', and to 'any right conferred by ... contract ... to undertake any economic activity in the energy sector', respectively.[48] While these provisions provide examples of investments, the Opinion goes on to clarify that they also add further requirements for classification as an investment. As such, under Article 1(6)(c), the claim to money is an investment provided that it arises from a contract which is itself associated with an investment; while under Article 1(6)(f), a right conferred by a contract is an investment provided that it was conferred to undertake an economic activity in the energy sector.[49]

The Opinion explains that a contractual claim, in particular where it arises from a contract for the sale of electricity, cannot be considered to be an 'investment' under Article 1(6)(c), as this provision does not refer to a simple commercial transaction.[50] The Advocate General also expressed the view that the definition developed in relation to the concept of 'investment' under the ICSID Convention, although this being a special treaty, contains the essential elements of what may constitute an investment.[51] Accordingly, the Opinion concludes that a claim to money is an investment under Article 1(6) of the ECT, only if it has arisen from a contract which involved a contribution on the part of the presumed investor and the expectation of a gain, which is not guaranteed.[52] This is, however, not the case for an electricity supply contract, as the Advocate General noted.[53]

As to Article 1(6)(f) of the ECT referring to 'any right conferred by ... contract ... to undertake any economic activity in the energy sector', the Opinion indicates that

---

44. Opinion, para. 91.
45. Opinion, para. 104.
46. Opinion, para. 104.
47. Opinion, para. 105.
48. Opinion, para. 106.
49. Opinion, para. 107.
50. Opinion, para. 112.
51. Opinion, para. 116.
52. Opinion, para. 117.
53. Opinion, para. 119.

Article 1(6) provides, in general terms, that an investment within the meaning of the ECT must be associated with an economic activity in the energy sector, which also applied to Article 1(6)(f).[54] This is apparent from the wording of the provision which refers to the words 'to undertake' and which indicates that the contractual right in question must have been conferred for the purposes of undertaking an economic activity in the energy sector.[55] However, the Opinion explains that when the claim is acquired after its creation by the original holder, such 'claim gives its holder not the right to undertake an economic activity in the energy sector, but only the right to claim payment for it'.[56] Consequently, the Advocate General concludes that Article 1(6)(f) of the ECT cannot be interpreted as meaning that a claim arising from an electricity supply contract and involving no contribution is an investment within the meaning of the ECT.[57]

The Advocate General turns then to the second question posed by the Cour d'Appel:

> Must [Article 26(1) of the ECT] be interpreted as meaning that the acquisition, by an investor of a Contracting Party, of a claim established by an economic operator which is not from one of the States that are Parties to that Treaty constitutes an investment?

The Advocate General begins by looking at Article 26(1) of the ECT which allows for the settlement of disputes between one Contracting Party and an investor from another Contracting Party where the dispute relates to an investment made by that investor:

> Disputes between a Contracting Party and an investor of another Contracting Party relating to an investment of the latter in the area of the former, which concern an alleged breach of an obligation of the former under Part III shall, if possible, be settled amicably.[58]

Further, as the emphasis of the question is whether there must be an investment *made* by an investor, the Advocate General resorted to Article 1(8) of the ECT, which defines the term 'making of investments'. Under this provision, the Advocate General states that 'an investment may be made by the acquisition of all or part of existing investments', but it 'does not, however, require that the existing investment in question was originally made in a State party to the ECT'.[59] In addition to this, the Opinion also relies on the provisions of Article 1(7) of the ECT which defines the notion of 'investor' with respect to both Contracting Parties and third States. The Advocate General emphasizes that it is 'clearly accepted that an investor may be from a third State not party to the ECT, without this implying that the investments he makes are not

---

54. Opinion, para. 121.
55. Opinion, para. 122.
56. Opinion, para. 123.
57. Opinion, para. 126.
58. Opinion, para. 133.
59. Opinion, para. 135.

existing investments within the meaning of the ECT'.[60] Consequently, as the Opinion concludes, the acquisition, by an operator from a Contracting Party to the ECT, of a claim established by an economic operator from a third State not a party to the ECT, represents the acquisition of an existing investment and therefore constitutes an investment made by an investor from a Contracting Party for the purposes of the ECT.[61] In reaching this conclusion, the Advocate General also commented on the fact that this particular situation may raise the possibility of an abuse of rights, but that while this possibility exists, this is not sufficient to exclude from the coverage of the ECT an investment acquired from an operator from a third State not a party to the ECT.[62]

Finally, the Opinion discussed the third question asked by the Cour d'Appel:

> Must [Article 26(1) of the ECT] be interpreted as meaning that a claim held by an investor, which arose from a contract for the sale of electricity supplied at the border of the host State, can constitute an investment made in the area of another Contracting Party, in the case where the investor does not carry out any economic activity in the territory of that latter Contracting Party?

With respect to this final question, the Advocate General noted that the investment at issue is held by a Ukrainian investor against a company established in Moldova. Under Article 1(10) of the ECT, 'area' is defined as 'the territory under its sovereignty'. As explained by the Advocate General, a claim held against a company established on Moldovan territory can be regarded as an investment made in the area of that Contracting Party, since the location of the debtor of the claim is sufficient to establish this.[63] The Opinion also noted that the same result would be achieved by upholding Moldova's argument that it is necessary also to ascertain the area where the investment with which the contract giving rise to the claim is associated was made.[64] Although in this case the electricity is supplied up to the border with Moldova, the electricity is ultimately fed into the Moldovan network and this is at the heart of the matter.[65] In conclusion, the Advocate General highlighted that Article 26(1) of the ECT must be interpreted as meaning that a claim held by an investor of one Contracting Party against an operator of another Contracting Party is an investment of the former in the area of the latter.[66]

The Opinion of the Advocate General, including on the definition of the notion of 'investment', was confirmed by the CJEU in the subsequent judgment of September 2021 ('Judgment').[67] CJEU first addressed the competence to respond to the questions posed by the Cour d'Appel, in the light of the underlying facts of the case. The court began by confirming that, in accordance with Article 267 of the TFEU, CJEU has jurisdiction to interpret the acts of the institutions, bodies, offices or agencies of the

---

60. Opinion, para. 138.
61. Opinion, para. 140.
62. Opinion, para. 142.
63. Opinion, para. 151.
64. Opinion, para. 152.
65. Opinion, para. 153.
66. Opinion, para. 154.
67. *Republic of Moldova v. Komstroy*, Judgment of the CJEU of 2 September 2021 in Case C-741/19.

EU.[68] Confirming the approach taken by the Advocate General, the court viewed the ECT as an act of its institutions, in the light of the Treaty of Lisbon giving exclusive competence to the EU for foreign direct investment, and shared competence as regards investment that is not direct.[69] However, CJEU emphasized that the court does not, in principle, have jurisdiction to interpret an international agreement as regards its application in the context of a dispute not covered by EU law, as it is the case in this present reference.[70] Nonetheless, when a provision of an international agreement would apply to situations covered by EU law and situations outside the scope of the EU law, the EU has the interest for the provision to be interpreted uniformly, 'whatever the circumstances in which it is to apply'.[71] Furthermore, the court held that the establishment of the seat of arbitration on the territory of an EU Member State triggers the application of EU law, with which the court must comply.[72] On the question concerning the interpretation of the definition of 'investment' under Article 1(6) of the ECT, the court agreed with the Advocate General and found that the contractual relationship between Moldtranselectro and Derimen concerned only the supply of electricity, which was generated by other Ukrainian operators that merely sold it to Derimen.[73] As such, the court concluded, a 'mere supply contract is a commercial transaction which cannot, in itself, constitute an "investment" within the meaning of Article 1(6) ECT, irrespective of whether an economic contribution is necessary in order for a given transaction to constitute an investment'.[74]

§10.03 DEALING WITH THE ELEPHANT IN THE ROOM: IMPLICATIONS OF CJEU'S APPROACH TO THE INTERPRETATION OF IIAS

The Opinion of the Advocate General and the CJEU Judgment in *Republic of Moldova v. Komstroy* are visibly in stark contrast with the reviewed court decisions interpreting similar jurisdictional requirements under IIAs. The approach of the national courts is to give proper deference to the principles and rules of public international law and, in particular, in addressing the interpretation of treaties and of their terms in accordance with the VCLT, as codifying the customary international law on this.[75] On the opposite end, the Judgment in *Republic of Moldova v. Komstroy* does not include any mention of such rules of treaty interpretation, while the Opinion, in one short paragraph, indicates that the interpretation of Articles 1(6)(c) and (f) is necessary to be done in accordance with Article 31(1) of the VCLT, 'in good faith in accordance with the ordinary meaning

---

68. Judgment, para. 22.
69. Judgment, paras 23–26.
70. Judgment, para. 28.
71. Judgment, para. 29.
72. Judgment, para. 34.
73. Judgment, para. 78.
74. Judgment, para. 79.
75. Further on the interpretation of treaties, *see* Richard Gardiner, *Treaty Interpretation* (Oxford University Press, 2008).

to be given to the terms of the treaty in their context and in the light of its object and purpose', without any further explanations on how that is done.[76]

This approach by the CJEU – addressing the interpretation of international multilateral treaties from the perspective of the EU law, without relying on the proper rules of treaty interpretation – must be further put in the context of the circumstances of the specific case. *Republic of Moldova v. Komstroy* is a case without readily visible connectors pointing to the competence of the CJEU. The CJEU itself admits this by noting that court does not, in principle, have jurisdiction to interpret an international agreement as regards its application in the context of a dispute not covered by EU law,[77] but that when a provision of an international agreement would apply to situations covered by EU law and situations outside the scope of the EU law, the EU has the interest for the provision to be interpreted uniformly, 'whatever the circumstances in which it is to apply'.[78]

Further to these observations, the CJEU noted a rather new and essential significance to the choice of the seat of arbitration in the post-*Achmea* world. As explained by CJEU, the establishment of the seat of arbitration on the territory of an EU Member State triggers the application of EU law, with which the court must comply.[79] In consideration of this, the applicable *lex loci arbitri* and the attitude of the national courts at the seat of arbitration must now be addressed as well in the context of the supranational law and the competence of the supranational courts.

The danger in endorsing the judgment in *Republic of Moldova v. Komstroy* in subsequent CJEU cases comes also from the potential of using this approach in the context of international multilateral treaties without EU participation, but to which the EU Member States are contracting States.

This future development can be previewed in the recent ECT cases before ICSID submitted against the Netherlands and concerning the phasing out of fossil fuel investments.[80] On 22 September 2021,[81] the European Commission responded by a letter to a request from the Netherlands to intervene as amicus curiae in the court proceedings before the German courts in the request for a declaratory judgment that *Achmea* should be given effect in the ICSID proceedings brought by RWE against the Netherlands under the ECT.[82] In its letter, the European Commission opined that the EU Member States judges should decide that the ICSID Convention is not applicable if they find it incompatible with the EU law, thus applying the principle of the supremacy of EU law. Subsequently, the Higher Regional Court of Cologne decided that the two intra-EU ICSID arbitrations brought against the Netherlands by Uniper and RWE are

---

76. Opinion, para. 109.
77. Judgment, para. 28.
78. Judgment, para. 29.
79. Judgment, para. 34.
80. *RWE AG and RWE Eemshaven Holding II BV v. Kingdom of the Netherlands*, ICSID Case No. ARB/21/4, and *Uniper SE, Uniper Benelux Holding B.V. and Uniper Benelux N.V. v. Kingdom of the Netherlands*, ICSID Case No. ARB/21/22.
81. European Commission Legal Service, Letter dated 22 September 2021, ARES (2021)5792228.
82. *RWE AG and RWE Eemshaven Holding II BV v. Kingdom of the Netherlands*, ICSID Case No. ARB/21/4.

inadmissible under German and EU law, since the investor-State arbitration provisions in Article 26 of the ECT are incompatible with EU law for disputes brought intra-EU.[83]

One can foresee here the danger of a referral to the CJEU so as to assess the compatibility of the ICSID Convention with the EU law, in the context of intra-EU investment disputes. Such an approach would, undoubtedly, result in a 'bilateralisa-tion' of a multilateral treaty: as European Commission has already advanced in its Letter of 22 September 2021: a multilateral treaty becomes a 'bundle of bilateral international obligations' between the respondent state and the investor's home state. Such an approach is, undoubtedly, at the minimum questionable in the context of the provisions of the VCLT.

---

83. Lisa Bohmer, German court declares ECT/ICSID arbitrations against the Netherlands to be inadmissible due to their intra-EU nature, Investment Arbitration Reporter, 8 September 2022.

Chapter 11

Dispute Resolution by 'Expert Decisions': Illustrated by the Norwegian Expert Procedure and the SCC Express

Amund Bjøranger Tørum

§11.01 INTRODUCTION

Arbitration is the preferred dispute resolution mechanism for disputes in international contracts. The typical feature of alternative methods for dispute resolution is that they aim to enable the parties to resolve their dispute faster and in a more cost-efficient manner.

Swift dispute resolution may be vital in certain contracts, typically in long-term contracts where a pending dispute may complicate or even undermine the essential spirit of cooperation. For example, disputed variation orders (DVOs) between a Contractor and its client may disrupt their cooperation and strain the liquidity of the Contractor. Similarly, disputes between the parties to a joint venture agreement may cause a deadlock, which again may lead to a most unfortunate outcome where the joint venture cannot fulfil its obligations to the end client.[1] A full-scale arbitration process is rarely cost-efficient and proportional in minor disputes.

For these reasons, *inter alia,* the Norwegian standard contract for offshore construction introduced a so-called expert procedure back in 1987.[2] A key feature of the

---

1. A recurring situation is that the participants to a joint venture disagree on cash-calls required to ensure the proper working capital to execute a project, typically in a situation with massive delays and cost overruns.
2. In the Norwegian Fabrication Contract of 1987 (NF 87). Another reason to introduce the expert procedure was to balance the Company's unilateral right to instruct the Contractor to carry out specific work, by providing the Contractor with a simplified path to a claim for additional compensation. *See* Kaasen, Tilvirkningskontrakter, 2018, p. 492.

expert procedure is that one or both of the parties to the contract are entitled to request an expert to decide provisionally: (i) whether the Variation Order Request (VOR) was submitted by the Contractor on a timely basis, and (ii) whether the work covered by a DVO is a part of the scope of work.[3]

Over the years, a number of such expert decisions have been provided in offshore construction projects concerning the Norwegian Continental Shelf.[4] In recent years a similar expert system has also been used in large (onshore) infrastructure projects involving international contractors.

The Norwegian offshore contracts also contain another alternative dispute resolution method to arbitration; the so-called Project Integrated Mediations (PRIME). This is a kind of permanent board created to assist the parties in amicably resolving disputes throughout (significant) projects.[5]

In 2021, for similar reasons, the Arbitration Institute of the Stockholm Chamber of Commerce (SCC) launched the 'SCC Express'. The scope and framework for this is set out in the SCC Rules for Express Dispute Assessment of May 2021 (the 'SCC Express Rules'), which are accompanied by the Guidelines to the SCC Rules for Express Dispute Assessment of May 2021 (the 'SCC Express Guidelines'). The SCC Express is a process based on consent and confidentiality, under which the parties receive a legal assessment of the dispute within twenty-one days, for a fixed fee (EUR 29,000).[6] The expert (the 'Neutral') must be neutral and shall provide a reasoned assessment of the disputed matters presented by the parties. The parties can agree to make the Neutral's assessment contractually binding or can instead choose to use the (non-binding) findings to guide settlement discussions or other ways forward.[7]

The SCC Express is not limited to certain issues in construction contracts.[8] Subject to either prior agreement or consent after the dispute has arisen,[9] it is available to parties willing to accept a more concentrated dispute resolution process with the benefit of greater time and cost-efficiency, who want to know (approximately) how a would-be-arbitrator might decide the case, or who trust each other to accept the outcome of the proceedings, without the need for legal enforcement of an arbitral

---

3. *See*, for example, the Norwegian Total Contract 2015 (NTK 15), Art. 16.3. In practice, only the Contractor will be interested in determining item (ii), whereas both parties may be interested in determining item (i).
4. The oil and gas activities on the Norwegian Continental Shelf have included some of the largest construction projects in the world and have led to significant domestic and international disputes. Some of the Expert Decisions have been published by the Scandinavian Institute for Maritime Law in the journal PetrIus.
5. *See*, for example, NTK 2015 Art. 37.
6. SCC Express Rules Art. 11 (of which EUR 25,000 is the fee of the Neutral).
7. SCC Express Rules Art. 2(4).
8. The SCC Express Guidelines' comments to Art. 2(1), however, indicate that the SCC Express is designed to, *inter alia*, address disputes arising '… in the context of a long-term contractual relationship between the parties, e.g. between a company and its key suppliers, or in ongoing projects …'.
9. SCC Express Rules Art. 2(2).

award.[10] The SCC Express is also available for parties who have not agreed to arbitrate under the rules of the SCC (or elsewhere).[11]

SCC Express was launched to fill a gap in the dispute resolution spectrum. Some features are derived from arbitration and mediation, while others are unique. Compared to mediation, the outcome of the SCC Express is a legal assessment, rather than a mutually acceptable compromise. Compared to an Arbitral Tribunal, the Neutral may play a more active and inquisitorial role, actively engaging with the parties and providing directions as to facts and issues to be addressed by them.[12]

In the following, I will address certain selected questions concerning expert decisions and share my experience on some recurring issues.

§11.02 THE PROCEDURES FOR COMMENCEMENT AND APPOINTMENT

As indicated, the Norwegian expert procedure in NTK 15 is not available until the Company has responded to a VOR by way of a DVO. The Company shall respond to a VOR by way of a Variation Order or a DVO within twenty-one days after receiving the VOR. However, if the Company has not responded in this manner within twenty-one days, a DVO shall be 'deemed' issued.[13] Hence, the Contractor will be able to trigger the Expert Procedure twenty-one days after having submitted the VOR, even if the Company does not respond to the VOR. These twenty-one days serve as a kind of grace period during which the Contractor cannot trigger the Expert Procedure, during which the parties can try to find an amicable solution.

One of the issues that may delay an arbitration process – in particular in ad hoc cases, which are still predominant in Norway[14] – is when the parties are not able to agree on the composition of the Arbitral Tribunal. Because the expert is required to render its decision within thirty days from its appointment,[15] time is of the essence. Therefore, the Norwegian expert procedure has traditionally provided for a particular approach to ensure the swift appointment of a neutral expert, namely a pre-agreed list of experts in prioritised order.[16] Such lists have traditionally been limited to highly regarded practitioners and law professors, being experienced arbitrators.

The SCC Express is, as indicated above, available at any time. The Neutral shall be appointed by the Board of the SCC.[17] The SCC Express Rules do not state that the parties are free to agree on a Neutral, but Article 6 (1) requires the Board to 'take into

---

10. SCC Express Guidelines s. 1. However, the parties may agree that the Neutral shall set out the findings in the form of an arbitral award; *see* below in section §11.04.
11. SCC Express Rules Art. 2(3).
12. SCC Express Guidelines s. 3.
13. NTK 15 Art. 16.2 first paragraph.
14. Arbitration in Norway is, however, in transitioning. *See* Tørum, Transitioning from Local Customs to International Best Practices in Norwegian and Nordic Arbitration, Festschrift to Henry John Mæland, 2019, pp. 433–446.
15. NTK 15 Art. 16.3 second paragraph.
16. In NTK 15, the list is set out in Appendix D. *See* more detail on the appointment procedure in Kaasen, Tilvirkningskontrakter, 2018, pp. 494–495.
17. SCC Express Rules Art. 2(1): 'Any party to a dispute may *request that the Board appoint* a neutral assessor (the "Neutral") …' (my emphasis).

consideration' proposals made by the parties. Due to the consensual nature of the SCC Express, the Board of the SCC will presumably accept a Neutral jointly suggested by the parties. The SCC Express Rules also provide for an appointment challenge procedure, with a tight preclusive deadline of forty-eight hours.[18]

Being a sole arbitrator may sometimes be a challenging task, but being (sole) expert under such a tight time schedule could be even more demanding. The latter explains why it may, in my opinion, be essential to select an expert with the following skills and experience (in the following order): (i) experience in managing disputes and experience in writing awards, (ii) up-to-date expertise in the relevant (standard) contracts and applicable law, (iii) a basic understanding of the relevant industry, (iv) a proper understanding of the technical aspects of the case, and (v) time to prioritise the case within the tight schedule.

The tight schedule does not normally allow the parties time to 'educate' the expert on all of the said qualifications. If the candidate is not an 'insider' in terms of items (i)–(iv), an appointment may eventually turn out to be an 'extreme sport' for both the expert and the parties. In practice, it may be necessary to compromise on some of the qualifications, typically because the candidates having the capabilities set out in items (i)–(iv) may be too busy to comply with item (v) on such short notice. My experience from Norway is, however, that the parties may be able to secure their preferred expert by postponing the deadline for providing the expert decision by a few weeks.

§11.03   CHALLENGES WITH A TIGHT SCHEDULE AND A WRITTEN PROCESS

The Norwegian expert procedures are, as a clear starting point, based on a purely written process. Each of the parties shall submit their pleading and the relevant documentation within seven days of the appointment of the expert, and they are entitled to make a second submission within seven days following their first submission.[19]

The tight schedule, combined with the written process, explains the narrow scope of the Norwegian expert procedure. Under NTK 15 Article 16.3, the expert can merely decide on two matters: (i) whether the VOR was submitted by the Contractor on a timely basis, and (ii) whether the work covered by a DVO is part of the scope of work. The expert cannot decide on the legal effects *if* he considers the disputed work to constitute a variation to the scope of work, for example, by determining the Contractor's claim for additional time and/or compensation.[20]

The written process is well adapted for determining whether the Contractor submitted a VOR on a timely basis within the preclusive deadline (twenty-one days) in Article 16.1. To determine when the deadline started to run is essentially a legal

---

18. SCC Express Rules Art. 6(4).
19. *See*, for example, NTK 15 Art. 16.3 second paragraph.
20. Kaasen, Tilvirkningskontrakter, 2018, p. 493.

question, and it is rarely necessary to present massive amounts of evidence and hearing witnesses in order to properly determine this issue.

Normally, the written process is also appropriate for deciding whether the work covered by a DVO is part of the scope of work, typically where the parties fundamentally disagree on the interpretation of the wording of the scope of work. In such cases, the expert may essentially apply the principles for interpretation of contracts.

There are, however, several examples in my practice where the assessment of the scope of work has turned out to be highly dependent on a complex factual matrix. For example, the parties may disagree on whether and to what extent the Company shared certain information with the Contractor before they both entered into the contract. This is a recurring issue in disputes concerning (alleged) unforeseen risks, unforeseen events, and incorrect or incomplete information concerning soil conditions etc.[21]

It might therefore be difficult for the expert to form a well-reasoned opinion on such matters based only on the parties' pleadings, without hearing witnesses etc. For this reason, it may sometimes be appropriate for the requested expert to ask for a video conference to learn more about the case before accepting an appointment to a case that might appear too complex to be (properly) resolved based merely on a written process within such a tight schedule. For the same reason, I sometimes reserve the right in the first case management conference to request further pleadings or a 'micro-hearing' via video conference to clarify certain topics if that should turn out to be necessary after considering the pleadings submitted by each of the parties.[22] In practice, however, it may be sufficient to schedule a second case management conference shortly after the parties' first submissions, in which the expert request the parties to clarify the topics in their second submissions.

Even though NTK 15 Article 16.3 does not state that the parties are required to submit their two submissions on the same date, this is how many parties seem to interpret the provision. In my opinion, the wording does not require such interpretation, and it is, in any case, an unfortunate interpretation. By not allowing the 'defendant', typically the Company, to comment on the first submission from the Contractor in its first submission, the precise scope and basis of the disagreement may not be as crystallised as it could and should have been; a step which could have clarified the case and benefitted the parties' rebuttals in their second submission.

As noted, the scope of the SCC Express is not limited to construction contracts and DVOs etc. The broad scope of the SCC Express means that it may include more complex disputes than the Norwegian expert procedure. At the same time, the SCC Express provides a more flexible procedural framework. For example, it does not limit

---

21. The other reason that such issues may be covered by the scope of the Norwegian expert procedure is that the preclusive variation order system in NTK 15 Art. 16.1 also applies, *inter alia*, to incorrect information from the company (Art. 6.4), force majeure (Art. 18.6) and the company's breach (Art. 27). *See*, more generally, Kaasen, Tilvirkningskontrakter, 2018, pp. 309–372, and Tørum, Sammenlignende analyser av fabrikasjon og entreprise: illustrert med endrings- og varslingsreglene og arbeidsplikten, Tidsskrift for Forretningsjuss, 2010, pp. 147–195.
22. NTK 15 does not, however, provide a right for the expert to request such a 'micro-hearing', *see* Kaasen, Tilvirkningskontrakter, 2018, p. 495, note 57.

the number of pleadings, and it is not necessarily an entirely written process. The Neutral shall, however, consider 'restricting the use of oral testimony and witness statements'.[23]

In this respect, the SCC Express differs significantly from the Norwegian expert procedure: Unless otherwise agreed, it is, as a clear starting point, a purely written process limited to two pleadings for each of the parties.

Furthermore, under the SCC Express, the Neutral shall consider 'limiting the scope and length of written submissions',[24] which may be useful for concentrating the case. By comparison, the Norwegian expert procedure does not provide for any limitations in this respect; however, it is rarely a problem that the pleadings are too extensive.

Under the SCC Express, the Neutral shall also consider taking on an active role by 'providing directions to the parties on facts and other issues they should address in their submissions'.[25] Under the Norwegian expert procedure, the expert should consider taking the same active approach, even if not set out in the contract.[26] In practice, it might, however, be difficult for the Neutral to provide appropriate directions in the initial phase, simply because proper directions often require a deeper understanding of the merits of the case that is rarely achieved before the parties have submitted their first submissions.

§11.04   BINDING DECISION

Under the SCC Express, the findings of the Neutral are not binding unless the parties agree otherwise.[27] There are two alternatives: The parties may (i) *ex ante* 'agree to make the findings of the Neutral contractually binding', or (ii) *ex post* agree to appoint the Neutral 'as an arbitrator to confirm the findings in an arbitral award'.

Essentially, the legal effect of choosing an alternative (i) or (ii) concerns recognition and enforcement. Alternative (i) is equivalent to an amicable (out-of-court) settlement, which cannot as such serve as a basis for enforcement.[28] By contrast, alternative (ii) entails the Neutral's findings being 'confirmed' in an arbitral award, making it recognisable and enforceable under, for example, the New York Convention on the Recognition and Enforcement of Foreign Arbitral Awards.[29]

---

23. SCC Express Rules Art. 7(5)(iii).
24. SCC Express Rules Art. 7(5)(ii).
25. SCC Express Rules Art. 7(5)(i).
26. Kaasen, Tilvirkningskontrakter, 2018, p. 495.
27. SCC Express Art. 2(4).
28. Unless the agreement can be considered as resulting from 'Mediation' and the parties belong to countries having ratified the United Convention on International Settlement Agreements Resulting from Mediation (the 'Singapore Convention on Mediation').
29. Provided that the process leading up to the Neutral's findings complied with the minimum requirements of an arbitral process under the New York Convention regarding 'due process' etc. The process set out in the SCC Express will presumably fulfil the minimum requirements set out in the New York Convention Art. V(1) if it is carried out according to the procedural requirements set out in SCC Express Art. 7 and the Neutral's (in this respect: the sole arbitrator's) findings are properly reasoned according to Art. 9(3). The most important ground

The Norwegian expert procedure provides a different approach. The provisional expert decision 'shall become final' if the decision has not been submitted to arbitration within six months following the date of the 'provisional' decision.[30] The Norwegian expert procedure does not explicitly set out whether such a 'binding' decision is merely contractually binding or does constitute an arbitral award.[31] However, in the absence of clear indications that the provision in NTK 15 Article 16.4 third paragraph constitutes an arbitration agreement,[32] it hardly qualifies as such.[33] The latter also seems to follow the approach of Article 16.4, under which the party not having succeeded under the expert decision – in order to prevent the expert decision from becoming binding – can commence arbitration proceedings. It would be awkward and circular if the parties had intended to agree to an expert decision to be an arbitral award – unless challenged by arbitration proceedings.

Even though a party may prevent the expert decision from becoming binding by commencing arbitration proceedings, the Norwegian experience is that the unsuccessful party does nevertheless accept the expert decision.[34] An important reason may be that until the losing party has been able to turn around the expert decision by way of arbitration proceedings, the other party will normally have the upper hand in the negotiations for an amicable solution,[35] in particular where a highly regarded expert provided a well-reasoned decision. Furthermore, unless the expert decision concerns a major part of the final settlement of the project, it will often be 'closed' as an integrated part of a 'global' settlement.

§11.05   CONCLUDING REMARKS

The Norwegian expert procedure serves as a swift and cost-efficient alternative to dispute resolution of certain recurring questions in construction contracts. There is, however, no reason to limit such a device to certain issues in construction contracts. The SCC Express, therefore, fills a gap in the dispute resolution spectrum. It is a

---

for refusal under the New York Convention is Art. V(1)(b), but its minimum requirements are not that strict; *see* Redfern/Hunter, International Arbitration, 2015, pp. 627–629.
30. NTK 15 Art. 16.4 third paragraph.
31. Even if the expert decision were to be considered an arbitral award, there would be nothing to *enforce* because the expert has no mandate under Art. 16 to determine the legal effects of a variation; Kaasen, Tilvirkningskontrakter, 2018, p. 500.
32. The Norwegian Arbitration Act s. 10 does not require a written arbitration agreement, but nevertheless requires certain clarity on what the parties have agreed to arbitrate, *see* Høgetveit Berg, Voldgiftsloven, 2006, pp. 130–131. By contrast, the New York Convention Art. II requires the arbitration agreement to be set out in writing; *see* Redfern/Hunter, International Arbitration, 2015, pp. 12–15.
33. Similarly Kaasen, Tilvirkningskontrakter, 2018, pp. 499–500, who states that a binding expert decision shall be considered a contractually binding agreement (p. 499 i.f.), and that the expert procedure, due to its simplicity and speed, will rarely fulfil the procedural requirements necessary to qualify as an arbitration process (p. 500).
34. I am not aware of statistics in this respect, but my understanding from Norwegian (offshore and onshore) projects is that there are very few examples (if any) that expert decisions under NF/NTK/NS have been set aside by way of subsequent court proceedings or arbitration awards.
35. Tørum, Sammenlignende analyser av fabrikasjon og entreprise: illustrert med endrings- og varslingsreglene og arbeidsplikten, Tidsskrift for Forretningsjuss, 2010, p. 163.

much-welcomed supplement to expedited arbitration, typically, where time is of the essence and the parties cannot agree on or wait for an expedited arbitration process.[36] A typical reason for the parties not being able to agree on an expedited arbitration process after a dispute has arisen is that they are not ready to accept a final arbitral award based merely on a 'quick and superficial' fast-track process.

At the same time, it is important to bear in mind the expert's evident challenges in providing a well-reasoned decision within such a tight schedule. The selection of the expert must therefore be tailor-made for the specific dispute. Swift expert decisions are most appropriate for less complex disputes that can be properly clarified in writing within the tight schedule.

---

36. Under the SCC Rules for Expedited Arbitration Art. 43, the final award shall be made no later than three months from the date the case was referred to the Arbitrator.

CHAPTER 12

The Subjective Scope of Arbitration Agreements under Norwegian and Danish Law

Johan Tufte-Kristensen

§12.01 INTRODUCTION

Privity of contract is recognized as a general doctrine across the Nordic countries. The doctrine limits the subjective scope of an agreement to the contracting parties. Accordingly, an agreement between A and B binds A and B; it does not bind C.

Arbitration agreements are subject to the doctrine as well.[1] If A and B have agreed to resolve their disputes arising out of X by arbitration, A may not initiate arbitration against C on the basis of A's agreement with B, and, vice versa, C may not initiate arbitration against A on that basis.

Reality is more complicated than the A-B-C example above. The subjective scope of agreements, including arbitration agreements, gives rise to frequent disputes, and the doctrine of privity does not always provide clear answers. Under some circumstances, C may be deemed a party to the agreement despite the fact that C did not initially sign and accept the agreement. Under other circumstances, the agreement is applicable to C even though C is not a party to the agreement.

---

1. On the subjective scope of agreements in general, *see* Oskar Mossberg, *Avtalets räckvidd I: Om avtals tredjemansverkningar, särskilt vid tredjemansavtal och direktkrav* (Iustus 2020); Vibe Ulfbeck, *Kontrakters relativitet—Det direkte ansvar i formueretten* (Gad Jura 2000). On the subjective scope of arbitration agreements, se Amund Bjøranger Tørum, *Voldgiftsavtalens subjektive grenser: Når kan den påberopes av eller overfor tredjemann?* in Ola Ø. Nisja and Borgar Høgetveit Berg (eds.), Avtalt prosess: Voldgift i praksis, 361 et seq. (Universitetsforlaget 2015).

The following sections aim at clarifying the subjective scope of arbitration agreements under Danish and Norwegian law. As explained, a party may transfer its rights under an arbitration agreement by way of assignment or subrogation, and the subjective scope of arbitration agreements may reach beyond the names on the signature page in a number of other specific situations too.

After having clarified the *general arguments and considerations* behind the rules and principles on the subjective scope of arbitration agreements (section §12.02) as well as the *modern Nordic approach to arbitration agreements* (section §12.03), the article will explain how the subjective scope of arbitration agreements may be effected by way of:

- succession by assignment or subrogation (section §12.04);
- universal succession (section §12.05);
- direct claims against prior parties (section §12.06);
- implied consent (section §12.07);
- relations to group companies (section §12.08); and
- certain other relations (section §12.09).

The article focuses on Norwegian and Danish law. These two legal systems are similar and comparable, both on a general level and within the specific areas of contract law and arbitration. Thus, the analysis is based on Danish and Norwegian legal sources, although a few Swedish legal sources are included as well.

§12.02   GENERAL ARGUMENTS AND CONSIDERATIONS

The subjective scope of arbitration agreements may generally be affected in two ways. First, rights or obligations under the agreements may be *transferred*. Second, the agreements may be *interpreted* as to include a party who did not sign the agreement. Either way, the subjective scope of an arbitration agreement involves fundamental considerations about, *inter alia*, party autonomy, access to justice, due process, costs and efficiency.

Whereas national courts serve the interests of society as a whole and all of society's individual citizens and entities, arbitration serves the interests of parties who have decided to resolve their specific dispute by arbitration—simply speaking, at least. Courts are available for almost any dispute, as long as the claimant sues the right defendant and meets the fundamental requirements of right of action. Thus, the national court system constitutes a common institution being generally available to anybody. The system is available for a tax dispute between a public authority and a private citizen as well as a post M&A dispute between several different plaintiffs and defendants.

Arbitration, however, is not a commonly available institution. Each arbitration and arbitral tribunal is set up to resolve a specific dispute between specific parties consenting to submit their dispute, typically arising out of a specific contract, to that specific process.

This fundamental difference between litigation and arbitration reflects, and is a reflection of, the procedural rules and practices applicable to the two types of dispute resolution. A conflicted judge is obliged to withdraw on his or her own motion, whereas a conflicted arbitrator is only obliged to withdraw if his or her disclosure gives rise to a challenge. The court is constituted without any involvement by the parties, whereas arbitral tribunals are typically constituted under the direct influence of the parties. Decisions by a first-instance court are appealable, whereas arbitral awards are final.

The differences have a natural impact on the "access requirements" applicable to each system. You do not need a contract to go to court, but you need a contract to arbitrate. Not any party will be bound by an arbitration agreement,[2] and the right to join a third party to arbitral proceedings already pending or to enforce an arbitral award against a third party is very limited. For the same fundamental reasons, the subjective scope of arbitration agreements is typically limited to the individuals or entities on the signature page of the underlying contract.

Despite close contractual relation between A, B and C, it may have significant unforeseen consequences for C to be bound by an arbitration agreement between A and B, which would prevent C from having disputes with A or B resolved by the ordinary courts. Vice versa, it may have significant unforeseen consequences for A to be bound by the arbitration agreement with B in a dispute with C, despite the fact that A actually signed an arbitration agreement with B.

However, it may be unnecessarily burdensome and inefficient to prevent A, B and C from resolving their tripartite dispute or any bipartite dispute between two of them by arbitration if they have all de facto accepted to resolve disputes between each other by arbitration.[3] Accordingly, arbitration agreements may under certain circumstances entitle or bind parties who were not originally parties to the agreements.

§12.03   THE MODERN NORDIC APPROACH TO ARBITRATION AGREEMENTS

Among Danish judges and scholars, the perception of arbitration agreements was rather skeptical compared to their perception of other commercial agreements until the mid-twentieth century. In 1937, a leading Danish practitioner described arbitration as unsafe (*"farlighed"*) in his monograph on voluntary arbitration.[4]

---

2. For example, under s. 6(1) of the Swedish Arbitration Act, s. 11(1) of the Norwegian Arbitration Act and s. 7(2) of the Danish Arbitration Act, a consumer is not bound by an arbitration agreement made before the dispute arose.
3. As stated by the Supreme Court of Norway in its decision of November 3, 1994 (Rt. 1994-1489), there are compelling arguments in favor of deciding several disputes arising out of the same agreement jointly (*"There are compelling arguments* [sterke reelle hensyn] *that several disputes arising out of the contractual relation be subject to a joint process, which must be in line with the purpose behind the arbitration clause."* (author's translation)).
4. Bernt Hjejle, *Frivillig Voldgift* (Levin & Munksgaard 1937), p. 69.

The Danish perception of arbitration is very different today.[5] Case law and literature from the latest decades reflects a widespread acceptance of arbitration as a due and fair dispute resolution system desired by many commercial parties.[6]

The perception does not only influence decisions on the conclusion and validity of arbitration agreements but also decisions on the interpretation and scope of arbitration agreements with respect to the issues and parties covered.[7]

Thus, as explained in the following sections, a variety of different grounds may make a court or tribunal deem an arbitration agreement signed by A and B applicable to C.

§12.04   SUCCESSION BY ASSIGNMENT OR SUBROGATION

Arguably, assignment and subrogation are among the simplest and most common ways to transfer rights under an agreement to someone who was not originally a party to the agreement.

Under Nordic principles of contract law, B may *assign* its claim against A to C. The assignment of a claim against a debtor to an assignee does not require consent from the debtor, so B is generally free to assign its claim against A to C, but the assignment does not grant C any additional rights. The assignee, C, "receives" the assignor's, B's, rights and claims against the debtor.

The same principle applies to claims or rights under an arbitration clause. If B is replaced by C in a contract originally made by A and B, C may assert its right to arbitrate under that agreement against A, and A may assert its right to arbitrate under the agreement against C.[8]

As opposed to the assignment of a right or claim, which does not require consent from the debtor, the assignment of *liabilities* requires the *creditor's* consent. Following this general principle, B may not assign its liabilities toward A to C without A's consent. However, the principle does not prevent an arbitration agreement from binding A and

---

5. Morten Frank, *Fortolkning af voldgiftsaftaler* (Karnov Group 2018), 54 et seq.
6. Judgment of April 11, 2014 by the Supreme Court of Denmark ("Højesterets dom af 11. april 2014 i sag 216/2013"), Ugeskrift for Retsvæsen 2014, 2042 et seq., 2045; Judgment of April 11, 2014 by the Supreme Court of Denmark ("Højesterets dom af 11. april 2014 i sag 217/2013"), 2–3; Niels Schiersing, *Voldgiftsloven med kommentarer* (Jurist- og Økonomforbundets forlag 2016), 140 et seq.; Jakob Juul and Peter Fauerholdt Thommesen, *Voldgiftsret* (3rd ed., Karnov Group 2017), 79–80 (mentioning both Denmark, England, Sweden and Norway); Jens Edvin A. Skoghøy, *Voldgift: konkurrent eller supplement til det alminnelige domstolsapparatet?*, in Ola Ø. Nisja and Borgar Høgetveit Berg (eds), Avtalt prosess: Voldgift i praksis, 349 et seq. (Universitetsforlaget 2015).
7. Juul and Thommesen, *supra* note 6, 84 et seq.
8. The principle was applied in a judgment of June 21, 2002 by the High Court of Western Denmark (Vestre Landsrets dom af 21. juni 2002 i anke 7. afd. nr. B-0528-02), Tidsskrift for Bolig- og Byggeret 2002, 410 et seq. The court held that the buyer was bound by an arbitration agreement between the seller and the original owner ("[...] *as a general rule, a party's successors in the substantive relation to which an arbitration clause relates are bound by an arbitration agreement to the same extent as the assignor.*" (author's translation)).

C as a consequence of the assumption of debt. If C assumes B's liabilities toward A, the arbitration agreement between A and B will normally bind C and A toward each other.[9]

An assignor's right to assign rights and liabilities under an arbitration agreement to an assignee is set out by case law and legal doctrine under Danish, Norwegian and Swedish law.[10]

In Norway, this right became statutory when the current Norwegian Arbitration Act entered into force in 2005.[11] Section 10(2) of the Act provides that unless otherwise agreed between the parties, *"the arbitration agreement shall be deemed to be assigned together with any assignment of the legal relationship to which the arbitration agreement relates."*[12] As explained in section §12.06 below, the scope of the provision is broader than merely covering assignment.

Similar to the *assignment* of a claim, C may *subrogate* B's claim against A. For example, a guarantor who paid the debtor's liabilities to the creditor may subrogate the creditor's claim against the debtor, and an insurer may subrogate the policyholder's claim against the debtor. Subrogation to a claim against a debtor does not require consent from the debtor either, and by subrogating to B's claim against A, C is entitled to invoke an arbitration agreement between A and B against A.

Accordingly, an arbitration agreement may be *assigned* to a party who was not originally a party to that agreement, and a party who was not originally a party to the agreement may *subrogate* the arbitration agreement.

In practice, arbitration agreements are never assigned or subrogated *in isolation*. An arbitration agreement typically forms part of a main contract or a set of contracts in which the arbitration agreement is included as a separate clause. When that main contract or contractual relationship is assigned, or when somebody subrogates it, the arbitration agreement is "part of the package."

The right to transfer rights and liabilities under an arbitration agreement by assignment or subrogation is rather uncontroversial. If B's rights and liabilities under a contract with A are transferred to C by assignment or subrogation, disputes between A and C falling within the arbitration agreement's *objective* scope will be subject to arbitration.

---

9. In a judgment of September 22, 2014, the High Court of Western Denmark extended an arbitration agreement between a creditor, A, and an original debtor, B, to cover the relation between A and a new debtor, C, because C thereby succeeded in the rights and obligations of the original debtor. ("[the new debtor] *has accepted being payment debtor on the construction project. By the assumption of debt,* [the new debtor] *has subrogated to* [the original debtor's] *rights and obligations, and the presented evidence* [...] *does not provide a basis for considering the agreement* [...] *non-binding due to the assumption of debt."* (author's translation)). *See* judgment of September 22, 2014 by the High Court of Western Denmark (Vestre Landsrets dom af 22. september 2014 i anke 6. afd. B-3301-12), Ugeskrift for Retsvæsen 2015, 209 et seq.

10. Judgment of October 15, 1997 by the Swedish Supreme Court (Högsta domstolens dom, 15. oktober 1997, målnummer Ö3174-95), Nytt Juridiskt Arkiv 1997, 866 et seq.; Stefan Lindskog, *Skiljeförfarande*, 150–151 (2nd ed., Norstedts Juridik 2012); Judgment of June 21, 2002 by the High Court of Western Denmark, *supra* note 9; Judgment of September 22, 2014 by the High Court of Western Denmark, *supra* note 10.

11. Act of May 14, 2004 No. 25 relating to Arbitration (Norwegian Arbitration Act).

12. *"Hvis ikke annet er avtalt mellom partene i voldgiftsavtalen, følger voldgiftsavtalen med ved overføring av det rettsforhold den omfatter."*

§12.05   UNIVERSAL SUCCESSION

Whereas singular succession implies an assignment or subrogation to single legal rights, universal succession implies an assignment and assumption of *all* rights and liabilities of a person or entity. Universal succession may be a consequence of, *inter alia*, bankruptcy, decease or a merger, and the succession implies a transfer of rights as well as liabilities.

In all Nordic countries, the universal succession of B's rights and liabilities to C would normally include the rights and liabilities under an arbitration agreement between A and B.[13] Accordingly, if B dies, any arbitration agreement between A and B may be upheld by A against B's estate, C. If the estate, C, brings a dispute covered by the agreement before the courts, the arbitration agreement will generally bar the jurisdiction of the court. Conversely, C may invoke the arbitration agreement against A.

The general right to transfer arbitration agreements by way of universal succession does not necessarily apply to bankruptcy cases. Disputes between the bankruptcy estate and the party to the arbitration agreement may involve significant public or third-party interests, and, thus, such disputes may be inarbitrable. For example, avoidance proceedings must be resolved before the courts despite any arbitration agreement with the bankrupt entity.[14] Nevertheless, the bankruptcy estate would normally be bound by the arbitration agreement if the issues covered by the agreement are independent of the bankruptcy and especially if the arbitration is initiated before the bankruptcy.[15]

§12.06   DIRECT CLAIMS AGAINST PRIOR PARTIES

If A sells a non-conforming product to B, which B resells to C, C may under certain circumstances claim remedies for breach of contract against A despite the absence of a contract between A and C. Similarly a developer may claim remedies from a sub-contractor despite the existence of a general contractor between the developer and the contractor in the chain of contracts.

---

13. SOU1994:81 (preparatory notes on the Swedish Arbitration Act), 93 (*"By universal succession, the arbitration agreement normally becomes applicable in relation to the succeeding party, e.g. an estate of a deceased person."* (author's translation)).

14. Decision of April 7, 1986 by the Danish Supreme Court (Højesterets Kæremålsudvalgs kendelse af 7. april 1986 i sag 472/1985), Ugeskrift for Retsvæsen 1986, 440 et seq. (*"The lawsuit is [...] commenced in the interest of the creditors and upon the probate court's accession. Accordingly, an arbitration and choice of court agreement between the parties cannot be invoked."* (author's translation)).

15. *Ibid.* (*"The arbitral proceedings concerned issues that could be decided independent of the bankruptcy, and at least in the present case in which the proceedings are initiated before the bankruptcy, the estate must be bound by the arbitration agreement."* (author's translation)); court order of April 25, 2013 by the High Court of Eastern Denmark (Østre Landsrets kendelse af 25. april 2013 i kære 16. afd. B-890-13) Ugeskrift for Retsvæsen 2013, 2238 et seq. (*"Because it was a customary clause of significant importance to the parties, and because the subject matter of the case merely concerns the justification of the claim, which is completely independent of the insolvency issues, the probate court does not find reason to deprive the arbitral tribunal from its competence to decide the present dispute."* (author's translation)).

The right to claim remedies from a prior party is established by case law and legal doctrine. There is no general right to do so. The right depends on the prior party's negligence and C's opportunity to subrogate B's claim against A.

The main features of a direct contract claim are similar to the main features of subrogation; instead of directing a claim against B, who will re-direct the claim against A, C goes straight to A, who would otherwise have been met with a claim from B. In most instances, the creditor's right to invoke an arbitration agreement against a prior party, and vice versa, is subject to the same principles as assignment and subrogation, but as explained by Tørum, the right to invoke arbitration agreements in relation to direct claims, and the underlying considerations, vary depending on the specific constellation.[16]

As mentioned in section §12.04 above, section 10(2) of the Norwegian Arbitration Act provides that unless otherwise agreed between the parties, "*the arbitration agreement shall be deemed to be assigned together with any assignment of the legal relationship to which the arbitration agreement relates.*"[17] Literally, the provision merely concerns the transfer of arbitration agreements by "*assignment,*" but as explained by Tørum and Woxholth, the scope of the provision is arguably broader than that.[18] According to the *travaux*, the provision amends the law as set out by the Norwegian Supreme Court in Rt-1994-1024 concerning a *direct claim*.[19] Accordingly, the explanatory notes indicate that section 10(2) of the Norwegian Arbitration Act extends the subjective scope of arbitration agreements in relation to direct claims.

If C raises a direct claim against A, C may normally invoke an arbitration agreement between A and B against A, and A may normally invoke an arbitration agreement between A and B against C. However, if A raises a direct claim against C, A may not necessarily invoke an arbitration agreement between A and B against C.[20]

A contractual chain may involve more than three parties. If A has made a contract with B, who has made a contract with C, who has made a contract with D, one or more bipartite arbitration agreements may bind the other parties in the chain.

In a judgment of April 11, 2014, the Supreme Court of Denmark dismissed an insurer's lawsuit against a technical consultant by reference to (a) an arbitration agreement between the insured developer and the lead consultant and (b) an arbitration agreement between the developer and the consultant.[21]

A property developer, B, had assigned a lead consultant, C, to assist in the building of a school. The lead consultant had assigned a technical consultant, D, to

---

16. Tørum, *supra* note 1.
17. "*Hvis ikke annet er avtalt mellom partene i voldgiftsavtalen, følger voldgiftsavtalen med ved overføring av det rettsforhold den omfatter.*"
18. Geir Woxholth, *Voldgift* (Gyldendal juridisk 2013), 342; Tørum, *supra* note 1, 367–369. On direct claims, *see* section §12.06 below.
19. NOU 2001: 33 ("*Utredning fra Tvistemålsutvalget oppnevnt ved kgl. res. 9. april 1999 avgitt til Justis- og politidepartementet 20. desember 2001*"), pp. 70–71.
20. The scenarios, requirements and considerations are not examined further in this chapter. For a thorough analysis, *see* Tørum, *supra* note 1, 369 et seq.
21. Judgment of April 11, 2014 by the Supreme Court of Denmark, *supra* note 8.

design the building's foundation. Due to an error in the foundation, a neighboring property was damaged. B's insurer, A, covered the damage and filed a lawsuit against D.

There were arbitration clauses in the agreements between B and C and between C and D. The insurer, A, who filed the lawsuit against D, had not signed any of these agreements, and the insured developer, B, had not signed any arbitration agreement with D. Nevertheless, the court accommodated D's request to dismiss the case by reference to the arbitration agreements between B and C and between C and D.[22]

The decision was based on two grounds. First, the court held that A, as B's insurer, had *subrogated* B's rights and obligations toward D. Second, the court considered whether the dispute would be subject to arbitration if it were a dispute between the developer, B, and the technical consultant, D, i.e., whether the developer would have been required to raise its claim against the technical consultant before the ordinary courts or before an arbitral tribunal.[23]

The court noted that the dispute fell within the objective scope of the arbitration agreement between B and C and the objective scope of the arbitration agreement between C and D. Under both of these agreements, disputes arising out of the performance of the project were subject to arbitration. The dispute at hand had arisen out of the performance of the project, so the court considered it covered by the general intent of the parties to arbitrate.[24]

For these reasons, the dispute between A, who had subrogated B's claims against C, and D were subject to arbitration despite the absence of arbitration agreements between A and B, between A and C, between A and D and between B and D.[25]

The right to invoke an arbitration agreement in relation to a direct claim will always depend on the circumstances in the specific case. Who invokes the agreement against whom? However, very simply speaking and as explained above, arbitration agreements are generally, but not always, "part of the package."

§12.07   IMPLIED CONSENT

The identification of the parties to an arbitration agreement—or any other agreement—may imply an element of interpretation. Under most contracts, the subjective scope is clear, but other contracts leave the court or tribunal with an element of discretion. Even when the subjective scope *seems* clear, specific circumstances may prove that the subjective scope covers parties who are not explicitly mentioned on the signature page. In that case, A, B and C are all deemed parties to the agreement despite the fact that only A and B have signed the agreement.

---

22. *Ibid.*, 2045.
23. *Ibid.* ("[...] it follows from general principles of obligations that a liability insurer who pays damages to an injured policyholder subrogates to the injured's (the developer's) rights and liabilities towards the technical consultant against whom the claim is made. [...] Then, the decisive question is whether the developer would have to pursue its claim against the technical consultant before courts or by arbitration." (author's translation)).
24. *Ibid.*
25. *Ibid.*

A party may be bound to an agreement by virtue of implied consent. Simply speaking, an implied consent requires an obvious reason to react. The absence of a response to an offer does not constitute an implied consent under Norwegian or Danish law, but A may be bound by its implied consent, *inter alia*, if A's conduct and a common usage or practice between the parties makes it reasonable for B to assume that A has accepted the terms of the agreement.

If a party is bound by its implied consent, the arbitration agreement is not transferred to a third party but rather extended by way of interpretation. The party *is* a party to the arbitration agreement.[26]

§12.08 RELATIONS TO GROUP COMPANIES

From a traditional legal perspective, the extension of the subjective scope of an arbitration agreement by way of *group affiliation* is rather controversial.

Nordic company law sets out a corporate veil between companies. Parent A and its subsidiary B are two different legal entities, both in terms of rights, liabilities, contracts, torts, procedural identity and enforcement. If parent A has made an arbitration agreement with C, the arbitration agreement does not bind A's subsidiary B. Accordingly, B cannot invoke the arbitration agreement against C, and C cannot invoke the arbitration agreement against B.

But this is merely the general rule because, under certain specific circumstances, an arbitration agreement may extend to a parent or subsidiary. The corporate veil is a necessary legal construction, but it is a construction after all. In reality, several companies in the same group may be involved in the same transactions, represented by the same directors, who attend the same meetings with the same counsel.[27]

If an arbitration agreement between a parent and C is de facto made by *the group* and C, it could be argued that other group members should be able to invoke the agreement against C, and that C should be able to invoke the agreement against other group members.

The arbitration agreement may be contained in a document that is only signed by the parent, A, and C, but if it clearly appears from the transaction history that group member B accepted to be bound, it could be argued that B is within the subjective scope of the agreement. Similarly, if it clearly appears from the transaction history that C accepted to be bound by an arbitration agreement with the non-signing group member, B, it could be argued that C is within the subjective scope of that agreement.

---

26. *See* e.g., the reasoning in court order of April 8, 2002 by the Supreme Court of Norway (Høyesteretts kjæremålsutvalgs kjennelse av 8. april 2002 i sak nr. 84-2002), Rt-2002-370 (the Supreme Court noted that the issue was not whether the arbitration agreement be extended to a non-party but whether the defendant was a party to the arbitration agreement. The claimant, who was a supplier of bunker fuel, claimed payment for the supplies to ships owned by the defendant, but the arbitration agreement was made by the claimant and the defendant's mangers.).

27. *See* e.g., Judgment of April 21, 1982 by the Supreme Court of Sweden (Högsta domstolens dom, 21. april 1982, målnummer Ö36-80), Nytt Juridiskt Arkiv 1982, 244 et seq. (A parent was liable to pay for deliveries to the subsidiary due to the parent's conduct).

In a court order of December 3, 1996, the Supreme Court of Denmark refused to set aside an arbitral award arising out of an agreement made by a subsidiary of one of the parties, i.e., not the party itself. The Supreme Court thereby extended the arbitration agreement to cover the subsidiary's parent. The arbitral tribunal had deemed the parent bound by the clause, and by refusing to set the award aside, the Supreme Court indirectly affirmed the tribunal's decision.[28]

The Supreme Court does not elaborate on the details of the transaction in its reasoning, but the details are described in the Norwegian tribunal's reasoning, which is outlined and quoted in the case summary. It follows from the tribunal's reasoning that the parent had been closely engaged in the negotiation and effectuation of the contract. The parent had issued a declaration to be jointly liable together with the subsidiary for the performance of the contract, and the parent did not object to being involved in the process until the subsidiary appeared to have difficulties paying its liabilities.[29]

Interestingly, the tribunal emphasized the economic and practical consequences for the parent, noting that the parent would be economically unaffected by being a party to the arbitration due to its joint liability with the subsidiary.[30] The Supreme Court did not explicitly repeat the tribunal's considerations but held that there was no reason to set the tribunal's *"well-reasoned"* award aside.[31]

Nevertheless, the due process considerations explained in section §12.02 above may give rise to concern about the extension of arbitration agreements to group companies. If the non-signing group member becomes bound by the arbitration agreement, that group member forfeits its right to a trial under the applicable procedural rules, which may, from that party's perspective, entail necessary safeguards such as a right to appeal.

---

28. Court order of December 3, 1996 by the Supreme Court of Denmark (Højesterets kendelse af 3. december 1996 i sag 325/1996), Ugeskrift for Retsvæsen 1997, 251 et seq.
29. *Ibid.*, 252 ("[...] *the handling of the case is conducted by* [the subsidiary] *and by* [the parent]. *The parent signs most of the contractual documents and appears as the main deliverer and source of resources to the other party to the contract. In its own declaration of 11.12.90, the parent has jointly backed the subsidiary's performance of the contract formally made between the subsidiary and* [the other party to the contract]. *It should further be noted that the Danish parent did not object to its role in the proceedings until the subsidiary's difficulties paying its liabilities came to light."* (author's translation)).
30. *Ibid.* ("*The consideration above is also supported by arguments on procedural economy* ["*reelle, prosessøkonomiske hensyn*"], *because the final outcome of the case will, economically, remain the same to the parent regardless of the determination of the company's position in the arbitral proceedings. It is clear under Norwegian law that a guarantor* ["*selvskyldnerkausjonist*"] *is bound by an arbitration agreement between the creditor and the debtor* ["*hovedmannen*"] *if the arbitration agreement was already made before the guarantee. The same is deemed the case under Danish law* [...]. *In the present case, the guarantee is derived from the subject matter, closely enough to naturally consider the declaration of guarantee an accession of or consent to the arbitration agreement by the guarantor."* (author's translation)).
31. *Ibid.*, 253 ("*The Supreme Court finds that the appellees have not pointed to any circumstances* [...] *providing a basis for setting aside the arbitral tribunal's well-reasoned decision, according to which* [the parent] *was deemed bound by the arbitration agreement in question, and according to which this company, thus, was deemed obliged to pay damages* [...] *to the appellor jointly with* [the subsidiary]." (author's translation)).

The extension of arbitration agreements to group companies has given rise to a recent decision by the Supreme Court of Norway. As illustrated by that decision, which arguably reflects both Norwegian and Danish law, group companies may be bound, but only under specific circumstances. In order to extend an arbitration agreement to a non-signing group company, a court or tribunal will conduct a thorough analysis and assessment of the specific circumstances.

The case concerned two different contractual relationships, one of which concerned a subsidiary, its parent and a buyer. The arbitration agreement was signed by the parent and the buyer, and the question was whether the subsidiary was entitled to invoke the arbitration agreement against the buyer.

After a thorough assessment, the Supreme Court dismissed the claim by reference to the arbitration agreement, despite the fact that the defendant, who was the subsidiary, was not a signatory to the agreement. Accordingly, the subsidiary successfully invoked the arbitration agreement against the buyer.

In its reasoning, the court noted the wording of the arbitration clause covering "[a]*ny dispute* [...] *relating to this Contract,*" which was, according to the court, "*general*" and without "*room for reading limitations into it.*"[32] Accordingly, the specific wording regarding the *objective* scope of the agreement appears to have influenced the court's determination of the subjective scope.

In determining whether the claims against the defendant would be subject to arbitration, the court assessed the relationship between the defendant and the agreement.[33] The court noted that there is a less strict standard for finding the requisite relationship with the agreement when the defendant is a member of the same corporate group as a signatory. In the court's view:

> the question here is not whether the Norwegian subsidiary can be identified with the parent company, but whether there are circumstances suggesting that [the subsidiary] must be deemed to have entered into the arbitration agreement. As emphasised by Woxholt, in corporate group cases, there may be reason to determine the agreement threshold on less strict terms than in other cases where the contractual party and the third party have no contractual obligations towards each other [...] I share this view. I also share his view that in this context, it is not a question of identification or of a variant of the theory on lifting of the corporate veil under company law.[34]

The court concurred with Woxholth's view that a "*third party*" may be bound by an arbitration clause "*if there has been a three-party constellation from the start, and the third party has been aware of the arbitration agreement.*"[35]

---

32. Judgment of October 10, 2017 by the Supreme Court of Norway (Høyesteretts dom av 10. oktober 2017 i sak nr. 2017/136) Rt. 2017-1932-A ("Skaugen"), para. 83 (the arbitration clause read, "*This Contract shall be governed by the Laws of Denmark. Any dispute arising out of or relating to this Contract shall be finally settled by arbitration in accordance with the Rules of Procedure of the Copenhagen Court of Arbitration.*").
33. *Ibid.*, para. 102.
34. *Ibid.*
35. Woxholth, *supra* note 19, 342.

Furthermore, the court noted the fact that the defendant had played an *"ancillary role in the contract negotiations"* that led to the agreement.[36] The claims against the defendant were of the same nature as the claims against the parent who had signed the agreement.[37]

For these reasons, the court dismissed the claim by reference to the arbitration agreement despite the fact that the defendant was not a signatory to that agreement.[38]

As illustrated by the decision, the extension of the subjective scope of an arbitration agreement to a non-signing group company depends on the terms of the agreement and the specific circumstances in question. The court or tribunal considers a number of factors, including the wording of the arbitration clause, the transaction history, and the relation between the parties in the specific dispute.

Courts and tribunals must be careful when extending arbitration agreements to non-signing group companies. There are good reasons why the resolution of a dispute by arbitration requires a contractual basis.[39] Nevertheless, in cases such as the Skaugen case, a strict approach to the subjective scope of the arbitration agreement, which prevents the agreement from being invoked by or against the non-signing subsidiary, could give rise to uncertainty and inefficiency.

§12.09   OTHER RELATIONS

When the subjective scope of an arbitration agreement extends to a group member, the extension is not merely a consequence of the corporate affiliation. Rather, the extension is a consequence of the overall relation between the parties and the transaction. When applying the same rationale to other relations, it could be argued that arbitration agreements may be extended to non-signing parties in several other situations.

For example, an arbitration agreement could be extended from covering only the shareholders of a company to covering the company itself.

Like the clear legal distinction between group companies, there is a clear legal distinction between the individual shareholders and the company. An agreement between shareholder A and shareholder B does not bind the company. Nevertheless, in a decision of October 28, 2013, the High Court of Western Denmark affirmed a decision

---

36. *Ibid.*, para. 105.
37. *Ibid.*, para. 104 (referring to the following premises in the High Court's decision: *"In the court of appeal's view, in our case there is a particularly close connection between the claim against the parent company, which is bound by the arbitration agreement, and the claim against the wholly-owned subsidiary, which has taken part in the negotiation of the contracts on behalf of the parent company. Although Skaugen contends that MTDN [MAN Norge] has committed independent tortious acts, the same legal basis and almost the same factual basis are, as the court of appeal sees it, asserted as basis for liability for MDT [MAN Germany] and MDTN [MAN Norge]. As concerns the claim in our case, MDTN must therefore also be bound by the arbitration clauses with regard to the purchase of the Hamburg engines and the two—stroke engines."*).
38. *Ibid.*, para. 132.
39. *See* section §12.02 above.

to dismiss a case by reference to an arbitration agreement in a shareholders' agreement, thereby extending the arbitration clause to a shareholder's claim against the company.

The shareholders' agreement was concluded between a number of shareholders. These shareholders owned company A. One of the shareholders, A, brought a lawsuit against company A. There was no arbitration agreement between shareholder A and company A. Nevertheless, the High Court held that a shareholder's claim against company A for the dividend was subject to the arbitration provision.[40]

The High Court noted that the dispute was within the scope of the agreement at issue. The court stated that *"a shareholder's claim for dividend from the company naturally must be considered to be comprised by the subject-matter regulated by the shareholders' agreement."*[41]

Next, the High Court addressed whether the claims against the company were subject to arbitration under the agreement, even though the company was not a party to the agreement. The High Court stated that *"[b]ased on an overall assessment of the shareholders' agreement it must also be taken as a fact that when concluding the shareholders' agreement, the shareholders assumed that a dispute such as this must also be settled by arbitration, although* [the shareholder's] *claim is not raised against the other shareholders directly, but against* [the company].*"*[42]

Thus, the court concluded that claims against the company, which was not a signatory to the agreement, were subject to arbitration under the agreement. The court reached its conclusion *"[b]ased on an overall assessment of the shareholders' agreement."*[43]

As the decision illustrates, a company may be bound by an arbitration agreement made by the entire group of shareholders. The decision would arguably have been different if the arbitration agreement had been made by a few individual shareholders instead of the entire group.

Now that Pandora's Box is open, Nordic courts and tribunals may extend arbitration agreements to other types of non-signing parties such as sellers, suppliers, service providers, buyers, lenders etc., but this would require exceptional circumstances and be a tiny exception to the general doctrine of privity of contract.

Half of the *Skaugen* case, i.e., the one described in section §12.08 above, concerned group companies. The other half concerned an engine supply contract between a shipyard and a buyer. A third party sought to invoke the arbitration

---

40. Judgment of October 28, 2013 by the High Court of Western Denmark ("Vestre Landsrets dom af 28. oktober 2013 i sag 9. afd. V.L. B-0008-13), 2.
41. *Ibid.* (*"The High Court agrees […] that a shareholder's claim of dividend from the company must naturally be deemed covered by the issues regulated by the shareholders' agreement."* (author's translation)).
42. *Ibid.* (*"Based on an overall assessment of the shareholders' agreement, the court assumes that the shareholders, when making this agreement, have assumed that a dispute as the present one must be resolved by arbitration despite the fact that* [the shareholder's] *claim is not put forward against the other shareholders but against* [the company]."*).
43. *Ibid.*

agreement against the buyer.[44] Once again, the court conducted a thorough assessment of the specific circumstances:

> [The third party] played a central role in the entry into of the contract between the Shipyard and [the buyer] for the supply of the Somargas engines. [The third party] instructed the Shipyard to enter into the contract with [the buyer], and it is set out in the complaint to the conciliation board that the negotiations of the purchase of engines to the relevant ships were mainly carried out with [the buyer's Norwegian subsidiary] where [the third party] was represented by its Norwegian management company. The complaint also states that the contracts for the purchase of engines were "formally" entered into with the Shipyard, but that [the third party] "was the legal and beneficial buyer of the engines."
>
> I am not disregarding the possibility that a third party also under Norwegian law may be bound by an arbitration clause by—like [the third party]—having actively participated in the contract negotiations. It seems natural that the party asserting its claim based on a contract between two third parties must at the same time respect any arbitration clause applicable between those parties.
>
> Nevertheless, I cannot see that this construction reaches as far as applying in a case such as ours, where [the third party] has not entered into the Shipyard's contract with [the buyer]. In this respect, I mention that the Shipyard has not incurred a loss due to [the third party's] increased fuel costs, and thus has no claim against [the buyer]. The Shipyard would only have had a claim if [the third party] first had directed its claim against the Shipyard, which in turn could have submitted a recourse claim against [the buyer]. But according to the contract between [the third party] and the Shipyard, the latter's liability for increased fuel costs is limited upwards to a discount of USD 200,000, which is only a small fraction of the loss, alternatively cancellation of the contract which was not an option when [the third party] submitted its claim. Thus, the claim submitted by [the third party] is a different claim than the claim the Shipyard could have submitted against [the buyer].

The court considered if the arbitration agreement could be extended to the third party by assignment, but "[a]ccording to what I have now said, there is also no reason—as the case stands—to argue that there has been an "assignment" of the legal relationship between the Shipyard and [the buyer]." In addition, the agreement was subject to a writing requirement. For that reason and due to the specific circumstances described above, the seller was not bound by the arbitration clause.[45]

As illustrated by the Supreme Court's reasoning, Pandora's Box is not wide open, but it is not fully closed either. Except for the relations dealt with in sections §12.04–§12.08 above, arbitration agreements are not extendable, unless the wording of the arbitration clause, the transaction history and the relation between the parties in the specific dispute makes extension the only reasonable solution in the specific case.

---

44. This third party was the subsidiary dealt with in the group company issue considered in the same case. *See* section §12.08 above.
45. Skaugen, *supra* note 33, para. 124.

§12.10 CONCLUSION

Like other agreements, arbitration agreements bind their parties and only their parties. In practice, an arbitration agreement will usually bind the entities identified on the signature pages of the underlying contract and no one else.

But there are a few exceptions. The rights and liabilities under an arbitration agreement may be transferred by way of *assignment, subrogation* and *universal succession*, and arbitration agreements may be invoked against prior parties by way of *direct claims.* An arbitration agreement may also be *extended* to a non-signing person or entity if that person or entity is deemed bound by *implied consent.*

Under certain specific circumstances, an arbitration agreement may bind a company by virtue of the company's *corporate affiliation* with a party to the agreement. Accordingly, a parent's arbitration agreement with a third party may bind the parent's subsidiary, and a subsidiary's arbitration agreement with a third party may bind the subsidiary's parent.

In addition, the subjective scope of an arbitration agreement may extend to non-signing parties in other specific situations, but only if the wording of the arbitration agreement, as well as the transaction history and the relation between the parties in the specific dispute, makes an extension the only reasonable solution. The extension of the subjective scope of an arbitration agreement on grounds of the intrinsic nature of the specific case should be exceptional.

CHAPTER 13

Ensuring Continuity of Contracts: Enforcing Self-Cleaning as a Tool to Combat Corruption Through Arbitration

Lauri Railas & Tero Poutala

§13.01 INTRODUCTION

The arbitration law scholarship includes a great number of corruption-related writings. However, what is an uncovered area is the application of arbitration for enforcing self-cleaning. Self-cleaning is a term used especially in public procurement law but may be applied for other corporate compliance purposes relating to restoring reliability. This article introduces a novel approach to apply the principle of self-cleaning in an arbitration context by examining whether contracts and the business relationship can be saved by the parties' action in cases where corruption is evident by analyzing the applicability of arbitration as a method of self-cleaning for rehabilitation. Based on our findings, we demonstrate how this is possible.

In the last ten years, contractual approaches to fight corruption have emerged and these apply the principle of proportionality to the need to call a contract terminated in case corruption is discovered. We are using the landmark International Chamber of Commerce (ICC) Anti-Corruption Clause 2012 ("the ICC Anti-Corruption Clause")[1] as an example. The ICC Clause purports to preserve the validity and continuity of the contract by providing remedies to the violations of the ICC Rules on Combatting Corruption 2011 ("ICC Anti-Corruption Rules").[2] The parties of a contract adhere to these Rules explicitly with a view to create an impact on their relationship. The key idea

---

1. ICC, *ICC Anti-corruption Clause*, 2012, https://iccwbo.org/content/uploads/sites/3/2012/10/ICC-Anti-corruption-Clause.pdf (accessed May 25, 2022).
2. ICC, *ICC Rules on Combating Corruption*, 2011 edition, https://iccwbo.org/content/uploads/sites/3/2011/10/ICC-Rules-on-Combating-Corruption-2011.pdf (accessed May 25, 2022).

is that a party to a contract could, in many, although not all, cases remedy its breach of contract constituted by not adhering to the Rules.

We are not talking about the criminal law consequences of corruption for those involved, or in most cases measuring whether the violations of law have occurred, which considerations derive from the applicable criminal law and apply measures of proof "beyond reasonable doubt." These matters are obviously not arbitrable. They are tried before general courts in accordance with criminal law. The application of criminal laws is based on the territoriality of the criminal offense, but some legal systems, most notably the United Kingdom (U.K.), have extended the jurisdiction of their courts to hear corruption cases by using what in private international law would be called "connecting factors" such as the British nationality of the suspect to consider the crimes having taken place in the U.K.

Instead, we are dealing with the effects of corruption on contractual relationships. The performance of major contracts is taken care of by several people in a company, or it may be subcontracted once or many times in a chain. Therefore, corruption may not be at all, or is only indirectly, attributable to the "directing mind" of the company concerned. In more stringent systems, even lesser involvement may constitute corruption. The diligence of the management may be measured by the existence of a system to recognize, control and report corruptive practices.

An arbitral tribunal, or a court,[3] may be seized to enforce the ICC Clause or similar contractual provision allowing a party in breach to self-clean, or resort may be had on legal provisions or principles potentially leading to similar conclusions, most notably the doctrine of good faith and fair dealing.[4] In these situations, the arbitral tribunal may be asked to uphold the validity of the contract but ordering or evaluating self-cleaning or remedial measures by the party in breach. This may be of utmost practical business relevance in many circumstances. Companies have extended compliance programs and want to promote integrity but may be faced with a situation where corruption takes place by employees or subcontractors. This article builds on a hypothetical case, which is partly based on an actual case or cases. For the sake of convenience, we assume that the parties have concluded a distributorship agreement based on "ICC Model Contract: Distributorship" of 2016.[5] The distributor in country B uses local agents, one of which resorts continuously to bribing the manager of a public sector client with a view to obtaining excessive orders under an ongoing framework agreement. A jealous colleague finds this out, the police start investigations, soon the press gets to know it and a small scandal is created. The principal in country A wants to terminate the contract with immediate effect.

---

3. For the sake of convenience, we assume that disputes are to be settled by way of arbitration, either institutional or ad hoc.
4. *See* Art. 1.7 of the UNIDROIT Principles of International Commercial Contracts, Art. 1:212 of the Principles of European Contract Law, Book II, Art. 1:212 of the Draft Common Frame of Reference, Art. 7(1) CISG. *See also* national law provisions such as § 242 BGB for Germany and Art. 1134.3 Code Civil for France.
5. ICC Publication No. E776E.

§13.02 ARBITRATING CASES INVOLVING CORRUPTION

[A] Jurisdiction of Arbitral Tribunals on Corruption Cases in Retrospect

Arbitration has traditionally been considered to be an inappropriate forum for deciding the claims of bribery and corruption. This was largely due to a restrictive view of arbitral jurisdiction and to the arbitral tribunals' lack of authority to impose criminal penalties. When faced with such issues, arbitral tribunals would refuse jurisdiction. A landmark case in this respect was ICC Case 1110 decided by Swedish Judge Gunnar Lagergren in 1963.[6]

An agent was commissioned by an English company to exert influence over members of the Argentinian government when bidding for public works contracts. The agent was promised a commission of 5% of contracts won with an understanding that a substantial part of the commission would be passed as bribes to public officials.

Judge Lagergren relied on Article V(2)(b) of the 1958 United Nations Convention on the Recognition and Enforcement of Foreign Arbitral Awards (the "New York Convention"). The New York Convention grants the state courts the power to refuse the recognition or enforcement of foreign arbitral awards on the grounds of being contrary to public policy in the country where recognition or enforcement is being sought. Judge Lagergren examined whether under the laws of different legal systems involved a contract contrary to public decency and morality could be submitted to arbitration. In line with the New York Convention allowing the courts of the country of enforcement to decline jurisdiction, Judge Lagergren considered being entitled to decline jurisdiction on public policy grounds.[7]

Since the award in ICC Case 1110, attitudes have changed, under the influence of the doctrines of the separability of the arbitration clause, *Kompetenz-Kompetenz* and public policy. Hence, subsequent arbitral tribunals have recognized the arbitrability of allegations of corruption and the powers to examine the merits of such allegations. For instance, in ICC Case 7047,[8] the award, rendered in 1996, considered allegations according to which part of a fee paid to a consultant to secure the sale of military equipment was to be used to bribe defense ministry officials. The arbitral tribunal assumed jurisdiction, analyzed the allegations made and issued an award on the merits holding that (i) a "mere suspicion" of bribery is not enough, (ii) the performance of the agreement did not violate the public policy of the state involved and (iii) lobbying by companies to obtain public contracts was not in itself illegal under Swiss law which was applicable. The award was challenged in England and Switzerland by raising allegations of bribery, but both the courts rejected the challenge on the above grounds.

---

6. Christian Albanesi & Emmanuel Jolivet, *Dealing with Corruption in Arbitration: A Review of ICC Experience*, International Court of Arbitration Bulletin, Volume 24, Supplement (Tackling Corruption in Arbitration 2013), 29; As regards investment arbitrations, *see* Joachim Drude, *Fiat Iustitia, Ne Pereat Mundus: A Novel Approach to Corruption and Investment Arbitration*, Journal of International Arbitration, Volume 35, Issue 6 (2018).
7. Albanesi & Jolivet, *supra* n. 6, at 29.
8. ICC Award No. 7047, ASA Bull. 1995, 301; Case reproduced in, https://www.trans-lex.org/207 047/_/icc-award-no-7047-asa-bull-1995-at-301-et-seq/ (accessed May 25, 2022).

Similarly, in an unpublished ICC award of 2003, an arbitration clause in a contract to bribe a public official to obtain a public works contract was held separate and valid.[9]

Nowadays, arbitral tribunals have a tendency to address issues of corruption by considering the admissibility of the claims, the legality of the contract or transnational public policy. Arbitral tribunals have consistently recognized that anti-corruption laws and treaties are an integral part of international public policy and have relied on these instruments to declare contracts tainted by corruption as being null and void.[10] National laws are criminal or civil laws, which must be taken into account as the applicable law (*lex causae*) or, as the case may be, as overriding mandatory laws of another state.[11] The public policy aspect relates to the recognition and enforcement of the arbitral award and is wider than the concept of overriding mandatory laws. International public policy is well covered by international conventions, which explicitly address the effect of corruption on contracts. For instance, Article 34 of the United Nations Convention against Corruption 2003[12] and Article 8 of the Council of Europe Civil Law Convention on Corruption 1999[13] ("Council of Europe Convention") do this. For the purposes of this writing, the Council of Europe Convention is more interesting as Article 8 (Validity of contracts) provides as follows:

(1) Each Party shall provide in its internal law for any contract or clause of a contract providing for corruption to be null and void.

(2) Each Party shall provide in its internal law for the possibility for all parties whose consent has been undermined by an act of corruption to be able to apply to the court for the contract to be declared void, notwithstanding their right to claim damages.

Without analyzing the actual adherence of states to the Council of Europe Convention, we could assume that it would define the limits of preserving contractual relationships in corruption cases. An arbitral tribunal could presumably not enforce a contractual term providing for corruption, or a contract obtained through corruption, at least against the will of the party whose consent has been undermined by corruption.

Yet, there remains a variety of situations in which corruption has "contaminated" the relationship by causing mistrust between the parties, although a big or major part of the contractual relationship has presumably not been affected by corruption. In our hypothetical case, a distributor in a country may be using agents locally and one of these has allegedly used bribes in his or her sales activity but the "directing mind" of

---

9. Albanesi & Jolivet, *supra* n. 6, at 27–30.
10. Albanesi & Jolivet, *supra* n. 6, at 30.
11. *See* Art. 9 of Rome I Regulation, Regulation (EC) No. 593/2008 of the European Parliament and of the Council of June 17, 2008 on the law applicable to contractual obligations (Rome I), OJ L 177, 4.7.2008, p. 6; Overriding mandatory laws are referred to as "laws of immediate application" or "*lois de police*" in French.
12. General Assembly resolution 58/4 of October 31, 2003, *see* the Convention at, https://www. unodc.org/documents/treaties/UNCAC/Publications/Convention/08-50026_E.pdf (accessed May 25, 2022).
13. *See* the Council of Europe Convention at, https://rm.coe.int/168007f3f6 (accessed May 25, 2022).

the distributor is not aware of it. The parties have anticipated this type of situation by inserting contractual provisions, which allow a party to remedy the breach of contract committed by way of corruption. Corruption is made a breach of contract, e.g., by incorporating the ICC Rules on Combatting Corruption 2011 or by tailor-made provisions. In the absence of such provisions, corruption could be considered a breach on the grounds of public policy or substantive provisions such as Article 25 of the United Nations Convention on Contracts for the International Sale of Goods (CISG).[14] In most cases, corruption in the transaction could turn off clients or investors, having also long supply chains in mind. Yet, it could nevertheless be reasonable to uphold the contractual relationship and clean it from the "contamination" caused by acts corruption.

[B]   Mandate of the Tribunal

Arbitration is one of the oldest dispute settlement mechanisms, being referred to in the Roman law era.[15] H.L.A. Hart has pointed out that "disputes as to whether an admitted rule has or has not been violated will always occur and will, in any but the smallest societies, continue interminably, if there is no agency specially empowered to ascertain finally, and authoritatively, the fact of violation."[16] It is submitted that arbitration can be used to declare self-cleaning measures in case of certain types of contractual breaches.

To successfully carry out the self-cleaning of corruption, the arbitral tribunal needs to be mandated to do so and to avoid exceeding it. The mandate of arbitral tribunal origins from the party autonomy and the arbitration agreement, which features the consensual nature of arbitration.[17] This mandate can have its origin in the model arbitration clauses, such as the Stockholm Chamber of Commerce Arbitration Clause or the ICC Arbitration Clause. Pursuant to the separability doctrine, an arbitration agreement lives a life of its own and is separate from the commercial contract.[18] If the tribunal's mandate is activated, then the tribunal may possess jurisdiction and hear parties' claims, including remedying the self-cleaning.

---

14. This Article provides as follows: A breach of contract committed by one of the parties is fundamental if it results in such detriment to the other party as substantially to deprive him of what he is entitled to expect under the contract, unless the party in breach did not foresee and a reasonable person of the same kind in the same circumstances would not have foreseen such a result.

15. Earl S. Wolaver, *The Historical Background of Commercial Arbitration*, University of Pennsylvania Law Review, Volume 83 (December 1934), 132.

16. H.L.A. Hart, *The Concept of Law* (Second Edition, Clarendon Press, Oxford, 1994), 93.

17. K. Hobér, *Extinctive Prescription and Applicable Law in Interstate Arbitration* (Iustus Förlag, 88 Skrifter från Juridiska fakulteten i Uppsala, 2001), 20.

18. The separability doctrine is often viewed in conjunction with the doctrine *Kompetenz-Kompetenz* meaning that an arbitral tribunal has competence to examine its own competence, *see* Art. 16(1) of the UNCITRAL Model Law on International Commercial Arbitration 1985, With amendments as adopted in 2006. The doctrine of separability has been included in national legislations or has been introduced by case law. In Sweden it was established by the Supreme

It is generally held that arbitral tribunals can have jurisdiction in corruption-related cases. Drude concluded in his investment arbitration-specific study that it is possible to afford protection to contracts (or investments) procured by corruption and not depriving the tribunal's jurisdiction or making the claims inadmissible, and thus, without going opposite to international (transnational) public policy.[19] The same analogy applies to the adjudication of commercial contracts,[20] especially if—based on the separability doctrine—the arbitration agreement is not infected by any illegality.[21] Respectively, these conditions include how domestic law regulates corruption and it means that the party autonomy is limited by the international public policy.[22] It goes without saying that the arbitration agreement is required to stay alive to enable the mandate of the tribunal, viz. it needs to stay within the limits of public policy.

An arbitral award is binding between the parties as a rule.[23] Such norms can be found in the domestic arbitration laws. The Arbitration Rules of the United Nations Commission on International Trade Law (UNCITRAL) Article 32(2) states that the award "shall be final and binding on the parties" as well as requires that the parties "undertake to carry out the award without delay."[24] This also gives the effect to be committed with the tribunal's jurisdiction and findings to cover claims related to corruption.

[C]   Public Policy and the Recognition and Enforcement

The effectiveness and wide recognition and enforcement are the cornerstones to use arbitration as a dispute settlement mechanism. Especially with cases having international elements, the New York Convention and *lex arbitri* become relevant. Analysis of the relevant recognition and enforcement norms is important to understand to what extent arbitration laws allow the recognition and enforcement of arbitral awards issued for self-cleaning purposes.

Court in 1936 in *AB Norrköpings Trikåfabrik v. AB Per Persson* (NJA 1936, p. 521). In Finland, reference could be made in this respect to the Supreme Court Cases KKO 1954 II 11, KKO 1988:55 and KKO 1996:61.

19. Drude, *supra* n. 6, at 718.
20. Michael Joachim Bonell & Olaf Meyer, *The Impact of Corruption on International Commercial Contracts: General Report*, in: Michael Joachim Bonell & Olaf Meyer eds., *The Impact of Corruption on International Commercial Contracts*, Ius Comparatum—Global Studies in Comparative Law, Volume 11 Springer (2015), 10–12.
21. Richard Kreindler & Francesca Gesualdi, *The Civil Law Consequences of Corruption under the UNIDROIT Principles of International Commercial Contracts: An Analysis in Light of International Arbitration Practice*, in: Michael Joachim Bonell & Olaf Meyer eds., *The Impact of Corruption on International Commercial Contracts*, Ius Comparatum—Global Studies in Comparative Law, vol. 11 Springer (2015), 397–399.
22. N. Blackaby, C. Partasides, A. Redfern & M. Hunter, *Redfern and Hunter on International Arbitration* (Oxford University Press, 2015), 197.
23. Hobér, *supra* n. 17, at 20.
24. United Nations, "*UNCITRAL Arbitration Rules*" (1998), General Assembly Resolution 31/98.

Around thirty years ago, Albert Jan van den Berg stated that the New York Convention had become "the most important Convention in the field of arbitration,"[25] applying to "the recognition and enforcement of arbitral awards made in the territory of a State other than the State where the recognition and enforcement of such awards are sought."[26] Article III of the New York Convention provides for the binding effect of awards. The law of the award determines when the award is to be considered binding.[27] This binding effect is given in the *exequatur*, where a domestic court reviews the foreign award, with the aim of declaration of enforceability,[28] or as a "declaration of enforceability of the recognized arbitral award,"[29] following the possible execution phase.

As is well known, there are exceptions provided in Article V of the New York Convention. It has been said that Article V is the heart of the New York Convention.[30] Article V is structured into two paragraphs: the first paragraph states that enforcement *may be refused only if*, while the second paragraph states that enforcement *may also be refused*, in listed exhaustive cases.[31] The general understanding is that Article V does not give the right to refusal in a case of error in law or in fact(s) by the arbitral tribunal, except for those listed as exceptions.[32] Needless to say, that public policy threshold of domestic arbitration law is of relevance and needs to be met, in many jurisdictions being similar to Articles 35 and 36 of the UNCITRAL Model Law on International Commercial Arbitration (1985 and 2006) and mirroring New York Convention Article V.

Although there is a limited possibility to set aside an international arbitral award in the Member States of the New York Convention, a contract that has been procured through corruption can violate public policy and may trigger setting aside.

---

25. A.J. van den Berg, *The New York Arbitration Convention of 1958: Towards a Uniform Judicial Interpretation* (Kluwer Law International, 1981).
26. Article I(1).
27. Dana H. Freyer & Hamid G. Gharavi, *Finality and Enforceability of Foreign Arbitral Awards: From "Double Exequatur" to the Enforcement of Annulled Awards: A Suggested Path to Uniformity Amidst Diversity*, ICSID Review—Foreign Investment Law Journal, Volume 13, Issue 1 (Spring 1998), 106–107.
28. Christoph Liebscher, *Preliminary Marks*, in: Wolff, Reinmar ed., *New York Convention on the Recognition and Enforcement of Foreign Arbitral Awards: Commentary*, Beck, Hart & Nomos (2012), 3.
29. Daniel Girsberger & Nathalie Voser, *International Arbitration: Comparative and Swiss Perspectives*, Third edition, Schulthess Juristische Medien AG (2016), 434.
30. Marike R.P. Paulsson, *The 1958 New York Convention in Action*, Kluwer Law International (2016), 157.
31. In total, Art. V contains seven exhaustive grounds for refusal: five in para. 1 and two in para. 2. Grounds for refusal according to Art. V are: (1)(A) incapacity, or invalidity of the arbitration agreement; (1)(B) violation of due process; (1)(C) excess of mandate by the tribunal; (1)(D) violation of arbitration agreement in terms of the composition of the arbitral tribunal or arbitral procedure; (1)(E) the award has not yet become binding on the parties, or it has been set aside or suspended; (2)(A) the subject matter is not arbitrable; and, (2)(B) violation of public policy.
32. G.B. Born, *International Commercial Arbitration* (Second edition, Kluwer Law International, 2014), 3707.

Article V.2(b) of the New York Convention stipulates the *public policy* exception. In 2002, the International Law Association published recommendations on the application of public policy as a ground for refusing the recognition or enforcement of international arbitral award.[33] In principle, an award can be contrary to public policy for both procedural and substantive reasons.[34] As provided above, Article V.2(b) of the Convention states that recognition and enforcement of an arbitral award may also be refused by the competent authority if it would be contrary to the public policy of that country. An explicit reference is made to public policy "of that country," i.e., the country where the award is being recognized and enforced. There seems to be a general understanding that this refers to a national public policy.[35] However, it has been held that the recognition and enforcement of a foreign arbitral award can be refused, if that is otherwise against the international public policy.[36] The Committee on International Commercial Arbitration of the International Law Association (published following the 2002 Delhi Conference) stated that the test to refuse recognition and enforcement of international arbitral awards "should be that of 'international public policy',"[37] which reflects the international tenets and values.[38] Generally, corruption can be understood to fall within the international public policy (as a narrower concept than domestic public policy).

Already decades ago, Lagergren noted that "corruption is an international evil; it is contrary to good morals and to an international public policy common to the community of nations."[39] Years after, the Committee on International Commercial Arbitration of the International Law Association stated that "bribery and corruption are generally considered to be *contra bonos mores*, and most courts will refuse to uphold agreements relating to corruption even when the parties and the acts of corruption are all foreign."[40] The Committee further noted that "Corruption might also be prescribed in legislation and have the status of *lois de police*," viz. being part of the mandatory provisions.[41] It is not sufficient to set aside an award based on a violation of a mere "mandatory rule," but there needs to be a violation of international public policy.[42]

---

33. International Law Association, *Recommendations on the Application of Public Policy as a Ground for Refusing Recognition or Enforcement of International Arbitral Awards*, Resolution 2/2002, New Delhi, India, 70th Conference, 2002, 1.
34. Reinmar Wolff, *Article V: [Grounds for Refusal of Recognition and Enforcement of Arbitral Awards]*, in: Reinmar Wolff ed., *New York Convention on the Recognition and Enforcement of Foreign Arbitral Awards: Commentary*, Beck, Hart & Nomos (2012), 413.
35. A.G. Maurer, *The Public Policy Exception under the New York Convention: History, Interpretation and Application* (Revisited Edition, JurisNet, 2013), 55–56.
36. International Law Association, *supra* n. 33, at 1.
37. International Law Association, *Final Report on Public Policy as a Bar to Enforcement of International Arbitral Awards*, New Delhi Conference 2002, para. 18.
38. C.H. Schreuer, et al., *The ICSID Convention: A Commentary* (Second edition, Cambridge University Press, 2009), 566.
39. ICC Case No. 1110, para. 20.
40. International Law Association, *supra* n. 37, para. 32.
41. International Law Association, *supra* n. 37, para. 32.
42. International Law Association, International Commercial Arbitration, *Annex: International Law Association Recommendations on the Application of Public Policy as a Ground for Refusing Recognition or Enforcement of International Arbitral Awards*, Resolution 2/2002, 3(a).

At first, it should be underlined that the possibility for public policy defense under the New York Convention has rarely caused refusal of enforcement.[43] However, that has not always been the case. In some ICC arbitrations, for instance, sanctions targeting bribery and corruption have been considered to either fall under international or Swiss public policy.[44] In Sweden, threatening physical security, bribery, and debts arising from gambling have been considered against Swedish public policy.[45] In *Robert G v. Johnny L*,[46] Supreme Court of Sweden refused to recognize and enforce a Slovenian arbitral award being against Swedish public policy because the legal relationships actually included simulated transactions. Although public policy arguments to refuse recognition and enforcement of arbitral awards have rarely been successful in Sweden[47] and many other states, it is generally held that corruption falls under international public policy.[48] A 2019 judgment by the Hague Court of Appeal in *Bariven S A v. Wells Ultimate Service LLC*[49] illustrates how an arbitral award can be set aside, if there is a contract procured through bribery or corruption violating public policy.[50] More than fifteen years ago, the arbitral tribunal in the World Duty Free Company held that:

> In light of domestic laws and international conventions relating to corruption, and in light of the decisions taken in this matter by courts and arbitral tribunals, this Tribunal is convinced that bribery is contrary to the international public policy of most, if not all, States or, to use another formula, to transnational public policy.[51]

The tribunal concluded that claims based on the contracts of corruption or on contracts obtained by corruption could not be upheld.[52] Based on these findings, corruption is a matter of public policy, and the tribunal needs to make sure that it does not adjudicate claims based on the contracts of corruption or on contracts obtained by corruption to meet the enforcement threshold. In any case, tribunal needs to carefully analyze relevant norms and apply them with reason on a case-by-case basis.[53] Yet, if we assume that the contract itself is unequivocally free from corruption, the tribunal has an avenue to render a binding and enforceable award.

---

43. Albert Jan van den Berg, *New York Convention of 1958: Refusals of Enforcement*, ICC International Court of Arbitration Bulletin, Volume 18, Issue 2 (2007), 18.
44. ICC Case No. 5622 (1988), s. 16; ICC Case No. 6248 (1990), s. 27.
45. K. Hobér, *International Commercial Arbitration in Sweden* (Oxford University Press, New York, 2011) 371; Government Bill 1998/99:35, 141, 150.
46. NJA 2002 C 45, Supreme Court of Sweden.
47. *See*, e.g., *Naftogaz v. IUGAS*, Decision of the Svea Court of Appeal, July 2, 2012, Case No. T 611-11: the Svea Court of Appeal rejected public policy argument in relation to gas supply issue.
48. Hobér, *supra* n. 45, at 59.
49. *Bariven S A v. Wells Ultimate Service LLC*, The Hague Court of Appeal, October 22, 2019.
50. J. Dunin-Wasowicz & S. Winters, *Does an Award Enforcing a Contract Procured Through Bribery Violate Public Policy? The Dutch Perspective*, Arbitration Committee Publications, https://www.ibanet.org/article/8d75e62e-0457-4e12-bca6-8118f13f955a (accessed May 25, 2022).
51. *World Duty Free Company v. Republic of Kenya*, ICSID Case No. ARB/00/7, Award—October 4, 2006, para. 157.
52. *World Duty Free Company v. Republic of Kenya*, *supra* n. 51, at para. 157.
53. Drude, *supra* n. 6, at 717.

§13.03   CONTRACTUAL CONSIDERATIONS

[A]   Key Principles: *Favor Contractus, Good Faith and Fair Dealing*

Preserving or ensuring the continuity and validity of contracts is an expression of the principle of *favor contractus*. This principle is said to be the underlying principle of international contract law instruments such as the CISG[54] and the UNIDROIT Principles for International Commercial Contracts[55] and probably of contract laws in general. The principle aims to preserve the contractual relationship by limiting the number of situations in which the existence or validity of the contract is questioned or in which it may be terminated.

Favor contractus appears in the provisions relating to contract formation and performance of contracts. In contract formation, it may appear as a reduced requirement for conformity between the offer and acceptance in the case of a battle of forms,[56] whereas in performance, it can be found behind the provisions concerning the grace period granted by the buyer to the seller to perform in Article 47 CISG.

For the purposes of this article, the treatment of hardship represents a benchmark to follow in f*avor contractus*. During the time of approximately one century since the end of World War I, statutory provisions have been shaped in national laws concerning the effects of changed circumstances on contractual relationships, the latest of them in France in 2016.[57] The need to address changed circumstances has created hardship clauses to be incorporated in contracts, and several compilations of contract law principles, such as the UNIDROIT Principles for International Commercial Contracts,[58] now address the issue. An increasing number of these rules of law provide that a court or arbitral tribunal may adjust the contract to restore its economic equilibrium.[59] Similarly, an arbitral tribunal could restore the integrity of a party by allowing self-cleaning measures in a corruption situation.

---

54. Bertram Keller, *Favor Contractus, Reading the CISG in Favor of a Contract*, in Camilla B. Andersen & Ulrich G. Schroeter eds., *Sharing International Commercial Law across National Boundaries*: Festschrift för Albert H. Kritzer on the Occasion of his Eightieth Birthday, Wildy, Sinnnons & Hill Publishing (2008), 247–266.
55. Nikole Cornet, *Evolving General Principles of International Commercial Contracts, the Unidroit Principles and Favor Contractus*, Maastrict European Private Law Institute Working Paper No. 2011/7.
56. Article 2.1.22 of the UNIDROIT Principles and § 2-207 of the Uniform Commercial Code of the United States.
57. *See* L. Railas, *Changing Circumstances and Contracts: Fairness in Action? University of Turku Covid-19 Supply Chain Update* at, https://sites.utu.fi/covid-supply-chains/wp-content/uploads/sites/714/2020/06/Changing-circumstances-and-contracts-fairness-in-action_10062020LR-1.pdf (accessed May 25, 2022) and T. Lutzi, *Introducing Imprévision into French Contract Law, Lessons to Be Learned from the German Codification in 2002* (Draft, Ius Commune Workshop on Contract Law, 2015), at 10, republished as amended in Multilatera Tobias Lutzi 2016, *Introducing Imprévision into French Contract Law A Paradigm Shift in Comparative Perspective*, in Styns/Jansen eds., *The French Contract Law Reform: A Source of Inspiration?* Intersentia (2016), 89–112.
58. Article 6.2 of the UNIDROIT Principles.
59. The ICC Model Hardship Clause 2020 makes it possible to opt the possibility by which a court or arbitral tribunal may adjust the contract to restore its equilibrium.

The observance of good faith and fair dealing are key in international contract law instruments. Provisions on hardship in national laws are partly the result of the application of good faith and fair dealing obligations.[60] In some countries, such as Italy, good faith provisions of the Civil Code may still be resorted to despite the existence of express provisions on the effects of changed circumstances on contractual relationships. Good faith and fair dealing can also be employed to tackle corruption through contracts in a way that not only condemns a conduct but helps to restore integrity in the relationship. It is submitted it would in some cases be against a party's good faith obligations not to allow a party to rehabilitate itself, considering the gravity of the offense.

[B] Why Is Corruption Relevant Also in a Contractual Context?

In the early 1760s, Adam Smith stated that a "greatly retarded commerce was the imperfection of the law and the uncertainty in its application."[61] Corruption is undoubtedly one of the biggest problems facing societies these days. It prevents natural competition in a marketplace and makes goods or services costlier. It has a detrimental effect on the morale, legality and transparency in a society and is an enemy to democratic decision-making. By undermining predictability in business transactions, corruption makes investments more hazardous and reduces growth and business opportunities. Corruption can take place in a business-to-government relationship, for example, by bribing representatives of a public procurement contracting authority. Also, the contemporary international business practice is moving toward a zero tolerance of corruption.[62] There may be no global definition of corruption, in the absence of which we restrict ourselves to what is stated in ICC Rules on Combatting Corruption 2011, which is largely based on the Organisation for Economic Co-operation and Development (OECD)[63] and United Nations Conventions. Although some national laws might be more stringent or permissive as regards corruption, particularly with regard to their application and enforcement, these international instruments should constitute benchmarks for the purposes of this article.

Combating corruption includes several measures, such as conventions, domestic legislation, and institutional arrangements. Companies are under increasing pressure to comply with anti-corruption laws that have been introduced by governments inspired by international conventions. These laws include the U.S. Foreign Corrupt

---

60. When it comes to the earliest expressions of *rebus sic stantibus* at the beginning of 1920's by the German doctrine of *Wegfall der Geschäftsgrundlage*, this doctrine requires a change of circumstances such that, acknowledging the possibility, the parties would not have concluded the contract and an equitable element meaning that it would not be equitable for a party (in line with his good faith obligations) to deny the other party any amendment of the contract to remedy the situation, Lutzi, *supra* n. 57, 10.
61. A. Smith, *Lectures on Jurisprudence* (Oxford University Press, 1978), 528.
62. Jeffrey R. Boles, *The Contract as Anti-corruption Platform for the Global Corporate Sector*, University of Pennsylvania Journal of Business Law, Volume 21, Issue 4 (2019), 809.
63. The OECD Convention on Combating Bribery of Foreign Public Officials (1997) https://www.oecd.org/corruption/oecdantibriberyconvention.htm (accessed May 25, 2022).

Practices Act[64] and Britain's Bribery Act of 2010.[65] Especially the latter has an international dimension stipulated in Article 12 which introduces a wider concept of territoriality by the involvement of persons having British citizenship or other connections with the U.K. wherever they are in the world. Persons having such a connection can be tried in criminal cases involving corruption before the U.K. courts. Moreover, multilateral development such as the World Bank issue procurement guidelines making lending to countries subject to the requirement that companies involved in corruption cases are blacklisted and excluded in public procurement award procedures in these countries, and companies wishing to participate in such procedures become sensitive of such a possibility. The issue has both a domestic and an international, cross-border dimension. As for the cross-border dimension, companies wishing to make their way with exports of goods or services are in some countries under pressure or tempted to offer bribes to the decision-makers of potential clients or other influential circles such as public authorities.

Irrespective of whether these actions are tried or penalized in the country where the bribery takes place, the domestic criminal legislation of the company may extend to such activity based on the nationality or domicile of the person committing the action. British law extends British criminal prosecution and jurisdiction to companies that operate in the U.K. irrespective of the nationality or domicile of the person committing the offense and the offense not having any other connection with the U.K. than the presence of the company there. The company has strict liability for the acts of any person associated with it (i.e., any employee, agent or subsidiary). However, a company can exonerate itself from liability by proving that it has put in place adequate procedures designed to prevent persons associated with it from undertaking this conduct.

[C]   The ICC Anti-Corruption Clause 2012 as a Business Method to Tackle Corruption?

[1]   The Need for a Contractual Solution

Based on increasing pressure from legislators and the public, companies are implementing policies to prevent corruption. Anti-corruption policies have found their way to corporate codes of conduct, which are usually incorporated into contracts by way of reference in the frame agreement or the general terms and conditions. Not adhering to such policies has become a ground for termination. Stringent policies are imposed on contracting partners, especially on agents and subcontractors. Many multinational companies impose extensive audit procedures on their subcontractors. Given these

---

64. The Foreign Corrupt Practices Act of 1977 (FCPA) (15 U.S.C. §§ 78dd-1, et seq.) is a United States federal law that prohibits U.S. citizens and entities from bribing foreign government officials to benefit their business interests, *see*, https://www.justice.gov/sites/default/files/criminal-fraud /legacy/2012/11/14/fcpa-english.pdf (accessed May 25, 2022).
65. The Bribery Act 2010, accessible: https://www.legislation.gov.uk/ukpga/2010/23/contents (accessed May 25, 2022).

developments, there was a need for a balanced contractual tool for anti-corruption. This contractual tool is typically an anti-corruption clause. One of the main functions of the anti-corruption clauses is to obtain protection from potential corruption conduct and shift possible damages, criminal penalties and fines to the corrupted parties and actors.[66]

[2]   The Clause Incorporates the ICC Rules on Combatting Corruption

In September 2012, the Executive Board of the ICC adopted the ICC Anti-Corruption Clause 2012, a document prepared as a joint effort by two ICC Commissions:

(1) the Commission on Corporate Responsibility and Anti-corruption, and
(2) the Commission on Business Law and Practice.[67]

The ICC has published anti-corruption rules for forty-five years as a tool for corporate self-regulation. As already stated, the ICC Rules in their latest form reflect the provisions of the OECD Convention on Combating Bribery of Foreign Public Officials in International Business Transactions (1997) and the United Nations Convention against Corruption (2003).

The aim of the Anti-Corruption Clause 2012 is to help businesspeople make essential reference to the ICC Rules on Combating Corruption 2011, with the aim of creating trust and preventing their contractual relationship from being affected by corruptive practices. Companies may include this clause in their agreements, whereby they undertake to comply with the ICC Rules.

[3]   Three Options

Two options are possible in this respect: either a short text with the technique of incorporation by reference of Part I of the ICC Rules on Combating Corruption 2011 (Option I) or the incorporation of the full text of the same Part I of the ICC Rules in their contract (Option II). Options I and II are essentially the same thing, but in some legal cultures, incorporation by reference may not be adequate to create legal effects.

Due to controversies about termination as a relief in the final days of preparations, a new Option III was added. According to this option, a company simply undertakes to maintain a corporate anti-corruption compliance program as described in Article 10 of the 2011 ICC Rules and not to abide by the full text of Part I of the Rules.

---

66. Boles, *supra* n. 62.
67. The drafting of the clause was done in a joint task force made up by François Vincke, Belgium, Vice Chair of the Commission on Corporate Responsibility and Anti-corruption; Jean-Pierre Méan, Switzerland, the Chairman of Amnesty International Switzerland and former Chief Compliance Officer of the European Bank for Reconstruction and Development; Christian Steinberger, Germany, Vice Chair of the Commission on Commercial Law and Practice and General Counsel of the German Metal Industry Federation; and Dr. Lauri Railas, a Finnish Attorney.

Companies adhering to Part I by choosing either Option I or Option II undertake that, at the date of the entering into force of the Contract, the company itself, its directors, officers or employees have not offered, promised, given, authorized, solicited or accepted any undue pecuniary or other advantage of any kind (or implied or inferred that they will or might do any such thing at any time in the future) in any way connected with the Contract and that it has taken reasonable measures to prevent subcontractors, agents or any other third parties, subject to its control or determining influence, from doing so.

"Corruption" or "corrupt practice(s)," as used in the clause, include (1) bribery, (2) extortion or solicitation, (3) trading in influence and (4) laundering the proceeds of these practices. These breaches against the rules are defined in detail in the clause. This is soft law that is independent of any national law but has counterparts in the legislation of most countries.

The parties submitting themselves to the clause agree, at all times in connection with and throughout the course of the contract and thereafter, that they will comply with and will take reasonable measures to ensure that their subcontractors, agents or other third parties, subject to their control or determining influence, will prohibit bribery, extortion or solicitation, trading in influence or laundering the proceeds of corrupt practices at all times and in any form, in relation with a public official at the international, national or local level, a political party, party official or candidate to political office, and a director, officer or employee of a party, whether these practices are engaged in directly or indirectly, including through third parties.

[4]   Interpretation of the ICC Clause

Practically all forms of corruption are caught by definition in the Clause. Additionally, the undertaking concerns both business-to-government and business-to-business relations. The undertakings of the parties relate to their activities by the time of the conclusion of the contract and during its entire lifespan and performance. It should be noted that the personnel of a party is subject to a definite undertaking whereas only reasonable measures should be taken to ensure that third parties, such as subcontractors or agents, subject to the determining influence of that company have not been involved in corruption or corrupt practices.

What this means is that a company is not required to prevent by all means any of its subcontractors, agents or other third parties from committing any corrupt practice. It shall, however, based on a periodical assessment of the risks it faces, put into place an effective corporate compliance program, adapted to its circumstances.

It shall also exercise, based on a structured risk management approach, appropriate due diligence in the selection of subcontractors, agents or other third parties, subject to its control or determining influence; and train its directors, officers and employees accordingly.

The clause contains both black-letter text and a commentary. In the commentary, detailed recommendations are made with a view to giving companies concrete advice on how to interpret the black-letter text.

For instance, the ICC recommends enterprises not to make "facilitation payments" (these are unofficial, improper, small payments made to a low-level official to secure or expedite the performance of a routine or necessary action to which the payer is legally entitled), unless their employees are confronted with exigent circumstances, such as duress or when the health, security or safety of their employees are at risk.

[5] Consequences of Non-Compliance

The failure to comply with the ICC rules may lead to consequences. It is possible that the officers of a company get caught by police and relevant criminal consequences follow. In the domestic laws of many countries, including Finland, a corporation may be prosecuted and face criminal sanctions, in practice, fines, and sometimes also confiscations. This obviously creates evidence for the consequences and sanctions in a contractual relationship but is not a precondition for that.

Paragraph 3 of both Options I and II provide that if a party, as a result of the exercise of a contractually-provided audit right, if any, of the other party's accounting books and financial records, or otherwise, brings evidence that the latter party has been engaging in (1) material or (2) several repeated breaches of the provisions of Part I of the ICC Rules, it will notify the latter party accordingly and require the party to take the necessary remedial action in a reasonable time and to inform it about such action.

If the latter party fails to take the necessary remedial action, or if such remedial action is not possible, it may invoke a defense by proving that by the time the evidence of breaches had arisen, it had put into place adequate anti-corruption preventive measures, as described in Article 10 of the ICC Rules, adapted to its particular circumstances and capable of detecting corruption and of promoting a culture of integrity in its organization. If no remedial action is taken or, as the case may be, the defense is not effectively invoked, the first party may, at its discretion, either suspend the contract or terminate it, it being understood that all amounts contractually due at the time of suspension or termination of the contract will remain payable, as far as permitted by applicable law.

As is clear from the preceding paragraph, the threshold of corruption having an impact on the sustainability of the contract is quite high. The consequences of minor violations of the ICC Rules than those envisaged above are not covered by the clause. The effect of such violations may have to be judged by other parts of the contract.

A question may arise as to what is meant by remedying a breach. How could one remedy a crime committed? The answer is not a simple one, and not all breaches can be remedied as such. The Commentary to the ICC Clause contains some examples of how a breach of a non-corruption obligation could be remedied. It is submitted that offenses that are not attributable to the "directing mind" of a company could be remedied by reorganization of work, increasing surveillance or, in worst cases, firing the people having committed the offense.

[6]   Parameters of Option III

Option III, which was added to the clause in the final part of the preparation, has a sanction mechanism. It essentially differs from Options I and II in that a company does not undertake that no corruption has taken place prior to the conclusion of the contract, during its validity or thereafter. There was a fear that random actions of insignificant employees would jeopardize the existence of a long-term contractual relationship in a situation where a contracting partner wants to get rid of a binding contract that has become disadvantageous due to commercial developments.

The obligation imposed by Option III on a company consists of the parties putting into place a corporate anti-corruption compliance program adapted to its circumstances and capable of detecting corruption and of promoting a culture of integrity in the organization. The program must be maintained and implemented throughout the lifetime of a contract, and the contracting partner must be informed regularly about the implementation of the program through statements of a qualified and named corporate representative (such as a compliance officer). Should the statements of the representative contain material deficiencies, the other party may trigger the remedy mechanism, failing which the contract may be suspended or terminated.

It is thought that the application of Option III will, in practice, lead to the same type of considerations. If a company gets caught in serious or repetitive corruption, its prevention systems are evidently not working very well. It is arguable, however, that remedy mechanisms are easier if the undertaking of a company is significantly less onerous.

Since the inception of the ICC Clause, it has been included in several ICC model contracts such as those for distributorship,[68] agency[69] and consultancy.[70] The ICC has chosen to incorporate the Clause by applying Option II, which could be construed to give Option II universal significance, even in cases where the ICC Clause is not incorporated, in other words as an expression of *lex mercatoria*.

It must be stressed that the clause does neither envisage nor in any way promote the idea of audit rights vis-à-vis the contracting partner. In fact, the clause is built on the idea that each party keeps its own yard clean, but indications of non-compliance may trigger the mechanism mentioned in paragraph 3 whereby a party needs to address the concerns of the other party in a suitable way.

§13.04   EU PUBLIC PROCUREMENT AS A MODEL WAY FORWARD

[A]   The Emergence of Self-Cleaning

Self-cleaning as a concept was originally linked to physical substances but has got a meaning in the context of compliance as well. The fundamental idea behind

---

68. *See supra* n. 5.
69. ICC Model Commercial Agency Contract, ICC Publication No. E766E.
70. ICC Model Contract, International Consulting Services, ICC Publication No. 787E.

self-cleaning in public procurement is to restore the candidate's reliability. The underlying idea is that an undertaking can restore the opportunity to participate in public tenders if it demonstrates that it has taken effective and preventive measures to ensure that wrongful acts will not occur again.[71]

It is common practice across Europe that candidates or tenderers who have committed criminal offenses or have proven to be unreliable on other grounds can be excluded from participating in public procurement procedures. This right of exclusion is enshrined in the European public procurement directives, and is based on the premise that criminal behavior, professional misconduct, and similar compliance breaches can render a candidate's integrity questionable and, therefore, the candidate unsuitable to be awarded a public contract. Having said that, the European legislators recognize that everyone deserves a second chance, also within the context of tender procedures, by introducing the "self-cleaning" option. This enables candidates or tenderers who have exhibited such misbehavior that would generally make them unsuitable for public contracts to demonstrate that they have changed for the better, by proving that they have adopted compliance measures remedying the consequences of their past behavior and preventing future misbehavior. The European Union (EU) system is a level playing field on the concept of self-cleaning. The European legislators mention specific measures to be taken follow Article 57 section 6 paragraph 2 of the Public Procurement Directive 2014/24/EU:

(i) compensation of damages caused by the criminal offense or misconduct;
(ii) a clarification of the facts and circumstances by means of active collaboration with the investigating authorities;
(iii) appropriate personnel, technical and organizational measures to prevent future misbehavior (e.g., the severance of all links with persons or organizations involved in the misbehavior, staff reorganization measures, the implementation of reporting and control systems, the creation of an internal audit structure to monitor compliance and the adoption of internal liability and compensation rules).

Article 57(6) can be understood as "the mechanism for adopting corrective measures" (i.e., *self-cleaning*).[72] When analyzing the situation, the measures shall be evaluated "taking into account the gravity and particular circumstances."[73] In other words, the analysis should be done on a case-by-case basis.[74] Although some EU Member States require these conditions to be met cumulatively, some Member States

---

71. Sue Arrowsmith, Hans-Joachim Priess & Pascal Friton, *Self-Cleaning as a Defence to Exclusions for Misconduct: An Emerging Concept in EC Public Procurement Law?*, Public Procurement Law Review, Volume 6 (2009), 2.
72. CJEU, June 19, 2019, Case C-41/18 (*Meca Srl v. Comune di Napoli*) ECLI:EU:C:2019:507, para. 40.
73. Directive 2014/24/EU of the European Parliament and of the Council of February 26, 2014 on public procurement and repealing Directive 2004/18/EC Text with EEA relevance, OJ L 94, 28.3.2014, pp. 65–242, Art. 57 s. 6 para. 2.
74. European Commission, *Notice on tools to fight collusion in public procurement and on guidance on how to apply the related exclusion ground* (2021/C 91/01), Official Journal of the European Union, May 18, 2021, C 91/1, s. 5.7.

consider it sufficient that only one (including Italy, Czech Republic, Romania, and the Netherlands) or two (e.g., Spain) conditions are met.[75] Even in the latter cases, the likelihood of successful self-cleaning increases when all three conditions are met.[76]

The burden of proof rests on the party seeking self-cleaning. To increase the likelihood of success, extensive evidence should be submitted.[77] It is easy for a company to prove that it has paid damages or undertaken organizational measures to prevent further corruption or bribery. The Court of Justice of the European Union (CJEU) held in Case C-387/19 that the threshold for self-cleaning includes that a party is "able to establish, to the satisfaction of the contracting authority, that the corrective measures taken restore its reliability."[78] If we follow the analogy provided by the CJEU, then it would be the party seeking self-cleaning from corruption to meet the burden of proof threshold before an arbitral tribunal.

[B]   Application of the ICC Clause Option II in Arbitration in a Hypothetical Self-Cleaning Case

In line with what has been stated above about *favor contractus* in hardship cases and allowing arbitrators to adapt the contract, it is submitted that arbitrators can also enforce contractual provisions such as the ICC Model Anti-Corruption Clause 2012 and allow self-cleaning to happen with a view to restore the cooperation between the parties in a situation where a party requests the arbitrators to declare the contract terminated. The idea behind self-cleaning in *favor contractus* context is to enhance the reliability and loyalty of the party.

When disputes relating to a contract are settled by arbitration, it is ultimately for an arbitral tribunal to determine whether a party has committed a material or several repeated breaches of ICC Rules, whether it has remedied the breaches or whether it is able to put up a defense of an effective corporate anti-corruptive mechanism. For the sake of clarity and our purpose, it is not relevant which mainstream arbitration agreement or rules are used. We submit that all those—combined with an anti-corruption clause—enable self-cleaning of corruption.

It is submitted that remedying breaches has its limits. If corruption is spelled out or presupposed in the contract, or an act of corruption has played a significant role by undermining the consent of a party, it would be against international public policy to enforce the contract or award the possibility for self-cleaning. In our hypothetical case, these were not at issue. The breach of ICC Rules by the distributor's regional agent could be evaluated in light of the ICC Rules.

---

75. Dentons *Guide to Self-Cleaning in European Public Procurement Procedures* (2021) available at https://www.dentons.com/en/insights/guides-reports-and-whitepapers/2021/april/13/guide-to-self-cleaning-in-european-public-procurement-procedures, accessed May 25, 2022, later 'Dentons', at 7.
76. Dentons, *supra* n. 75, at 7.
77. Dentons, *supra* n. 75, at 7.
78. CJEU, January 14, 2021, Case C-387/19 (*RTS infra BVBA Aannemingsbedrijf Norré-Behaegel BVBA v. Vlaams Gewest*) ECLI:EU:C:2021:13, para. 49.

In our example, the distributor's agent has bribed a client's manager continuously, and this would probably trigger the application of the ICC Clause Option II as several repeated breaches of the ICC Rules had occurred.

The ICC Rules, however, state that only reasonable measures should be taken by a company to ensure that third parties, such as subcontractors or agents, subject to the determining influence of the company, have not been involved in corruption or corrupt practices. The company is not required to prevent by every means any of its subcontractors, agents or other third parties from committing any corrupt practice. It shall, however, based on a periodical assessment of the risks it faces, put into place an effective corporate compliance program, adapted to its circumstances. It shall also exercise, based on a structured risk management approach, appropriate due diligence in the selection of subcontractors, agents or other third parties, subject to its control or determining influence; and train its directors, officers, and employees accordingly.

The burden of proof issue is of utmost importance. Unlike in the UK Bribery Act 2010, it would have to be the party invoking breach of the ICC Rules to prove that this has happened. The arbitrators would have to decide burden of proof issues on the basis of the rules of law applicable to the merits of the case. It is, therefore, up to the arbitrators to determine whether the requirement of "beyond reasonable doubt" or any other level of proof would apply. Arbitrators would have to consider whether an act of corruption is attributable to the company as such or not. The UK Bribery Act imposes strict liability on the company for persons associated with it, whereas the United States and Finnish laws limit corporate criminal liability to circumstances in which a person who is the "directing mind" of the company is guilty of the offense. Therefore, although the arbitrators do not apply criminal law to award penalties, they may have to apply it in a contractual setting.

Once a breach is established, it would be up to the party in breach of the ICC Rules to prove that a possibility of self-cleaning is possible and to suggest remedies for the breach. The arbitral tribunal would have to evaluate the proposed measures and the ultimate compliance with them. When it comes to remedying a breach or putting up a defense of an effective anti-corruptive mechanism, the party invoking these should eventually bear the burden of proof of their effectiveness subject to the rules of law applicable to the merits of the case.

What happens, in effect, is that an arbitral tribunal would apply criminal law in a contractual context. The characterizations of offenses are given in an ICC document which largely reiterates international conventions. The traditional approach of contract law requiring a fundamental breach for the termination of contract is largely useless since the concept as known, for example, by Article 25 CISG builds on commercial expectations relating to the contract. Breaches of ethical values can obviously lead to sinister economic consequences by way of sanctions, blacklisting or public condemnation, but can also operate independently of such considerations. If the tribunal would then consider that not all conditions to self-cleaning are met, meaning that the measures are insufficient, then a statement of the reasons should be elaborated in the award.[79]

If we now consider that the arbitral tribunal would render an arbitral award to declare whether the party complies—or not—with the self-cleaning requirements, the tribunal needs to avoid going to the area of "international public policy" to render an enforceable award. Following a clue from previous practice, these parameters include that the claims are not based on the contracts of corruption and contracts may not have been obtained by corruption. In other words, the contract needs to be alive and not contrary to international public policy.

As with hardship, where the arbitral tribunal might adjust the contract to restore its equilibrium, the arbitral tribunal in a self-cleaning case would help to restore the integrity of a party. In the end, however, it falls on the rules of law applicable to the merits of the case to determine, whether a party must in practice remain in a contractual relationship, or whether it can terminate the contract and incur liability.

§13.05   CONCLUSIONS

Arbitration has survived at least from the Roman era and there are no signs that the flame will be extinguished. Quite the opposite, we have noted a global trend of emerging the scope of arbitration practice to various ambiences, including the disputes of international taxation and adjustment of contracts, and especially operating between public and private laws is axiomatic. Arbitrators are empowered with an imperative role to ascertain disputes of a varying kind with final and binding effect. At the end of the day, the arbitration business serves society and keeps the ball rolling.

It is submitted that there are situations in which arbitrators have a role in enforcing self-cleaning measures at least based on contractual commitments by the parties which are in line with international public policy. By doing so, arbitrators ensure the continuity of such contracts by building on the sound parts of the contract and "picking up, throwing into the fire, and burning up unsound branches"[80] of it, meaning the unsound parts.

Our findings suggest that the tribunal can have jurisdiction in most cases to hear claims with self-cleaning purposes, unless the international public policy is violated. A European Procurement self-cleaning framework provides a recognized cumulative threshold to be met, viz. damages caused by offense have been compensated, there is evidence of active collaboration with the investigating authorities, and the party has taken appropriate measures to prevent future misbehavior. Burden of proof to meet that threshold is on the party to be self-cleaned. These criteria may offer guidelines, or at least inspiration, to arbitrations addressing corruption. The tribunal may render an enforceable award in this remedy under certain conditions. This means that the claims are not based on a contract or on contracts obtained by corruption, viz. respecting the

---

79. Cf. Public Procurement Directive 2014/24, Art. 57 s. 6 para. 3.
80. John 15.

public policy domain. This can be done on a case-by-case basis, applying relevant norms with a sound application.

Arbitrators may hear the request of a party to allow for remedying a breach committed through corruption by fixing such measures, including a timetable and sufficient proof of complying with the orders contained in the award. At the same time, the arbitrators should be able to award other remedies, most notably damages sustained by the aggrieved party through loss of reputation or other consequences. It could be possible that the arbitral tribunal or another one could be resorted to evaluate compliance with the orders at a later stage.

CHAPTER 14

Corruption and Arbitration: Swedish Perspectives Against a French Backdrop

Simon Arvmyren & Chloé Heydarian[*]

§14.01 INTRODUCTION

Corruption is an unwanted reality from which arbitration is not spared. Many of the most common business sectors in arbitration are the most exposed to corruption; such as, construction, infrastructure, defence and natural resources. There is a risk that dubious parties will try to find a 'safe haven' in arbitration by exploiting the privacy and integrity of arbitration proceedings.

In most jurisdictions, corruption falls under the concept of international public policy (or *ordre public international*), the violation of which will render an award invalid or unenforceable. If contested, a national court will review the award, but the depth of the review differs among jurisdictions. Some jurisdictions have adopted a *minimalist approach* (e.g., Switzerland and the United Kingdom), while others have adopted a *maximalist approach* (e.g., France and the Netherlands).[1] The minimalist approach can be defined as a review based only on the facts established in the award. This excludes the possibility to correct or supplement the arbitrators' findings ex officio, even if such facts were established in a manner that is manifestly incorrect or contrary to the law.[2] The maximalist approach allows a court to go beyond the findings laid down in the award. The maximalist approach is neither limited to the evidence

[*] We, the authors, extend our thanks to Anna Nyström, Wilhelm Rönnqvist, Carl Sundberg, Johan Persson Ed and Anna Magnusson Glans for their valuable input, support and good discussions during work with this chapter.
1. The terms 'minimalist approach' and 'maximalist approach' are not official terms or fixed in the sense that commentators will always use and define them in the same way. In this chapter we only use the terms to discuss the scope of the courts' review of an award in relation to facts. Other factors, such as standard of proof, are discussed separately from these terms.
2. *Alexander Brothers v. Alstom*, 4A_136/2016 (Swiss Federal Court, 3 November 2016).

produced before the arbitrators nor bound by their findings, assessments or qualifications.[3]

Using French case law as a comparative backdrop, this chapter seeks to study whether Swedish courts lean towards the minimalist or the maximalist approach, and to what extent Swedish law puts a duty of activity on arbitrators to raise issues regarding corruption ex officio and on their own initiative (sua sponte).

§14.02   WHAT IS CORRUPTION AND WHY IS IT RELEVANT FOR ARBITRATION?

Arbitration is a much-preferred form of commercial dispute resolution due to, among other things, its private nature. In arbitration, the parties are free to choose the arbitrators as well as the rules, place and language of the proceedings.[4] However, the possibility to adapt the procedure to the wishes of the parties comes with both pros and cons.[5] Owing to the private (and sometimes confidential) nature of arbitration, there is generally no public transparency or control of the process and the flexibility of arbitration can be used to reduce the public influence to a minimum, for example, by waiving the right to invoke certain grounds for challenging an award.[6] As a result, the incentives to confront and pursue corruption may be lower in arbitration than court litigation. One could even argue that the private nature of arbitration leads to a greater risk that corruption is realised, facilitated or rewarded when using arbitration compared to using court litigation.[7]

Transparency International defines corruption as 'the abuse of entrusted power for private gain'.[8] The definition is relatively general, which seems unavoidable given that corruption comes in many forms. Article 1 of the ICC Rules on Combating Corruption (2011) stipulates four main categories of prohibited practices: (i) bribery, (ii) extortion or solicitation, (iii) trading in influence and (iv) laundering the proceeds of such corrupt practices.[9] Corruption can be manifested through payments, undue advantage or excessive gifts and hospitality, such as luxury items or travel, which may be given to employees of companies or public entities to influence business decisions or secure an advantage. In relation to agents or intermediaries, bribes may be disguised

---

3. CA Paris Ch.1, 28 May 2019, No. 16/11182 and Cour de Cassation, 29 September 2021, No. 19-19.769.
4. L. Heuman, *Arbitration Law of Sweden: Practice and Procedure* (Huntington, N.Y.: Juris Publishing, Cop. 2003) 13.
5. J. Kvart and B. Olsson, *Tvistlösning genom skiljeförfarande* (Juno, Version 3 2012) 15–16.
6. Cf. s. 51 of the SAA.
7. Cf. International Chamber of Commerce (ICC), International Court of Arbitration, *Tackling Corruption in Arbitration* (Bulletin, Volume 24, Supplement, 2013), 14.
8. Transparency International, *What is corruption?*, https://www.transparency.org/en/what-is-corruption (accessed 13 April 2022). Transparency international is a global civil society organisation that leads the fight against corruption. The organisations have over 90 offices worldwide with an international secretariat in Berlin.
9. *'These ICC Rules are intended as a method of self-regulation by business against the background of applicable national law and key international legal instruments'*, in ICC Rules on Combating Corruption (2011), 4.

as a fee or commission. If a fee or commission exceeds what is considered as the industry standard it might be identified as a bribe.[10]

Extortion and solicitation can take the form of a demand for a bribe that may be coupled with a threat if the demand is refused. It may involve requests for payments or gifts in return for making decisions or conducting specific business-related tasks. Trading in influence is the sort of corruption illustrated by a business employee bribing a public official with the expectation to receive an undue advantage from the public authority in return. In relation to giving remuneration for receiving confidential information, other forms of corruption, such as insider trading,[11] might be a better label. Embezzlement occurs when employees misappropriate anything of value that was entrusted to them because of their position. There are also more subtle measures that may be considered as corruption, such as favouritism, nepotism, cronyism and clientelism, which all concern situations when a person or a group of persons are given unfair preferential treatment at the expense of others. Collusion is yet another form of corruption, which can be defined as a secret agreement for an illegal purpose. Collusion can be manifested through, for example, a labour union employee and a member of the company's management team exchanging favours that result in the employee's interests not being accurately represented.[12] It can also be illustrated by parties agreeing to make up a phoney dispute and resolve it in arbitration, to try to circumvent national law and launder money through obligations laid down in an award.[13]

All in all, the concept of corruption in business is very broad and can occur at different levels of corporate activity or spheres of influence. It goes well beyond what falls within the concept of bribery. This being so, we have, for the purposes of this chapter, limited the concept of corruption to the act of bribing public officials or private individuals in order to obtain a contract (unless stated otherwise).

§14.03 COMPARATIVE BACKDROP FROM THE FRENCH PERSPECTIVE

[A] Introduction

One issue that cuts across the board when discussing corruption in arbitration is the scope and standard of review to be applied by national courts when awards are challenged based on allegations of corruption. In a recent decision of 23 March 2022 (the *Belokon* case), the French Cour de Cassation may have put an end to the question of how thorough a review of an award should be in relation to international public policy in France.[14]

---

10. UNODC, United Nations Office on Drugs and Crime, *Forms and manifestations of private sector corruption*, https://www.unodc.org/e4j/en/anti-corruption/module-5/key-issues/forms-and-manifestations-of-private-sector-corruption.html (accessed 13 April 2022).
11. *Ibid.*
12. *Ibid.*
13. *See, e.g.,* NJA 2002 Note C 45.
14. Cour de Cassation, 29 September 2021, No. 19-19.769.

[B]   The *Belokon* Case

The judgment of 23 March 2022 of the Court de Cassation closed the Belokon saga, which started more than ten years ago. In 2007, a Latvian citizen, Mr Belokon, acquired the National Bank of the Kyrgyz Republic and renamed it Manas Bank. Political tensions later led to the fall of the Kyrgyz Republic's president and the new government placed Manas Bank under temporary administration and eventually a receivership. Criminal proceedings followed. In 2011, Mr Belokon commenced arbitration based on Article 9.2(d) of the bilateral investment treaty between the Republic of Latvia and the Kyrgyz Republic and Article 3 of the UNCITRAL[15] Arbitration Rules. By an award rendered in Paris in 2014, the tribunal ordered the Kyrgyz Republic to pay approximately USD 15 million in damages to Mr Belokon's. In so doing, the tribunal, among other things, rejected the Kyrgyz Republic's allegations that Mr Belokon had been involved in money laundering.[16]

The Kyrgyz Republic brought an action to have the award set aside at the Paris Court of Appeal.[17] The court set aside the award based on the conclusion that recognising the award would make Mr Belekon benefit from the result of criminal activities in a manner that would be in 'manifest, effective and concrete' violation of international public policy. For its reasons, the court raised ex officio that it has an obligation to investigate whether enforcement of an award might breach international public policy.

Mr Belokon appealed the judgment to the Cour de Cassation. The Cour de Cassation quoted the Paris Court of Appeal's statement that as a matter of principle money laundering cannot be tolerated by the French legal system, even in an international context, and especially since the fight against money laundering is part of international consensus, as expressed in particular by the United Nations Convention against Corruption.

The Cour de Cassation concluded that it was possible to qualify Mr Belokon's acts as money laundering based on 'serious, precise and conclusive evidence'.[18] The Paris Court of Appeal had already established that the connection between Mr Belokon and the son of the former president of the Kyrgyz Republic, Mr Bekiev, had been 'inappropriate'. Mr Bakiev occupied the top floor of the bank's building without a rental contract and without paying rental fees and other costs. The set-up was characterised by the Paris Court of Appeal as a misuse of social assets.[19] The Paris Court of Appeal had established that it was the privileged connection with the holder of economic power that guaranteed Mr Belokon freedom from 'real control' of his activities, which in turn facilitated money laundering. The Paris Court of Appeal concluded that the overwhelming success of Manas Bank, in such a short time and in such a poor country, could not be explained by normal banking practices.

---

15. The United Nations Commission on International Trade Law (UNCITRAL).
16. *Valeriy Belokon v. The Kyrgyz Republic*, UNCITRAL Award, 24 October 2014.
17. CA Paris Ch.1, 21 February 2017, No. 15/01650.
18. In French 'grave, précis et concordant'.
19. In French 'abus de biens sociaux'.

By its judgment in the *Belokon* case, the Cour de Cassation recognised the maximalist approach by adopting the view of the Paris Court of Appeal that the court's investigation of possible breach of international public policy was neither limited to the evidence produced before the arbitrators nor bound by the findings, assessments and qualifications made by them. The court's primary duty, in this respect, had been to ensure that the evidence presented before it complied with the principles of contradiction and equality of arms. Finally, the Cour de Cassation concluded that the Paris Court of Appeal had not revisited the merits of the award. Instead, the court had made its own assessment regarding the limited question of whether there was 'serious, precise and conclusive evidence' showing that recognition of the award would allow Mr Belokon to benefit from money laundering.

[C] The *Belokon* Case in Relation to Previous Case Law

The impact of the *Belokon* case in the French panorama cannot be fully appreciated without seeing a few cases such as the *Indagro* case or the infamous *Alstom* saga which have paved the way towards a maximalist approach.

[D] The *Indagro* Case

Before the *Belokon* case, the Cour de Cassation rendered another judgment (the *Indagro* case),[20] which was also on appeal from the Paris Court of Appeal.[21] The two companies Indagro and Ancienne Maison Marcel Bauche (Bauche) had entered into a contract for the sale of urea granules from Russia to Benin and Togo. There was a delay in the underloading of the vessel carrying the goods and Indagro claimed demurrage. Bauche initiated arbitration.[22] During the arbitration, which was seated in London, Bauche alleged that its purchasing agent had been bribed during the conclusion of the contract. In parallel, Bauche also brought an action based on the same allegation before the Paris Criminal Court. The sole arbitrator decided to suspend the arbitration proceedings in anticipation of the judgment of the criminal court, but on the condition that Bauche put up as security an amount corresponding to the litigious claim. Bauche agreed to post security but was unable to renew it at a later stage. As a result of this, the sole arbitrator ruled against Bauche.

Bauche brought an action to set aside the award before the Paris Court of Appeal on the argument that allowing enforcement of the award would be contrary to international public policy. In support of its action, Bauche relied on the judgment from the Paris Criminal Court, which had been rendered after the award. The sentence confirmed that the purchasing agent had indeed been bribed.[23] The Paris Court of Appeal stated that the principle of res judicata in criminal cases makes such cases

---

20. Cour de Cassation, 13 September 2017, Nos 16-25.657 and 16-26.445.
21. CA Paris Ch.1, 27 September 2016, No. 15/12614.
22. *Indagro v. Bauche*, Final Award, 6 May 2015.
23. Tribunal Correctionnel de Paris, 12 May 2016.

binding in subsequent civil processes. Thus, the Paris Court of Appeal was not bound by the findings of the sole arbitrator and set aside the award by application of international public policy. The court used the maximalist approach. Indagro appealed the judgment, but the Cour de Cassation also found that the award was in violation of international public policy and confirmed that the judgment of the Paris Criminal Court had res judicata effect. Among other things, the Cour de Cassation concluded that the court's review of the award 'cannot be conditioned by the attitude of a party before the arbitrator'.

[E]   The *Alstom* Cases

The lengthy dispute between Alstom Transport and Alstom Network (Alstom), on the one side, and Alexander Brothers Ltd (ABL), on the other, came before the review of various different national courts. Alstom tried to set aside the award in front of the Swiss Federal Tribunal in 2018, the Paris Court of Appeal in 2019, the High Court of Justice of England and Wales in 2020 and finally, the Cour de Cassation in 2021. In short, the English and Swiss courts favoured the minimalist approach, while the Paris Court of Appeal, unsurprisingly, favoured the maximalist approach.

[F]   Background

Alstom had signed three consultancy agreements with ABL regarding tenders for rail transport equipment in China. The agreements provided for staggering success fees if Alstom won the tenders. Alstom was awarded all three contracts by the Chinese Minister of Transport and paid the first terms of two contracts in 2006 and 2008 but did not pay the remaining balance and made no payment under the third contract. ABL commenced arbitration in Geneva in 2013.[24] During the arbitration, neither of the parties raised the allegation that the contracts were obtained through bribery. Alstom did not state that it had proof of acts of corruption, but expressed 'softer' concerns relating to ABL not having complied with Alstom's so-called Ethics and Compliance Policy and that Alstom was unable to pay ABL due to the risk of ABL possibly having been engaged in corrupt practices in the performance of the consultancy contracts and the subsequent risk for criminal prosecution. The arbitrators ordered Alstom to pay ABL.

[G]   The Swiss Federal Tribunal

Unsatisfied with the decision, Alstom tried to set aside the award in the Swiss Federal Tribunal, arguing that the enforcement of the award would breach international public policy.[25] The Swiss Federal Tribunal adopted a minimalist approach and upheld the

---

24. *Alexander Brothers Ltd. v. Alstom Transport S.A. and Alstom Network UK Ltd.*, Award, 29 January 2016.
25. *Alexander Brothers v. Alstom*, 4A_136/2016, Swiss Federal Court, 3 November 2016.

award. It stated that the decision was based on the facts established in the award and that the court cannot correct or supplement the arbitrators' findings ex officio, even if the facts have been established in a manner that is manifestly incorrect or contrary to the law. The court added that its 'mission' is only to examine if objections against an award are well-founded. Allowing the parties to make factual allegations other than those established in the award would not comply with the court's function (other than in exceptional cases), even if such new factual allegations were established by evidence that had been submitted in the arbitration.

[H]   The High Court of Justice of England and Wales

Alstom made the same allegations in its application to resist enforcement before the High Court of Justice of England and Wales (the High Court).[26] The High Court stated that Alstom 'could and should' have raised the issue of corruption before the tribunal as it 'had in its mind, and had the materials for, a bribery case', but that 'there is no explanation why this was not done'.[27] Unlike the Paris Court of Appeal, the High Court concluded that the evidence relied on was not particularly strong and that Alstom's allegations were 'entirely unspecific and based on suspicions and inferences'.[28] Therefore, the High Court concluded that there were no such 'exceptional circumstances' that would allow enforcement to be refused. The High Court also declared that there are several levels of seriousness of corruption.[29] In the present dispute, the bribery was considered as incidental, 'not planned, not contracted for, not suspected', and thus according to the court 'somewhat less serious'.[30]

[I]   The Paris Court of Appeal and the Cour de Cassation

Following the decision of the Swiss Federal Court, ABL also sought enforcement before the Paris Court of Appeal.[31] The Paris Court of Appeal took the maximalist approach and noted that while the court is not the judge of the contract, it is the judge when it comes to the incorporation of the award into the national legal order. The review of the Paris Court of Appeal aimed to ensure that the recognition or enforcement of the award did not result in a 'manifest, effective and concrete' violation of international public policy. The court analysed the facts of the case on an ex officio basis and concluded that Alstom's payments to ABL had been used by ABL to bribe Chinese government officials and that sums payable under the award were 'intended to finance or remunerate acts

---

26. *Alexander Brothers Limited (Hong Kong S.A.R) v. (1) Alstom Transport SA (2) Alstom Network UK Limited* [2020] EWHC 1584.
27. *Alexander Brothers Limited (Hong Kong S.A.R) v. (1) Alstom Transport SA (2) Alstom Network UK Limited* [2020] EWHC 1584, at para. 174.
28. *Ibid.*
29. *Ibid.*, at para. 159.
30. *Ibid.*
31. CA Paris Ch.1, 28 May 2018, No. 16/11182.

of bribery'. The Paris Court of Appeal refused to enforce the award by applying international public policy.

The Cour de Cassation reversed the decision, finding that the Paris Court of Appeal had misunderstood a witness transcript, thereby wrongly refusing to enforce the award.[32] The Cour de Cassation rendered a so-called arrêt de cassation avec renvoi, which means that the Cour de Cassation sent the case back to another lower court (the Versailles Court of Appeal) for a retrial. It would seem that it was not the approach regarding the scope and standard of review in relation to the international public policy taken by the Paris Court of Appeal that was problematic, but the appreciation of evidence.

[J]   Discussion

The *Belokon case* confirms that the Cour de Cassation has taken a further step towards the maximalist approach. An adoption of the maximalist approach would mean that, going forward, the Paris Court of Appeal will be allowed to independently investigate all elements, factual and legal, relevant to an issue of international public policy in the context of corruption.[33] A further indication that the Cour de Cassation is creating a uniformed approach, is that it does not require the violation to be 'manifest, concrete and effective' or 'flagrant, concrete and effective', as previously stressed by the Paris Court of Appeal.[34] Instead, the Cour de Cassation simply seems to adopt the wording of Article 1520, paragraph 5 of the French Code of Civil Procedure, which states that 'an arbitral award may only be set aside when recognition or enforcement of the award is contrary to international public policy' as a sufficient standard. As Professor Pierre Mayer has rightly pointed out, the relevant question is not whether an award violates international public policy, but whether the *recognition of the award* would be compatible with international public policy.[35] However, we note that the Cour de Cassation has decided not to publish the *Belokon case* in the *Rapport annuel de la Cour de Cassation*, which references the most important cases. We think that additional cases are needed to finally determine whether the maximalist approach has fully triumphed and to which extent.

At first, the minimalist approach might be perceived as more arbitration friendly since it does not allow room for a court to raise issues outside the scope of the parties' causes of action. However, the potential negative long-term effects of arbitration of the minimalist approach could lead to the opposite conclusion. In cases where the

---

32. Cour de Cassation, 29 September 2021, No. 19-19.769.
33. T. Granier, *Une nouvelle confirmation du contrôle effectif et concret de la conformité à l'ordre public de la reconnaissance et de l'exécution des sentences internationales en matière de corruption privée, et une application discutable de l'article 519 CPC, note sous Paris, Pôle 1 – Ch. 1, 30 juin 2020*, Revue de l'Arbitrage (© Comité Français de l'Arbitrage; Comité Français de l'Arbitrage 2021, Volume 2021 Issue 1) 133, pp. 129–144.
34. CA Paris Ch.1 18 November 2004, No. 2002/19606, CA Paris Ch.1, 30 June 2020, No. 17/22515, CA Paris Ch.1, 16 January 2018, No. 15/21703.
35. S. Arvmyren's notes from the speech by Professor P. Mayer at the meeting of the ICC Commission on Arbitration and ADR on 29 March 2022.

arbitrators do not raise the issue of corruption despite numerous indicators, such as in the *Alstom* case, there is a risk that awards that violate international public policy become enforceable, which in turn may be detrimental to the perception, integrity and legitimacy of arbitration in the longer run. The maximalist approach is, however, not a flawless alternative. Why should a party that has stayed silent during the arbitration suddenly be allowed to successfully contest the award by invoking international public policy? The maximalist approach arguably benefits a party that, for tactical or obstructive purposes, chooses to 'save' an allegation of corruption for possible set aside proceedings or as a basis for opposing enforcement. That is of course undesirable, since it causes unnecessary further legal proceedings.

§14.04 POSSIBLE MEANS OF CONTROLLING CORRUPTION IN ARBITRATION UNDER SWEDISH LAW

[A] Introduction

It is a reasonable starting point that rules governing arbitration must serve the purpose of preventing arbitration from being used to realise, facilitate or reward corruption. It is also a reasonable starting point that such rules must be adapted to the reality of the arbitrators responsible for the award and the proceedings, but also take into account that the arbitrators' mandate is contractually based. It would be naïve, and probably counterproductive, to think that arbitrators should (or could) police arbitrations with the same authority and diligence as public enforcement agencies are expected to do.

The means of controlling corruption in arbitration should not go beyond the usual means of ensuring that arbitration proceedings are conducted within acceptable standards of rule of law and due process, and that awards do not give rise to offensive results. Controlling corruption in arbitration should be limited to the same means of control as already exist.[36] The increasing awareness of corruption globally may, however, lead to a need to reassess the methods and standards of how such means of control shall be understood and applied. For example, the arbitrator may have a *duty of activity* with respect to facts that indicate corruption, which goes further than in relation to other facts and that is stricter than has previously been believed to be the case. Swedish arbitration law should take into consideration the developments in other jurisdictions.

In the following, when we talk about 'controlling corruption', we mean such means of control already exist under Swedish law to prevent arbitration from being used to realise, facilitate or reward corruption.

---

36. Cf. ICC, National Sweden Committee's answers to the Questionnaire from ICC Commission on Arbitration and ADR Task Force, *Addressing Issues of Corruption in International Arbitration*, November 2021, 6, http://www.rettig.icc.se/wp-content/uploads/2021/11/Corruption-report-The-Swedish-National-Committee-Nov2021.pdf (accessed 13 April 2022).

[B]   Controlling Corruption by Setting Aside the Award

The ultimate, and perhaps most obvious, means of controlling corruption is the possibility to *set aside* an award that is, in some respect, the result of corruption. Setting aside the award would effectively reverse the corruptive implications of the award. The legal effect of setting aside an award is that the award will be annulled and lose all legal effect, sending the issue decided by the arbitrators back to an absolute zero point.

Swedish law distinguishes between two legal concepts for setting aside an award which are dealt with in two separate provisions of the Swedish Arbitration Act (SAA) (sections 33 and 34 of the SAA). The first legal concept protects third-party interests (such as aspects of competition law, intellectual property law or family law) or interests that are subject to the legitimate state monopoly over those parts of the legal system that uphold civilian authority (such as criminal law, tax law, other fields of administrative law, the protection of fundamental rights and some particular aspects of private law). An award that infringes such third-party or public interest is *invalid*, a nullity, and may be set aside without restriction in time. The legal concept of invalid awards deals, among other things, with cases of an issue *not being arbitrable* or an issue being *contrary to Swedish public policy*.[37]

The second legal concept for setting aside an award protects various aspects of party interest and is subject to strict time limits with respect to bringing an action to set aside (a challenge of the award).[38] The legal concept of *challengeable* awards deals, among other things, with cases of an issue not being covered by a valid arbitration agreement, an arbitrator not being impartial and independent or the occurrence of procedural errors affecting the outcome of the dispute.[39]

[C]   Controlling Corruption by Refusing Enforcement

Given that the possibility of setting aside an award is limited to the seat of arbitration, the controlling function by national courts over foreign awards can only be exercised at the enforcement stage.

In order to enforce a foreign award in Sweden, one must first apply to the Stockholm appellate court (the Svea Court of Appeal) for a declaration of recognition and enforceability of the award. The conditions for declaring an award enforceable are set out in sections 53–55 of the SAA. Section 55 provides that an application for recognition and enforceability shall be rejected if the court finds that the award includes the determination of an issue that may not be decided by arbitrators under Swedish law (arbitrability) or that it would clearly be incompatible with the basic principles of the Swedish legal system to enforce the award (public policy). The bases for refusing enforcement under section 55 of the SAA mirror the bases for setting aside an award due to it being invalid. Furthermore, section 54 of the SAA contains a

---

37. Section 33 of the SAA.
38. Section 34 of the SAA.
39. *Ibid.*

possibility to refuse enforceability if the party against whom the award is raised can prove, for example, that the arbitration agreement is invalid, that the party was not given proper notice of the arbitration or the appointment of an arbitrator, or that the party was otherwise unable to properly present its case. This section protects the party interest of not having to tolerate an award that is challengeable.

[D]   The Minimalist or Maximalist Approach?

Under Swedish law, set aside and enforcement proceedings are subject to standard rules of civil procedure, which provide that the parties can submit and invoke new facts and evidence, including facts and evidence beyond what was submitted in the arbitration. Under the so-called principle of free assessment of evidence, the court is free to assess the evidentiary value of such new evidence. This is what courts regularly do and it indicates a maximalist approach, although the court may of course assess that new evidence will not outweigh the assessment made in the award. We believe that although Swedish courts would likely be prevented from using the minimalist approach in the strict sense, the actual assessment might result in an outcome similar to what would have been the case if a minimalist approach was used.

In the Supreme Court Case NJA 2015 p. 433, concerning an application for recognition and enforceability of an award, the Supreme Court stated that a court should raise and assess, on its own motion, circumstances that have been disclosed in the matter that may lead to the application of public policy.[40] With 'the matter', the court referred to the matter before the court, thus not limiting itself to what had been disclosed in the arbitration. The Supreme Court also expressed, however, that the court's obligation does not go beyond this duty of activity (to 'raise and assess'), and it is not the function of the court to independently attempt to find or research circumstances. One could say that the court should not assume the role of the police or a public prosecutor.

In one sense, the Swedish approach is even more maximalist than, for example, the French approach since under Swedish procedural law, a sentence following criminal proceedings would not have a res judicata effect in a subsequent arbitration or in a case before civil court, even if exactly the same allegations of corruption are raised.[41] Under Swedish law, this would, among other things, be an effect of the parties not being the same in criminal proceedings, which is between the state (the public prosecutor) and the defendant, and in the civil case. A sentence has strong evidentiary value, but in theory, the court would be able to go beyond the conclusions in the criminal proceedings if something new and material comes up (it goes without saying,

---

40. *See* Svea Court of Appeal, Judgment of 22 April 2021 in Case No. T 603-1 where the court emphasised that although the departure point is the arbitrators' assessment of the evidence, the court has to make an independent assessment with respect to evidence that had not been presented in the arbitration.
41. ICC, National Sweden Committee's answers to the Questionnaire from ICC Commission on Arbitration and ADR Task Force, *Addressing Issues of Corruption in International Arbitration*, *supra*, 1–8, 2.

however, that a sentence cannot be reversed in a civil case). At the same time, Sweden and France are similar in the sense that in both jurisdictions, a court is not bound by the arbitrators' findings if corruption has taken place.[42] The stricter application of the res judicata principle in France, making a sentence in criminal proceedings binding upon a civil court seems to be more a question of method and principle, than having a different view on the maximalist approach. Thus, in our opinion, there is no doubt that Swedish law adheres to the maximalist approach when it comes to such bases for an action to set aside or refuse enforcement that would render the award invalid, but also in relation to other party interests that are axiomatic to arbitration; such as the existence of a valid arbitration agreement or that an arbitrator must be impartial.[43]

[E]   Arbitrability as the Legal Basis for Controlling Corruption

Under section 33(1) of the SAA, an award is invalid and shall be set aside if the issue determined by the award is not arbitrable. As a main rule in Sweden, disputes which are arbitrable are those that the parties can resolve through settlement.[44] With respect to issues of corruption, the departure point seems to be that an issue involving an allegation of corruption is capable of settlement and thus arbitrable. One author, Professor Kaj Hobér, states that an allegation of bribery and corruption does not deprive the arbitrators of jurisdiction due to non-arbitrability.[45] Another author, former Supreme Court Justice Stefan Lindskog, confirms the international tendency to move the concept of arbitrability from a procedural context to more of an issue of substantive law.[46] In Lindskog's opinion, arbitrators tend to accept jurisdiction over an issue involving an allegation of corruption, but rejecting the claim on the merits.[47] Lindskog argues that rejecting a claim on the merits prevents immorality in a more effective way, which seems to be in contrast with previous ideas.[48]

An ICC Sweden national committee report discusses cases involving some form of corruption, fraud or alleged illegality. The authors conclude that there is a high

---

42. *Ibid.*
43. Other commentators have expressed the opposite belief, arguing that Swedish law lies nearer to the minimalist approach as adopted in the UK. However, this conclusion seems to be based on a confusion of the scope of the courts' review of an award in relation to facts and the applicable standard of proof. *See* C. Sanderson, *GE Pays Out after Losing Corruption Challenge in Legacy Case*, Global Arbitration Review https://globalarbitrationreview.com/article/ge-pays-out-after-losing-corruption-challenge-in-legacy-case (accessed 6 May 2022).
44. *See* s. 1(1) of the SAA and Prop. 1998/99:35, 48.
45. K. Hobér, *International Commercial Arbitration in Sweden* (Second edition, Oxford University Press 2021) 117.
46. S. Lindskog, *Skiljeförfarande: en kommentar* (Juno, Version 3 1 June 2020) Chapter 33, 4.4.1.
47. *Ibid.*
48. Cf. the illustrative statements by Lagergren in the ICC Case No. 1100. The Swedish Judge Gunnar Lagergren acted as a sole arbitrator and declared that he did not have jurisdiction to decide over a dispute in which the main contract resulted from bribery. Contrary to some of the criticisms of this decision, Lagergren rejected the idea that issues of corruption were not for arbitrators. In his opinion there were well-founded indicators of corruption, but they remained unproven and the parties refused to cooperate. He averred: 'In these conditions, I cannot deal with the request to order performance of the contract. What can I do? I can only say that I have no jurisdiction.'

threshold for the arbitrators to find themselves lacking jurisdiction on the basis that the case is not arbitrable.[49] In this respect, we note that the prevailing view internationally seems to be that when jurisdiction is challenged due to an allegation of corruption, the dispute will still be considered arbitrable.[50] This is supported by an unpublished ICC award from 2003,[51] in which the arbitrators found that the contract in dispute was invalid since its purpose was to bribe a public official in order to obtain another contract. The arbitrators applied the doctrine of separability and concluded that the arbitration agreement was separate and, as such, remained valid.[52]

Having said the above, it is questionable whether *all* disputes involving corruption are arbitrable, without considering the extent and severity of the corruption. We note that Swedish courts have in several cases pointed to the necessity of a *real legal relationship* between the parties as a condition for a court, or arbitrators, to be able to adjudicate the issue. In NJA 2002 note C 45, two brothers had colluded with each other in order to establish an award confirming the transfer of ownership of a real estate property from one brother to the other, thereby excluding the property from being included in the first brothers' bankruptcy estate. For its reasons, the Supreme Court implied that the brothers had created a fictitious transfer document to deceive the bankruptcy estate. The court refused to enforce the award and concluded that it did not reflect a real legal relationship.[53] In NJA 2015 p. 433, the Supreme Court identified several factors indicating that the disputed agreement was a sham agreement and noted that courts shall not assist in enforcing awards where it would be highly offensive to do so. In a case from the Stockholm Court of Appeal (the *Stati* case),[54] the court stressed the importance of a real legal relationship between the parties, despite finally concluding that a fraudulent scheme together with falsified evidence was, on the facts of that case, not enough to conclude the absence of a real legal relationship.[55]

It is possible that in a situation where the corruption is so severe or collusive that the contract must be considered a sham or not reflecting a real legal relationship, the issue could be considered as not arbitrable. But, it would also be possible to see it as an issue of public policy which might be an easier route.

---

49. ICC, National Sweden Committee's answers to the Questionnaire from ICC Commission on Arbitration and ADR Task Force, *Addressing Issues of Corruption in International Arbitration*, *supra*, 1–8, 8.
50. International Chamber of Commerce (ICC), International Court of Arbitration, *Tackling Corruption in Arbitration*, Bulletin, Volume 24, Supplement (2013), 13.
51. *See* C. Albanesi and E. Jolivet, 'Dealing with Corruption in Arbitration: A Review of ICC Experience', in International Chamber of Commerce (ICC) (ed.), International Court of Arbitration, *Tackling Corruption in Arbitration*, Bulletin, Volume 24, Supplement (2013), 27–38, 30.
52. *Ibid.*
53. ICC, National Sweden Committee's answers to the Questionnaire from ICC Commission on Arbitration and ADR Task Force, *Addressing Issues of Corruption in International Arbitration*, *supra*, 1–8, 7.
54. Svea Court of Appeal, Judgment of 9 December 2016 in Case No. T 2675-14.
55. ICC, National Sweden Committee's answers to the Questionnaire from ICC Commission on Arbitration and ADR Task Force, *Addressing Issues of Corruption in International Arbitration*, *supra*, 1–8, 7.

[F]   Public Policy as the Legal Basis for Controlling Corruption

The French legal system makes a distinction between 'national' public policy and 'international' public policy (*ordre public international*).[56] In Sweden, the topic is not extensively discussed. In theory, it might be possible to make a distinction, but this chapter does not pretend to bring a solution. One author, Hobér, points out that 'in practice it would seem likely that if application of any law or rule would be deemed to be contrary to international public policy such application would in all likelihood also violate the national public policy'.[57] In the context of corruption, we believe that under most legal systems corruption is considered to fall within the standard of international public policy as an example of immoral and socially destructive behaviour.[58] It is generally accepted that corruption goes against 'fundamental rules of law' and 'principles of natural justice'.[59] This being so, the possibility of setting aside an award based on public policy is still intended to be applied restrictively by the courts.[60]

Under section 33(2) of the SAA 'an award is invalid if the award, or the manner in which the award arose, is clearly incompatible with the basic principles of the Swedish legal system'. This was further elaborated upon in the preparatory works, which stated, among other things, that section 33(2) of the SAA is applicable when the award orders a party to perform a payment that is an agreed-upon bribe.[61] It is possible to consider corruption as a matter of public policy under Swedish law.[62] An award may also come in conflict with public policy if the contract in question is considered to be a so-called *pactum turpe*, an illegal or immoral contract,[63] or enforces a right based on a *pactum turpe*.[64] Under Swedish law, the doctrine of *pactum turpe* is a

---

56. Under French law, ordre public international is defined as 'the principles of universal justice considered in French opinion as endowed with absolute international value', French in the original, 'principes de justice universelle considérés dans l'opinion française comme doués de valeur internationale absolue', *Lautour case*, Cour de Cassation, 25 May 1948.
57. K. Hobér, *International Commercial Arbitration in Sweden* (Second edition, Oxford University Press 2021) 53.
58. P.L. Ullmer, *The Arbitrator's Dilemma: Does the Potential Arbitrator's Duty to Investigate Corruption on His/Her Own Initiative Create Conflicts with the Parties' Due Process Rights?* (Master Thesis, Stockholm University 2021) 11.
59. P. Lalive, 'Transnational (or Truly Transnational) Public Policy', in Comparative Arbitration Practice and Public Policy in Arbitration, Pieters Sanders Edition, ICCA Congress Series, Volume 3 (ICCA & Kluwer Law International 1987), 290–291.
    M. Hwang and K. Lim, *Corruption in Arbitration: Law and Reality*, Asian International Arbitration Journal (© Singapore International Arbitration Centre (in co-operation with Kluwer Law International); Kluwer Law International 2012, Volume 8 Issue 1), 1–119, 101.
    World Duty Free Company Limited v. Republic of Kenya, ICSID Case No. ARB/00/7, Award 4 October 2006, para. [148].
    Final Award in ICC Case No. 13914 (Extract) para. 230.
60. *See* SOU 1994:81, *Skiljedomsutredningen*, 289; Prop. 1998/99:35, 142; Svea Court of Appeal, Judgment of 22 April 2021 in Case No. T 603-19.
61. *See* Prop. 1998/99:35, 234.
62. *See* Svea Court of Appeal, Judgment of 22 April 2021 in Case No. T 603-19.
63. F. Andersson et al., *Arbitration in Sweden* (Jure 2011) 62.
64. Prop 1998/99:35, 141.

'super-mandatory' norm, which applies irrespective of the law otherwise applicable to the contract.[65]

As in most jurisdictions, Swedish legal theory makes a distinction between procedural and substantive public policy.[66] This is confirmed by Professor Lars Heuman, who divides public policy into the said two categories.[67] Another author, Lindskog, states that procedural public policy means that something in the procedure does not live up to the necessary requirements for the rule of law; and that substantive public policy means that the content of an award is in some way contrary to the foundations of the Swedish legal system.[68]

[G] Procedural Public Policy

Fundamental procedural principles, such as due process, impartiality, the right to legal representation and the right to be heard, may all raise public policy concerns.[69] If a party influences one or more arbitrators to take a certain action by using bribery or another criminal act, procedural public policy may be applicable.[70] Procedural public policy may also be applicable if an arbitration clause contains provisions that constitute a serious deviation from fundamental procedural principles.[71]

However, not all serious procedural shortcomings amount to an award being contrary to procedural public policy. In the Government official report preceding the SAA, the committee suggested that awards based on *false evidence*, such as an expert or a witness committing perjury or falsified documents being relied upon, should be considered contrary to public policy.[72] The suggestion was not adopted in the final Government proposal. In choosing between the interest of substantively correct awards and the parties' interest in having the dispute resolved quickly, the legislature considered that the latter outweighed the first. It was an explicit objective of the SAA to satisfy, to the greatest extent possible, the interest of having a final and binding award through a speedy and efficient proceeding.[73]

---

65. F. Andersson et al., *Arbitration in Sweden* (Jure 2011) 62.
66. *See* Prop. 1998/99:35, 232; SOU 1994:81, *Skiljedomsutredningen,* 289.
67. L. Heuman, *Skiljemannarätt* (Norstedts Juridik AB, edition 1:6, 1999) 600.
68. S. Lindskog, *Skiljeförfarande: en kommentar,* Chapter 33-4.2.1–4.2.3.
69. S.A. Budok, S.U Gürman and C.Ç. Kadıoglu, *International vs. Domestic Public Policy in International Arbitration: Where Does It Begin, Where Does It End?* (Lexology 2019) 31–33, 31, https://www.lexology.com/library/detail.aspx?g = 8edc0dee-29e9-45e9-9879-e0b4deb80105 (accessed 13 April 2022).
70. L. Heuman, *Skiljemannarätt,* 600; SOU 1994:81, *Skiljedomsutredningen,* 172, 182 and 289; Prop. 1998/99:35, 142, 150 and 234.
71. L. Heuman, *Skiljemannarätt,* 601; SOU 1994:81, *Skiljedomsutredningen,* 172 and 289; Prop. 1998/99:35, 142, 150 and 234.
72. SOU 1994:81, *Skiljedomsutredningen,* 182.
73. *See* Prop. 1998/99:35, 149.

[H]   Substantive Public Policy

The situation that an award is contrary to substantive public policy constitutes an exception to the rule that an award may not be reviewed on the merits and represents one of those exceptional instances when it is more important to have a decision that reflects the true condition of things than to preserve the finality of the award.[74] This implies that courts should apply substantive public policy restrictively. Objections based on substantive public policy should relate to the principles of *'pacta sunt servanda*, good faith, abuse of right, prohibition of bribery and corrupt practices, and protection of individual rights'.[75] Specific examples of the latter are when the award allocates criminally acquired funds or if an arbitrator has failed to comply with some mandatory rule of law, regarding a third-party or public interest, at least if the arbitrators have failed to apply a particularly important legal standard.[76] It is also possible that offensive cases of incorrect application of the law, assessment of evidence and other things may in exceptional cases cause an award to be invalid as being contrary to substantive public policy if the result of the award is truly unreasonable.[77]

§14.05   THE ARBITRATORS' OBLIGATION TO ENDEAVOUR TO ACHIEVE AN AWARD THAT IS NOT INVALID, CHALLENGEABLE OR UNENFORCEABLE

[A]   Introduction

The basis upon which an arbitration comes into existence is the arbitration agreement[78] and accordingly the arbitrators' mandate is also *contractually based*. Under section 27(1) of the SAA, there is a mandatory procedural requirement that the dispute referred to the arbitrators shall be decided by an award. This requirement also encapsulates a contractual undertaking by the arbitrators, but besides some supplementary provisions concerning the formal content[79] the SAA does not provide for any particular standard of quality of an award.[80] Where the quality of performance is left undetermined, general principles of Swedish contract law assumes that the performance shall be of *normal standard*[81] or, in other words, of a standard that is reasonable and not less than

---

74. N. Voser and A. George, *Revision of an Srbitral Award*, ASA No. 38 Post Award Issues, 43–74, 43, https://www.swlegal.ch/media/filer_public/32/63/32637dcf-3c36-46a1-b8bf-98f3cdf21573 /09-chapter-3.pdf (accessed 13 April 2022).
75. S.A. Budak and S.U. Gürman, *International vs. Domestic Public Policy in International Arbitration: Where Does It Begin, Where Does It End?* (Lexology 2019) 31–33, 31, https://www.lexology .com/library/detail.aspx?g = 8edc0dee-29e9-45e9-9879-e0b4deb80105 (accessed 13 April 2022).
76. S. Lindskog, *Skiljeförfarande: en kommentar*, Chapter 33-4.2.2.
77. *Ibid.*
78. S. Lindskog, *Skiljeförfarande: en kommentar*, 724. Here disregarding the rare instances of statutory based arbitration.
79. *See* s. 31 of the SAA.
80. Cf. S. Lindskog, *Skiljeförfarande: en kommentar*, 710.
81. *See* for example K. Rodhe, *Obligationsrätt* (1956) 219 et seq.; J. Ramberg and J. Herre, *Internationella köplagen (CISG): en kommentar*, ss 7.2.2 and 7.2.4, Juno (accessed 29 June

average in the circumstances.[82] In our opinion, this principle provides an appropriate starting point for the standard of quality applicable to awards;[83] a standard that arbitrators have an obligation to endeavour to achieve in order to preserve the integrity of the arbitration.[84]

The purpose of this article is not to set out all elements of what the normal standard of an award should be,[85] but an award that is invalid, challengeable or unenforceable would, in our opinion, not fulfil the requirement of being of normal standard.[86] The arbitrators must, as a minimum, endeavour to achieve an award that is free from such encumbrances. In our opinion, this shall mean that the arbitrators have a duty of activity with respect to such facts or indicators of fact, such as corruption, that threatens the achievement of an award that is invalid, challengeable or unenforceable.

[B]   Procedural Guidance

The rules and steps of the arbitration process are laid down by the arbitration agreement together with any additional procedural agreements between the parties, as supplemented by the SAA and other sources of law. As a starting point, procedural rules are binding for the arbitrators, but they also provide the arbitrators with certain powers or tools. Some rules allow for a fair portion of discretion. An important instrument to exercise control over the arbitration process and protect the integrity of the arbitration is the arbitrators' obligation, and corresponding right, to use procedural

---

2022); T. Sandström, *Mönster i förmögenhetsrätten*, ss 5, 112, footnote 6 and 7, Juno (accessed 29 June 2022); J. Kihlman, *Fel*, s. 1.6.2., Juno (accessed 29 June 2022); Arrhed, *Offentlig upphandling av komplexa IT-tjänster*, ss 5.3, 78, footnote 20, Juno (accessed 29 June 2022); and cf. Norwegian law V. Hagstrøm, *Obligasjonsrett* (Second edition 2011) 166–175.

82. Cf. Art. 5.1.6 UNIDROIT Principles 2016 and Art. 6:108 Principles of European Contract Law.
83. Cf. A. Gomez-Acebo, 'Chapter 3: The Right to Make a Unilateral Appointment', in *Party-Appointed Arbitrators in International Commercial Arbitration*, International Arbitration Law Library, Volume 34 (© Kluwer Law International; Kluwer Law International 2016), 39–68, footnote 101, 'a good award is an award which is right and can be enforced. "Right" means right on the merits, the materialisation in each particular case that justice is done. A bad award is one that is wrong in its decision on the merits or is not enforceable (at least in some places)'.
84. We note that to some extent the parties can dispose of the standard of an award by way of agreement, which can lead to tricky considerations; for example, if the respondent does not participate in the arbitration or takes a passive approach. Cf. S. Lindskog, *Skiljeförfarande: en kommentar*, IV:0-5.3.7, in particular on 720–722, commentary to 8 §, Allmänna anmärkningar.
85. Cf. S. Lindskog, *Skiljeförfarande: en kommentar*, Chapter IV, in particular on 723–732. Lindskog does not relate standard of the award to the contractual norm of normal standard, but reasons along the same lines, stating, among other things, that the dispositive part of the award must be 'adequate' and provide for an order that is enforceable, or a declaration that can serve as basis for further adjunction (on 724). Lindskog also notes that it must be assumed that arbitrators 'should' provide reasons for the determination of issues referred to them, since it would improve the 'quality' of the award (on 727).
86. Cf. s. 9 of the Swedish Promissory Notes Act, which contains a rule regarding the standard of quality in relation to monetary obligations; determining the standard to be that the obligation must be 'valid' (*veritas*), but not that the obligation must be 'good' (*bonitas*) in the sense that the obligor will actually perform the obligation. Depending on the contractual context, s. 9 of the Promissory Notes Act can be applied to other types of obligations. Cf. E.M. Runesson, *Licens till patent och företagshemligheter i avtals- och kontraktsrätten*, 96 et seq.

guidance (Swedish: *materiell processledning*) in order to actively deal with issues that arise during the proceedings.

By way of analogy, the obligation to pursue procedural guidance finds its legal support in section 8 of Chapter 42 and section 4 of Chapter 43 of the Swedish Code of Civil Procedure, which prescribes that a court shall, from what is demanded under the circumstances, endeavour to achieve that the issues in dispute are clarified and that the parties specify everything they want to rely on in the proceedings. The court shall exercise procedural guidance by asking questions and making statements with the aim of remedying ambiguities and incompleteness in the parties' submissions. The extent to which the court shall pursue procedural guidance is determined, on the one hand, by the parties' right to an effective remedy before court and, on the other hand, by the court's duty to remain impartial.[87] The use of procedural guidance shall be applied restrictively and it should, in principle, be limited to aiding the parties, to the extent necessary, to *clarify* their request for relief, the various bases for the request and what evidence they wish to adduce.[88] Procedural guidance is primarily to be used during the preparatory steps of the proceedings and thus before the evidentiary hearing.[89] The court's obligation to pursue procedural guidance is stricter in relation to mandatory law, typically protecting third-party or public interests.[90] It is a fair assumption that the court's duty of activity is also stricter in relation to indicators of corruption.

There are some differences in how procedural guidance is to be used in arbitration compared to court proceedings. For several reasons, arbitrators should use procedural guidance more restrictedly than a court. In arbitration, many of the interests that justify procedural guidance are not as prevalent. For example, although it may appear somewhat cynical, the arbitrators are not, at least not to the same extent as a court, guided by the same higher purpose of achieving a decision that is right on the merits[91] (although arbitrators would of course also be inclined to reach a correct outcome given the finality of an award). This perspective is mirrored by the fact that an award cannot be appealed, but only set aside under certain rather limited conditions. Also, arbitrators do not have to consider that less restricted procedural guidance could save the courts' resources and thus have a positive economic effect on public spending.[92] The more restricted approach in arbitration seems to have been confirmed by the Supreme Court in older case law, where the court stated that it is uncertain whether an omission to exercise procedural guidance by arbitrators constitutes a ground for setting aside an award.[93] Naturally, a more extensive obligation for arbitrators to exercise procedural guidance would limit party autonomy and possibly the speediness of arbitration proceedings.[94] Exercising procedural guidance should reflect the parties' reasonable expectations on the arbitration process.

---

87. *See* Prop. 1986/87:89, 105.
88. *See* Prop. 1986/87:89, 106.
89. *See* Prop. 1986/87:89, 216.
90. *See* Prop. 1986/87:89, 104, 108, 196 and 217.
91. B. Lindell, *Alternativ tvistlösning* (First edition, Iustus 2000) 173–175.
92. *Ibid.*
93. *See* NJA 1973 p. 740.
94. B. Lindell, *supra*, 175.

Independence and impartiality will in practice be considered with a higher degree of sensitivity than in relation to judges, which coincides with the fact that arbitration is based on trust in the arbitrators.[95] It is axiomatic that an arbitrator must be impartial,[96] and under Swedish law this principle is laid down in sections 7–9 of the SAA. The meaning of impartiality and independence is, among other things, that the arbitrator shall act without considering the parties' material interests.[97] As regards the use of procedural guidance, Lindskog claims that the use of procedural guidance cannot be deemed to damage the confidence in the arbitrator, if the parties are treated equally.[98] However, it has been suggested that procedural guidance should in general be exercised with caution, not be perceived as lacking objectivity.[99] If the arbitrators are uncertain whether to use procedural guidance, they should limit themselves to such measures that are necessary, but without risking helping one of the parties to improve its case.

That being said, we submit that arbitrators do have duty of activity and that they shall use procedural guidance to raise issues on their own initiative (sua sponte) if something wrong threatens the achievement of an award of normal standard.[100] Deliberate or careless inactivity, causing a forthcoming award to be possible to set aside is not desirable and should not be a protected approach to arbitration proceedings. This seems to be particularly true considering Swedish courts being likely to use the maximalist approach in line with the French case law described above. The duty of activity must be especially strong in cases where the arbitrators perceive indicators that would render the award invalid under section 33 of the SAA, such as indicators of something being contrary to public policy or outside the scope of arbitrability. We believe this view to have solid support.[101] The arbitrators should actively raise issues regarding a well-founded suspicion that the claim is the result of corruption (such as a bribe) and doing so would normally not compromise the arbitrator's independence and impartiality,[102] at least as long as the issue is raised in a neutral manner preserving the

---

95. Cf. B. Lindell, *Alternativ till rättskipning: förhandling, medling, processförlikning, tvistlösnings-snämnder och skiljeförfarande* (First edition, Iustus 2020) 300–301.
96. *Halliburton Company v. Chubb Bermuda Insurance Ltd*, UK Supreme Court [2020] UKSC 48.
97. S. Lindskog, *Skiljeförfarande: en kommentar*, commentary to 8 §, Allmänna anmärkningar.
98. S. Lindskog, *supra*, Särskilda fall.
99. *See* SOU 1982:26, 121.
100. Cf. Svea Court of Appeal, Judgment of 22 April 2021 in Case No. T 603-19; *see also* ICC, National Sweden Committee's answers to the Questionnaire from ICC Commission on Arbitration and ADR Task Force, *Addressing Issues of Corruption in International Arbitration*, *supra*, 1, 3–5.
101. NJA 2015 p. 433; S. Lindskog, *Skiljeförfarande: en kommentar*, Chapter 33-3.3.2; F. Madsen, *Kompetenz-Kompetenz in Swedish Arbitration Law Is Being Recast, How Should It Be Done?*, SvJT 2016 653–673, 655.
102. In could be submitted that the arbitrators' choice to address corruption may endanger the principle of equal treatment by giving 'guidance' to one the parties. However, in the *Metal-Tech v. Uzbekistan* case it was stated that '[t]he idea […] is not to punish one party at the cost of the other, but rather to ensure the promotion of the rule of law, which entails that a court or tribunal cannot grant assistance to a party that has engaged in a corrupt act'. *See Metal-Tech Ltd. v. Republic of Uzbekistan*, ICSID Case No. ARB/10/3, Award 4 October 2013, para. [389].

parties' right to be heard.[103] We note, however, that arbitrators do not have an obligation to report suspicions of corruption to any relevant authorities.[104]

[C] The Principle of *Iura Novit Curia*

As an alternative to procedural guidance as a method for controlling issues of corruption in arbitration, the arbitrators could possibly also deal with problems from a substantive perspective using the principle of *iura novit curia* (in the arbitration context sometimes also called the principle of *iura novit arbiter*). The principle of *iura novit curia* could be said to mean three things. First, that the parties do not have to prove the content of the applicable law.[105] Second, that the court is generally not confined to the legal qualifications and arguments that the parties have made in the proceeding as applied to the pleaded facts.[106] And third, that a court can rule *non ultra petita*, interpreting or construing the request for relief sought, as long as that the judgment does go beyond or provides for something else than sought by the plaintiff.[107]

According to Supreme Court Justice Eric M. Runesson, *iura novit curia* in its first meaning does not apply in international arbitrations seated in Sweden, unless the parties and the arbitrators agree otherwise. As regards the second and third meaning, *iura novit curia* will apply in international arbitration seated in Sweden, again, unless the parties and the arbitrators agree otherwise.[108] Runesson recognises that this view leads to a wide mandate for the arbitrators, but that they do not have to stretch their mandate to the outer limits.[109] If the arbitrators would choose to use their mandate in a wide manner, their decision-making process must also not violate the adversarial nature of the proceedings.[110] This means that the arbitrators, as a starting point, shall give the parties a reasonable opportunity to be heard and that the arbitrators must avoid rendering an award with a surprising outcome caused by surprising reasoning, since such an award may be set aside due to a procedural error.[111] Runesson states that 'the significance of the surprise is that the parties by an objective assessment had no reason to address the possibility of the reasoning in their pleadings and submissions. In this way due process has been violated in the sense that the parties have not been given a reasonable opportunity to be heard'.[112]

---

103. *See* in D. Baizeau and T. Hayes, 'The Arbitral Tribunal's Duty and Power to Address Corruption Sua Sponte', in Andrea Menaker (ed.), *International Arbitration and the Rule of Law: Contribution and Conformity*, ICCA Congress Series, Volume 19 (© Kluwer Law International; ICCA & Kluwer Law International 2017), 225–265, 246.
104. ICC, National Sweden Committee's answers to the Questionnaire from ICC Commission on Arbitration and ADR Task Force, *supra*, 6.
105. E. Runesson, *Jura Novit Curia and Due Process with Particular Regard to Arbitration in Sweden*, Juridisk Tidsskrift, Nr 1 2017/18, 172–196, 172.
106. E. Runesson, *supra*, 172.
107. *Ibid.*
108. *Ibid.*
109. *Ibid.*
110. *Ibid.*
111. *Ibid.*
112. E. Runesson, *supra*, 190.

The idea that arbitrators should not use a surprising application of the law is supported by Finn Madsen.[113] This view also reflects the attitude of Swedish courts as regards the application of *iura novit curia*, namely that courts are obliged to inform the parties of such legal rules that have not been addressed by the parties but may be of significance for the outcome of the case.[114] It can be argued that the arbitrator also has a certain duty to draw attention to rules that the parties have not introduced.[115] We believe that the arbitrators will have a duty to draw the parties' attention to, for example, that contracts falling within the category of *pactum turpe* are ineffective. This could be done using the principle of *iura novit curia*. Similarly, if the arbitrators conclude that a claim is based on an undertaking to pay a bribe, the reasonable outcome should be that the claim is rejected on the merits.[116] Also, in such cases, the arbitrators can use the principle of *iura novit curia* to draw the parties' attention to legal rules and regulations that make it impossible for the arbitrators to uphold such a claim, since an outcome to the contrary would probably be considered as surprising.

[D] The Standard of Proof

Faced with a suspicion of corruption the arbitrators will find themselves in the dilemma of, on the one hand, potentially failing to perform their obligation to endeavour to achieve an award of normal standard (free from encumbrances) unless they react actively to the suspicion, and, on the other hand, potentially over-reacting and thereby – ironically – causing a forthcoming award to be challengeable as a result of the arbitrators exceeding their mandate or losing their impartiality. So, when should the arbitrators do something actively and when should they wait and see? Unfortunately, it appears impossible to establish a simple rule that can be applied in all circumstances, but some guidance can be given.

As said, the arbitrators' mandate is *contractually based*. Although the obligation to endeavour to achieve an award free from encumbrances is an obligation towards *both* the claimant and the respondent, failure to react actively to a suspicion of corruption will often benefit one of the parties (typically the claimant) and be a detriment to the other party (typically the respondent). In a certain sense, the arbitrators will make a choice between the interest of one party against the interest of the other; and inactivity will favour the party being responsible for the existence of corruption. Under section 29 of the Promissory Notes Act, which applies by way of analogy to most types of contractual obligations,[117] a party that is in the position of

---

113. F. Madsen, *Concerning the Principle of Jura Novit Curia in Arbitration from a Swedish Perspective*, Scandinavian Studies in Law, Volume 63, 196–218, 218. https://scandinavianlaw .se/pdf/63-10.pdf (accessed 13 April 2022).
114. *See*, e.g., NJA 1989 p. 614, 1993 p. 13 and 2017 N7.
115. SOU 1994:81, *Skiljedomsutredningen*, 150.
116. S. Lindskog, *Skiljeförfarande: en kommentar*, commentary to 1 §, *Särskilda frågor*.
117. *See* G. Wallin and J. Herre, *Lagen om skuldebrev m.m.: En kommentar* (Fourth edition, 2018) 243.

having to choose between two possible recipients of the same performance shall be considered to have performed to the correct recipient unless the performing party *knew* or had *reasonable cause to suspect* that said recipient was no longer entitled to the performance.[118] In our opinion, this rule provides a good and normative starting point for which standard of proof to apply in the situation of the arbitrators being faced with an indicator of corruption. Thus, if a suspicion of corruption is well-founded, in the sense that the arbitrators have reasonable cause to suspect corruption, the arbitrators must react actively.

Internationally the view seems to be that the arbitrators must, at least, raise an issue of corruption on their own initiative if they have a 'strong suspicion',[119] and not merely if they have a suspicion of corruption.[120] We agree that a mere suspicion is not enough, but we are, tentatively, somewhat sceptical towards a very high threshold, since we believe that arbitrators who react actively to a well-founded suspicion of corruption will not automatically form themselves an opinion that amounts to a conviction, and we see no reason why a well-founded suspicion of corruption shall be exempted from being brought to the parties' attention.

It is a different matter that another standard of proof must be applied when deciding whether an allegation of corruption can be proven to exist as a fact. On this point, Swedish law is clear.[121] The applicable standard of proof is the same as is generally applied for factual allegations in civil cases which the parties can resolve through settlement.[122] The party alleging corruption must prove (or show) (Swedish: *styrka* or *visa*) the allegation, which is a high standard of proof although not as high as the standard applied in criminal cases; that the offence must be proven beyond a reasonable doubt. In the present context, we note that some arbitrators have, however, taken the position that if 'reasonable doubts' remain, then it is not possible to establish the occurrence of bribery.[123]

---

118. *See* s. 29 of the Promissory Notes Act which is applied by analogy to other contractual performances. It reads (unofficial translation): 'Where the debtor pays the transferor, notwithstanding that a non-negotiable promissory note has been transferred, such payment shall be valid, provided that the debtor neither knew that the transferor was no longer entitled to receive payment nor had reasonable cause to suspect so.'
119. B.M. Cremades and D.J.A. Cairns, 'Trans-national Public Policy in International Arbitral Decision-Making: The Cases of Bribery, Money Laundering and Fraud', in *Dossier of the ICC Institute of World Business Law: Arbitration – Money Laundering, Corruption and Fraud* (2003), 1–30, 20.
120. ICC Case 7047 in C. Albanesi and E. Jolivet, 'Dealing with Corruption in Arbitration: A Review of ICC Experience', in International Chamber of Commerce (ICC) (ed.), International Court of Arbitration, *Tackling Corruption in Arbitration*, Bulletin, Volume 24, Supplement (2013), 27–38, 29.
    EDF (Services) Limited v. Romania, Award, ICSID Case No. ARB/05/13, 8 October 2009.
121. *See* Svea Court of Appeal, Judgment of 22 April 2021 in Case No. T 603-19; ICC National Sweden Committee's answers to the Questionnaire from ICC Commission on Arbitration and ADR Task Force, *supra*, 1–8, 3.
122. Svea Court of Appeal, Judgment of 22 April 2021 in Case No. T 603-19.
123. *Oil Field of Texas, Inc. v. The Government of the Islamic Republic of Iran* and *National Iranian Oil Company*, IUSCT Case No. 43, para. 25.

[E] The Red Flags Method

A suspicion can be described as the apprehension or imagination of the existence of something wrong, based only on inconclusive or slight evidence, or possibly even no evidence. It goes without saying that the mere suspicion of corruption must be an unsatisfactory basis to give rise to a duty for the arbitrators to react actively, and the mere suspicion does not attain the standard of proof of reasonable cause to suspect. This view finds some support in an ICC case where the arbitrators accepted jurisdiction over the dispute despite the allegation of bribery. In the award, the tribunal argued that, among other things, that a 'mere suspicion' of bribery was not enough.[124] In order to trigger activity, the suspicion needs to be based on an indicator or set of indicators of corruption that makes the suspicion conclusive or well-founded.

Indicators used to analyse the existence of corruption are better known under the name *red flags* and the method of using indicators could be called the *red flags method*. Colloquially, one could say that red flags are 'warning signs' which give the arbitrators hints as to the true nature of, for example, an agreement used to disguise corrupt activity behind a seemingly legitimate layer.[125] The list of red flags for identifying corruption is extensive,[126] and includes, among other things, the place of business or the place of performance of the agreement, which could be considered a high-risk country according to the Corruption Perception Index.[127] One author, Vladimir Khvalei, has grouped red flags into three categories that, according to the author, should trigger the arbitrators to pursue various degrees of activity.[128] First, 'light' red flags should trigger an arbitrator to investigate issues of corruption further.[129] Second, a medium category which creates a presumption of corruption.[130] And third, a serious category which shifts the burden of proof to the party under suspicion to disprove corruption.[131] There is not enough room in this chapter to discuss Khvalei's categories, but they are at least helpful for understanding the problem. Red flags include, but are not limited to: (i) the identity of the parties (typically state or publicly owned entities

---

124. ICC Case 7047 in C. Albanesi and E. Jolivet, 'Dealing with Corruption in Arbitration: A Review of ICC Experience', in International Chamber of Commerce (ICC) (ed.), International Court of Arbitration, *Tackling Corruption in Arbitration*, Bulletin, Volume 24, Supplement (2013), 27–38, 29.

125. V. Khvalei, 'Using Red Flags to Prevent Arbitration from Becoming a Safe Harbour for Contracts that Disguise Corruption', in International Chamber of Commerce (ICC) (ed.), International Court of Arbitration, *Tackling Corruption in Arbitration*, Bulletin, Volume 24, Supplement (2013), 15–26, 15.

126. ICC Case No. 8891. ICC Guidelines on Agents, Intermediaries and Third Parties (2010). https://iccwbo.org/content/uploads/sites/3/2017/02/ICC-Guidelines-on-Agents-and-Third-parties-ENGLISH-2010.

127. Corruption Perception Index. https://www.transparency.org/en/cpi/2021 (accessed 13 April 2022).

128. V. Khvalei, 'Using Red Flags to Prevent Arbitration from Becoming a Safe Harbour for Contracts that Disguise Corruption', in International Chamber of Commerce (ICC) (ed.), International Court of Arbitration, *Tackling Corruption in Arbitration*, Bulletin, Volume 24, Supplement (2013), 15–26, 15, 22 and 25.

129. *Ibid.*

130. *Ibid.*

131. *Ibid.*

whose real owners are difficult to identify); (ii) the location of the parties' dealings (in a country or a sector sensitive to corruption); (iii) the remuneration (timing, excessively high rates of commission, payments overseas, etc.); and (iv) the services to be provided (ill-defined and intangible); the parties' business activity (no evidence of real or prior activity, lack of qualified personnel and actual offices).[132] This information is very often available to the arbitrators through the case file. Khvalei submits that, based on a brief examination of the case bearing red flags in mind, arbitrators will easily be able to determine whether there is a strong indication of corruption.[133]

Other authors submit that red flags are not, on their own, sufficient to support the existence of corruption without first seeking explanations from the parties, but that they can serve to trigger activity by the arbitrators.[134] Of course, there can be no fixed idea of how many red flags should be present in order to attain reasonable cause to suspect corruption and trigger activity, but certainly, the more that are present, the greater the suspicion and the degree of activity that is justified.[135] To our knowledge, no case in Sweden has touched upon the issue of red flags or used such a method.[136] However, having seen the red flags method being used in other jurisdictions, such as France,[137] and in the absence of a better method, we believe the red flags method to be an appropriate tool also for a Swedish context.

§14.06   SUMMARY OF CONCLUSIONS

In our opinion, the raised awareness of corruption in arbitration will benefit arbitration as the preferred dispute resolution method for international trade, but if these questions are not taken seriously arbitration will risk coming under increased scrutiny. With this chapter, we submit that Swedish law is in most aspects aligned with French law when it comes to the choice between the minimalist approach and the maximalist

---

132. V. Khvalei, 'Using Red Flags to Prevent Arbitration from Becoming a Safe Harbour for Contracts that Disguise Corruption', in International Chamber of Commerce (ICC) (ed.), International Court of Arbitration, *Tackling Corruption in Arbitration*, Bulletin, Volume 24, Supplement (2013), 15–26, 15.

133. V. Khvalei, 'Using Red Flags to Prevent Arbitration from Becoming a Safe Harbour for Contracts that Disguise Corruption', in International Chamber of Commerce (ICC) (ed.), International Court of Arbitration, *Tackling Corruption in Arbitration*, Bulletin, Volume 24, Supplement (2013), 15–26, 17.

134. P.Y. Tschanz and J-M. Vulliemin, *Chronique de jurisprudence étrangère: Suisse*, 2001 Rev. Arb. 4, Comité Français de l'Arbitrage.

135. *See* in D. Baizeau and T. Hayes, 'The Arbitral Tribunal's Duty and Power to Address Corruption Sua Sponte', in Andrea Menaker (ed.), *International Arbitration and the Rule of Law: Contribution and Conformity*, ICCA Congress Series, Volume 19 (© Kluwer Law International; ICCA & Kluwer Law International 2017), 225–265, 251.

136. ICC National Sweden Committee's answers to the Questionnaire from ICC Commission on Arbitration and ADR Task Force, *supra*, 1–8, 6.

137. Paris CA Ch.1, 18/02568, 17 November 2020. The Paris Court of Appeal indirectly confirms the use of the 'red flags' test and circumstantial evidence ('faisceau d'indices graves, précis et concordants') to determine whether the underlying contract was procured by corruption.
    See also Paris Court of Appeal, 10 April 2018, No. 16/11182; Paris Court of Appeal, 15 September 2020, No. 19/09058.

approach. Both in the *Belokon case*[138] and in NJA 2015 p. 433, the French Cour de Cassation and the Swedish Supreme Court, respectively, have used the maximalist approach. To us, the maximalist approach must be the only reasonable approach if the means of control that are available to prevent corruption in arbitration shall be given true impact.

We also submit that Swedish law, with the maximalist approach as a backdrop, puts an obligation on arbitrators to endeavour to achieve an award of 'normal standard', free from encumbrances in the sense that the award is not invalid, challengeable or unenforceable. We believe that such an obligation would reflect the reasonable expectations of the parties and help protect the integrity of the arbitration. In the context of corruption, this obligation should be understood to put a duty of activity on the arbitrators whereby the arbitrators can use procedural guidance or the principle of *iura novit curia* to raise well-founded concerns. The applicable standard of proof for triggering activity should be when the arbitrators know or have reasonable cause to suspect the existence of corruption. If the standard of proof is attained, the arbitrators must react and endeavour to prevent that corruption will result in an award that is invalid, challengeable or unenforceable. The specific action to be taken will depend on the circumstances. For evaluating indicators of corruption, the arbitrators can be aided by the red flags method which provides some structure and good guidance.

---

138. Cour de Cassation, 29 September 2021, No. 19-19.769.

CHAPTER 15

Arbitration and Public Procurement: A Match?

Olof Larsberger

§15.01 INTRODUCTION

In 2020, the annual turnover of the sectors subject to public procurement in Sweden alone exceeded SEK 800 billion.[1] There is, therefore, no question that public procurement plays a major role in the Swedish economy. The aim of the public procurement rules is to govern the procurement process from 'A–Z', i.e., from the first decision of the contracting authority to commence a procurement, all the way through to the establishment of a contractual relationship between the contracting authority/entity and the winning bidder but, ever since the rules were first introduced in the early 1990s, they have repeatedly been accused of being complex and inflexible.

In 2020 alone, there were over 3,500 public procurement judicial review cases submitted to Swedish administrative courts.[2] In addition, Swedish civil courts frequently try public procurement-related damages claims and contract disputes. It is no exaggeration to state that private enforcement in the public procurement field is a reality in Sweden. Some commentators suggest that the significant number of public procurement judicial review cases every year – as well as other types of public procurement disputes – is explained by the alleged complexity and inflexibility of the rules. Others regard it as a sign of the high value and importance of public contracts among suppliers. A third explanation might be judicial availability. General *access to justice* – at least as to review cases – must be deemed to be high in Sweden and the awareness among suppliers of these circumstances is, one must assume, fairly high.

---

1. *See* statistics published on The Swedish Agency for Public Procurement's website: https://www.upphandlingsmyndigheten.se/statistik-som-utvecklar-den-offentliga-affaren/fortsatt-okat-intresse-for-offentliga-upphandlingar/.
2. *Ibid.*

Irrespective of the reason, public procurement undoubtedly also plays a major role in Swedish judicial life. Similarly, irrespective of the aim of the public procurement rules as such, the great number of disputes has to some extent, in practice, transformed the public procurement field into a litigation field. Indeed, there are obvious interactions between public procurement and litigation. But what about public procurement and *arbitration*?

As a dispute resolution lawyer with one foot in the public procurement field and the other in litigation/arbitration, I have a long-standing interest in the possible interactions between these different fields of law. What role, if any, may arbitration as a dispute resolution mechanism play in the public procurement field? The scope of this chapter is to explore this subject. The general questions probed are the following:

(a) How may arbitration play a role in public procurement-related disputes *de lege lata* (and, possibly, *de lege ferenda*)?
(b) What are the possible implications in and/or overall challenges to using arbitration as a dispute resolution mechanism in the public procurement field?

In order to approach the subject and the questions above, an introduction to the public procurement rules – including the judicial remedies available under these rules – for the, one assumes, more arbitration law-focused reader is required (*see* section §15.02).

Thereafter, an attempt will be made to identify some of the possible answers to questions (a) and (b) above (*see* section §15.03).

Finally, I will conclude with some closing remarks (*see* section §15.04).

My research and findings are limited to a Swedish law perspective.

§15.02   PUBLIC PROCUREMENT RULES: AN OVERVIEW

[A]   Background, Purpose and Overall Content

Different types of public bodies (governmental authorities, municipalities, state- and municipality-owned companies etc.) have different kinds of functions and, depending on the situation, play different roles. In order to be able to perform the duties assigned to them, they are entrusted with certain powers in relation to the public, such as, the power to decide on taxes, different kinds of permissions, benefits. Some public bodies might even be entrusted with the power to use force, if necessary.

When a public body wishes to acquire something, it takes on another role. It acts as a *contracting authority* and enters into a contractual relationship with a supplier governed by private law. Therefore, once such a contractual relationship is established, the public body – i.e., the contracting authority – is to be regarded in the same way as any other party to a commercial contract, with the rights and obligations deriving from such a contract. However, *the route* to the establishment of such a commercial contract is regulated and subject to certain legislation: the public procurement rules.[3]

The Swedish public procurement rules emanate from European Union (EU) law. The central EU directives in the field[4] are implemented into Swedish law through four different acts:

(1) Swedish Public Procurement Act (2016:1145) (the SPPA).[5]
(2) Swedish Utilities Procurement Act (2016:1146).[6]
(3) Swedish Concession Procurement Act (2016:1147).[7]
(4) Swedish Defence and Security Procurement Act (2011:1029).[8]

Which act is applicable depends on the nature of the contract awarded and the sector in which the contracting authority is active. The overall purpose of the acts remains the same:[9] to regulate (with some exceptions)[10] the public tender and submit it to a step-by-step procedure, from the decision to pursue the acquisition, through to the final result of such an acquisition, namely the entry into a contract with the selected supplier. From an EU perspective, the aim of the rules is to facilitate cross-border trade between the EU Member States, i.e., the establishment and maintenance of the EU inner market.[11] Thus, the acquisition of the public tender should be open to competition. The rules emanate from five fundamental principles:[12]

(1) *Principle of non-discrimination*: the prohibition to discriminate suppliers based on nationality. For example, a Swedish contracting authority is prohibited from including requirements that only Swedish suppliers will satisfy.
(2) *Principle of equal treatment*: all suppliers must be given the same opportunities and in all other ways be treated in the same manner.
(3) *Principle of proportionality*: the defined requirements in a procurement must be proportional and must not go beyond what is necessary for the procurement in question.

---

3. Henceforth, the term 'public contract' will be used for a contract between a contracting authority and a supplier (post a competitive procurement or via a direct award). Further, the public procurement rules also cover framework agreement. However, henceforth references will only be made to contract.
4. (i) Directive 2009/81/EC ('Defence and Security Procurement Directive'); (ii) Directive 2014/23/EU ('Concession Procurement Directive'); (iii) Directive 2014/24/EU ('Public Procurement Directive'); (iv) Directive 2014/25/EU ('Utilities Procurement Directive'); and (v) Directives 89/665/EEC, 92/13/EC and 2007/66/EC ('Remedies Directives').
5. Sw: Lagen (2016:1145) om offentlig upphandling.
6. Sw: Lagen (2016:1146) om upphandling inom försörjningssektorerna.
7. Sw: Lagen (2016:1147) om upphandling av koncessioner.
8. Sw: Lagen (2011:1029) om upphandling på försvars- och säkerhetsområdet.
9. Henceforth on a Swedish domestic level, references will be made to the SPPA alone. However, corresponding provisions are to be found in the other acts as well.
10. *See* Chapter 3 of the SPPA.
11. *See*, e.g., Arrowsmith: *The Law of Public and Utilities Procurement: Regulation in the EU and UK* (3rd edition, Oxford 2014) pp. 150–155.
12. Chapter 4, s. 1 of the SPPA.

(4) *Principle of transparency*: all procurements must be conducted in a transparent and non-secret manner. All the requirements must be clearly established in the tender documentation, and, arguably, the most important rule emanating from this principle is the obligation to publish a procurement and inform the participating suppliers in writing about the result.

(5) *Principle of mutual treatment:* Certificates etc. issued by authorities in one EU Member State must be recognized and applicable in other EU and EEA[13] states.

Several types of procurement procedures exist, e.g., the *open procedure* and *negotiated procedure*. The freedom of the contracting authorities to choose the procurement procedure differs between the various procurement acts. In a procurement where the SPPA is applicable (which is the case in the majority of procurements), the use of a negotiated procedure is limited to more complex procurements.

The nature of a procurement, and the different steps involved, differ, depending on the procedure. Heavily simplified, and in a nutshell, a procurement comprises, *inter alia,* the following elements:

– *Publication of the procurement*: the announcement to the market and its suppliers of the commencement of the procurement.

– *Publication of the procurement documents:* depending on the type of process, the procurement documents are published either in connection with the publication of the procurement or on a step-by-step basis during the process. The procurement document must include all information necessary to the procurement and its conditions, such as mandatory requirements (in relation to the suppliers as well as the subject of the acquisition), evaluation principles and award criteria, contract drafts etc.

– *Qualification of suppliers*: pursuant to the qualification criteria set out in the procurement.

– *Tender stage*: the suppliers formulate and submit their tenders. In an *open procedure,* none of the content of the procurement documents, including the terms and conditions of the contract draft, is open for negotiation. Any supplier who wishes to participate is left to submit its tender in accordance with the procurement documentation. In a *negotiated procedure,* this stage includes negotiations with the qualified suppliers, meaning that not everything contained in the procurement documents is 'set in stone', some of it is open for negotiation. However, specified minimum requirements and award criteria cannot be subject to negotiation. Further, any negotiations must be conducted in accordance with the fundamental principles, implying, *inter alia,* that all participating suppliers must be given the same opportunities, information etc.

– *Evaluation and award stage*: the contracting authority evaluates the tenders pursuant to the award criteria specified in the procurement document and

---

13. European Economic Area.

awards the contract to the winning supplier. Only suppliers who fulfil all mandatory requirements may be selected and awarded the contract.

– *Standstill period:* following the announcement of the award, the contracting authority is prevented from entering into the contract during a standstill period (normally ten days). During the standstill period, the procurement is open for challenge in court (*see* further section §15.02[B][2]). If the procurement is challenged, the standstill period is automatically prolonged during the court procedure in the first instance.[14]

– *Establishment of contract:* after the end of the standstill period, or after the dismissal of any judicial review application and such ruling having become legally binding, the contracting authority and the winning supplier may enter into the contract. The procurement comes to an end and is replaced by a contractual relationship between the contracting authority and the winning supplier.

Needless to say, bearing in mind the aim of the public procurement rules and the obligation to open up the public acquisition to competition, the failure to publish a procurement when required constitutes one of the most serious breaches of the public procurement rules. For a public body to ignore the potential competition and, without publication, reach out to one supplier alone, clearly violates the principles of equal treatment and transparency, and is commonly referred to as an *illegal direct award of contracts.*[15]

Further, since the nature of the public procurement rules is to regulate the procurement, they no longer apply once the contract in question has been entered into between the contracting authority and the winning supplier, and the procurement is finalized. From that point onwards, the relationship between the contracting authority and the supplier is governed by contract law. However, there are exceptions to this rule. Generally, no *substantial modifications*[16] may be made to public contracts. If a public contract is substantially modified, the modified contract is, from a public procurement law perspective, to be regarded as a *new* contract which, in turn, must not be entered into without publication and a call for competition. Entering into a contract without a call for competition – i.e., an unlawful direct award – is regarded as one of the most serious breaches of the public procurement rules.

Example 1: Let us assume that a contracting authority conducts a procurement for a certain goods, '*X*'. The contracting authority enters into a contract with the winning supplier and a contractual relationship, governed by contract law, is established between them. The contracting authority is satisfied with the performance of the supplier and wishes to extend the cooperation by expanding the contract to include the purchase of another goods, '*Y*'. From a contract/private

---

14. An interim relief, preventing the contracting authority from entering into contract, is required in the higher instances.
15. Sw: otillåten direktupphandling.
16. Chapter 17, ss 9–13, of the SPPA contain a catalogue of lawful modifications (modifications of lesser value, modifications in accordance with a review of option clause etc.).

law perspective, such modification of the contract hardly raises any concerns. But from a public procurement law perspective, by introducing Y into the contract, the contracting authority has, arguably, entered into a new contract without a call for competition, i.e., it has committed an unlawful direct award.

It is submitted that the prohibition to modify public contracts or framework agreements substantially makes perfect sense. Indeed, if a contract is substantially modified during the contract period, it is no longer equal to the one published for competition in the first place. The key question is the following: would the contract have attracted other suppliers if it had included the modification from the beginning? Going back to Example 1: would other suppliers have been interested in participating and submitting tenders had the contract included not only goods X but also goods Y, at the time of the procurement?

[B]   Judicial Remedies

[1]   General

Judicial remedies form an important part of the public procurement law system. These rules emanate from the Remedies Directives, and are included in all the Swedish public procurement acts. The rules enable suppliers to act against alleged breaches of the public procurement rules in three different ways:[17]

(1) Remedy 1: Apply for judicial review of a procurement.
(2) Remedy 2: Apply for judicial review of the validity of a contract.
(3) Remedy 3: Claim damages.

Remedies 1–3 consist of the application of EU directive-based legislation in the domestic court system. The ultimate interpreter of EU legislation is the Court of Justice of the European Union (the CJEU). A key aspect of the CJEU's interpretative functions is the preliminary ruling procedure pursuant to Article 267 of the Treaty on the Functioning of the European Treaty (the EU Treaty). The availability of preliminary rulings is a cornerstone for ensuring an effective and uniform interpretation of EU law, including its public procurement rules. This issue will be returned to at a later stage in this chapter.

[2]   Remedy 1: Judicial Review of a Procurement

Remedy 1, judicial review of a procurement, is by far the most common. Around 7.6% (1,356 of 17,938) of all procurements published in 2020 were reviewed.[18]

---

17. The public procurement acts also provide for a fourth type of court procedure, actions for procurement fines. Such actions are brought by Swedish Competition Authority (the SCA) against a contracting authority for certain types of public procurement law violations. A procurement fine action does not preclude a suppler from bringing judicial review cases or to claim damages.
18. *See* note 1 above.

As a general rule, when a contracting authority has awarded a contract, it must send an award notice to all participating suppliers.[19] As stated, the contracting authority is prohibited from entering into the contract during a standstill period and during that period, an application for a review of the procurement in question may be submitted.[20] The competent court is the Administrative Court[21] of the court district in which the contracting authority is established.[22] Hence, the jurisdiction lies with the administrative courts[23] and the Administrative Procedure Act (1971:291)[24] applies to the procedure.

For a supplier to be successful, it must demonstrate two things: (i) a public procurement law violation; and (ii) that such violation has caused or may cause the supplier harm. Hence, there must be a causal link between the alleged public procurement violation and the alleged harm to the supplier. If the application is successful, the court will decide that the procurement shall be (i) recommenced; or (ii) corrected.[25]

[3]   Remedy 2: Judicial Review of the Validity of a Contract

Once a contracting authority has entered into a contract, the *procurement* which proceeded such contract may not be subject to a judicial review. In such a scenario, the door to Remedy 1 closes, but another door opens (primarily in case of an illegal direct award): Remedy 2 – judicial review of *the validity of the contract* (commonly referred to as 'invalidity cases').[26] If a supplier is successful in such a review case, the court will declare the contract null and void.[27] The invalidity works retroactively – i.e., *ex tunc*[28] – with the effect that all performances under the contract (payments, deliveries etc.), shall, as a main rule, be reversed.

Like procurement cases, invalidity cases fall within the jurisdiction of the administrative courts.[29] Hence, in these cases, an *administrative* court has the power to declare *a binding contract under private law* null and void. The invalidity as such must be interpreted in a private law sense, and a contract which has been declared invalid may not be enforced in court. However, it is crucial to bear in mind that a public contract is not null and void per se due to a public procurement violation: the invalidity is a result of the administrative court's decision. Therefore, without a (successful) invalidity action, the contract is not invalid.

---

19. Chapter 12, s. 12 of the SPPA.
20. Chapter 20, s. 1 of the SPPA.
21. Sw: Förvaltningsrätt.
22. Chapter 20, s. 5 of the SPPA.
23. Sw: allmänna förvaltningsdomstolar.
24. Sw: Förvaltningsprocesslagen (1971:291).
25. Chapter 20, s. 6 of the SPPA.
26. Sw: Ogiltighetstalan.
27. Chapter 20, s. 13 of the SPPA.
28. *See*, e.g., the *travail prépatoire*, proposition 2009/10:180, p. 136.
29. Chapter 20, s. 5 of the SPPA.

The possibility for a supplier to bring an invalidity action should be regarded as a tool to combat illegal direct awards.[30] It is notable that, in illegal direct award cases,[31] harm is not a prerequisite to assent. A supplier must claim to have suffered (or have run the risk of suffering) harm to have standing, but, unlike in the review of procurement cases, there is no need to show harm or risk of harm. Hence, the mere fact that the contracting authority had entered into a contract without prior publication, when such publication was required, is sufficient to declare the contract null and void.

[4]   Remedy 3: Damages

Remedy 3 – the right of a supplier to be compensated for harm caused by a public procurement law violation[32] – exists in a different procedural landscape than the judicial review cases. The jurisdiction has switched from the administrative courts to the general courts,[33] and the district courts[34] are the first instance courts. Chapter 20 section 21 of the SPPA provides that a claim for damages *must* be instituted at a general court. The procedure is regulated by the Swedish Code of Judicial Procedure (1942:740)[35] (the SCJP) applies to the procedure.

Notwithstanding the fact that an action for damages on public procurement law grounds *is* a damages claim (and, thus, falls within the jurisdiction of the general court system), it differs from other actions for damages. It is not a claim for contractual damages.[36] On the contrary, a missed contractual relationship between the claimant and the contracting authority – caused by an alleged illegal direct award to the benefit of one of the claimant's competitors – often forms the very basis of such a damages claim. However, despite the absence of a contractual relationship, the action cannot be considered a pure non-contractual damage claim.[37] It is 'something in between' and may be best described as a 'quasi-contractual' damage claim.[38] Depending on the circumstances, any supplier deprived from entering into a contract with a contracting authority due to a violation of public procurement law is entitled to compensation up to the amount of the positive contract interest.[39]

---

30. *See*, e.g., directive 2007/66/EC, preamble ss 13 and 14. *See also* the *travail prépatoire*, proposition 2009/10:180, p. 130.
31. Invalidity actions may be invoked in certain other situations as well, e.g., when a contracting authority has violated the stand still period by entering into contract during that period (*see* Chapter 20, s. 13 para. 2 of the SPPA).
32. The public procurement acts explicitly provide for such compensation (*see* Chapter 20, s. 20 of the SPPA).
33. Sw: allmänna domstolar.
34. Sw: tingsrätter.
35. Sw: rättegångsbalken (1942:740).
36. Sw: Inomobligatoriskt skadestånd.
37. Sw: Utomobligatoriskt skadestånd.
38. In Swedish case law regarding damages of public procurement law grounds, a procurement has been characterized as a 'quasi-contractual' relationship between the contracting authority and the suppliers (*see* the Swedish Supreme Court's ruling in NJA 1998 p. 873).
39. Sw: Positiva kontraktsintresset. Regarding damages on public procurements grounds, *see* further e.g., Andersson et al.: *Lagen om offentlig upphandling: En kommentar* (Juno Version 3), commentary to Chapter 20, s. 20 of the SPPA, and references made therein.

[C]   Post-procurement Contract Disputes

When a procurement is finalized and the contract has been entered into, the contracting authority takes the role of a contractual party, with the winning supplier as the counterparty. Thus, it is a contractual relationship governed by private law, and subject to the rights and obligations of the contract. Like any party to a commercial contract, a contracting authority might have different types of disagreements with its counterparty, ultimately resulting in a contractual dispute. Further, like any other party to a commercial relationship, the contracting authority has an interest in effective mechanisms to resolve such contractual disputes.

The SPPAs are silent as to the question of how any post-procurement contract disputes between the contracting authority and the winning supplier ought to be resolved. Hence, general civil procedure rules apply. Pursuant to Chapter 10 section 2 of the SJCP, in civil cases 'the Crown may be sued at the place where the public authority charged with attending to the suit has its seat'. In order words, the competent court in action against the Swedish state is the court where the public authority, representing the state, has its seat. In addition, the general rule in Chapter 10 section 1 of the SJCP stipulates that the competent court for civil cases, in general, is the court for the place where the defendant resides.

As stated, the procurement documentation normally includes a draft contract, including general terms and conditions, as well as dispute resolution clauses. From a public procurement law perspective (in an open procedure), the content of the draft contract takes the form of mandatory requirements which the suppliers have to accept in order to participate.[40] Hence, in practice, it is up to the contracting authority, during the establishment of the procurement documentation, to decide the form of the resolution of any post-procurement contract disputes between the contracting authority and the winning supplier. Commonly, contracting authorities make use of the possibility set out in Chapter 10 section 17 of the SJCP to convey exclusive jurisdiction upon the court where the contracting authority resides. As discussed below, a contracting authority may also choose arbitration as the form of resolving post-procurement contract disputes (*see* further section §15.03[B]).

§15.03   POSSIBLE AREAS OF INTERACTION AND IMPLICATIONS

[A]   Identification

With the introduction of the public procurement rules in the previous section in mind, we come to the very heart of this chapter: are there any areas of possible interaction between public procurement and arbitration? Is there a 'match' between these separate fields of law? In sections §15.02[B]–§15.02[C], the different cases where contracting

---

40. However, certain terms and conditions as such may be in violation with the public procurement rules (e.g., the principle of proportionality) and, consequently, open for a challenge in a review procedure.

authorities might face court procedures were examined. The author asked himself whether arbitration could be an alternative to court procedures in any, or all, of these cases. In the search for possible answers, the following 'scenarios' were identified:

- – Scenario 1: Arbitration as an alternative to litigation in judicial review of procurement cases.
- – Scenario 2: Arbitration as an alternative to litigation in non-contractual damages cases.
- – Scenario 3: Arbitration as a way to solve post-procurement contract disputes between the contracting authority and the winning supplier.

In the following sections §15.03[B]–§15.03[C], Scenarios 1 and 2 will be explored briefly, while Scenario 3 will be examined in more detail.

[B]   Scenarios 1 and 2: Arbitration as an Alternative to Litigation in (i) Judicial Review of Procurement Cases and (ii) Non-contractual Damages Cases

[1]   Scenario 1

The idea behind *Scenario 1* is not the author's own. To the author's knowledge, it was first launched in the Swedish legal debate by two public procurement lawyers, Johan Stern and Björn Bergström of Ramberg Advokater. In an article published in 2017,[41] Stern and Bergström argued – in the light of the increasing and burdensome number of judicial review cases before the Swedish administrative court system – that arbitration *de lege ferenda* could be a tool for achieving more cost-effective and less time-consuming judicial review procedures. Concretely, the authors' proposed that contracting authorities should be given the opportunity to formulate a mandatory requirement in a procurement, stating that any judicial review would be subject to arbitration. Correspondingly, arbitral tribunals should be entrusted to handle judicial review cases. Stern and Bergström admitted that their proposal would require legislative amendments[42] but argued that such amendments could be made in a way (the article does not reveal how) that would make arbitration compatible with the Remedies Directives.

The Remedies Directives provide for a review procedure carried out by a 'body'.[43] No references are made to arbitral tribunals, but the Remedies Directives explicitly provide that bodies other than courts may be given the responsibility to carry out review procedures. Article 2(9) of 89/665/EEC, as amended by Directive 2007/66/EC, reads (author's emphasis):

---

41. https://upphandling24.se/tre-konkreta-forslag-att-hantera-overprovningsproblematiken/.
42. Obviously, e.g., the exclusive jurisdiction of the administrative courts set out in the public procurement acts as described in section §15.02[B][2] above.
43. Sw: Prövningsorgan.

Where bodies responsible for review procedures *are not judicial in character,*[44] written reasons for their decisions shall always be given. Furthermore, in such a case, provision must be made to guarantee procedures whereby *any allegedly illegal measure taken* by the review body or *any alleged defect in the exercise of the powers* conferred on it can be the *subject of judicial review or review by another body which is a court or tribunal within the meaning of Article 234 of the Treaty* and independent of both the contracting authority and the review body.

The members of such an independent body shall be appointed and leave office under the same conditions as members of the judiciary as regards the authority responsible for their appointment, their period of office, and their removal. At least the President of this independent body shall have the same legal and professional qualifications as members of the judiciary. The independent body shall take its decisions following a procedure in which both sides are heard, and these decisions shall, by means determined by each Member State, be legally binding.

It could be argued that it would indeed be possible, by legislative amendments, to establish that arbitral tribunals could be considered 'bodies' within the meaning of the Remedies Directives.[45] This could potentially be done within the provisions on challenge actions[46] contained in sections 33–36 of the Swedish Arbitration Act (the SAA), thus satisfying the request contained in the Remedies Directive, as quoted above, that 'any allegedly illegal measure taken by the review body or any alleged defect in the exercise of the powers conferred on it' may be subject to a judicial review by a 'court or tribunal within the meaning of Article 234 of the Treaty'.[47] Further, according to CJEU case law, different types of bodies – arbitral tribunals included – can be regarded as a court or tribunal within the meaning of Article 267 of the EU Treaty, provided that (i) they are established by law; (ii) they are permanent; (iii) their jurisdiction is compulsory; (iv) their procedure is *inter partes*; (v) they apply rules of law; and (vi) they are independent.[48]

Admittedly, careful in-depth analysis must, naturally, be conducted to create a system *de lege ferenda* where arbitration is used in judicial review of a procurement. It is not the author's aim to deliver all the legislative 'solutions' in this regard, within the

---

44. The Swedish version of the beginning of the first paragraph reads: '*Om de behöriga prövningsorganen inte är domstolar ...*'.
45. To satisfy the requirements in the Remedies Directives (for standstill periods, interim measures etc.), similar rules as the current ones applicable in administrative courts would have to apply in any arbitration procedure.
46. Sw: klandertalan.
47. Now Art. 267 of the EU Treaty. To the author's understanding, a regular appeal model, similar to the on applicable in compulsory arbitration in buy-out of minority shareholders cases (*see* Chapter 22 s. 24 of the Swedish Companies Act (2005:551)) (Sw: Aktiebolagslag (2005:551)) could, alternatively, be considered.
48. Case C-555/13, *Merck Canada Inc. v. Accord Healthcare Ltd et al.*, paras 15–25, and references made therein. The CJEU (para. 17) also made clear that a 'conventional arbitration tribunal', due to its non-compulsory character – is *not* a court or tribunal within the meaning of Art. 267 of the EU Treaty (author's underscores): 'It should also be stated that a conventional arbitration tribunal is not a "court or tribunal of a Member State" within the meaning of Article 267 TFEU where the parties are under no obligation, in law or in fact, to refer their disputes to arbitration and the public authorities of the Member State concerned are not involved in the decision to opt for arbitration nor required to intervene of their own accord in the proceedings before the arbitrator [...].'

framework of this chapter. However, to the author's understanding – and provided that the requirement in the Remedies Directives regarding standstill periods and interim measures are met – arbitration could *de lege ferenda* be used in the judicial review of procurement. This would be the case if one were to apply either of the two following, alternative viewpoints regarding the legal status of arbitral tribunals:

    (c) The arbitral tribunal is *not* a court or tribunal within the meaning of Article 267 of the EU Treaty (i.e. because its jurisdiction is not exclusive) but with the possibility of a judicial review by a court.

    (d) The arbitral tribunal *is* a court or tribunal within the meaning of Article 267 of the EU Treaty (which implies that its jurisdiction must be exclusive by law, which would then preclude a contracting authority from choosing arbitration (via a mandatory requirement in the procurement) at its own will).

[2]   *Scenario 2*

The idea behind *Scenario 2* is to use arbitration as a way to solve a non-contractual damages claim between a supplier and a contracting authority.

> *Example 2*: Assume that a supplier, '*X*', accuses a contracting authority, '*Y*', of having breached the public procurement rules, e.g., in the form of an alleged illegal direct award. X claims it has suffered losses due to the public procurement violation and wants compensation. No contractual relationship exists between X and Y. However, X and Y share a common wish to have the dispute tried by arbitration rather than by court (e.g., to save time). Hence, X and Y enter into an arbitration agreement regarding the damages claim.

Arguably, legislative amendments would also be required for Scenario 2 to become a reality. Indeed, Chapter 20 section 21 of the SPPA (as referred to in section §15.02[B][4] above) could well be interpreted such that non-contractual damages claims on public procurement grounds fall within the exclusive jurisdiction of the general courts. However, on the contrary, the provision might be regarded as merely a dividing line between the administrative court procedure and civil procedure.[49] Viewed from that perspective, the provision would, arguably, not preclude the parties to a non-contractual damages dispute on public procurement grounds to agree on arbitration.[50] To the author's knowledge, the question has not been tried. Further, arbitration would be compatible with the Remedies Directives, provided that arbitral tribunals could be regarded as 'bodies' within the meaning of these directives (*see* section §15.03 [B] [1]).

---

49. Administrative courts do not have jurisdiction on damages claim and such claims, in presented in an administrative court, must be dismissed (Sundsvall Administrative Court of Appeal, Case 2489-13).
50. Indeed, in the light of the liberty of the parties to settle the dispute, it could be well questioned why they should be prohibited from agreeing on arbitration.

[3]   Implications?

A common denominator of Scenarios 1 and 2 is the application by arbitral tribunals of the public procurement rules, i.e., EU directive-based law. Would this raise any problems? The short answer would – based on the author's conclusions from a Remedies Directives perspective in sections §15.03[B][1]–§15.03[B][2] –, simply be: 'no'. However, in light of the latest developments in the case law of the CJEU – commencing with the landmark *Achmea* case[51] – the question remains justified and must be addressed, or at least touched upon.

Naturally, one must bear in mind that *Achmea* and the cases following it – the *Komstroy*[52] and the *PL Holding Sàrl* cases[53] – concerned investment treaties disputes, and the question regarding the compatibility with EU law of submitting such disputes to arbitration. It could be argued that the rulings should be examined in this specific context and that they should not have any 'spill-over effects' to other possible areas of interaction between EU law and arbitration. This may be correct. However, the author cannot completely ignore the universal wordings of the CJEU. For example, paragraphs 45 and 46 of *PL Holding Sàrl* read (author's emphasis):

> By concluding such an agreement, the Member States which are parties to it *agree to remove from the jurisdiction of their own courts* and, therefore, from the system of judicial remedies which the second subparagraph of Article 19(1) TEU requires them to establish in the fields covered by EU law [...] *disputes which may concern the application or interpretation of EU law.* Such an agreement is, therefore, capable of *preventing those disputes from being resolved in a manner that guarantees the full effectiveness of that law.*
>
>   It is common ground that the arbitration clause in Article 9 of the BIT is, like the clause at issue in the case which gave rise to the judgment of 6 March 2018, Achmea (C-284/16, EU:C:2018:158), capable of leading to a situation *in which an arbitration body rules in disputes which may concern the application or interpretation of EU law.* Accordingly, that arbitration clause is such as to call into question not only the principle of mutual trust between the Member States but also the *preservation of the particular nature of EU law, ensured by the preliminary ruling procedure provided for in Article 267 TFEU* [...].

What is the CJEU telling us? Is the message limited to the case of an arbitration clause in an investment treaty with an EU Member State as a party, and the incompatibility of such arrangement with EU law? Is merely the 'Member State issue' the problem here? Or, on a more universal level, that any arbitration clause in any contract – or even any arbitration arrangement – which leads to 'a situation in which an arbitration body rules in disputes which may concern the application or interpretation of EU law' will prevent 'those disputes from being resolved in a manner that guarantees the full effectiveness of that law' and is therefore incompatible with EU law? If the latter, is the dividing line between compatibility and incompatibility with EU law whether an arbitration arrangement would permit a preliminary ruling procedure or

---

51. Case C-706/17.
52. Case C-741/19.
53. Case C-109/20.

whether it would not? If so, that would take us back to the question of whether an arbitral tribunal can be regarded as a court or a tribunal within the meaning of Article 267 of the EU Treaty.

If the findings of the CJEU in *PL Holding Sàrl* in line with the above are to be universally applied, it is likely that a floodgate will open. In its most extreme form, such a scenario would run the risk of establishing a great barrier between EU law and arbitration. Needless to say, that would have a much greater impact than, and go far beyond, the question of the possibilities of the public procurement rules being applied and interpreted by arbitral tribunals. Indeed, the 'extreme form scenario' – arguably highly unlikely – would be contrary to current Swedish legislation as well as to a general view that EU law, e.g., EU competition rules, in fact, is arbitrable.[54] Future developments will have to tell. It is sufficient for the purposes of this chapter, to conclude that the current uncertainty regarding the relationship between arbitration and EU law would probably have an adverse effect on any legislative amendments (if they were ever to be considered by the legislator) enabling Scenario 1 (and Scenario 2 in case arbitration in that scenario is not possible already *de lege lata* – *see* section §15.03 [B] [2]) to become a reality.

[C]   Scenario 3: Arbitration as a Post-procurement Dispute Resolution Mechanism

[1]   *General*

In preparing for this chapter, the author searched for statistics regarding the use of arbitration clauses in public contracts, and contacted the SCA, the regulatory body on public procurement issues in Sweden, to request such statistics. The SCA in turn suggested contacting the Swedish National Agency for Public Procurement. That agency was also unable to help. The officer spoken to, who was specialized in collecting public procurement statistics, had not heard of such statistics.

The author turned to the Swedish legal literature. Was there anything written on the use of arbitration clauses in public contracts and the frequency of such use? The results were scant. One work on the law applicable to municipality-owned companies was found, which touched on the subject.[55] The authors of that work, while not rejecting the use of arbitration clauses in public contracts, argued that contracting authorities should, in most cases, refrain from such use in public procurement.[56] Now, what would the reason be for such restrictive attitude towards arbitration as a dispute resolution mechanism in commercial relationships involving public bodies? According to the authors, one of the major advantages of arbitration – the possibility to keep the

---

54. *See*, e.g., Lindskog: *Skiljeförfarande: En kommentar* (Juno Version 3), 1 § ss 4.2–4.3. *See also* e.g., Karlsson et al.: *Konkurrensrätt: En handbok* (Juno Version 6), s. 6. Pursuant to s. 1, 3 paragraph, of the SAA, arbitrators may rule on the civil law effects of competition law as between the parties.
55. Adrell et al., *Juridik i kommunala bolag: En praktisk guide* (Juno Version 2).
56. *Ibid.*, s. 10.5.2.

procedure confidential – does not apply to bodies which are subject to the principle of public access to official records.[57] In a way, this is true.[58] However, many advantages of arbitration remain applicable to contracting authorities, in their capacity as parties to commercial contracts. It might be, for example, the time efficiency of arbitration and/or the possibility of selecting arbitrators, the latter potentially a critical issue in highly technically complex procurements resulting in highly technically complex contracts. It might also be the question of enforcement, potentially a critical issue in public procurements which attract foreign suppliers. Arbitration could undoubtedly be beneficial to contracting authorities as a way of solving contract disputes. There should be space for Scenario 3.

And *there is* room for Scenario 3. It really exists *de lege lata*. Contracting authorities *do*, from time to time, include arbitration clauses in the draft contract in the procurement documents, making the arbitration agreement a mandatory requirement which every participating supplier must accept, to have a chance of being selected and awarded the contract.[59] Correspondingly, provisions making arbitration the mechanism to solve any post-procurement disputes arising from the contract are sometimes included.[60] Hence, the question is not what the conditions or possible implications are for Scenario 3 to become a reality. Rather, one can ask whether there are any implications for Scenario 3 to *continue to be a reality* and what challenges, if any, arise from the fact that a contract subject to arbitration is the product of public procurement. These questions will be addressed below.

[2] Possible Implications and Challenges

The author once heard, probably during his time as a law student at Uppsala University, that law, in fact, was nothing but 'frozen' politics. Political wills and visions are formulated and transformed into legislation, and subsequently handed over to the judicial system. Heavily simplified, maybe, and some would even say inaccurate. But

---

57. Sw: offentlighetsprincipen.
58. In the author's view, the question of the principle of public access to official records should not be exaggerated. Indeed, to some extents, the commercial relationship with a body which are subject to the principle of public access to official records would possible be covered by provisions in the Swedish Public Access to Information and Security Act (2009:400) (Sw: Offentlighets- och sekretesslagen (2009:400)). Further, an arbitration as such does not guarantee secrecy for any party, public or private. For example, an award may be made public, via the court system, in case of a challenge action.
59. It can be noticed that procurements pertaining to arbitration as such are excepted from the public procurement rules (Chapter 3, s. 21 of the SPPA).
60. One, recently well-observed, example is AB Storstockholms Lokaltrafik's (SL) procurement of a metro signalling system in 2010. The contract included an arbitration clause (stipulating SCC rules) and was eventually awarded to Hitachi Rail Sweden STS Sweden AB ('Ansaldo'). Many years later, in 2017, SL rescinded (Sw: hävde) the contract and the parties ended up in arbitration. In a separate award, rendered on 25 February 2021, the arbitral tribunal ruled that the rescindment of SL constituted a breach of contract and that Ansaldo was entitled compensation for damages and certain costs. In a final award, rendered on 10 December 2021, Ansaldo was awarded 500 MSEK. SL has initiated a challenge action (Svea Court of Appeal, Cases T-4968-21; pending).

still appealing to any legal positivist: The law depends on politics – the former is the result of the latter – and does not exist by nature. But despite their close relationship, politics and law are not the same. They co-exist and might interact, but they are different disciplines and must not be confused.

The relationship between politics and law raises the issue of the relationship between the public procurement rules and the subsequent contractual relationship between the contracting authority and the winning supplier. Such a contractual relationship emanates from the public procurement rules. It is 'frozen' public procurement, the result of a competitive tender procedure and the application of the principles of equal treatment, transparency etc. The parties to a public contract might feel the presence of the public procurement rules during the performance of the contract, like a watchdog in the shadow. As noted above, the public procurement rules prohibit public contracts from being substantially modified.

However, it is crucial to keep in mind that, notwithstanding its origins, the contract between a contracting authority and a supplier is *not* governed by the public procurement rules: it is subject to private law. The public procurement rules and private law might face each other and even interact, but they are not the same.[61] Any contract dispute between a contracting authority and a supplier will primarily be resolved in accordance with the contract, and pursuant to private law and its principles. That, in turn, leads to the first conclusion in this section: It is submitted that any possible implications regarding the application of EU law by arbitral tribunals as discussed above (*see* section §15.03[B][3]) are not relevant here. In Scenario 3, an arbitral tribunal will *not* apply the public procurement rules as such.

Do any implications or other challenges, i.e., risks of clashes between the public procurement rules and arbitration, remain? Could the watchdog potentially come out from the shadows, barking angrily? Maybe. To exemplify.

Example 3: Assume that a contracting authority '*X*', after conducting a public procurement, has entered into a contract with a supplier, '*Y*'. The dispute resolution clause in the contract stipulates that any disputes shall be resolved by litigation. X and Y end up in disagreements over certain performances under the contract. However, they agree on the advantages of having the dispute resolved by arbitration. Hence, X and Y enter into a supplementary contract, amending the dispute resolution clause from litigation to arbitration. Supplier Z finds out about the modification of the contract and initiates an invalidity action on the argument that the modification is substantial. Maybe Z was a former participant in the procurement and now argues it would have been able to offer a more attractive price and, hence, submit a more competitive tender, had arbitration been a prerequisite in the first place. Or maybe Z did not participate in the procurement

---

61. Several of the provisions in the public procurement act have a 'private law dimension' insofar they prescribe how actions under private law, should be carried out, and also limit the private law freedom of the contracting authority. *See*, e.g., Chapter 7, s. 2 of the SPPA which stipulate that a framework agreement may have a term exceeding four years only if there are specific reasons therefore, and Chapter 10, s. 10 of the SPPA which stipulates that a contracting authority shall state the period during which the supplier shall be bound by its tender.

and now argues it would have done so, had arbitration been a prerequisite in the first place (maybe Z is a non-Swedish supplier who, for some reason, wants to avoid ending up in a contract dispute before Swedish courts).

Example 4: Assume that the same X and Y have entered into the contract, but without previous publication and call for competition, perhaps because X argued that the acquisition is covered by an exception from the scope of the public procurement rules. The contract includes an arbitration clause. The same Z finds out about the contract between X and Y and initiates an invalidity action.

Now, assume that Z is successful with the invalidity actions in examples 3 and 4. The contract is declared null and void by an administrative court. What about the arbitration agreement in such a scenario? While the answer, from an arbitration law perspective, might require a complex analysis and thoughts on *the principle of separability* and other, different, considerations, the answer from a public procurement law perspective is, to the author's understanding, straight-forward: the arbitration agreement is invalid *ex tunc* under private law and cannot successfully be invoked. But what happens if an arbitral tribunal has already rendered an award prior to the decision on invalidity? Here, things become complicated. Obviously, if the arbitration agreement is deemed to be null and void *ex tunc*, it is deemed never to have existed. Consequently, the award cannot be regarded as being based on an arbitration agreement, and, if so, any enforcement of the award would, to the author's understanding, be impossible.[62]

Naturally, the potential clash between arbitration and the public procurement rules might have additional angles and is certainly open for further and more in-depth analysis. The intention for the purpose of this chapter is merely to address the subject and touch upon its surface. Finally, however, in this section, a few words are required regarding the interpretation of public contracts, which is what any arbitrator appointed to solve a post-procurement contract dispute must do. Although the public procurement rules are not directly applicable in a post-procurement contractual relationship between a contracting authority and a supplier, the specific origin of a public contract must not be ignored when interpreting it. As the Swedish Supreme Court expressed it in a recent landmark ruling in this field, NJA 2021 p. 643: an interpretation of a public contract must be made pursuant to an overall assessment of the contract and its purpose, taking into consideration the public procurement context of the contract.

For example, the aim to identify the *common will of the parties*, crucial in contractual interpretation pursuant to Swedish law, is often irrelevant for public contracts. The reason is simple: it is the contracting authority that – by identification of the scope of the procurement and stipulation of the mandatory requirements – has 'run the show' (albeit restricted by the public procurement rules and the fundamental principles of these rules). The supplier is a mere passenger, forced to accept the prerequisites in the procurement. Although, admittedly, the influence of the supplier will vary, depending on the procurement procedure used, the public procurement

---

62. Chapter 3, s. 15 of the Swedish Enforcement Code (1981:774) (Sw: Utsökningsbalk (1981:774)).

procedure can very seldom be compared with the procedure preceding a private commercial contract conducted by two equal parties.

Another example is the relevance – or rather irrelevance – of *subsequent actions* taken by the parties when interpreting a public contract.[63] Obviously, a natural reply from any contracting authority to an argument of a supplier that subsequent actions should be taken into consideration when interpreting a public contract would be that such interpretation in fact would be equal to a *modification of the contract*, in breach of the public procurement rules and never intended by the contracting authority. Hence, the public procurement rules might still be of relevance during the contract period, not in the way of *application* but as contract *interpretation*.

Additional examples may be added but I leave it here with the following conclusion: Any arbitrator appointed to solve a public contract dispute should have the ability to navigate in the specific legal terrain from which the contract in question emanated – the public procurement field.

§15.04   FINAL REMARKS

This chapter was borne out of the author asking himself what different roles arbitration might play in public procurement-related disputes. To refer to the title of this chapter: is there a match between arbitration and public procurement? The possibilities *de lege ferenda* of using arbitration in the judicial review of procurement cases, and non-contractual damages claims on public procurement law grounds, were explored, and the article concluded with a discussion of arbitration as a post-procurement contract dispute resolution mechanism *de lege lata*. If there is a match between arbitration and public procurement, it is primarily to be found in the latter.

The conclusion probably needs an immediate modification. As stated, public procurement rules are not directly applicable in a post-procurement contractual relationship between a contracting authority and a supplier. Hence, the arbitration match is with a public procurement *environment* rather than with the public procurement *rules*.

Just like any other parties to a commercial contract, a contracting authority might identify the benefits of arbitration for a specific contract, and, indeed, has the right to choose it as the mechanism for resolving disputes arising from such a contract. From this perspective, arbitration certainly plays a role in public procurement-related disputes. But the watchdog will always be there, in the shadows. And the arbitrators set to rule on a post-procurement contract dispute will have to take notice of its potential bark. And bite!

---

63. *See*, e.g., Ramberg, *Allmän avtalsrätt* (Juno Version 11), Chapter 9, s. 7.

STOCKHOLM ARBITRATION YEARBOOK

1. Axel Calissendorff & Patrik Schöldström (eds), *Stockholm Arbitration Yearbook 2019*, 2019 (ISBN 978-94-035-0692-0).
2. Axel Calissendorff & Patrik Schöldström (eds), *Stockholm Arbitration Yearbook 2020*, 2020 (ISBN 978-94-035-2410-8).
3. Axel Calissendorff & Patrik Schöldström (eds), *Stockholm Arbitration Yearbook 2021*, 2021 (ISBN 978-94-035-3524-1).
4. Axel Calissendorff & Patrik Schöldström (eds), *Stockholm Arbitration Yearbook 2022*, 2022 (ISBN 978-94-035-1876-3).